The Right to Be Rural

The Right to Be Rural

KAREN R. FOSTER & JENNIFER JARMAN, Editors

UNIVERSITY *of* ALBERTA PRESS

Published by

University of Alberta Press
1–16 Rutherford Library South
11204 89 Avenue NW
Edmonton, Alberta, Canada T6G 2J4
Amiskwacîwâskahican | Treaty 6 | Métis Territory
uap.ualberta.ca

LIBRARY AND ARCHIVES CANADA
CATALOGUING IN PUBLICATION

Title: The right to be rural / Karen R. Foster and
     Jennifer Jarman, editors.
Names: Foster, Karen R., editor. | Jarman, Jennifer,
     editor.
Description: Includes bibliographical references
     and index.
Identifiers: Canadiana (print) 20210310057 |
     Canadiana (ebook) 20210310448 |
     ISBN 9781772125832 (softcover) |
     ISBN 9781772125948 (EPUB) |
     ISBN 9781772125955 (PDF)
Subjects: LCSH: Rural conditions. | LCSH: Sociology,
     Rural. | LCSH: Rural development. | LCSH:
     Rural development—Sociological aspects.
Classification: LCC HT421 .R54 2021 |
     DDC 307.72—dc23

First edition, first printing, 2022.
First printed and bound in Canada by Houghton
Boston Printers, Saskatoon, Saskatchewan.
Copyediting and proofreading by Angela Pietrobon.
Indexing by Judy Dunlop.

University of Alberta Press is committed to
protecting our natural environment. As part of our
efforts, this book is printed on Enviro Paper: it
contains 100% post-consumer recycled fibres and is
acid- and chlorine-free.

University of Alberta Press gratefully acknowledges
the support received for its publishing program
from the Government of Canada, the Canada
Council for the Arts, and the Government of Alberta
through the Alberta Media Fund.

Contents

III The Right to Rural Health

IV The Right to Rural Representation

V The Right to Rural Policy

VI The Right to Rural Mobility

Acknowledgments

THIS BOOK HAS BEEN ENRICHED by its engagement with the scholarly and practitioner communities that come together in the Canadian Sociology Association, the International Sociology Association, and the Canadian Rural Revitalization Foundation. The conferences held by each of these groups provided a venue for contributors to workshop their chapters and get to know one another. At the time of publication, when COVID-19 has prohibited most of our usual conferences, the value of just being together to share ideas is especially clear.

We thank Mat Buntin at University of Alberta Press for shepherding us through this process, and Doug Hildebrand for encouraging us to submit the proposal. We are grateful to Hannah Main, a PHD student in the Department of Sociology and Social Anthropology, who proofread and formatted the final manuscript.

Geographies of Citizenship, Equity, Opportunity, and Choice

KAREN R. FOSTER & JENNIFER JARMAN

IS THERE A RIGHT TO BE RURAL? If there is, how might it manifest and what does it mean in the everyday lives of rural people, those who govern rural places, and those who depend on rural societies for food, recreation, access to nature, and natural resources? What are its limitations and contingencies? How is the right to be rural claimed, protected, and enforced? Conversely, if there is no right to be rural, what codified rights can be meaningfully asserted and realized in rural communities, and what ones cannot? Does living outside densely populated areas affect access to services that are supposed to be universal? If citizenship rights have a spatial character, what are the implications for the principles of equity and access that underpin most legal charters and declarations, at state and international levels? These questions, and their attendant tensions and dilemmas, offer a productive framework for studying and understanding the many demographic, social, economic, environmental, and political challenges faced by rural communities worldwide. The framework of rights, mobilized in countless other causes, also helps highlight underappreciated facets of community creativity and resilience in the face of these challenges. It might also be a foundation for strategic action to direct resources and tailor public policy to rural places.

This edited collection is meant as a first step toward a rights-based understanding of rural futures. It assesses the theories and concepts of rights and citizenship in elucidating rural challenges and identifying practical solutions and routes for advocacy. Collectively, the chapters that follow demonstrate the value of applying a rights framework to climate change, neoliberal social and economic policies, economic globalization, restructuring and de-industrialization, population aging and out-migration, food security and sovereignty, and the host of other issues dramatically changing small town and rural life. Most of these issues stem from, and exacerbate aging, shrinking, or stagnating rural populations. And, as Jarman noted a few years ago, "when jobs are simply lost, young people are the first to depart for better prospects, creating a skewed age structure with communities composed principally of old people" (2017, p. 104). In some cases, the resulting out-migration threatens the very survival of communities. This book builds from the premise that, because such challenges are altering the relationship between rural citizens and their states, it is time to analyze and articulate rural decline, survival, and sustainability using the language of rights. By "rights," we mean to conjure up what the sociologist Margaret Somers understands as legal claims "brought to bear on a state," which come together in the "bundle" or "package" we call "citizenship"—the "status" that confers rights on people and asks for some duties in return (Somers, 2008, p. 67). We also draw on T. H. Marshall's tone-setting 1950 essay, in which citizenship is a status that accords equal rights as well as duties to the people who hold it, and in which rights are understood to comprise civil, political, and social rights—the latter including the right to a decent standard of living.

As one of us has written on this topic before:

> Marshall and the hundreds of others who have analyzed citizenship in his wake tell us that although what it means to be a citizen has and continues to evolve, citizenship is, at its core, the relationship between people and the nation-state to which they belong, as expressed, if only partially, through the rights and duties each expects of the other. To be a citizen of a particular state is to be able to hold that state accountable, and to be held accountable by that state...There's a degree of nuance and specificity to what we have coded into law, and what we expect of states and their citizens that is unwritten, unsaid, and mostly unexamined—until it becomes controversial, as...it does in the question of how to sustain rural communities (Foster, 2018, p. 372).

One major change in the experience and codification of citizenship, according to scholars who have studied it in the later half of the twentieth century and after, is a shift toward a more contingent and contractual citizenship and away from the automatic, universal, or equalizing one envisioned, if not realized, in Marshall's time. Margaret Somers, for example, finds in the contemporary United States a "contractualized citizenship." Instead of a broad set of universal entitlements or birthrights, American citizenship today is earned only by productive members of society, and productivity is defined narrowly as employment. As Somers puts it, "this is the model by which the structurally unemployed become *contractual malfeasants*" (2008, p. 3), "judged to have let down their end of the citizenship contract" and "deemed unworthy of the 'earned privileges' that comprise citizenship" (Foster, 2018, p. 373). This is not a uniquely American phenomenon. As Foster has argued before, drawing on case studies from Canada,

> *those who are deemed unnecessary for the operation of economy and society, possibly even a burden to it...are therefore denied, through direct and horrifying neglect, or banal, slow-moving, bureaucratic indifference, some or all of the goods and protections that other scholarship lumps under citizenship (2018, p. 373).*

Importantly, for the editors and authors of this collection, this perspective on transformations in rights and citizenship illuminates structural facets of the rural experience, where in many cases, people live in rural communities because there was once waged work available to them. Marshall argued that modern citizenship flourished because it helped capital expansion—it articulated the rights and mobility that people, and capital itself, need for private property and freedom of choice in employment. In rural communities around the world, companies arrive in search of deep pools of available labour, and then abandon their workers when circumstances change. And so, processes of industrialization, deindustrialization, economic restructuring, and urbanization have occurred or are occurring on a global scale. In rural communities, shuttered mines, fallowed or converted farmland, idle mills, empty manufacturing plants, and boarded-up main streets are no accidents of culture. They are signs that companies have moved on, but people have not. Those left behind—who are asked "Why do you live here?" or "How can you live here?"—even if they are employed, are placed among the contractual malfeasants and denied the full rights of citizenship, by virtue of where they continue to live. This alone is a compelling reason to study rural life in terms of citizenship and rights. Fortunately, some other extant works on rights and rurality provide an even stronger foundation for a rights-based analysis of rural issues, and they approach the matter in a productive variety of ways.

Two of these works, which our title will call to mind for many readers, are Henri Lefebvre's 1968 (in French) essay, *La Droit de la Ville*, published in English in 1996 as *The Right to the City*, and the geographer David Harvey's 2008 article, "The Right to the City." Lefebvre's essay, embraced by activists and academics in its wake, posits the "right to the city" as a "cry and demand," but is otherwise rather abstract about what this might mean. Subsequent scholars have attempted to flesh out the concept. In Harvey's piece, we find the notion of a right "far more than the individual liberty to access urban resources: ...a right to change ourselves by changing the city" (2008, p. 23). Harvey makes the case that the right to the city—the right to change ourselves by changing it—has been denied to "us" ordinary people and is worth fighting for. This argument rests on the premise that urbanization, comprising the making and remaking of cities, has historically been a classed process, with capitalist and bourgeois interests directing where people can reasonably live, what cityscapes look like, and what activities go on in them. According to Harvey, urban infrastructure and even neighbourhood layouts and lifestyles are all but dictated by capitalist expansion, and by its particular requirement of surplus value (i.e., profit) via surplus production. Echoing our argument above, Harvey shows that people live and concentrate where workers are needed, and then infrastructure concentrates where people live. The motor of urbanization, in Harvey's work, is revealed to be capital expansion; the motor of further urban development and change is identified as "accumulation by dispossession"—the "capture of land from low-income populations" (2008, p. 34) for the purposes of making profit, establishing and expanding industry, increasing productivity, and securing control over natural and human resources.

The right to the city, it follows, is currently "too narrowly confined, restricted in most cases to a small political and economic elite who are in a position to shape cities more and more after their own desires" (Harvey, 2008, p. 38). The only hope, according to Harvey, is in a "global struggle, predominantly with finance capital...over the accumulation by dispossession visited upon the least well-off and the developmental drive that seeks to colonize space for the affluent" (2008, p. 39).

It is easy, particularly from the interdisciplinary vantage point of rural studies, to see how a right to the rural could parallel the right to the city. Indeed, Lefebvre's path-breaking essay mentions a "right to the countryside," but characterizes it as a disappearing, "largely agrarian" piece of the past, the rural a place of "scarcity and penury" to be absorbed by a better city (1996, p. 150). However, importantly, Lefebvre's formulation did not equate the city with urban space, but rather he sought to understand the city as something more like a political imaginary. This might be useful, but if we want to build the case for a right to rural life, we have to look elsewhere, too. Laura Barraclough (2013) has attempted to flesh out the idea of a right to the countryside by building on those who have taken up Lefebvre's "slogan," but she notes that most of the latter have, "contrary to Lefebvre's own arguments," asserted that the "right to the city is properly—and exclusively—applied to *cities*" (2013, p. 1047). In Barraclough's brief interpretation, Lefebvre made space for rural people in his formulation of the right to the city. As she explains, "given that the lives of people in the countryside are overwhelmingly structured by decision-making in cities, rural people also have a right to the city that is not at all linked to their urban inhabitance" (2013, p. 1048). However, Barraclough asks whether there is a further, more specific right to the countryside, rather than only a right to the city that belongs to rural people, too. She proposes that a right to rural life might, for example, "more explicitly [protect] human relationships to the natural environment" (2013, p. 1049).

The chapters in this collection take up the question of the right to be rural, asking whether we can meaningfully think about rights to nature and natural resources in rural places, rural livelihoods, public services in rural and remote communities, political representation, technologies, and connectivity. The chapter authors acknowledge the gaps that exist between the citizenship rights, freedoms, and obligations enshrined in the national constitutions of their case study geographies as well as in international declarations and the realities of rural life in a diversity of places. From Nova Scotia and Newfoundland to Poland, and from northern Ontario to India, Denmark, Spain, Zimbabwe, and Ethiopia, their detailed examinations of what is happening in rural communities show that rights to personal security, education, health, income, and association may only be weakly maintained in rural places with small populations, where external actors deem it too costly or inefficient to deliver a universal standard of services and amenities. Their studies assess the demonstrable impacts that weakly enforced rights frameworks have in small, peripheral communities outside urban zones, and contemplate the changes that could realize stated commitments to universal human rights and access to public services in rural communities.

The first three chapters in this volume present case studies of rural education. Across the world, education is considered a fundamental human right, and schools are viewed as sites that create citizens. But what these visions mean in practice is inconsistent. In case studies of education, the spatial character of rights and citizenship is immediately clear. Katie K. Macleod's case study of a small rural Acadian community in Nova Scotia, Canada, in chapter 2, highlights the challenges around access to French language education, which are themselves framed by issues of rurality. For over a century, needing to work on family farms meant that many rural children were kept out of school in Pomquet, Nova Scotia. At the same time, difficulties in getting appropriately trained teachers to settle in the town have been present since the outset. One result has been a gradual loss of control to urban areas, which has in turn diminished the distinctively Acadian regional dialect of Pomquet French by emphasizing French language learning that is more generally understood at national and international levels. Interestingly, MacLeod further shows that many changes to education that are problematic at a local level have actually been driven by the needs and interests of wealthier urban children who want (or whose families want them) to become bilingual due to the advantages it brings. The chapter offers a fascinating look at how intersections of class, language, and geography shape the delivery, experience, and control of rural education in ways that may hold lessons for any dual language society.

In chapter 3, Laura Domingo-Peñafiel, Laura Farré-Riera, and Núria Simó-Gil look at rural learning contexts in relation to the learning of citizenship in three rural schools in Catalonia, Spain. They argue that their case studies demonstrate how guaranteeing more democratic, inclusive, and participatory practices in secondary schools can foster broader forms of social inclusion and social cohesion. In this chapter, Lawy and Biesta's 2006 ideas of "citizenship-as-practice" come to the fore, in an emphasis on voluntary action and experiential learning as methods of developing youth citizenship. Domingo-Peñafiel and her co-authors show us three schools facing somewhat different challenges, and reveal different ways of "learning citizenship" by exploring tensions in the curriculum and school climate, and the influence that school governance, and in particular, participatory school culture, has on the learning and practicing of democratic habits. In their view, students who learn how to handle controversial subject matters learn how to cooperate and participate at political levels beyond the school. Human relationships and feelings of belonging are shown to be important, and accordingly, small rural schools are argued to build fruitful collaborations between families and community agents that foster democratic practices and thus develop meaningful citizenship. The implicit extension of this argument is that rural school consolidation and closure—and the practice of commuting rural students to nearby urban schools—might be damaging to the development of meaningful citizenship.

Ario Seto's case study offers another angle on the rural school's role in citizenship making, taking us back across the Atlantic Ocean to rural Newfoundland, Canada, in chapter 4. He explores Newfoundland's history in order to provide the context for present-day struggles between teachers and students over what constitutes appropriate sources of authority for understanding our complex world. Drawing upon interviews with rural teachers, he documents the strategies that some teachers are using both in "hallway conversations" and the formal classroom to empower students to use and critically assess online information, and connects the challenges posed by fake news to the project—typically ascribed to teachers—of developing responsible citizens. Seto's research highlights the added pressures on rural teachers to support students' growth as citizens in communities where the school might be one of only very few local civic organizations and where it must compete with social media's comparatively placeless and often sensationalized content.

In chapter 5, Gregory R. L. Hadley bridges the topic of rural education into the topic of rural livelihoods, opening a set of chapters on the latter. He starts from a problem faced by many rural schools: low enrollments and the potential of closure. This problem, common in his case study of three communities in the province of Nova Scotia, Canada, diminishes the educational opportunities for those who remain in rural areas, but it also constrains citizenship, which, to be fully exercised, requires stability and community cohesiveness. Hadley proposes that enhancing the entrepreneurial skillsets of rural youth can help improve the prospects for young people to stay in rural areas and can strengthen community ties more broadly. Refusing to cede entrepreneurialism to neoliberalism, Hadley argues that an entrepreneurial mindset, conceived as more than the rational calculations of homo economicus, can allow rural young people to react to opportunities available in rural areas and make them more resourceful, creative, agentic, and able to use social capital. Drawing on survey and interview data from a sample of Nova Scotian students in three communities, Hadley's chapter assesses the presence of entrepreneurial knowledge, skills, and attitudes among rural high school students. The author then reflects on three themes: entrepreneurial personalities, community connections, and complicated school experiences. In doing so, Hadley identifies structural challenges faced by rural youth and recommends a better engaged pedagogy that underpins and develops a well-rounded, more-than-economic entrepreneurialism to promote rural retention and revitalization.

Pallavi V. Das moves the focus more directly toward labour, engaging intensely with David Harvey's (2008) writing in her chapter on small-scale producers in a coastal fishing community in Chilika, India (chapter 6). Seizing specifically on the theory of capital accumulation, she notes that rural areas are important spaces for capital accumulation, as well as the homes for many people. However, rural people are losing access to many of these spaces in a process that is similar to, but also different from, the urban process and experience that exemplifies Harvey's theory of accumulation by dispossession. Das shows how rural people are losing access due to two factors: first, degraded natural resources that affect their livelihoods, and reduced control over the decisions relating to these degraded natural resources; and second, capitalist mechanisms such as broader market fluctuations in fish prices. Das argues that the right to be rural shares with Harvey's right to the city the need to establish democratic management of land and resources. For Das, this is the crux of the right to be rural. She offers a definition of rural in terms of social-ecological spaces and highlights the class cleavages that further delimit who can enter and meaningfully shape which spaces. The chapter shows the complexity of the interactions among the state, local elites, and shrimp farmers. This chapter also has a clear application of Laura Barraclough's (2013) idea of the right to the rural.

The next three chapters—7 through 10—are conceptualized as examinations of the right to a rural life course, from birth to old age. Sarah Rudrum, Lesley Frank, and Kayla McCarney begin the section by describing the evolution of maternity care in rural communities, with a focus on rural midwifery and hospital births in Nova Scotia, Canada. Drawing on focus groups with rural women in the context of a stalled rural midwifery pilot program in the province, they highlight how access to different kinds of maternity care options impacts women's health, feelings of belonging, decisions about where to live, and the sustainability of rural life itself. Their chapter shows how the centralization and medicalization of birth have occurred in tandem, resulting in fewer options for women giving birth outside major cities, and the downloading of ironically increased costs of birthing and maternity care to individual mothers and their families. Their case study provides the evidence to consider where the right to be born in, and give birth in, rural communities might fit under the umbrella of a right to be rural.

Kathleen Kevany and Al Lauzon's chapter on rural food systems and security in Canada (chapter 8) shifts our attention from the beginning to the end of human lives. Their contribution synthesizes scholarly arguments and evidence pertaining to older adults' food security and insecurity in rural communities, illuminating the structural conditions that enable and constrain an individual's nutrition. They describe neoliberal shifts in Canadian agricultural, social, and economic policy that benefit industrial agriculture and enable farmland consolidation, connecting these high-level changes to the transformation of food systems and, in turn, to alterations in the way people in rural communities are able to feed themselves and their families. Specifically, they argue that a more heavily industrialized, globalized food system increases local food insecurity, and they focus on how this impacts older people who might have mobility limitations, less social support, and health problems that would benefit from better dietary choice. They critique extant "solutions" to food insecurity, chief among them Canada's food banks, which they show to be insufficient for a variety of reasons, such as the mobility required to access them and the nutritional quality of the food they distribute. Their argument is that, given the critical importance of nutritious food to humans' overall health, a right to be rural entails a right to nutrient-dense food in sufficient quantities.

In chapter 9, Katja Rinne-Koski and Sulevi Riukulehto connect the focus on older adults in rural settings with the thread of belonging, arguing for a relational approach to citizenship that draws attention to the two sides of belonging—belonging to a place, and having a place belong to you. The authors search for this sense of citizenship in the narratives of older people living in rural Finland and find a "multifaceted" interpretation of "home"—as a building, an emotion, a site of interaction, and a place for events—which in turn shapes a similarly multifaceted sense of belonging and rural citizenship. Their research underscores the importance of more subjective feelings of place and belonging alongside the objective matters of service and resource allocation highlighted by the previous two chapters. But it also points to practical policy solutions: if we acknowledge the critical importance of feelings of belonging to the full development of citizenship, enjoyment of its attendant rights, and exercise of its attendant duties, we must allocate resources and design public infrastructure with social cohesion and community development valued as highly as any other factor. When it comes to older persons, we must invest in the infrastructure (housing, transportation, and supports) to enable them to age in the places where they feel they belong.

Chapters 10 through 12 maintain the focus on subjectivity and agency, each addressing the topic of rural political citizenship through a case study of how rural citizens, as polities, influence rural governance. Worldwide, the full exercise of citizenship typically hinges on a person's ability to participate in political life, including organizing with other citizens to advocate and effect change as well as running in or voting in elections. Ilona Matysiak begins a section of the book focused on rural political participation and representation with a qualitative, interview-based study of citizenship behaviours in rural Poland. She analyzes her data for evidence of individualization and civic engagement, asking whether her sample of 92 educated 25 to 34-year-olds living in rural Poland reflect a culture of increasing individualization and consumerism, or one of active citizenship. She finds a diversity of rural experiences and offers a helpful typology for interpreting rural citizenship as a verb—something that is done, rather than held or bestowed—as well as some thoughts on what can be done to encourage more active citizenship from rural young adults, particularly those with young families. Her recommendations underscore the fact that people and communities need support to develop and contribute to their democracies and fully exercise their political citizenship.

Chapter 11, from Rachel McLay and Howard Ramos, pans out from the in-depth study of youth to a macro examination of a regional population. They seek to trouble the persistent characterization of rural societies as politically backwards—conservative, closed, traditional, and parochial. Using results from a 2019 telephone survey of Atlantic Canadians, they show that, at least in Canada's easternmost provinces, the notion that rural blocs support conservative ideologies, vote in hyper-conservative governments, and are less politically progressive than their urban counterparts is not true. Rather, their data reveal that rural residents are more likely to be economically progressive (favouring redistribution, for example) and just slightly less likely to be socially progressive (such as being open to increased immigration). Moreover, they found interesting rural–urban similarities and differences in political actions, such as protesting, boycotting, and voting. These findings, which highlight the heterogeneity of rural populations, are particularly important at a time when much divisive politics around the world is attributed to rural–urban divides, and often blamed on anti-cosmopolitan rural people. Moreover, they support the hypothesis that there is actually latent potential for a coordinated, rural-led movement to coalesce around the notion of a right to be rural.

However, in chapter 12, Satenia Zimmermann and her co-authors remind us that "rural" is not homogeneous, and that intra-rural inequalities in representation, civic participation, and self-determination will complicate any efforts to mobilize communities around a rights-based framework. The chapter examines the role of Indigenous communities in the governance of resource development. This is one of the most critical areas of rural citizenship in Canada, where Indigenous communities, First Nations, and their supporters have been locked in contentious battles over who has the right to extract and transport oil from and over ancestral Indigenous lands. Zimmermann et al. discuss the evolution of different models of Indigenous citizenship and ask how Canada's recent adoption of the United Nations Declaration on the Rights of Indigenous Peoples (2007) affects the complicated question of consent in the development of natural resource projects in certain rural areas in Northwestern Ontario, Canada. The interviews presented and analyzed illustrate how the process of consent—a key aspect of the democratic governance of economic affairs—is viewed by Indigenous people active in land, environmental, resource management, and/or forestry, and First Nations governance. This is an important perspective outside rural studies, too, since so much of the literature on the duty to consult has been written by members of Canada's legal community. It highlights the fact that rights have the potential to infringe on each other, and that balancing competing rights claims is a necessary part of any rights-based movement or analytical framework.

Chapters 13 through 16 keep the focus on governance, but the authors move further from action in the arena of electoral politics and governance into the arena of policy development, with case studies that collectively highlight the need for a rural lens in public policy. Ray D. Bollman's chapter (13) makes the case most explicitly with its attempt to operationalize rurality as a function of "density and distance-to-density"—a spatial concept that sets the parameters for a community's access to publicly-funded services. He argues that the more sparsely populated a community is and the further it is from a densely populated area (a town or city), the more in theory it costs a central government to deliver public services to or in that community. Bollman applies this concept to health care in Canada, ruminating on how density and distance-to-density already shape the discourse around rural health care delivery and negatively affect access to health care services. Optimistically, his chapter points to innovative ways of overcoming rural spatial challenges, and shows how thinking about rural as a spatial concept offers a means of de-politicizing conversations about rural public service delivery. Moreover, doing so can open the door to interesting technical solutions to rural service challenges. Bollman suggests that there are, for example, untapped tech- nological possibilities as well as promising, old-fashioned methods of ensuring access and service sustainability in the face of the urbanization of resources and people. Importantly, Bollman's rigorous attempt at operationalizing rurality might offer a more objective basis for resource allocation at provincial and national levels, and a way of exposing some arbitrary inequities in access to services that are supposed to be universally accessible.

The impact of urbanization on policy development stays in focus in chapter 14. Authors Jeofrey Matai and Innocent Chirisa argue that the myriad challenges faced by rural communities around the world are a function of unregulated, unplanned processes of globalization and urbanization as well as urban-centric public policy. They propose that spatial planning, with close attention to the needs, rights, and resources of rural populations, can be an important tool for enhancing the rights of rural citizens. Drawing on interviews with key informants and document analysis in Zimbabwe, they assert that proper spatial planning can counter some of the dominant forces driving both urbanization and globalization, as well as the creation of poverty and inequality traps. Combining these findings with Bollman's contribution, a rights-based spatial planning perspective emerges as a possible way to bring a rural lens to policymaking without necessarily naming it as such.

S. Ashleigh Weeden's chapter (15) narrows the focus to telecommunications and tech policy and regulation in rural communities, extending the discussion of service provision begun in previous chapters, and building on the other authors' critique of urban centrism in policy development. While so much of the current public discourse about rural telecommunications is about the need to extend network coverage to rural locations, Weeden considers more deeply what the right to be rural means in a digitally-mediated world and, using a case study from rural Ontario, Canada, discusses some of the difficulties with "smart" technology. She concludes that rural decision-makers should be thoughtful about what type of technology they adopt, particularly considering the surveillance potential of smart technology projects, and make choices that enhance rather than restrict the depth of political citizenship in rural areas.

Eshetayehu Kinfu and Logan Cochrane conclude the section on rural policy, returning the focus to Africa and land in chapter 16. They examine how rural lands in Ethiopia are administratively reclassified as "urban," so that rural land becomes urban without anyone transferring their residence. Since there are two different land tenure systems in play—one for rural, one for urban—this has serious consequences for landowners and users. Especially problematic is the fact that there is no tenure system governing peri-urban regions, leaving those who live and work in transitioning areas at risk of losing their property, access, and right to make changes on the land. Kinfu and Cochrane use Marshall's concept of social rights to highlight land reclassification's contribution to inequality of opportunity and related impacts on citizenship. Overall, the chapter shows the impact of urban-centric policy and the need for a rural policy lens, because it reveals that urbanites' rights are dominant over those of rural people, who, despite multiple generations of being on land, now have their relationships to their land curtailed by its reclassification for political and economic ends. Importantly, the chapter also explores two types of resistance and suggests that, at least in some instances, people can navigate change in a positive way.

The final three chapters share a focus on the right to a rural mobility, offering case studies of different means of migration to and recognition within and as rural communities. In chapter 17, Stacey Haugen asks the critical question of what the right to be rural means for displaced people who find themselves settling in rural Canada. Her research provides a much-needed addition to the literature on the issues relating to refugees who settle in Canada, as the preponderance of this literature focuses heavily on the refugee experiences and situations in urban contexts. Haugen explains how and why rural areas in Canada have been active in sponsoring and helping refugees to settle. Her interview material illuminates the shared goals of sponsors, community members, and members of refugee families, but also draws out some areas where goals and aspirations conflict. Furthermore, it reveals the importance of ideas of market-based citizenship in creating support for or criticism of refugees in relation to questions on how refugees prioritize their objectives as they settle in. It points to the need for rural government supports on par with those available to refugees in urban areas, as it highlights the negative consequences of relying exclusively on private networks of volunteers to act as gatekeepers between rural refugees and the communities they settle in.

Issues of mobility intersect with spatial injustice, economy, and labour again in chapter 18. Authors Clement Chipenda and Tom Tom draw upon Marshall's ideas about social citizenship rights to analyze the consequences of a major land reform in Zimbabwe, in terms of its effects on the lives of migrant workers and their descendants. They analyze the land reform's consequences in three areas of Zimbabwean citizenship: political participation and organization; economic rights including access to, and ownership of, land resources; and civil rights, meaning access to civic essentials, such as local burial societies and microfinance associations. Chipenda and Tom conclude by suggesting that there has actually been increased participation in some areas of the political realm after the land reform, but that ownership still remains problematic and participation in local civic associations is low. Their chapter underlines the importance of ensuring that citizenship rights are extended to marginalized groups, such as migrant labourers, and reinforces the point made in previous chapters that rural communities have their own internal inequities in addition to the inequities between rural and urban places.

Mobility and home and land ownership remain in view in chapter 19, where authors Jens Kaae Fisker, Annette Aagaard Thuesen, and Egon Bjørnshave Noe elucidate how problems in mortgage-lending work to deny mortgages to people who would like to live in some rural areas in Denmark. Even if people are able to pay for the homes they desire, the rural areas where they want (and in theory, have the basic right) to live can be deemed too risky by the mortgage lender. The effect, as this chapter shows, is that rural areas are being "redlined" by mortgage practices. Fisker and his co-authors frame this as a classic "wicked problem" (Rittel & Webber, 1973), in which there is no malicious intent, but there is a serious effect nevertheless. The authors then go on to develop a multiperspective understanding of the rural redlining phenomenon, drawing on Nancy Fraser's (2009) and Edward Soja's (2010) ideas of social and spatial injustice, respectively, and developing an exploration of the relationship of endogenous to exogenous geographies. The chapter reflects the right to be rural theme through an analysis of the problem of not being rural, but becoming rural, by identifying the serious barriers imposed on those who wish to move into a rural area and finance a home purchase. Just as Haugen's chapter on refugee policies and practices reveals how communities and government policies can play a gatekeeping role in determining who lives in rural spaces, on what terms, and with what access to critical resources, Fisker et al. show that regulatory policies and assumptions of actors outside the policy arena can have a dramatic effect on people's ability to move freely into rural geographies. This point reaffirms the need for a rural lens in public policy, but also in corporate practices, especially in the context of weakly regulated capitalism.

Taken collectively, the chapters in this book advance our understanding of the issues and challenges facing rural communities around the world. At the outset of this project, we extended a challenge to the authors who participated. We asked them to consider whether there is a "right to be rural," and if so, to elaborate on how it manifests and whether this term can be used to create a productive framework for the many interconnected aspects of the study of rural societies today. The response to our call for papers was significant, as has been the response to calls for conference sessions that we have run subsequently using the same term.

In the context of the ongoing COVID-19 pandemic, the notion of a right to be rural has taken on new significance, as city dwellers have flocked to rural areas worldwide as tourists, seasonal residents, and increasingly, permanent residents to escape dense populations and high infection rates in cities. As one of this volume's contributors put it in a recent article, "the coronavirus pandemic has escalated existing tensions in a complicated, ongoing negotiation between the 'right to be rural' and trends toward 'disaster gentrification' driven by urban flight" (Weeden, 2020). In some locales, the mass movement away from densely populated areas toward rural and remote ones has revealed the sticky problem of who has the right to be rural—permanent residents? Cottagers? Tourists? The differences between these groups are important, especially in deindustrialized rural zones where permanent residents have less economic capital and thus fewer resources to put toward mobility and choice, and seasonal residents and tourists have more social and economic advantages. The latter groups' right to go where they please, and where they own or rent property, has trumped permanent rural residents' right to health and safety. In other locales, COVID-19 has had an effect on low-income families from high-density suburbs, who are reshaping their own futures and shifting out of problematic situations in urban centres in a reverse migration to more affordable, less dense, rural locations. These shifts in the direction of migration from rural-to-urban and then urban-to-rural also heighten the problems of inadequate rural health provision and inadequate school provision, as well as strengthen the demand for better services of all sorts, including the rural broadband that often connects people to online employment opportunities in their former communities.

While there are obviously many differences in the struggles the researchers are exploring in this book, some significant themes emerge. What we can see from these chapters is that based on the research being done in rural communities around the world, there is a feeling that there should be a right to be rural. Furthermore, active democratic citizenship and a rural policy lens are viewed as the main routes to stronger and healthier rural lives.

Yet, a question remains: if there is a right to be rural, what ought to be done about it? The chapters provide multiple examples of what it means to have reduced citizenship rights in rural areas. In some, rural districts are being absorbed into urban areas with serious diminution of land rights; in others, the natural resources upon which rural lives depend are being damaged, or there is a lack of adequate spatial planning that balances resources between urban and rural locations. In still others, there is a lack of clarity about what constitutes consent, and how consultation processes concerning natural resource development and land planning should proceed as a result. Throughout these varied cases, we can clearly see that there are already significant global efforts to claim, protect, and enforce the rights of rural peoples, and that there are important inequities in core rural and urban service. Citizenship does have a rural/urban distinction.

What is less clear is whether the right to be rural is possible to operationalize, or mostly an aspirational statement. The same lack of clarity, we note, is found across any arena where rights are invoked in advocacy. They are nice ideas, but most are quite difficult to enforce. However, they have shown up as a meaningful principle around which people with diverse interests will mobilize. In rural communities, we see parallels of what Karl Marx (1978) called a "class in itself" (meaning one that has the potential for united action), as opposed to a "class for itself" (one that is unified and in motion around a broader purpose), and we propose that this distinction might be useful in understanding calls for a significant strengthening of a rural framework of legally supported rights to be rural, and for their reception. In other words, there are many examples in this book that support the need for a right to be rural to be articulated and developed, but, as yet, little evidence of a united front that links all these issues together into a coherent, global force against the power of urbanized capital and that pressures for the putting into place of a legal architecture of rights underpinned by the power of enforcement mechanisms. One way to anchor such a movement might be to amplify calls for a rural lens in policy development, and another would be to seek to strengthen measures that encourage and enable widespread civic participation. We return to these possible ways forward in our conclusion at the end of this book.

References

Barraclough, L. (2013). Is there also a right to the countryside? *Antipode, 45*(5), 1047–1049.

Harvey, D. (2008). The right to the city. *The City Reader, 6*(1), 23–40.

Foster, K. (2018). The right to be rural. *The Dalhousie Review, 98*(3), 369–375.

Fraser, N. (2009). *Scales of justice: Reimagining political space in a globalizing world.* Columbia University Press.

Jarman, J. (2017). What are the challenges of economic transition? Exploring the consequences of regional dynamics and global shifts. In M. Hird & G. Pavlich (Eds.), *Questioning sociology: Canadian perspectives* (3rd ed., pp. 96–105). Oxford University Press.

Lefebvre, H. (1996). *The right to the city: Writings on cities.* (E. Kofman & E. Lebas, Trans.). Blackwell.

Marshall, T. H. (1950). Citizenship and social class. In *Citizenship and social class, and other essays* (pp. 1–85). Cambridge University Press.

Marx, K. (1978). The coming upheaval, excerpt from *The poverty of philosophy.* In R. Tucker (Ed.), *The Marx/Engels reader* (2nd ed., pp. 218–219). W. W. Norton.

Rittel, H. W. J., & Webber, M. M. (1973). Dilemmas in a general theory of planning. *Policy Sciences, 4*(2), 155–169.

Somers, M. (2008). *Genealogies of citizenship: States, markets, statelessness and the right to have rights.* Cambridge University Press.

Soja, E. (2010). *Seeking spatial justice.* University of Minnesota Press.

United Nations Declaration on the Rights of Indigenous Peoples (UNDRIP). (September 13, 2007). https://www.un.org/development/desa/indigenouspeoples/declaration-on-the-rights-of-indigenous-peoples.html

Weeden, S. A. (2020, May 21). Do you have a right to go to the cottage during the coronavirus pandemic? *The Conversation.* https://theconversation.com/do-you-have-a-right-to-go-to-the-cottage-during-the-coronavirus-pandemic-138702

I
The Right to Rural Education

2

The Right to Language in Rural Nova Scotia, Canada

KATIE K. MACLEOD

IN CANADA, regionalism has shaped the identities of the people and created a sense of attachment and belonging to geographic spaces (Buckner, 2000; Pocius, 1991).[1] There is significant disparity between Canadian regions. Regional disparities have been attributed to geographic, economic, and cultural factors (Allen, Massey, & Cochrane, 1998; McKay, 2000). Atlantic Canada, as an identifiable region, has within it identities that are constructed on foundations of rurality. Atlantic Canada is Canada's easternmost region, consisting of the provinces of Nova Scotia, New Brunswick, Prince Edward Island, and Newfoundland and Labrador, and contains within it distinct ethnic, linguistic, provincial, political, and Indigenous identities. Regional differences become defined not only by economic development and underdevelopment but also within political ideologies that are inherently attached to contemporary capitalist ideologies (Harvey, 2008; Ornstein, 1986). Within Atlantic Canada, some regions can also be defined as more rural than others; the less rural areas in the region benefit, relatively speaking, socially and economically "through neo-liberal governing practices" (Brodie, 2002, p. 377).

Regionalism within Atlantic Canada has developed over the last four centuries. The region began as individual colonies, which then became provinces with similar concerns about the development of a centralized government.

Acadians became the first permanent settlers of the region in 1604 (Griffiths, 2005; Muise, 1993). In the century following their arrival, Acadians developed an autonomous political identity that emerged from their limited contact with France, alliances with the Indigenous Mi'kmaw population, and unique agricultural advancements (Griffiths, 2005; MacLeod, 2015). Between the years 1755 and 1762, approximately 14,100 Acadians were deported from the colony of Acadie (Faragher, 2006; White, 2005). British authorities viewed the Acadians as a threat to their colony and exiled them from the region now called Nova Scotia. Some Acadians were able to escape, fleeing their pursuers and often hiding among Mi'kmaw allies, but most were deported on ships destined for locations along the east coast of the United States and France (Faragher, 2006; Griffiths, 2005; Johnston, 2007). In 1764, many Acadians returned, resettling in small pockets throughout the Atlantic provinces after the Royal Proclamation of 1763 was issued. Today, there are 23,700 Acadians in Nova Scotia (Statistics Canada, 2016).

Within Atlantic Canada, Acadian identities are based within rurality and the larger context of the region. Acadians are able to demonstrate the practical use of regional frameworks in that they are able to define distinctiveness within groups beyond the local level through the incorporation of strong ethnic identities and cultural traditions (Forbes, 1983; McKay, 2000). Strong identities and social movements have aided Acadians in their goal to implement French-language education in Atlantic Canada, even though it serves a minority population—a goal that was not readily supported by provincial and national agendas.

This chapter focuses on research conducted in the 900-person Acadian community of Pomquet, located in Antigonish County, Nova Scotia. This community predates the founding of Canada and has had a strong commitment to providing French-language education since well before the reorientation of language rights in Canada. As we will see, teachers and community members have long aimed to provide children in the village with a proper education that includes culturally and linguistically appropriate content, despite a lack of both resources and provincial and national support. This case study explores the intersections of rural and linguistic minority rights to demonstrate how state interests can both benefit and work against the efforts of a community at the local level.

Context

Located within the Municipality of the County of Antigonish, Pomquet is a small rural community with few businesses, aside from a handful of farms, tourist destinations, and bed and breakfasts. It was founded in 1773 by five Acadian families who returned to the area post deportation. It has a small church, community centre, and school that serve its 900 citizens. Antigonish acts as a service hub to the many small communities that surround it. Many people who live in Pomquet work either in Antigonish or in Alberta's oil sector because of the lack of industry in the community.

During my fieldwork in Pomquet, education was an ongoing conversation. Teachers, students, parents, and community members were passionate about education and its role in the community. Participants identified three central problems associated with rural French-language education in Pomquet: 1) the length of time it took the province to provide French curriculum to the community's school; 2) the loss of ownership and connection with the school that the community felt as a result of a jurisdictional change in education; and 3) the influx of anglophone students to the school in Pomquet in recent years. These central problems tie into an examination of the social component of citizenship and the right for Pomquet residents to have culturally and linguistically appropriate education as citizens despite their rural position (Marshall, 1950).

In the Canadian federal system, power is shared between the federal and provincial governments. This division of powers permits individual provinces to sustain a degree of authority over the policy and legislation of their region (Breton, 2005). Within this model, provincial governments oversee education, except for education on First Nations reserves.

Primary and secondary education are fundamental rights of citizenship in Canada, but education is predominantly a provincial responsibility. Rural education in particular presents both unique challenges and definitive advantages for students, and for communities in which schools often act as hubs of community engagement and activity. The extent to which French-language education in each province is successfully implemented is one way to assess challenges and advantages in accessing French-language education. Grounded in the narrative of social citizenship rights, French-language education was developed in Nova Scotia during the late 1980s and early 1990s in response to the educational needs of some of its citizens. It was envisioned as benefitting all Acadians and francophones within the province. This move toward language equality in the province also engaged with the larger national rights of citizen equality that emerged in section 23 of the Canadian Charter of Rights and Freedoms in 1982 (Brodie, 2002). Prior to 1982, language rights were not on the state agenda, and thus nor was the responsibility to provide francophone citizens in Canada with education in their native language. In fact, provinces discouraged offering that education (Heller, 2008; Heller et al., 2016). In the Education Act of 1841, Nova Scotia allowed French as a language of instruction in schools, but the curriculum remained in English (Buckner, 1993, p. 79; Ross & Deveau, 1992, p. 96).

In light of the foregoing, this chapter has two central purposes: 1) to provide an historical overview of how education developed in the rural Acadian community of Pomquet, Nova Scotia, and to demonstrate the narratives of ownership and belonging that emerged alongside this process; and 2) to examine the shift that occurred when francophone language education became a central focus of national policy—an agenda that was not necessarily aligned with Pomquet citizenship solidarities. I conclude with a discussion of how citizenship's exclusionary practices, such as not providing adequate or culturally appropriate education to a rural linguistic minority, can result in language loss. In the case of this study, the discussion reveals that the educational priorities of Nova Scotia have never been in line with the educational priorities of the community of Pomquet.

Data for this study was collected through semi-structured interviews, participant observation, and archival research throughout 2016 and 2017 in the community of Pomquet. I spoke with parents, past and current teachers, former members of the school board, and community members. Semi-structured interviews and life history interviews were audio-recorded and transcribed. The coded themes of education, language, and rurality were then analyzed for the purposes of this chapter. Archival materials and life history interviews provide a foundation for an examination of how education in Pomquet evolved throughout its history, and semi-structured interviews and participant observation inform an analysis of the shift to community education regulated by the Conseil scolaire acadien provincial (CSAP), the francophone school board, in the late twentieth and twenty-first centuries. The research collectively provides insight into the impact this transition has had on the community and overall education of children.

Early Education in Pomquet

In the initial settlement of Pomquet in the eighteenth century, it was difficult to organize education in the community: many children were needed at home to work on the farms. Due to its rural locale, it was also difficult to find French teachers to work in the community, and many families were unable to afford the taxes associated with education. At the time, there was little access to minority language education throughout Atlantic Canada (Buckner, 1993). In 1816, however, missionary Father Antoine Maneau established the first school in Pomquet for the parishioners of Pomquet, Tracadie, and Havre Boucher (Rennie et al., 1980).

This initial school produced a foundation for francophone education for the three Acadian settlements in the region. In 1823, three nuns established another school called "Le Petit Couvent"; however, in 1835, after the three sisters had moved to Tracadie and no longer ran the school, the building was listed as vacant. In 1848, there were two schools in Pomquet—École du Lac (with 24 students) and another located in Monks Head (with 31 students).

Presented with a need to preserve Acadian culture and provide education at a wider scale to francophones in Atlantic Canada, the urban elite in Moncton, New Brunswick started a church-centred Acadian Renaissance that resulted in the Acadian nationalist movement between the 1870s and 1880s (Buckner, 1993; Muise, 1993). In 1864, Saint Joseph's College opened in Memramcook, New Brunswick, becoming chartered in 1868 (Buckner, 1993; Richard, 2006). Many of the Acadian elites that were part of the Acadian Renaissance attended Saint Joseph's College, as did their children after them (Buckner, 1993). This Renaissance occurred during a key period of nation-building in Canada that saw the development of national and multicultural politics. Acadian newspapers began to be produced in the 1880s in both New Brunswick and Nova Scotia, leading to increased communication between Acadian communities (Fingard, 1993; Kymlicka, 2001; Taylor, 1994).

Schools and churches became key places for nationalist narratives to permeate communities. As a result, early education and schooling in Pomquet were linked to the church and influenced by the attachment of local priests to the Acadian Renaissance. Advocacy on the part of priests in continuing to promote rural Acadian life as well as natural population increases also ensured the longevity of Acadian communities, despite external threats (Fingard, 1993). In the 1870s, there was little French schooling across the Maritimes; however, with a larger Acadian population than Nova Scotia and Prince Edward Island, New Brunswick was more successful at achieving rights for Acadians (Buckner, 1993). By contrast, a standard English curriculum became compulsory across Nova Scotia in 1864, which was also implemented in the French schools in the 1870s (Buckner, 1993).

Education provided employment opportunities to young Acadian women who were studying to become teachers at convents in Atlantic Canada and Quebec in the French language rather than in English. As a result, many Acadian teachers who came to Pomquet, most of whom settled in the community, were able to teach in French despite the English curriculum. In 1916, the Pomquet school district was divided into three areas: Lower Pomquet, Upper Pomquet, and Monks Head. Monks Head School was built in 1916, and the others were constructed shortly after that. An addition to Lower Pomquet School was built in the 1940s. All three schools offered a mix of French and English. However, many residents with whom I spoke who had attended these schools during the 1940s and into the 1950s remember school as difficult because many of the teachers were English and most people in Pomquet at the time only spoke French at home. Many community members recounted stories of struggling to adjust to the English language and English resources used at school. It remained difficult for the community to recruit teachers qualified to teach French (Benoit, n.d.). If the community was able to secure a francophone teacher, classes were often taught in French, but with English materials. These francophone teachers shouldered the burden of translating curriculum, lessons, and reading materials into French for their students.

This experience with inadequate educational supports in Pomquet became more challenging with the centralization of education. Education is mainly a provincial responsibility, meaning educational language policy changes from province to province. In the late nineteenth and twentieth centuries, some provinces allowed French-language instruction, but in some regions within these provinces, it was still not permitted (Heller et al., 2016). In Pomquet, schools remained in the Antigonish School District and followed an English curriculum. The major shift in French education services came with changes to national policy in the 1960s. These changes fall under what Marshall describes as the social component of citizenship—that is, to being granted the right to "a modicum of economic welfare and security to the right to share to the full in the social heritage and to live the life of a civilized being according to the standards prevailing in the society. The institutions most closely connected with it are the educational system and the social services" (Marshall, 1950, p. 69).

In 1969, the Official Languages Act addressed the language rights of francophone minorities, granting the French language equal status with English (Woehrling, 1985). This shift at the national level resulted in a growing acceptance of French language being spoken among the dominant English-speaking population, and this indeed led the provincial governments in both New Brunswick and Nova Scotia to provide French education and French social resources to Acadians. In Nova Scotia, the Conseil scolaire acadien provincial spans the province and has schools in rural Acadian communities and in urban centres. There is also an Acadian post-secondary institution, Université Sainte-Anne, in Church Point, Nova Scotia, and representation under the Department of Acadian Affairs within the Nova Scotia provincial government. These examples demonstrate how the provincial legislation and policy at the national level have been used to benefit the Acadians as an ethnonationalist group. However, these services are not always distributed equally.

Negotiating Minority Education Rights

Rural education poses unique challenges to both students and educators, particularly as they relate to securing and maintaining facilities that meet the needs of rural students (Eastwood & Lipton, 2000; Wallin, 2008). These challenges include teacher and administrator recruitment and retention, access to resources and adequate space, and capacity for growth. Furthermore, schools within the CSAP system generally lack extra-curricular activities, especially sporting activities, because of the small class sizes and distance between schools within the school board (DiGiorgio, 2006).[2]

The challenges associated with rural education increase with the added dimension of minority language and rights. In 1961, the Pomquet Consolidated School (hereafter, Pomquet School) was constructed. The school provided a much-demanded and much-needed new education facility in the community. This school became the centre of community activity. A sense of community pride was tied to this building and what it represented as far as improving the education of children in Pomquet. The curriculum, however, was English, and the teachers at Pomquet School thus continued to promote the importance of French education within the community of Pomquet. Two retired teachers I spoke with, both of whom had moved.Pomquet for work from other Acadian communities, remembered the difficulties with using the English curriculum provided by the province. They noted that it required more effort on their part to offer the students in Pomquet an adequate education because most did not speak or read English, so there was a lot of preparation involved in translating materials and providing bilingual education.[3] The teachers worked to educate the children of Pomquet in French when possible, which speaks to these teachers' desire to create language programs that would reflect the community's language ideologies (Cormier, Bourque, & Jolicoeur, 2014).

A few years after the construction of Pomquet School, the teachers lobbied for the Grade 9 students to be able to attend Antigonish East School in Monastery because they would have separate teachers for science and math, as well as access to labs and other facilities that Pomquet School did not have. Students in Grade 9 and above were the first to be sent to Antigonish East School in Monastery, followed by those from Grades 7 and 8.[4] By 1965, students were required to attend Grades 7 to 12 outside the community, as Pomquet School was reduced to Kindergarten to

Grade 6.[5] Students who attended school in Antigonish or Monastery in the 1960s experienced discrimination based on linguistic and geographic differences. During this period, anglophone students began to define students from Pomquet by their rurality and language. These negative experiences, associated with increased assimilation into the dominant culture through attending school outside of the community, account for some of the language loss in the community.[6] In addition, a significant amount of out-migration to the eastern United States for work between 1940 and 1960 as well as increased economic dependency on Antigonish adversely affected the francophone composition of the village and impacted the sustainability of the French language in the region.[7]

Throughout the next few decades, there was a significant shift in identity politics in Canada. In 1968, the Fédération acadienne de la Nouvelle-Écosse (FANE) was founded in the province "to promote the growth and global development of the Acadian and Francophone community of Nova Scotia" (FANE, 2016). In 1982, as part of the revisionist Canadian constitution, several changes were made to promote federalism, multiculturalism, immigration, Indigenous rights, and francophone rights (DiGiorgio, 2006; Kelly, 2001). Within the Constitution Act, 1982, section 23 of the Canadian Charter of Rights and Freedoms addresses the topic of minority language education rights. Section 23 goes a step further than the equal status that was given to the French language in the Official Languages Act in 1969 by explicitly addressing the rights of francophone minorities (Woehrling, 1985). In Nova Scotia, there was already activity to create Acadian schools, and by 1986, within five different school districts, there were 19 designated Acadian schools. However, much of the authority within these schools remained with the English school boards that operated them (Goreham & Dougherty, 1998).

Between 1960 and 1980, these national political shifts coincided with increases in Acadian nationalism, cultural politics, and language revival in Pomquet. In the 1980s, the FANE founded a branch in Pomquet, known today as la Société acadienne Sainte-Croix. This resulted in a significant identity shift within the community that emerged out of the larger national language agenda in Canada. The presence of the FANE in Pomquet promoted both historical and nationalistic Acadian narratives that did not necessarily permeate the community during the height of the Acadian Renaissance in the 1880s. The establishment of the FANE led to citizens of Pomquet experiencing increased identification with elements of Acadian nationalism and the importance of language and French education. It also ushered in new opportunities for the community to engage with Acadian nationalism and its attendant language politics.

The curriculum at Pomquet School remained predominantly English throughout the 1980s, despite these local and national political changes, until Pomquet School was granted French immersion programming within the English school board in 1990. In 1992, Pomquet School gained Acadian school status, which meant it became a French-language school. Different from French immersion programs, which provide anglophone children with the advantages of bilingualism in French and English in Canada (Hart & Lapkin, 1998; Wise, 2011), French-language schools aim to cater to the needs of francophone students. The implementation of Acadian schools in Nova Scotia under the English school boards resulted in tensions around jurisdiction, decision-making, and infrastructure across the province (Goreham & Dougherty, 1998).

Thus, after several public consultations, in 1995, a French-language school board with the jurisdiction to manage minority language educational facilities was formed alongside a new Education Act for the province (Goreham & Dougherty, 1998; Nova Scotia Department of Education, 1995). The Conseil scolaire acadien provincial (CSAP) was founded in 1996 (CSAP, 2018). That same year, Pomquet School became part of the CSAP. Although the government consulted with communities, education remained under provincial jurisdiction, and therefore in the control of the anglophone majority (DiGiorgio, 2006). The transition to Acadian school status and the move to the new French-language school board ensured children in Pomquet would continue to be educated in French.

Conflicting Solidarities in Language Education

In 2001, École Acadienne de Pomquet was constructed, and it has offered Kindergarten to Grade 12 from the beginning. Thus, since then, students have been able to complete their entire elementary and secondary school education in the community. Many community members, past and current teachers, and members of the school board viewed the construction of the new school as a major achievement for the community. Others believed that it came too late to save the French language in Pomquet.

Since the community did not have the same feelings of ownership over and belonging to École Acadienne de Pomquet that they had developed at Pomquet Consolidated School, the move to the new provincially operated French-language school presented new challenges for residents and students. Many within the community did not feel welcome or like they belonged at the school. As one participant reflected:

In the 1970s, Pomquet began hosting an annual winter carnival at the school. We
had concerts; we had suppers, we had parades, we had snow sculpting—a nice variety
of activities. Everything, everything was in French. And they were very, very popular
and drew a lot of people. They went on until the 1990s. Then for some reason, when
we got our new francophone school, the emphasis turned more on the school and less
on the community. When we had them [the activities] at the Consolidated School,
the whole community was involved.[8]

Moreover, some participants described the relationship between the school and the community as turbulent; these community members explained that the school no longer served local interests and instead supported a pre-constructed agenda created at the provincial level. This state-based nationalism in the distribution of language education also resulted in Pomquet as a community losing a degree of control over their school and the ways in which it was able to meet particular community needs as it shifted to CSAP jurisdiction (Taylor, 1994). The divide that occurred with the jurisdictional change raises new questions about the link between culture and language as they pertain to Acadian identities in the twenty-first century. With the construction of École Acadienne de Pomquet, the community and teachers were no longer the authority on *how* language and culture were taught in the school.

Citizens of Pomquet lobbied for a CSAP school, and many viewed it as a benefit to the community. It was an opportunity for children in the community to complete, once again, their primary and secondary education in the community rather than having to travel to Antigonish. Contrary to the intent of French-language schools, École Acadienne de Pomquet has experienced an influx of anglophone students in recent years. Teachers have noted that students from Pomquet at the school made up (and still make up) a minority of the students. It is also important to note that by the school's construction in 2001, many children native to Pomquet would have already experienced significant language loss. Thus, many parents wish for their children to be educated in French today, and Pomquet is the only school in the area that offers full French-language education. The student populations of CSAP schools, particularly those within urban areas or that are surrounded by anglophone communities, are becoming English dominant. Moreover, the sociocultural environment in Nova Scotia is English dominant, which places increased challenges on these schools and communities when it comes to maintaining the French language (Cormier, Bourque, & Jolicoeur, 2014).

Despite the dominance of English in the sociocultural environment, many anglophones see a benefit in schooling their children in French. There is an emphasis on "choice" when enrolling children in Acadian schools (DiGiorgio, 2006). Describing another CSAP school in the province, DiGiorgio (2006) notes that the school in her study emphasizes aspects that are not available elsewhere in the English public school; in this case, it is a system that offers a more valuable product (the French language) that will ensure students' success later in life. This is also true of other schools within CSAP, in that they emphasize supporting Acadians or French heritage, smaller class sizes, familial spirit, and a willingness to help children succeed. These elements of the CSAP system are what make the schools attractive to parents outside of Pomquet. Contrary to this perspective, recent studies on French immersion programs in Canada have revealed segregationist and exclusionary practices that do not support all learners and that benefit the status quo (Arnett & Mady, 2018; Willms, 2008).

The increase of students from outside communities has resulted in École Acadienne de Pomquet outgrowing its space because of the student demand for education in French. After reaching its capacity in the last few years, some students are now housed in portable classrooms behind the school. After a significant amount of lobbying by parents and teachers, in April 2018 the school was approved for a multi-year expansion. The citizens have, yet again, become responsible for raising the proper attention to ensure their school receives an expansion so it has adequate space for students to receive an appropriate education.

Since the transition to École Acadienne de Pomquet, the community, educators, and students have found themselves grappling with new challenges. The main challenge is educating students with little foundation in the French language, while simultaneously revitalizing Pomquet's declining French-speaking population. The CSAP school also came with a new mandate to promote Acadian and francophone culture. This mandate is in line with liberal state nationalism in Canada, which aims to define and promote cultural difference (Mackey, 2002). It is supported by national policies that benefitted Pomquet from the 1960s to the 1980s, and unlike other forms of regional and cultural nationalism, Acadian nationalism does not threaten the nation-state. Despite being in line with the school's mandate, the promotion of culture and language has become increasingly difficult for teachers because Acadians are a minority in the school population and, moreover, there is little interaction between the school and the community. The cultural differences that were, from the beginning, important factors in promoting culture and language (in this case, Acadian culture and language) have become lost in the large, dominant English population that attends the school.

Conclusion

This chapter has highlighted the issues that have arisen concerning access to French-language education in Pomquet, Nova Scotia, with particular attention to the divide that emerged between community ownership and response to state policy. Pomquet's rurality has created unique barriers to the implementation of a French-language school that might not have been present in more urban centres or in Acadian communities with stronger connections to cultural and linguistic politics. This case study demonstrates the impact rural citizenship has on accessing both language and education rights. Citizens of Pomquet have fought for their schools and their language since the establishment of their community in the late eighteenth century. The hard work of teachers and parents has ensured that students in the community are educated in their language, despite the lack of an adequate and linguistically appropriate curriculum in the province. Even with the implementation of supportive policies at the national level after the 1960s, the "state" or province was not able to provide sufficient resources for French-language education in Pomquet, and as a result, there was substantial language loss and the community school now favours those from more urban areas. The community no longer owns its education, nor does it have the control to develop it for the community's benefit.

Exclusionary practices of citizenship have led to a significant degree of language loss for this rural linguistic minority because the educational priorities of the province have not been in line with the educational priorities of the community. That is, national policies have focused on supporting bilingualism for all, rather than the maintenance of francophone areas and distinct dialects that can become lost through assimilation with the dominant culture. Concerned citizens in this study noted that the French taught in École Acadienne de Pomquet today is not Pomquet French, and they argued that their dialect has largely been lost due to the various social factors outlined in this chapter.

State processes have led to an increased awareness of the need for funded francophone education in Nova Scotia. State and corporate interests tend to combine to benefit the interests of the upper class within urban areas (Harvey, 2008). Such erosion of social citizenship rights through neoliberalism impacts a small community and its connection to the language (Brenner, Peck, & Nik, 2010; Brodie, 2002). Provincial and national agendas do not necessarily support the needs of an ethnic or linguistic minority, especially in rural contexts. It is evident, through this case study, that in Pomquet rural and linguistic minority rights have not been taken into consideration by the state. With the jurisdictional shift in education, minority rights in Pomquet have not been fully considered. Although Pomquet was initially influenced by national shifts in language policy, the community's linguistic minority rights have not been fully supported by these processes; rather, it is their rural position and the authority that community members have held within their schools that have allowed the language to flourish within the education system.

Notes

1. The research presented in this chapter was supported by the Social Sciences and Humanities Research Council of Canada, 767-2015-1379, 2015.
2. Participant interview, June 22, 2017.
3. Participant interview, September 28, 2016; participant interview, October 3, 2016.
4. Participant interview, September 28, 2016.
5. In Nova Scotia, Kindergarten is called Primary.
6. Participant interviews, September 28, 2016; participant interview, October 2, 2016.
7. Participant interview, February 2, 2018; participant interview, May 17, 2018.
8. Participant interview, October 3, 2016.

References

Allen, J., Massey, D. B., & Cochrane, A. (1998). *Rethinking the region*. Routledge.

Arnett, K., & Mady, C. (2018). Exemption and exclusion from French second language programs in Canada: Consideration of novice teachers' rationales. *Exceptionality Education International, 28*, 86–99.

Benoit, P. (n.d.). *Historie de Pomquet*. Pomquet, NS: Pomquet Heritage Museum.

Brenner, N., Peck, J., & Nik T. (2010). After neoliberalization? *Globalizations, 7*(3), 327–345.

Breton, R. (2005). *Ethnic relations in Canada: Institutional dynamics* (Vol. 44). McGill-Queen's University Press.

Brodie, J. (2002). Citizenship and solidarity: Reflections on the Canadian way. *Citizenship Studies, 6*(4), 377–394.

Buckner, P. A. (1993). The 1870s: Political integration. In E. R. Forbes & D. A. Muise (Eds.), *The Atlantic provinces in confederation* (pp. 48–81). University of Toronto Press.

Buckner, P. A. (2000). "Limited identities" revisited: Regionalism and nationalism in Canadian history. *Acadiensis, 30*(1), 4–15.

Conseil scolaire acadien provincial (CSAP). (2018). *Notre histoire*. https://csap.ca/le-csap/notre-histoire

Cormier, M., Bourque, J., & Jolicoeur, M. (2014). (Re)-introduction to French: Four education models to revitalise an endangered group in Eastern Canada. *International Journal of Bilingual Education and Bilingualism, 17*(2), 160–177.

DiGiorgio, C. (2006). What happens after the law is passed? Marketing to parent demands in a Canadian francophone school. *Journal of School Choice, 1*(3), 91–113.

Eastwood, R., & Lipton, M. (2000). *Rural-urban dimensions of inequality change.* WIDER Working Paper 200. UNU-WIDER.

Faragher, J. M. (2006). *A great and noble scheme: The tragic story of the expulsion of the French Acadians from their American homeland.* W. W. Norton & Company.

Fédération acadienne de la Nouvelle-Écosse (FANE). (2016). *Qui sommes-nous?* https://www.acadiene.ca/home/qui-sommes-nous/

Fingard, J. (1993). The 1880s: Paradoxes of progress. In E. R. Forbes & D. A. Muise (Eds.), *The Atlantic provinces in confederation* (pp. 82–116). University of Toronto Press.

Forbes, E. R. (1983). *Aspects of maritime regionalism.* Canadian Historical Association.

Goreham, R., & Dougherty, S. (1998). *School governance: The implementation of Section 23 of the Charter.* Office of the Commissioner of Official Languages.

Griffiths, N. (2005). *From migrant to Acadian: A North American border people, 1604–1755.* McGill-Queen's University Press.

Hart, D., & Lapkin, S. (1998). Issues of social-class bias in access to French immersion education. In S. Lapkin (Ed.), *French as a second language education in Canada: Recent empirical studies* (pp. 324–350). University of Toronto Press.

Harvey, D. (2008). The right to the city. *New Left Review, 23,* 23–40.

Heller, M. (2008). Language and the nation-state: Challenges to sociolinguistic theory and practice. *Journal of Sociolinguistics, 12*(4), 504–524.

Heller, M., Bell, L. A., Daveluy, M., McLaughlin, M., & Noël, H. (2016). *Sustaining the nation: The making and moving of language and nation.* Oxford University Press.

Johnston, A. J. (2007). The Acadian deportation in a comparative context: An introduction. *Journal of the Royal Nova Scotia Historical Society, 10,* 114.

Kelly, J. B. (2001). Reconciling rights and federalism during review of the Charter of Rights and Freedoms: The Supreme Court of Canada and the centralization thesis. 1982 to 1999. *Canadian Journal of Political Science/Revue canadienne de science politique, 34*(2), 321–355.

Kymlicka, W. (2001). *Politics in the vernacular: Nationalism, multiculturalism, and citizenship.* Oxford University Press.

Mackey, E. (2002). *The house of difference: Cultural politics and national identity in Canada* (2nd ed.). University of Toronto Press.

MacLeod, K. K. (2015). Emergence and progression of Acadian ethnic and political identities: Alliance and land-based inter-peoples relations in early Acadia to today. *Totem: The University of Western Ontario Journal of Anthropology, 23*(1), 7.

Marshall, T. H. (1950). Citizenship and social class. In *Citizenship and social class, and other essays* (pp. 1–85). Cambridge University Press.

McKay, I. (2000). A note on "region" in writing the history of Atlantic Canada. *Acadiensis, 29*(2), 89–101.

Muise, D. A. (1993). The 1860s: Forging the bonds of union. In E. R. Forbes & D. A. Muise (Eds.), *The Atlantic provinces in confederation* (pp. 13–47). University of Toronto Press.

Nova Scotia Department of Education. (1995). *Education horizons: White Paper on restructuring the education system*.

Ornstein, M. D. (1986). Regionalism and Canadian political ideology. In R. J. Brym (Ed.), *Regionalism in Canada* (pp. 47-88). Irwin Pub.

Pocius, G. L. (1991). *A place to belong: Community order and everyday space in Calvert, Newfoundland*. McGill-Queen's University Press.

Rennie, C., Doiron, C., Morell, L., & Morell, P. (1980). *La tradition orale de Pomquet*. Pomquet, NS: Société Sainte-Croix.

Richard, C. (2006). Le récit de la Déportation comme mythe de création dans l'idéologie des Conventions nationales acadiennes (1881-1937). *Acadiensis, 36*(1), 69-81.

Ross, S., & Deveau, J. A. (1992). *The Acadians of Nova Scotia: past and present*. Nimbus Pub Limited.

Statistics Canada. (2016). Census Profile, 2016 Census. Nova Scotia. Population, urban and rural, by province and territory. Summary table: Population and demography, All subtopics. Last updated June 18, 2019. https://www12.statcan.gc.ca/census-recensement/2016/dp-pd/prof/details/page.cfm

Taylor, C. (1994). The politics of recognition. In A. Gutman (Ed.), *Multiculturalism: Examining the politics of recognition* (pp. 25-73). Princeton University Press.

Wallin, D. (2008). A comparative analysis of the educational priorities and capacity of rural school districts. *Educational Management Administration & Leadership, 36*(4), 566-587.

White, S. (2005). The true number of Acadians. In R. G. LeBlanc (Ed.), *Du grand dérangement à la déportation: nouvelles perspectives historiques* (pp. 21-56). Chaire d'études acadiennes, Université de Moncton.

Willms, J. D. (2008). The case for universal French instruction. *Policy Options, 29*(7), 91-96.

Wise, N. (2011). Access to special education for exceptional students in French immersion programs: An equity issue. *Canadian Journal of Applied Linguistics/Revue canadienne de linguistique appliquée, 14*(1), 177-193.

Woehrling, J. (1985). Minority cultural and linguistic rights and equality rights in the Canadian Charter of Rights and Freedoms. *McGill Law Journal, 31*, 50-92.

3

Experiencing an Active Citizenship

Democratic and Inclusive Practices in
Three Rural Secondary Schools in Spain

LAURA DOMINGO-PEÑAFIEL, LAURA FARRÉ-RIERA & NÚRIA SIMÓ-GIL

Introduction

The following chapter outlines and analyzes the range of democratic practices in three Catalan secondary schools located in rural areas. The question that guides our research is: how can rural educational contexts contribute to the learning of citizenship? In order to give an answer to this great rural challenge, we investigate some educational experiences based on principles related to the experience of citizenship and highlight the possibilities and limits they present.

This chapter is based on two Spanish research projects. The first project, "Demoskole: Democracy, Participation and Inclusive Education in Secondary Schools,"[1] which ran a three-year research program starting in 2013, analyzed the participatory and democratic processes in five different educational schools (one rural, two semi-rural, and two urban). This research aimed to contribute to developing new ways to achieve democracy and participation in secondary schools to improve inclusion and social cohesion. The second project, "Democ: Community Service as an Innovative Social Practice in the Local World: Analysis and Proposals for Improvement,"[2] focused on one specific rural secondary school to analyze its service learning project and how community engagement promoted collaboration between the secondary school and social entities within the municipality. Furthermore, the foundation of the Democ project arose from the Demoskole research, in order to achieve the common goal of guaranteeing more democratic, inclusive, and participatory practices in secondary schools.

Methodologically, the two research projects were grounded in the interpretive paradigm, deepening the knowledge of a concrete reality by gathering together the opinions and experiences of all members of the educational community. The qualitative data collection tools used in both projects were: a) a review of official school documents; b) interviews; c) focus groups; and d) observations. The purpose was to collect and to analyze the points of view of each educational centre's agents about different educational experiences that promote student participation in order to move toward more inclusive and democratic contexts.

Regarding this, and through the lens of rural citizenship, we selected three secondary schools for children aged between 12 and 16 (from first to fourth grade of ESO —Compulsory Secondary Education) located in small, non-isolated Catalan villages. Catalonia has an area of 32,107 square kilometres with 7,600,267 inhabitants (Idescat, 2019), and is organized into four provinces. From a demographic point of view, 95% of the population lives in urban regions. Nonetheless, based on geographic data, Catalonia can be considered a rural area because out of its 946 municipalities, 71.85%, or 680, are small municipalities (Aldomà, 2009).

This chapter is organized into five sections that provide: (a) an outline of the need to promote the learning of democracy in schools from the perspective of citizenship as a practice; (b) an analysis of the legal framework in which education for citizenship is registered, as well as the opportunities through which to live it; (c) summaries of three case studies in rural and semi-rural secondary schools, which describe and analyze different practices of democratic participation as spaces of citizenship; and (d) an in-depth analysis of service learning experiences that points out the opportunities and difficulties involved in learning citizenship outside of the urban context. In the last section, the main conclusions show that citizenship is learned through democratic experiences, and specifically through service learning projects.

Promoting Democracy in Schools from the Perspective of Active Citizenship

Nowadays, many citizens seek an active, critical, and committed role in confronting the social conflicts and inequalities of today's world. The debate surrounding education for democracy, according to Crouch (2004), arises out of the deterioration of government institutions and principles of equity. Even though some essential elements for democratic empowerment have been stripped away by economic powers, schools must take up the challenge of teaching democracy and connecting the idea of empowering a community to practice democracy through citizenship. Bosniak (2000) has categorized the study of modern citizenship into four dominant perspectives: citizenship as legal status, rights, participation, and identity and solidarity. According to Mansouri and Kirpitchenko (2016), citizenship highlights the role of civic participation and engagement in the life of the political community. Thus, we understand citizenship education in schools as a way of life, as a process (Osler & Starkey, 2003), and not as a result to be achieved in the future, because in schools individuals function as citizens (Biesta et al., 2009).

Democracy and Education

In the current social and political contexts, the definition of democracy in schools is both ambiguous and problematic. The conception of what democracy should involve can all too easily be reduced to the presence of pupil and/or teacher representatives in school governing bodies, where their ability to influence school life is limited to participating in discussions about relatively peripheral matters (Simó et al., 2016). We propose that schools ought to promote some democratic form of life in which deliberation and democratic decision-making, resolution of conflicts, responsible cooperation, and participation are deemed essential in maintaining democratic forms of life.

The starting point of schooling is that children and youth should have the power to express their points of view and opinions on all matters affecting them, or on those that influence the context of schools. This means that students have to be able to participate in their schools as citizens, which is the path that could ensure democratic well-being in educational centres (McLellan et al., 1999; Samdal et al., 1998).

Democracy is not simply a form of government but rather a relational process, fundamentally, a "mode of associated living, a conjoined communicated experience" (Dewey, 1966, p. 87). It is only in this way that trust can be built, allowing relationships in which all participants—in this case, pupils and teachers—feel that they are full partners (Thornberg & Elvstrand, 2012).

According to Feu, Serra, Canimas, Lázaro, and Simó-Gil (2017), the concept of school democracy can be understood from four dimensions. The first is governance, which involves community members' participation in all the bodies and processes related to decision-making. This affects the relationship between members of the educational community and allows them to develop a common interest.

The second dimension is habitance, which refers to the set of actions that make the educational community, and especially students, feel good and able to fulfill their main task: to be autonomous citizens who have good judgment, relate well with others, are happy, and can successfully complete the various stages of the education system. This involves three fundamental aspects: the minimum conditions that make possible the participation of each member of the school community; the receptiveness and quality of members' shared life and a sense of well-being in participatory contexts; and the kind of relationships that take place in educational centres between all members.

The third dimension is otherness, which is understood as being embodied in the practices, discourses, initiatives, policies, and projects that are established in order to recognize (respect, welcome, include) and positively assess the "other" (the minority, the unconventional, the counter-hegemonic, etc.). In this respect, the term diversity can also be used as a synonym. Democratic practice consists not only of tolerating the other, but also of giving them visibility and normalized treatment, resituating the relations of power and domination between the hegemonic and the peripheral. These three dimensions demand a transversal fourth dimension, ethos, which is understood as the humanist values and virtues needed to make this democracy possible (Feu et al., 2017).

Citizenship Education in Democratic Schools

In the twenty-first century, citizenship education has been established, in most countries of the European Union, as an educational initiative designed to achieve a fairer society with values such as justice, peace, and tolerance. Furthermore, there are diverse contexts in which to learn practices of citizenship and experience it actively at the same time: the school is the only institution that enables this citizenship learning for all youth (Edelstein, 2011). Thus, citizenship education ostensibly provides social and civic rights and principles that support the practice of democratic citizenship to achieve a more cohesive, inclusive, and equitable society. In fact, education is arguably the most powerful and effective way to guarantee the exercise of democratic, responsible, and critical citizenship, as well as promote the active and civic participation of youth.

Our research has focused on how youth participation in schools can enable individuals to learn citizenship in a democratic way. Taking into account the four dimensions of democracy discussed above, we must bear in mind that it is not possible to have citizenship education that does not include cognitive learning on what democracy is and how to experience it. As Edelstein (2011) asserts, school practices must combine efforts and methodologies to promote learning about democracy, through democracy, and for democracy.

Based on the idea that youth must be able to exercise their citizenship within their schools, we adopt the concept of "citizenship-as-practice" (Lawy & Biesta, 2006) and connect it to the quotidian dynamics of the democratic experiences that young people encounter both inside and outside the school. We disagree with the concept of "citizenship-as-achievement," and of the school path that represents a narrow perspective of the citizenship concept. This last concept involves understanding that individuals can only exercise citizenship once they have experienced a certain educational trajectory and development of maturity. This approach excludes children and youth from the opportunity to live and learn from their current condition as citizens (Lawy & Biesta, 2006). As Meehan has suggested, active citizenship stands for a combination of "voluntary action and experiential learning" (2010, p. 115). Moreover, this view of active citizenship provides a more integral and global perspective on what it means to be a citizen.

Analysis of the Spanish Legal Framework for Citizenship Education

In analyzing the legal framework in Spain, we can see that educational laws have changed with each new government, generating instability surrounding educational policies. Thus, each law on education has forced educational centres to adapt their reality to the new characteristics and demands. Specifically, in recent years, citizenship education has been one of the subjects at the centre of the struggle, conditioning the progress toward citizenship education.

Even though the government had begun to implement subjects related to ethical and civic education, it was not until the Organic Law of Education (LOE) of 2006 that three specific subjects—citizenship education, ethical and civic education, and ethical values—within the formal curriculum were introduced and integrated in the curriculum around citizenship and human rights when a left-wing party governed in Spain. These subjects became compulsory, accessible, and fixed within school schedules. The LOE was intended to help develop social and democratic rights as part of the set of aims of education to contribute to the formation of new citizens. Specifically, the preamble of the law points out that citizenship education must be a subject that facilitates shared spaces for all students related to social and democratic citizenship in a global context (Parareda-Pallarès et al., 2016). This subject was contested by right-wing political parties and by most conservative religious powers in Spain. In 2011, this situation changed (Gómez &

García, 2013) when a right-wing political party won the election, and launched, in 2013, a new Organic Law for Improving the Educational Quality (LOMCE)—the current law today. It was considered more important to integrate components of civic education and values in all curriculum subjects in a transversal way, hence justifying the decision to remove the specific subjects of citizenship and human rights from the school context.

This situation has caused inconsistencies regarding curricular, methodological, and organizational decisions that secondary schools must assume in relation to teaching citizenship (Parareda-Pallarès et al., 2016). These schools have been concerned about finding areas within the curriculum to articulate different democratic experiences of citizenship in the absence of specific subjects.

In this context, we have identified some difficulties in promoting the active engagement of children as citizens in schools. First, the successive changes in educational laws have generated a climate of uncertainty related to civic and ethical education; and second, the limited areas dedicated to citizenship education in curriculums have increased the difficulty in achieving this type of educational practice. If one of the main objectives of education is to promote youth participation in an active and democratic attitude within society, it is foundational to recognize them as citizens of the present and not only as citizens of the future (Lawy & Biesta, 2006). But how can teachers confront this challenge? In the next section, we present three case studies that each trace educational experiences within the school environment that promote different opportunities for a democratic form of life.

Democratic Participation for Citizenship Education in Three Rural Secondary Schools

During the Demoskole research project, we asked representatives from participating secondary schools what experiences they considered most relevant in terms of democracy and the participation of their students in school. They told us about situations in which they thought the students had played a key role, moments that promoted the establishment of horizontal relations between teachers, students, and the community, and so forth. All three schools implemented a focus on democratic education that we analyze and discuss below.

Rural Secondary School A
In school A, our proposal looked at creating citizenship activities that would link the curriculum and the community. School A was opened as a cooperative

learning project for ESO and with the willingness to ensure educational success for all, from an inclusive perspective. The school is located in a small town (of less than 3,000 inhabitants) in the province of Barcelona, near Vic, a city of about 40,000 inhabitants in central Catalonia. At the time of our research, the school accommodated some 300 students from the town and the nearby rural community. Its main objectives were the academic and personal improvement of all their students and the development of social skills essential for the learning of citizenship, such as solidarity, responsibility, social entrepreneurship, and respect for diversity (Simó-Gil, Tort-Bardolet, Barniol, & Pietx, 2018). This secondary school participated in our two research projects, as mentioned at the beginning of the chapter. We conducted analysis and made suggestions for improving the service learning projects as they developed. Apart from this, the most noteworthy activities involving citizenship education in this school were:

1. Cooperative work groups in all school subjects. The organization of these groups affected the school timetable (some classes were in two-hour blocks), the arrangement of the classrooms—the pupils were always in groups of four—and the type of work they did, since tasks were collaboratively carried out.

2. Individual tutoring. Each teacher acted as an individual tutor to 10-12 pupils and each student was able to talk with their tutor whenever they needed to. The school encouraged students to lead procedures and take initiative to maintain a relationship with their tutor. On some occasions, the student's family also participated in these meetings with the teacher.

3. School support brigades. Every pupil took responsibility for a school service and worked with a team to deliver it. The teams included, for example, the green team—maintenance and gardening; teaching team—support for pupils with academic difficulties; bicycle team—cycle repairs; interior team—decoration; mouse team—computing; and the class representative team, among others.

4. Collaborative evaluation. Pupils participated in the process of their own evaluation, using self- and co-assessment. They used evaluation rubrics for a lot of activities, and some items were developed together with teachers as a team evaluation.

5. Service learning projects. The pupils did educational work with the community to effectively promote positive change in society. During the Democ project, as presented below, we analyzed the activities and

how community engagement promoted collaboration between the secondary school and the social entities of the municipality.

Semi-Rural Secondary School B

In school B, we focused on the experience of citizenship as the foundation of the school's project. School B was founded 12 years ago and covers ESO. It was created by a group of professors concerned with the organizational and pedagogical system of ESO. Located in a municipality of the interior in the north-east of Catalonia with less than 10,000 inhabitants, it accommodates students of diverse origin from this locality and the neighbouring areas. This school presented a pedagogical project closer to the learning of citizenship from an integral perspective, which included the experience of democratic values like respect, the evaluation of the efforts made by students, and spaces for participation within the school context. The school's activities related to citizenry were:

1. Project work. This occupied between six and eight hours a week and involved pupils working in cooperative groups of four. Here the pupils could recognize that their opinions were important because group work involves debate, decision-making, self-management, and coordination between group members.
2. Good morning sessions. This activity took place during the first 15 minutes of the school day. All the pupils in the same year assembled in a classroom to discuss and listen to something that had happened, an important piece of news, or a saying that either the teachers or the pupils wanted to explore together.
3. Pupil council. This body, set up by the school, was made up of pupils, class representatives, and others, from all the groups of the same year, and was tasked with making decisions about matters that would affect the pupils in general.
4. Service learning project. This activity combined learning objectives with community service so that local entities of the municipality could effect positive change within the community.

Rural Secondary School C

In school C, we concentrated on curriculum proposals that would promote citizenship. As it is the only secondary school in the area, this high school receives all ESO students from a small village (2,700 inhabitants) in the province of Barcelona, to the northwest of the city of Vic, and from other nearby rural municipalities (small towns and villages). This creates in the young people a territorial identity, in that the pupils all have a common feeling of belonging to that territory. The school was created in the 1995–96 academic year, and its relatively small size, with a total of 270 boys and girls, makes it a familiar (small and friendly) institution with a climate of coexistence with few conflicts—three outstanding qualities shared by the different sectors of the educational community. In this school, we highlighted three training spaces related to the community work axis that connected the activities of the school with the community.

1. Theater project. In the fourth year of ESO (in which pupils are 16 years old), a student play was organized with the aim of raising money for the end-of-the-school-year trip. The entire education community participated in this experience, including families, students, and some teachers, with decision-making processes shared between them.

2. Small groups for attention to diversity. These were organized taking into account students' learning difficulties in diverse subjects like Catalan, Spanish, and math. Teachers valued this strategy because they could offer more individualized attention to the students.

3. Outside community activities. Voluntary activities were conducted in the community, such as organizing concerts or races for the people of the town. Fourth-year secondary school students and their families played a key role, since they sought to do activities that would allow them to raise money for the end-of-the-year trip.

Analyzing Different Practices of Democratic Participation as Spaces of Citizenship

In our research for the Demoskole project, we found a correlation between the experience of democracy through democratic educational spaces and learning citizenship. While in school C specific, proposed activities were developed that would convey the learning of citizenship, schools A and B approached such learning from an institutional perspective. In the latter case, it was not only some activities that allowed for this learning; it was all the work of the school.

The schools that generated spaces for debate, opinions, and decision-making from students, as in cases A and B, lived democratic processes through activities and methodologies such as cooperative groups, projects, support teams for teachers, and tutoring. This strategy particularly promotes learning through democracy (Edelstein, 2011), whereby democratic experiences are offered and lived in order to acquire sustainable democratic habits. For example, schools A and B generated more situations in which decisions were valued from different points of view. They also encouraged learning for democracy (Edelstein, 2011) through service learning activities, where a link with the environment is promoted, in the community.

Our research shows that citizenship learning cannot be separated from the concept of democracy. Although the experience of citizenship takes different forms, the will of each school's community to live in a subjective and shared way is necessary. As Biesta et al. (2009) propose, for example, young people should feel what it means to "live citizenship." This way of promoting and living democracy requires understanding human relationships in a specific way, especially when they relate to people of different ages who occupy different positions in a framework that, by definition, is hierarchical. For all of these reasons, we consider that the experience of citizenship in schools requires that educators equip themselves with elements that allow students to live transversally, in all the spaces of the school.

Along these lines, service learning experiences are presented below as a practice that permeated the educational project of school A and that allowed the pupils to experience citizenship in the rural world.

Community Engagement in the Service Learning Experience: Opportunities and Difficulties

The analysis of service learning experience formed part of the Democ project, with the aim of investigating the participation of young people in different projects that were being developed in rural secondary school A. We chose this school because of its powerful community projects and the integration of these projects in its own school curriculum. Specifically, we worked collaboratively with this school and some social entities to investigate the participatory processes of students and the inclusive and civic practices that service learning experience might guarantee.

As a publicly owned school, school A encouraged a respectful and close relationship with the community as a way to promote the civic, engaged, and active participation of youth through service learning methodology. This methodology combines a process of learning and community service in a single and well-articulated project, where students work on the needs of their community with the aim of improving it (Service-Learning Promotion Center, 2019). Through this methodology, the school guaranteed, first, the acquisition and development of personal skills and competences in the classroom (10 hours), and second, social action within community entities (10 hours minimum) (Simó-Gil et al., 2018). In fact, the main purpose of this experience was to detect a real need in the community context and then to design and implement different activities and proposals to respond to that need. This school had a wide range of projects (nearly 20 each year) with different focuses and sensibilities, such as digital literacy for elderly people, aid given to entities through student collaboration, the restoration of some nature paths in collaboration with the local town hall, and projects of cooperation with Rwanda through a Catalan NGO.

Service learning projects encourage young people to make decisions about what activities to develop within social entities and institutions, such as NGOs, schools, and senior citizens' centres, and how, so dialogue becomes a crucial tool through which to establish agreements between students, teachers, and members of community entities. Consequently, students' participation in different social projects with different institutions to achieve improvement as a collective plays a key role. Therefore, these projects can be considered as educational projects with social utility, because of the combination of peda-gogical intentions with social values (Furco, 1996). Service learning projects are powerful in schools where the dimensions of democracy—governance, habi-tance, and otherness—are present. By definition, students experience some kind of governance when they make decisions about the projects. When developing service learning projects, it is also necessary to ensure that the climate (habi-tance) is safe for everyone so that students can experience trust in their actions, and that otherness is clearly understood in a positive way so that all students can find their own place in the groups to which they belong. Considering these dimensions, the role of the students is to be active agents who put into play their knowledge and capacities in order to serve and develop some kind of impact for their community. Thus, they experience a genuine participation in real contexts (Simovska, 2004, 2007). This practice therefore fosters their autonomy, placing them at the centre of educational activity (Blitzer-Golombek, 2009), which promotes the learning of citizenship as a way of living, as a process, and not as a result to achieve in the future (Biesta & Lawy, 2006; Lawy & Biesta, 2006). All of this ensures a civic and engaged student experience in an active exercise of citizenship.

Conclusion

In light of our field work, we want to highlight five characteristics of the three schools studied to resolve the central question of this chapter: how can rural educational contexts contribute to the learning of active citizenship?

First, results showed that schools that promote more democratic educational practices encourage learning through democracy (Edelstein, 2011) and promote participation in a democratic school community. The pupils took more responsibility in their learning process in dealing with new situations, and thus they acquired sustainable democratic habits (Dewey, 1966). Following Edelstein (2011), we observed in these schools that the more that skills, practices, and learning processes are experientially linked in the learning community, the more they are embedded in a participatory school culture. The students developed strategies like searching for data, debating, giving opinions, and using dialogue to discuss controversial subjects, and the students' decisions were respected and valued by the different agents in the community. This way of working broadened governance in the schools (Feu et al., 2017), specifically in schools A and B. As we referred to above, learning methodologies were organized in these educational centres as a way to deepen the integrated approach of linking knowledge from different curricular areas to overcome the fragmented approach of disciplinary school curricula. In these conditions, learning for democracy, as Edelstein (2011) argues, means to include democratic forms of life based on cooperation and participation in local, national, and transnational contexts.

A second point worth noting is that the three schools shared the issue of taking care of human relationships, which involves making sure that student participation is valued both inside and outside the classroom. The existence of relationships based on trust and more horizontal forms of collaboration between the teachers and pupils led to a sense of well-being. This, in turn, had an effect on the atmosphere within these schools, and on relationships of proximity between the different members of the community. Thus, in schools where there were less rigid disciplinary structures, the participation of students was more active and the climate based on trust increased. In short, a democratic climate in these schools contributed to the development of responsibility and individual student participation in school activities, which made up the habitance dimension (Feu et al., 2017) in each school. As John-Akinola, Gavin, O'Higgins, and Gabhainn (2013) point out, this feeling of belonging, developed from interpersonal relationships, makes it possible to have a higher degree of commitment to and participation in school life.

Third, the small schools were more permeable to collaborations with families and community agents. This is where rurality specifically comes into play. Entering and leaving a small school is easier, and the educators know and benefit from the educational and social points of view of community members. We found differences between the three schools, but they all tried to offer individual opportunities for each student. In this context, a significant tension emerges in the recognition of otherness (Feu et al., 2017) when minority groups do not share the majority's preferences. In these situations, the schools that are more explicit in widening participation in decision-making to a more heterogeneous core of students broaden the degree of adhesion and the students' feeling of belonging to the school.

We also want to emphasize the importance of each school's educational project and how the sense of commitment within the community was reflected in it. Although the management team of each school had studied how to promote relationships with the community, albeit in a singular way and with different intensities, all three schools lived their involvement with the community as a democratic community experience. Hence, our investigation showed that schools A and B had clearly chosen this option in the curriculum and in the school's project. This way of living democracy within the school context made a difference in terms of citizenship education in these schools. In short, we found them to be schools in which the dimensions of governance, habitance, and otherness were present in their ways of organizing educational activities, along with a large dose of ethics, awareness, and reflexivity. It is only through these dimensions that it is possible to enable teachers, students, and families to participate fully in a school's democratic processes, thus influencing the fourth dimension, the ethos (Feu et al., 2017).

Another point to consider is that the cases analyzed show that it is possible to live citizenship as a democratic experience when management teams have a clear educational project. This can be achieved in a tangential or occasional way, as in the case of school C, or in a more integral or global way, such as in schools A and B, but in all cases, it is necessary to have the teachers' support and the involvement of the educational community—despite the fact that the Spanish legal framework understands "the education of citizenship" as a result of the future (Lawy & Biesta, 2006), and does not consider young people to be full citizens who live citizenship in all contexts and among their peers in educational centres. The results of our research show that democratic processes cannot be automatically implemented—neither spontaneously nor by chance. They require a strong certainty to be able to move forward toward more participatory and open processes. This requires a strong institutional commitment (Fielding & Rudduck, 2002), to organize new structures, new activities, and a rethinking of the internal workings of each institution.

Finally, we want to highlight the role of school A in community development. Through this school's service learning project, we identified three impacts of these projects on rural contexts: 1) a sense of co-responsibility among the social agents, students, and teachers for the detection of community needs and also interest in the actions that young people carry out for the community; 2) involvement in the coordination between the agents for the successful progress of the service; and 3) improvements in the nearby area that young people carry out through the community actions they develop. These impacts are fundamental to the experience of citizenship as a practice (Lawy & Biesta, 2006). Active citizenship is thus a process that is under construction in the school, not in the future.

In conclusion, these two research projects have given us the opportunity to show some ways to transform difficulties into possibilities to advance toward a more democratic school. As we have shown in this chapter, schools need to overcome different obstacles as a consequence of living an active citizenship (Meehan, 2010). Learning citizenship is a way to experience democracy through participation in school life and in the community. This is challenging, but these three rural schools have shown us how to deal with tensions in the curricula, in the school climate, and in the role of teachers and pupils that has emerged from experiencing active citizenship.

Notes

1. Demoskole integrated two coordinated projects. The first was aimed at primary schools and was coordinated by Jordi Feu (University of Girona), and the second looked at secondary schools and was coordinated by Núria Simó-Gil (Educational Research Group of UVic-UCC). Both were financed by the Spanish Ministry of Education (Ref: EDU 2012-39556-C02-01/02).
2. Democ's project was run by the Educational Research Group of UVic-UCC. It was financed by the Catalan Government (Ref: 2016 DEMOC 00012).

References

Aldomà, I. (2009). *Atles de la nova ruralitat*. Fundació del Món Rural.

Biesta, G., & Lawy, R. (2006). From teaching citizenship to learning democracy: Overcoming individualism in research, policy and practice. *Cambridge Journal of Education, 36*(1), 63-79.

Biesta, G., Lawy, R., & Kelly, N. (2009). Understanding young people's citizenship learning in everyday life: The role of contexts, relationships and dispositions. *Education, Citizenship and Social Justice, 4*(1), 5-24. https://doi.org/10.1177/1746197908099374

Blitzer-Golombek, S. (2009). Children as citizens. *Journal of Community Practice*, 14(1-2), 11-30.

Bosniak, L. (2000). Citizenship denationalized. *Indiana Journal of Global Legal Studies*, 7(2), 447-509.

Crouch, C. (2004). *Post-democracy. After the crisis*. Polity.

Dewey, J. (1966). *Democracy and education: An Introduction to the philosophy of education*. Free Press.

Edelstein, W. (2011). Education for democracy: Reasons and strategies. *European Journal of Education*, 46(1), 127-137.

Feu, J., Serra, C., Canimas, J., Lázaro, L., & Simó-Gil, N. (2017). Democracy and education: A theoretical proposal for the analysis of democratic practices in schools. *Studies in Philosophy and Education, 36*(6), 647-661. http://dx.doi.org/10.1007/s11217-017-9570-7

Fielding, M., & Rudduck, J. (2002, September 12-14). *The transformative potential of student voice: Confronting the power issues*. Paper presented at the annual conference of the British Educational Research Association, Exeter, England.

Furco, A. (1996). Service-learning: A balanced approach to experiential education. In B. Taylor and Corporation for National Service (Eds.), *Expanding boundaries: Serving and learning* (pp. 2-6). Washington, DC: Corporation for National Service.

Gómez, A. E., & García C. R. (2013). El debate en torno a la educación para la ciudadanía en España. Una cuestión más ideológica que curricular. *Enseñanza de las Ciencias Sociales, 12*, 127-140.

Idescat. (2019). *Institut d'Estadística de Catalunya*. https://www.idescat.cat

John-Akinola, Y. O., Gavin, A., O'Higgins, S. E., & Gabhainn, S. N. (2013). Taking part in school life: Views of children. *Health Education, 114*, 20-42.

Lawy, R., & Biesta, G. (2006). Citizenship-as-practice: The educational implications of an inclusive and relational understanding of citizenship. *British Journal of Educational Studies, 54*(1), 34-50.

Mansouri, F., & Kirpitchenko, L. (2016). Practices of active citizenship among migrant youth: Beyond conventionalities. *Social Identities, 22*(3), 307-323. https://doi.org/10.1080/13504630.2015.1119680

McLellan, L., Rissel, C., Donnelly, N., & Bauman, A. (1999). Health behaviour and the school environment in New South Wales, Australia. *Social Science and Medicine, 49*(5), 611-619.

Meehan, E. (2010). Active citizenship: For integrating the immigrants. In B. Crick & A. Lockyer (Eds.), *Active citizenship: What could it achieve and how?* (pp. 112-128). Edinburgh University Press.

Organic Law of Education (LOE) 2/2006, 3rd May, BOE number 106, 7899 (2006).

Organic Law for Improving the Educational Quality (LOMCE) 8/2013, 9th December, BOE number 295, 12886 (2013).

Osler, A., & Starkey, H. (2003). Learning for cosmopolitan citizenship: Theoretical debates and young people's experiences. *Educational Review, 55*(3), 243-254. http://dx.doi.org/10.1080/0013191032000118901

Parareda-Pallarès, A., Simó-Gil, N., Domingo-Peñafiel, L., & Soler-Mata, J. (2016). La Complejidad de vivir la ciudadanía en el Aula: Análisis en cuatro centros de secundaria. *Revista Internacional de Educación para la Justicia Social, 5*(1), 121-138. https://doi.org/10.15366/riejs2016.5.1

Samdal, O., Nutbeam, D., Wold, B., & Kannas, L. (1998). Achieving health and educational goals through schools: A study of the importance of the school climate and the students' satisfaction with school. *Health Education Research, 13*(3), 383-397.

Service-Learning Promotion Center. (2019). *Què és l'A PS?* www.aprenentatgeservei.cat

Simó, N., Parareda, A., & Domingo, L. (2016). Towards a democratic school: The experience of secondary school pupils. *Improving Schools, 19*(3), 181-196. https://doi.org/10.1177/1365480216631080

Simó-Gil, N., Tort-Bardolet, A., Barniol, M., & Pietx, T. (2018). Learning democracy in a new secondary school. *Power and Education, 10*(2), 166-180. https://doi.org/10.1177/1757743818756912

Simovska, V. (2004). Student participation: A democratic education perspective—Experience from the health-promoting schools in Macedonia. *Health Education Research, 19*(2), 198-207.

Simovska, V. (2007). The changing meanings of participation in school-based health education and health promotion: The participants' voices. *Health Education Research, 22*(6), 864-878.

Thornberg, R., & Elvstrand, H. (2012). Children's experiences of democracy, participation, and trust in school. *International Journal of Educational Research, 53*, 44-54. https://doi.org/10.1016/j.ijer.2011.12.010

4

Hallway Pedagogy and Resource Loss

Countering Fake News in Rural Canadian Schools

ARIO SETO

Introduction

"I can tell you a lot of stories about the nonsense my students get from social media and want to chat about later at school," said MJ5M, a teacher on Newfoundland and Labrador's Burin Peninsula, Canada, when I asked him if he had ever encountered the circulation of fake news or other problematic social media content among his students.[1] He continued on to say that it had become a daily experience for him, as a social studies teacher, to counter the disinformation that students read from various internet sources. Four teachers from four different schools in the region also narrated similar stories, and two of them recounted the experience of correcting students who had written their homework based on online "alternative facts." The proliferation of problematic online content—fake news, disinformation, misinformation, alternative facts, and racism, prejudice, and bigotry—has increased teachers' workloads as they find themselves on the frontline of countering such circulations. In rural settings, as this chapter will elaborate, teachers sometimes feel that they are "left alone," as teacher FK6F put it, in cultivating students as critical citizens, since there are fewer civic organizations in rural areas.[2]

The presence of civic organizations, according to the teachers, could be a critical social forum for students to experience differences, to engage in socio-political discussions, and therefore to learn to be responsible citizens by assessing facts from various perspectives. The interviewed teachers believed that such opportunities are necessary to expose students to people from different backgrounds and with different opinions, and thus to foster understanding of the notions of tolerance and indifference. These civic values that students could acquire from civic organizations, they believed, would be the first step in converting the literacy they learn in the classroom into knowledge. Accordingly, this chapter discusses the challenges associated with ensuring critical citizenship education (Giroux, 1984, 2005) in rural areas, both in and outside the classroom, in the context of how rural students should have the same opportunities as their urban counterparts to acquire civic training in a wider social sphere in the wake of the rising circulation of problematic online content.

This chapter addresses this issue across five sections. The next section describes the socio-cultural context in which rural education in Newfoundland takes place. It is followed by the third section, which focuses on the challenges that students and teachers face in pooling the necessary resources to maintain teaching activities. The fourth and fifth sections then discuss the strategies that rural teachers have initiated to counter the circulation of problematic online content with their students by becoming their mentors both at school and in the community.

The ethnographic research for this chapter was conducted on the Burin Peninsula, Newfoundland and Labrador, Canada, between September 2018 and March 2019. Besides participant observation in school environments, seven in-depth interviews were conducted with teachers. Since the anonymity of schools, teachers, and students is protected by law (Access to Information and Privacy Act, 2015), the schools and teachers in this research are not named. The names of the teachers are coded using a selected two-letter identifier, years of teaching experience (with "r" used for retiree), and gender.

The Rural Context

In terms of landmass, Canada is one of the largest countries in the world, second only to Russia. However, for economic and resource access reasons, around 81% of Canadians in 2015 lived in cities, which the Canadian government defines as places of more than 1,000 residents, or centralized urban areas (Martel, 2015). By contrast, with 41% of its population inhabiting the rural areas, in the province of

Newfoundland and Labrador, the urban–rural ratio is more balanced when compared to other provinces. With a total area of 405,720 square kilometres, Newfoundlanders and Labradorians are scattered across rural towns, which they call "communities."

Newfoundland became a lucrative destination for European settlers in the early sixteenth century because it is located next to one of the world's richest fishing grounds, the Grand Banks. With the fishery as the primary livelihood, they created coastal settlements around the bays of the island and used boats as their means of transportation to obtain supplies and visit acquaintances or family members in neighbouring communities. Even today, some rural areas in Newfoundland and Labrador remain only accessible by ferry services provided by the government. Access to communities is subject to harsh weather conditions over the winter months, when boat schedules might be interrupted and local roads might become unusable (Policy and Planning Division, 2010). Apart from boats, mobility around the island has also been limited to cars since the Newfoundland Railway Company went bankrupt in 1988. Coach service operates between several major hubs on the island, but its reliability is also affected by fluctuating weather conditions. In Newfoundland, isolation is not only a social construction, but a reality of nature.

With the land being too acidic to sustain agriculture (Fisheries, Forestry and Agriculture Agency, 2018), fishery was the province's major industry for almost 500 years until the codfish moratorium began in July 1992. The moratorium was declared in the wake of years of overfishing that also led to the strict regulation of other commercial fishing licenses (Fife, 2014). At that time, nearly 30,000 people lost their jobs and related industries on the island collapsed. Limited job security has consequently pushed the province's labour force toward out-migration (MacDonald et al., 2013). Between the start of the moratorium until 2020, the province recorded a population decline of approximately 58,000 people. The census shows that out-migration affects both genders, but is prevalent among a higher proportion of men, particularly working-age men between the ages of 25 and 39 (Newfoundland and Labrador Statistics Agency, 2020). A member of a local development association on the Burin Peninsula explained to me, however, that the actual out-migration might be greater than the official number recorded by Statistics Canada since some workers leave the province to work elsewhere but maintain factual residency on the island. This economic and demographic decline disrupted the preservation of the community's social and cultural institutions. As Sider described, "fish plant employment [was] gone, the village grocery store closed...cars [were put] up on blocks for the winter...[the] telephone [was] given up...As income, ways of working, and community collapse, and kin and friends and neighbors leave, people are increasingly unable to meet the demands of their own culture" (2006, p. 258). Elizabeth Murphy, a community organizer of a community-based Economuseum explained to me that community centres rely greatly on local seniors to run the community's affairs.

The limited human resources for social institutions resulted in a decreased number of civic activities for young people. During my fieldwork on the Burin Peninsula, several young Newfoundlanders narrated their everyday life regularities, explaining that since they had nothing else to do, they would simply stay at home and entertain themselves with either online activities or television. Youth activities are highly dependent on volunteerism and some communities lack the formal institutions to regulate these activities (see also Sheppard & Anderson, 2016, p. 40). As communities such as his go through a process of decline, AM8M, a teacher who organized community sports, expressed his concern that young rural Newfoundlanders end up lacking civil society experiences. "Even just organizing sports teams, we lack people," expressed MJ5M, a volunteer high-school sports coach, on the issue. Sports, according to him, can teach students about "solidarity" and being "fair," regardless of players' skills, class, and cultural differences. He framed participation in community sports as a virtue that should thrive among students as young citizens in progressive democratic settings to counter the circulation of problematic online content.

The decrease in regular community activities also signifies a decline in civic forums. AM8M gave an example of how young people used to be able to chat with seniors during community activities, which provided them with the opportunity to exchange ideas. For instance, he narrated how older members of the community, who could remember the ravages of polio and tuberculosis in Newfoundland in the 1950s and 1960s, would quickly oppose online content that undermined the benefits of vaccination circulating on popular fake news outlets (see also Kitta, 2018). These rural teachers lamented that such forums and civic experiences are crucial for helping students receive a "reality check," as MJ5M expressed, to counter what they read online. They opined that such experiences could offer students the practical training to become responsible citizens—a subject they have learned about in the classroom—particularly against the background of the limitations of rural schools, as the next section describes.

Rural Education

In times of economic decline, the Government of Newfoundland and Labrador and the Canadian government in general tend to turn to education policies as a remedy (Corbett, 2004). Both the federal and provincial governments view education as a solution that will equip citizens with the labour skills necessary to navigate economic uncertainty. Education is therefore a state's prescribed mechanism of control used to provide citizens with a certain formal way of overcoming their economic struggles. Accordingly, schooling is conceptualized simply as bait for a better future in a simple economic sense (Atkin, 2003; Overton, 1995). The risk of such a development agenda is what Giroux (2012) pointed out as a "crisis in public values," that is, when the state leans toward policies in which education is relegated to a support system for capitalist business values and self-interest. In this schooling ideology, such policies hinder schools' creativity in offering educational opportunities that might be necessary for students in the face of social change (see also Giroux, 1984).

Although Giroux's studies focused on education in the United States and should be applied carefully in examining Canadian cases, his concerns about capitalist ideology as a management platform for safeguarding education are congruent with the problem of rural school management in general. When they have to decide between the costs associated with the school's role in crafting public values and those of school administration, governments tend to opt for the latter. In this policy logic, teachers and school activities are dependent on budget efficiency, which is thus a pivotal aspect of the provision of rural education. This problem can be found throughout Newfoundland and Labrador. Since the moratorium and the subsequent out-migration, the number of students enrolled in school has declined and many rural schools have closed (Mulcahy, 2009; Stevens, 2006).[3] For example, in 2018, the provincial government closed one school with no expected enrollment, saving around $77,000 annually (McCabe, 2018). Consolidations have also saved the province money. With budget as a decisive factor, the provincial government is at risk of prioritizing cost above the integrity of education, which has prevented schools from improving on their educational programs (Mulcahy, 2009). For example, while music is an exemplary subject for teaching students about non-violent behaviour, according to MA8M, music education has been declining in recent years, and where programs remain, there are no certain strategies to solve the problem of aging musical instruments and the shortage of music teachers (see also Sheppard & Anderson, 2016, p. 46).

These challenges of rural schooling realities emerge because rural schools are subjected to policies that are made in and designed for urban settings. Mulcahy has underscored the urban bias of rural school development design as "policies of consolidation, centralization, and standardization have been relentlessly implemented" (2009, p. 25). Even when rural education policy is successful, the measurement of "success" is problematic. If the expectation is that such outcomes will comprise the province's general elevation in the face of economic problems caused by the moratorium, the result is ambiguous: successful education is then perceived by students as a "ticket out" of challenging rural life, rather than a means to ensure that they can stay where they grew up, as the teachers interviewed for this study admitted (see also Atkin, 2003). Successful students, or those with better social capital, tend to leave the community to pursue better jobs as the region lacks jobs. Education does not stop out-migration from the rural community. This means that education policies should not only focus on vertical mobility, but should also seek out ways to provide opportunities for students to become resilient and carve out strategies to remain in their rural communities.

Besides school closures, such a resource allocation approach also locates education as an expense rather than an investment, which has made recruiting and retaining teachers difficult (Riggs, 1987). The lack of human resources limits the degree of achievement that teachers are expected to be able to meet as outlined by the Department of Education's curriculum requirements (Mulcahy, 2007; Patterson et al., 2006). Preparing a rural-capable teacher, as part of professional development, with sufficient training in understanding the construction of the rural world is another issue to raise (Barter 2008).[4] Newhook (2016) found that rural teachers perceive their challenges and the burden of the workload to be larger when compared to their colleagues who teach in urban areas, such as in the St. John's metropolitan area or larger towns. She explained that in addition to more challenges in multi-grade teaching, teachers in rural areas also have to deal with long-distance commuting, the lack of material resources, and "difficulties in work-life separation in the community" (Newhook, 2016, p. 90).

Small rural schools are often stretched beyond what their resources allow. Keeping the school open often corresponds with an increased teaching load, since many rural Newfoundland schools use multi-graded classrooms, or composite classes, with different curriculums. As such, any further demands on the system exhaust the already limited resources. In the post-truth era, the teachers in this study believed that they should be generating extensive and vigilant supervision for students as the latter learn to sift through facts and alternative facts. They expressed that countering fake news cannot work if it only becomes the task of those teaching social studies. M A 8 M, also a vice principal, underscored that since problematic online content is becoming more "scienti-ficesque"—common current examples including the anti-vaccine campaign and the flat-earth conviction—debunking it requires more coordination with science teachers. The problem is that such coordination requires extra time and hours of meetings—an extra workload that teachers cannot afford to take on. With long commutes, extra-curricular activities, and supervision outside of class time, the minimum labour force of rural teachers that the government provides is already exhausted, he added.

A classic strategy to counter the resource limitation is distance education. The Government of Newfoundland and Labrador has implemented distance education through the Centre for Distance Learning and Innovation (C D L I) since the turn of the millennium (Barbour, 2005; Mulcahy, 2009). Schools in Newfoundland initially struggled to access digital technology (Barbour, 2007), but the problem was resolved when the provincial government started to provide satellite dishes that offered a stable internet connection (Atkin, 2003). In 2018, I found that an updated computer lab with virtual classroom applications had become the stan-dard equipment for rural schools in the province.

Infrastructure is the least of teachers' concerns. Steven's (2006) study found that the problem with e-learning is a social one. On one hand, there is an ambiva-lence whereby students might actually be satisfied with distance education as it has made it possible for the student to know and work with "one of the best teachers" (Steven, 2006, p. 123) on the other end of the line. On the other hand, students also experience a sense of social alienation. On one occasion, I met a student who was completing her distance-education sessions for Biology and French sitting alone in the computer lab. When I asked whether she was enjoying the learning expe-rience, she said that she felt lonely at first. Intriguingly, she also wondered about why she still had to go into the school to complete her distance-learning sessions, with a schoolteacher checking on her now and then, when she could complete them at home. When I was visiting during her C D L I session, one of the teachers went into the computer lab for less than five minutes to check on her. Compulsory class attendance in a segregated designated lab seems ironic, since the presence of a teacher in such technological learning experiences is just in passing; the teacher's physical presence seemed irrelevant to this student. With their everyday independent study experience, students gain confidence in their ability to master their subjects using the technology provided without the presence of a teacher.

This raises the issue of the teacher as a figure of authority who can validate information, since students are getting used to computer-assisted learning on their own, without the presence of a teacher.

Hallway Pedagogy

Students' mounting confidence in their independent study abilities, as described in the previous section, creates a new challenge for rural teachers when it comes to convincing students to reject fake news and alternative facts. During a Q&A session after I, as a guest speaker, presented methods on debunking fake news at a Burin Peninsula school, several students expressed their fondness for reading conspiracy theories on social media and even the dark web. One of the students said that it was "fun" to read them because they offered the other side of the story. The entertainment dimension in the positive acceptance of alternative facts is not a new issue. But it is alarming for public morality when it becomes a method of negation against the construction of factual information. Marchi (2012) found that, as they prefer to source news from Facebook, teenagers in the United States have begun to reject journalistic objectivity, as they consider that most news outlets, regardless of differences in politics and points of view, will broadcast similar news. Such tolerance of the degree of "objectivity" of facts has provided the possibility for readers to read any news simply as a spectacle, instead of as a form of information gathering (Mihailidis & Viotty, 2017). Responding to such issues, BM8M shared with me his experience that sometimes his students initially "do not care" if the content they read is true or not. In any given situation, however, he saw such problems as an opportunity to have a deeper "discussion of a world issue" with the students.

Returning to my Q&A session, the accompanying teacher for my session told me after the class that students were aware of close reading techniques and were digitally literate—which they also had demonstrated during my Q&A session—as they had learned about the subjects at school. She nevertheless added that in addition to the skills of digital literacy, in order to reverse students' receptiveness to fake news, they need to be willing to reject such circulations. As long as it is fun, she asserted, students will continue reading problematic online content. All the other teachers I interviewed at other schools confirmed her assessment of the popular circulation of misinformation and disinformation among students. This phenomenon raises the issue that the problems of fake news and alternative facts have extended beyond mere questions of digital literacy. Sociologically, such practices present a new challenge to the construction of public morality, as, left unchecked, they foster complacency with dishonesty.

Agosto (2018) argued that as an educational institution, the school already has the infrastructure for literacy education, with the library as a centre and teachers as the gatekeepers to information. Through these actors and agents, students are expected to learn close reading and to be critical of how news and information are presented (Luhtala & Whiting, 2018). These approaches, however, undermine the fact that students' encounter with information is not simply confined to the school and library, since they also continuously read other sources beyond the school environments. Subsequently, the hegemony of teachers and schools is being contested by social media circulations and "alternative" news producers.

The circulation of fake news and alternative facts among students varies across two distinct categories, which I identify as muted and expressive. In muted circulation, students do not discuss what they have read online in the classroom or at school. MC4F shared that she had not realized the prevalence of fake news circulation until she had asked her students, around a year ago, what they had recently read. She had found students were prone to reading untrustworthy websites, such as those stemming from conspiracy theorists. As replacement teachers who had worked at different schools, MJ5M and BM8M confirmed her findings. In their experience, students might not use such fake news to complete their school assignments, but they indeed use "alternative facts" narratives in their small talk between classes and outside the school.

MJ5M narrated a contrasting situation, emblematic of expressive circulation. For him, it was clear that some students are convinced by problematic online content, as they had expressively used it to justify their opinions during discussions on current politics, such as job creation, carbon tax policies, and immigration, and current debates about the validity of science, such as the issue of vaccination side effects and climate change. Another expressive use of fake news is when students actually cite the material for their schoolwork. Three other teachers interviewed for this research recounted that students were indeed using such alternative-facts-based sources for coursework. For example, one of FK6F's students wrote a paper in English class with sources from conspiracy websites on the use of radio-frequency identification in schools as a form of government control.[5]

In countering such issues, teachers have to find ways to convince students to reject problematic online content. A common strategy is to conduct deeper

discussions on the issue, as BM8M mentioned. Discussions are, however, not
without challenges. FK6F explained that a traditional method of discussion,
such as the philosophical chairs method where discussion is directed to examine
if the class should "agree" or "disagree" with the discussed subject, is only ill-
perceived by students, as they think that teachers are simply offering contrasting
facts of their own or their own opinion, rather than actual facts. She recalled a
moment when she was debunking Alex Jones' conspiracy theories in a valida-
tion session in which she could tell that students did not take her information
seriously. She expressed, "Luckily I had students who are aware of Alex Jones
[as a far-right conspiracy theorist], and could share their voice [of disagree-
ment] and give further examples of his out-there theories." It was only then that
the classroom shifted into a discussion forum in which most students participated. Her "lucky" experience echoes Giroux's (2005) suggestion that education
cannot focus on individual cases or achievements—in this case, accepting valid
facts—but rather on reaching collective goals as group projects. Teachers, accordingly, cannot only be the only agents in countering fake news. They need to find
students with whom they can partner.

The teachers interviewed for this study shared similar "beyond-formal"
pedagogical knowledge that, in their experience, students who believe in alternative facts are more open to changing their opinions when teachers personally
approach them outside the classroom. This method is what MA8M coined as
the "hallway conversation," an informal conversation between teachers and
students in the school's hallways. All the teachers agreed that hallway pedagogy
makes teachers more accessible to students. In my observation, this approach
of informal message delivery actually transforms the roles of educators from
that of "teachers" into "mentors." Both parties are more relaxed in expressing
their opinions and they can use colloquial language. MJ5M expressed that in
the hallway, teachers can also informally but directly advise students on what
is "right" and "wrong"—leniency that should be avoided in the student-centred
learning method, where teachers in the classroom are urged not to directly tell
students that they are wrong.

PV4F also argued that students seemed to be appreciative of the teacher's
information given during hallway conversations, possibly because such admissions "did not take place in front of their peers" in the classroom. By having
small talks in the hallway, students are more willing to dismiss their own opinions because, in this smaller social setting, they do not need to publicly admit
in front of their peers that they have made a mistake in assessing a fact, thus
avoiding being mocked as "stupid" by their friends. On the effectiveness of

hallway conversations, CM4F reflected that "critical thinking is still the best way." She pointed out that her students, "[eventually] feel betrayed by fake news." She formulated that the "dehumanizing" aspects of problematic online content can become an opportunity for teachers to reclaim respect from their students. Contrary to the online environment, in the hallway setting, teachers are approachable human mentors in the eyes of the students. In a larger context, such an approach thus provides a possibility for the teachers and schools to reclaim their position as the gatekeepers of legitimate information.

Surveying more than 400 students in Italy, Lenzi and her team (2014) found that to encourage more civic engagement from students and to craft the value of becoming a responsible citizen among them, schools should deliver a "democratic school climate" (pp. 252, 254) where civic discussions on democratic principles and civic participation flourish. All the teachers interviewed for this research nonetheless warned that the effectiveness of out-of-classroom conversations to support the democratic school climate is still limited to a school site since hallway conversations are bound to the virtual division between the school's critical ecology and the reception of unrestricted alternative facts outside the school. JM5M described the situation as being "a hard one to talk about. Teachers are encouraged not to have any real connection outside the school structure. It is very important to teach digital safety and citizenship but the best we can do is provide the tools and hope they are used outside school." BM8M expressed similar concerns about this: "That is not to say we do not care, but we are encouraged to keep a distance and keep our lives professionally separate."

Considering this communication barrier and since teachers cannot address any education issues alone (see also Waddock, 1995), teachers had expected that the community would step up to create further democratic learning spaces. The problem is, they alleged, rural communities lack a variety of civic activities. As a result of population decline, communities have fewer volunteers to organize youth activities and are unable to maintain a pool of capable partners. All interviewed teachers for this study had the view that in urban schools, parents and students would at least have more opportunities to be exposed to the community's civic projects, through which students could encounter other educated members of the society as there would be more social organizations. In rural Newfoundland, many of the organizations that served young people in the pre-moratorium years, such as youth clubs and the Canadian cadet movement, among others, are either struggling to attract new members because of the low population base or have disappeared from the landscape entirely. An example is the 4-H youth club, which grew rapidly in the 1960s across Newfoundland

and Labrador under the Department of Education's Division of Community Leadership Development, and which now has only five clubs in the province (The Telegram, 2018; see also, 4-H Newfoundland & Labrador, 2021a, 2021b). Citing the 4-H members' pledge, "My head to clear thinking, my heart to greater loyalty, my hands to larger service, my health to better living, for my Club, my Community, and my Country" (see also 4-H Newfoundland & Labrador, 2021a), M E I F, a retired teacher, explained that the independent non-profit youth organization, which focuses on leadership and citizenship, helps students understand the notion of co-existence and how to be responsible citizens through various group activities and experiential learning.

Since rural life differs from that experienced in urban centres, where education policy is shaped, studies (e.g., Barter, 2008; Sheppard & Anderson, 2016; Singh & Devine, 2013) on rural education in Newfoundland and Labrador have underscored the importance of the community's involvement in shaping schooling activities and learning experiences. Community participation brings awareness to the community of the struggles the school faces in dealing with the limited educational resources. Community involvement can provide the school with socio-cultural insight and educational context. This, in turn, could mobilize community members to offer the school the potential capacity they have to help the school adopt better learning strategies. Since school transformation is related to social change in the communities where they live, this dialogue between the school and related communities can provide information on the community dynamic and how the communities are changing. Integrating these insights in the classroom will shape a sense of place for students' learning subjects.

Although the public recognizes the importance of a collaborative approach to crafting school governance, there is still asymmetric participation and schools are often expected to be the main institution that responds to social change. For example, the recommendations outlined in the *Report of the Panel on the Status of Public Education in Newfoundland and Labrador 2015–16* (Sheppard & Anderson, 2016) pointed out what the government should do to enhance school capacity and provided less attention to community educational support building. This results in imbalanced governmental support for community educational capacity building and a condition that relies on teachers, and their teaching capacities, as the sole agents responsive to social change and, accordingly, mitigates the risk that students will perceive the school as an enclave that does not reflect the community's transformation. This is where the discrepancy between the current realities in the community and previous studies emerge. As this study exemplified, the observed school and teachers are responding quickly to counter problematic online content and innovatively generating new methods for knowledge transfer, while the community is falling behind as it lacks the needed and relevant social organizations to support the effort.

The provisional findings described in this chapter are not an attempt to revive Putnam's (2000) concern that communities are collapsing because they are being replaced by online sociability. Communities on the Burin Peninsula are still motivated to maintain their existing activities and create new centres. Retired teacher M E1F, for example, has pooled nearby human resources and applied to the government for some funding to further develop a regional museum. In this museum, young Newfoundlanders can engage with various cultural activities in which they learn cooperation, leadership, and other democratic values. The museum also has a communal garden, where students plant organic vegetables common to the traditional Newfoundland diet and harvest them annually. In the program, community members teach students the importance of food security while delivering the message of the importance that personal actions can have in tackling climate change. Yet, such examples are sporadic engagements and not a sustainable practice as they rely heavily on informal voluntarism and individual support. Exemplifying the case of 4-H, M E1F warned about how the program ended. "We got tired. The Wells' [the premier during the moratorium] government cut the budget and the support staffs were let go and us, volunteers, got stuck with all the paperwork and planning," she said.

Unfortunately, teachers are also rather helpless in finding a sustainable solution for the communities, as they recognize the lack of support available for communities to create new civic activities for students. Some teachers, like M A 8 M, M J 5 M, and P V 4 F, expressed that the best they could do was doing volunteer work in the community. The three teachers volunteered in the community's youth sports clubs where their students were also members. In such off-school sites, hallway conversation and knowledge transfer continue to transpire.

By engaging in deeper hallway conversations and volunteering in community activities, rural teachers have shown their ability to go beyond regular teaching tasks in countering problematic online content. In doing so, they have recognized the limitations of digital literacy and critical pedagogy—two methods that the students have learned to respond to problematic online content. Their efforts echo Giroux's (1983, 2005) call for teachers to be innovative, beyond the prescription of the existent teaching pedagogy, based on students' local-context reactions during teaching. While they may lack the budget and resources they need, they have nonetheless found ways to play the role of what Giroux described as promoting "character development in students, to teach them a clear sense of right and wrong" (2005, p. 19), by engaging in hallway conversations and getting involved in the community's activities. Such methods, however, are dependent on teachers' initiative and their own resources, as they have to use their private time and even financial resources to do so. Not to mention, these activities outside of school add more weight to the already-demanding teaching workload. PV4F asserted also that teachers with families face additional difficulties in investing such efforts in voluntarism, as their children need to be given the first priority when it comes to their time and attention. Countering problematic online content is thus not only an issue of school capacity, but also a problem for rural communities and the state to solve to ensure the democratic and scientific competencies of future generations through sustainable capacity building in the community.

Conclusion

The struggles of rural teachers in countering problematic online content and the circulation of alternative facts among students reveal that the issue needs to be approached beyond digital literacy and critical pedagogy. Teachers' best practices for redirecting students' reception of alternative facts demonstrate how everyday life practices can bring science back into content circulation. To this end, rural teachers in places like the Burin Peninsula have invested extra labour to innovatively address this issue by extending the discussion from the classroom to the hallway and sites outside of the school.

What makes the cases in this chapter a rural problem is that the teachers are "alone"—to use the expressions of the interviewed teachers—since the rural community and the state lack the social organizations, civic activities, and necessary policies to support their efforts. Similar to the communities where they teach, they feel isolated and unaccompanied by needed public activities that could sustain their job to ensure that students have a sound understanding of what it means to be a critical and responsible citizen. Unlike in urban settings where a larger society, various associations, and political groups are more accessible, rural communities are vulnerable in terms of their limited access to the resources that could provide support for students to learn social and civic skills. In such a setting, there is a pressing call for the state to deliver more balanced attention to support the presence of a democratic environment and civic activities in rural communities. As it is with their urban counterparts, rural communities have the right to progressive educational environments, including activities for young citizens, where teachers can be supported by local civic organizations.

As resources are not only limited in schools but also in terms of volunteers, rural communities also require various other community-based supports to sustain such endeavours. With the rise of urban migration, Canadian communities are facing resource loss and consequently a rural maintenance problem, including in stewarding progressive civic organizations that can sustain citizenship training. This is not because of a lack of trying by those who live in these communities, but because it is too large a load for them to manage on their own, especially as the state increases the demands it places on the shoulders of volunteers with, for example, paperwork and bureaucratic insurance requirements. The current resource loss has made communities like those of the Burin Peninsula suffer in terms of their ability to maintain their role as an educating space. Against this background, although the interviewed rural Newfoundland teachers are innovative in countering the weakness of digital literacy lessons and classroom-based discussions of public morality—a subject that has become increasingly important in debunking the justification of dishonesty in the wake of fake news and alternative facts circulation—their methods have yet to be proven methodologically sustainable.

Notes

1.   This research was funded by the German Research Foundation (*Deutsche Forschungsgemeinschaft*) as part of the funding for the Collaborative Research Center 1095 "Discourses of Weakness and Resource Regimes" at Goethe University Frankfurt, Germany. The author would like to deeply thank the teachers interviewed for this research and the two anonymous reviewers for their helpful suggestions.
2.   According to MA8M, workload has become an issue for Canadian rural teachers as they have to not only teach, but also coach and supervise extra-curricular activities and participate in breakfast programs, among numerous other duties, regardless of their human resources shortage when compared to their colleagues in urban areas.
3.   Confirmed with data set processing (Department of Education, 2018).
4.   See also Staszenski and Smits (2008) for cases of the teacher-technology encounter in Alberta.
5.   See, for example, the Snopes website at https://www.snopes.com.

References

4-H Newfoundland & Labrador. (2021a). Who we are, 4-H Motto, 4-H Pledge. https://4-hnl.ca/who-we-are

4-H Newfoundland & Labrador. (2021b). *History of 4-H Newfoundland.* https://web.archive.org/
web/20160306174148/https://4hnl.ca/what-is-4-h/history-of-4-h-newfoundland/

Access to Information and Protection of Privacy Act. (2015). House of Assembly of Newfoundland
and Labrador. https://assembly.nl.ca/legislation/sr/statutes/a01-2.htm#1

Agosto, D. (2018). *Information literacy and libraries in the age of fake news.* ABC-CLIO.

Atkin, C. (2003). Rural communities: Human and symbolic capital development, fields apart.
Compare: A Journal of Comparative and International Education, 33(4), 507–518.

Barbour, M. (2005). From telematics to web-based: The progression of distance education in
Newfoundland and Labrador. *British Journal of Educational Technology, 36*(6), 1055–1058.

Barbour, M. (2007). Portrait of rural virtual schooling. *Canadian Journal of Educational Administration
and Policy, 59*, 1–21.

Barter, B. (2008). Rural education: Learning to be rural teachers. *Journal of Workplace Learning,
20*(7/8), 468–479. https://doi.org/10.1108/13665620810900292

Corbett, M. (2004). "It was fine, if you wanted to leave": Educational ambivalence in a Nova Scotian
coastal community 1963–1998. *Anthropology & Education Quarterly, 35*(4), 451–471.

Department of Education. (2018). *Education and early childhood development: Education statistics, 1990–
2000.* Government of Newfoundland and Labrador. https://www.gov.nl.ca/education/
fastfacts/

Fife, W. (2014). Fault-lines and fishing: Bioregulation as social struggle on island Newfoundland.
Anthropologica, 56(1), 101–116.

Fisheries, Forestry and Agriculture Agency. (2018). Soil Survey. Government of Newfoundland and
Labrador. https://www.gov.nl.ca/ffa/faa/agrifoods/land/soils/soilsurvey/

Giroux, H. A. (1983). *Ideology, culture, and process of schooling.* Temple University Press/ Farmer Press.

Giroux, H. A. (1984). Public philosophy and the crisis in education. *Harvard Educational Review, 54*(2),
186–195. https://doi.org/10.17763/haer.54.2.a0163830n3237732

Giroux, H. A. (2005). *Schooling and the struggle for public life: Democracy's promise and education's
challenge.* (2nd ed.). Paradigm Publishers.

Giroux, H. A. (2012). *Education and the crisis of public values: Challenging the assault on teachers, students,
and public education.* Peter Lang.

Kitta, A. (2018). Alternative health websites and fake news: Taking a stab at definition, genre, and
belief. *The Journal of American Folklore, 131*(522), 405–412.

Lenzi, M., Vieno, A., Sharkey, J., Mayworm, A., Scacchi, L., Pastore, M., & Santinello, M. (2014). How
school can teach civic engagement besides civic education: The role of democratic school
climate. *American Journal of Community Psychology, 54*(3–4), 251–261. https://doi.org/10.1007/
s10464-014-9669-8

Luhtala, M., & Whiting, J. (2018). *News literacy: The keys to combating fake news.* Libraries Unlimited.

MacDonald, M., Sinclair, P., & Walsh, D. (2013). Labour migration and mobility in Newfoundland:
Social transformation and community in three rural areas. In J. R. Parkins & M. G. Reed
(Eds.), *Social transformation in rural Canada: Community, cultures, and collective action* (pp. 110–130).
UBC Press.

Marchi, R. (2012). With Facebook, blogs, and fake news, teens reject journalistic "objectivity."
Journal of Communication Inquiry, 36(3), 246–262. https://doi.org/10.1177/0196859912458700

Martel, L. (2015). Canada goes urban. In Minister Responsible for Statistics Canada (Ed.), *Canada Megatrends* (pp. 1-5). Minister Responsible for Statistics Canada.

McCabe, M. (2018, February 4). 4 communities keep schools as small as 9 students. *CBC.ca*. https://www.cbc.ca/news/canada/newfoundland-labrador/communities-keep-schools-despite-costs-programs-1.4519143

Mihailidis, P., & Viotty, S. (2017). Spreadable spectacle in digital culture: Civic expression, fake news, and the role of media literacies in "post-fact" society. *American Behavioral Scientist, 61*(4), 441-454. https://doi.org/10.1177/0002764217701217

Mulcahy, D. M. (2007). Current issues in rural education in Newfoundland and Labrador. *Education in Rural Australia, 17*(1), 17-39.

Mulcahy, D. M. (2009). Developing government policies for successful rural education in Canada. In T. Lyons, J.-Y. Choi, & G. McPhan (Eds.), *Improving equity in rural education* (pp. 23-32). Armidale: SIMERR National Centre.

Newfoundland and Labrador Statistics Agency. (2020). *Census dataset: Table 17-10-0009-01*. Government of Newfoundland and Labrador. https://www.stats.gov.nl.ca/Statistics/Statistics.aspx?Topic=population

Newhook, J. T. (2016). Teaching "in town" or "around the bay": Comparing rural and urban primary/elementary teachers' workload concerns in Newfoundland and Labrador, Canada. *Policy and Practice in Health and Safety, 8*(1), 77-94. https://doi.org/10.1080/14774003.2010.11667743

Overton, J. (1995). Moral education of the poor: Adult education and land settlement schemes in Newfoundland in the 1930s. *Newfoundland Studies, 11*(2), 250-282.

Patterson, J. A., Koenigs, A., Mohn, G., & Rasmussen, C. (2006). Working against ourselves: Decision making in a small rural school district. *Journal of Educational Administration, 44*(2), 142-158. https://doi.org/10.1108/09578230610652033

Policy and Planning Division. (2010). *Evaluation of the 24-hour snow clearing pilot project*. Department of Transportation and Works, Government of Newfoundland and Labrador. https://www.gov.nl.ca/ti/files/publications-evaluation-24-hour-snow-clearing-pilot-project.pdf

Putnam, R. D. (2000). *Bowling alone: The collapse and revival of American community*. Simon & Schuster.

Riggs, F. T. (1987). *Report of the small schools study project*. Government of Newfoundland and Labrador.

Sheppard, B., & Anderson, K. (2016). *Better together: The final report of the panel on the status of public education in Newfoundland and Labrador 2015-16*. Government of Newfoundland & Labrador.

Sider, G. (2006). The production of race, locality, and state: An anthropology. *Anthropologica, 48*(2), 247-263.

Singh, A., & Devine, M. (2013). *Rural transformation and Newfoundland and Labrador diaspora: Grandparents, grandparenting, community and school relations*. SensePublishers.

Staszenski, D., & Smits, H. (2008). *Complementary social sciences courses in the Alberta high school curriculum: A conceptual review*. Alberta Education Curriculum Branch.

Stevens, K. (2006). Rural schools as regional centres of elearning and the management of digital knowledge: The case of Newfoundland and Labrador. *International Journal of Education and Development using Information and Communication Technology, 2*(4), 119-127.

The Telegram. (2018, April 12). Province continuing financial support for 4-H Newfoundland and Labrador. https://www.thetelegram.com/news/local/province-continuing-financial-support-for-4-h-newfoundland-and-labrador-201337/

Waddock, S. A. (1995). Not by schools alone: Sharing responsibility for America's education reform. Praeger.

II

The Right to Rural Livelihoods

5

Stemming the Tide

Youth Entrepreneurial Citizenship in Rural Nova Scotia, Canada

GREGORY R. L. HADLEY

Introduction

Under siege by declining enrolments, fuelled by a considerable shift in demographics, many school boards in Nova Scotia, Canada have voted to permanently
shutter an increasing number of public schools. In 2016, one of the province's
school boards voted to close 17 schools over a five-year period (Grant, 2016). The
justifications for these, and the closures that came before and after, were generally economic, and stemmed from figures that revealed some schools were
operating at as little as 30% capacity (Strait Regional School Board [SRCE], 2016).
The rationale, however in dispute, was relatively simple: there were not enough
students attending these schools to justify the expenses associated with their
operation.

School closure has become a central issue in rural Canadian communities,
with many viewing it as a sign of the larger collapse of the rural experience.
It is tied up with out-migration-fuelled population decline, which continues
to take a distressing toll on rural Canada. Viewing school closures as a further
blow to the vitality of their respective communities, townspeople in many areas
have rallied with a galvanized intent and taken to print, social media, and the
streets in protest of the demise of the community school. Seen through the lens

of the right to be rural, the civic reaction to school closures in rural communities becomes a plea for the right to receive education close to home, to be taught by teachers who are likely to live nearby, and to have one's school bear some connection to the place one calls home. It is grounded in the belief that travelling outside the community to attend school cuts one more thread connecting young people to their rural homes and facilitates their eventual out-migration. It is premised on the assumption that a community without a school will fail to attract new families, and thus will be doomed to shrink perpetually. But it glosses over a problematic feature of rural schools: their urban-centric curriculum, which has been found in numerous studies to strengthen the discursive association between cities and success, such that students "learn to leave" (Corbett, 2007). The more appropriate civic fight, therefore, might be to keep local schools open *and* ensure that their curriculum is appropriate for the place and makes staying both appealing and possible.

The entanglements of rural schools, out-migration, rights, and citizenship are manifold. Education is widely understood as a human right, but few if any constitutions make promises about how close a school must be to a person's home. Education is the key to unlocking other universal rights, such as the right to a sufficient livelihood, as well as important for developing the capacity to exercise full citizenship rights *and* duties. The right to mobility may help guarantee the right to access education, but what of the right to *stay* and be educated in place with a curriculum relevant to local community needs and labour markets? This chapter touches on all of these intersecting puzzles and issues, by assessing the potential role of entrepreneurial knowledge, skills, and attitudes (KSA) in rural education, population retention, and youth citizenship behaviours. Subsequently, the research reveals that rural youth are, indeed, entrepreneurial and actively use their entrepreneurialism in curricular and extra-curricular contexts. This is interpreted as an underutilized opportunity related to matters of rural social stability and vitality.

A Matter for Research

In 2016, while working as a public high school teacher, I found myself at a well-attended local school board meeting where a special vote was planned on motions to close two elementary schools. An online petition, combined with ample news coverage, had mounted pressure on school board officials to amend, or even strike down, the motion to close the schools. The meeting, throughout its duration, was tense. Under the weight of considerable public pressure, its special vote was rejected. The two schools slated for closure will remain open for the immediate future.

As a classroom teacher, I would routinely listen to students speak of plans to leave their rural communities in pursuit of educational or career opportunities, none of which existed, or even could exist, in the communities they called home. As population figures demonstrate, this leads to a necessity to leave in pursuit of a more urban and, ostensibly, economically prosperous and cosmopolitan life (Corbett, 2007; Statistics Canada, 2011).

Given these experiences, the research summarized in this chapter seeks to understand why young people leave rural Nova Scotia, how their experiences and attitudes influence their departures, and how education might serve as a mechanism to disrupt out-migration. A key presupposition helps support this research: young people from rural areas would stay in their rural community if their various personal and professional wants could be satisfied. Didkowsky (2016) articulated a similar point in her research, resulting in what she coined as "youth-place compatibility." What she meant was that young people are, by and large, willing to live in a rural area, as long as it is compatible—that is, significant compromises to their educational and career aspirations do not have to be made. My research seeks to confront those compromises before a decision to leave is made, and theorizes that helping young people develop a range of entrepreneurial knowledge, skills, and attitudes could result in more citizenship behaviours, promote stronger bonds to place, and, when combined with a sense of self-determination, compel a young person to remain in a rural area, or entice them to return if they have left.

This theory is intriguing because schools are, as Corbett (2007) argues, effective mechanisms for educating young people *away* from small communities, and toward areas where the technical knowledge acquired in school is better purposed. It follows that a key challenge in rural settings, over and above keeping schools open, is finding pedagogical methods that endow the specific skill sets to allow young people the agency to better dictate the terms of their future as it relates to living in rural areas. I propose that the notion of entrepreneurialism holds the potential to merge the often-underlying affinity for a rural home held by young people with KSAs that can support uncertain educational, recreational, or employment realities (MacKinnon & Looker, 1998).

Importantly, this study does not align entrepreneurship with the creation of a business venture; rather, it situates it as a phenomenon that exists between the influences of broader sociological forces and the capacities of the individual.

As Watson (2012) writes, entrepreneurship can be understood as "the making of adventurous, creative or innovative exchanges, trades or 'deals' between entrepreneurial actors' home 'enterprises' and other parties with which those enterprises trade" (p. 311). Even those "home enterprises" are decoupled, in Watson's definition, from businesses per se (p. 312). This study accepts Watson's definition, and recognizes the importance of the individual through the mobilization of the entrepreneurial mindset. The latter is a descriptor that considers the various traits, behaviours, and attitudes held by entrepreneurs, and McGrath and MacMillan (2000) define it as "the ability to rapidly sense, act and mobilize, even under uncertain conditions" (p. 14). This mindset is often associated in the research with a suite of KSAS held by entrepreneurs. Among the more prevalent in the research include higher levels of creativity, resourcefulness, and innovation, integrated with high achievement motivation, tolerance for uncertainty, and ability to mobilize social capital (Geldhof et al., 2014). Each of these KSAS, in a broad sense, is useful, but could be particularly relevant in areas facing greater uncertainty or reduced social or economic opportunities. Combined with Watson's sociological definition, we can come to see entrepreneurialism as encompassing all of these skills, which can be applied and useful not only in the establishment of business enterprises, but in many other arenas and pursuits.

Nevertheless, it is important to note the common criticisms of entrepreneurialism. This study has been undertaken with the assumption that entrepreneurialism can serve as a progressive social and economic force for the common good. Yet it is necessary to acknowledge those elements of entrepreneurialism that have sown the seeds of economic, environmental, and social disparity that we endure in the modern world. Under the banner of neoliberalism, the entrepreneur can be less concerned with matters of the public good and more aligned with what Burchell (1996) calls "responsibilization," where the individual enjoys the maximum freedom to rationally conduct themselves (p. 29). Lemke (2001) argues that "this responsibilization conveniently annihilates notions of the 'public' in favour of the responsible individual who maximizes his or her own interests and engages in personal self-care" (p. 201). These conditions move avarice and human and environmental exploitation from a mere abstraction to a calculable pursuit. This has, unfortunately, resulted in many of the concerns associated with the contemporaneous critiques of modern capitalism. It even underlies many of the challenges facing rural communities and the fleeting nature of their economic gains.

This inquiry, however, has elected to frame entrepreneurialism in what we might call small terms. Small entrepreneurialism thinks and acts locally, with the intention of fostering community-centric economic development through job creation and enhanced social cohesiveness. In this model, entrepreneurialism is seen as a vehicle for stabilization and construction and not as a harbinger of social, economic, and environmental collapse. With this definition out front, the next section is a literature review that draws on select scholarship that has developed or mobilized ideas of youth entrepreneurship, youth citizenship, or entrepreneurial citizenship, bringing these together to advance the concept of youth entrepreneurial citizenship. After that, I introduce the empirical research to ground the preceding discussion.

Understanding Youth Entrepreneurial Citizenship

The understanding of what it means to be an entrepreneurial citizen is at the root of this study. As argued earlier, it is important to adopt a broad definition of entrepreneurship that resists a more myopic, business-centric manifesta-tion. Indeed, to be an entrepreneur is to employ a range of knowledge, skills, and attitudes that, in some circumstances, can be beneficial to a business venture, but that, in their totality, reflect behaviour and action associated with so-called modern-day competencies. These competencies include a propensity for creativity and innovation, problem-solving ability, social and emotional literacy, and communicative mastery, as well as internal locus of control, persistence, and analytical thinking. When employed, these competencies are linked to a wide range of desirable behaviours and outcomes that, as this study will argue, are beneficial to citizenship development, particularly among young people.

As noted by Damon and Lerner (2008), the study of youth entrepreneurship remains in its infancy, a statement still true today over a decade later. In fact, studies that examine entrepreneurship as it relates to young people are diffi-cult to locate, with the bulk of the literature circling the topic and offering no resultant substantive contributions to the nuances that separate entrepreneur-ship behaviours between young and old. In some of the literature (Baum & Locke, 2004; Schmitt-Rodermund, 2004), entrepreneurial behaviours are not exclu-sively linked with venture development, but manifest in a variety of areas that span from school achievement to community involvement. What seems clear, from a behavioural perspective, is that young people who exhibit an aptitude for entrepreneurialism combine individual, contextual, and intra-individual competencies that are strengthened over time. The net result is a cache of entre-preneurial capacities linked with personal and professional success later in life (Damon, 2008).

Geldhof and colleagues (2013) developed a complimentary set of markers for youth entrepreneurialism, four of which are of direct interest to the notion of rural entrepreneurial citizenship: self-regulation, innovation orientation, commitment to goal setting, and exposure to entrepreneurial pursuits. Damon and Lerner (2008) concluded that youth entrepreneurialism is earmarked by "resourcefulness, persistence, know-how, and a tolerance of risk and temporary set-backs" (p. 114).

Extensive work in the broader field of entrepreneurship (e.g., Curtin & Reynolds, 2004) has positioned the practice, largely, as the sum total of behaviour and action from the individual. While there is no denying the intra-individual forces (e.g., persistence, creativity, tolerance for uncertainty) that enhance entrepreneurial propensity, consideration must also be given to the broader, macro-level forces that either promote or stymie entrepreneurial action. In this vein, Thornton (1999) situates entrepreneurship theory as divided among two schools: the supply side explanations and the demand side. In demand side explanations, entrepreneurial action occurs to fill "the number and nature of... entrepreneurial roles" (p. 20) in society. In other words, the demand for entrepreneurs brings them into being. The work of Hindle (2010) is an example of such an explanation, particularly where he invokes the metaphor of the gardener:

> despite their undoubted importance to the gardening process, the gardener cannot control such macro-environment climatic variables as wind, rainfall and temperature. Similarly, an entrepreneur who is and wishes to remain a member of a particular community is subject to many possibilities and limitations (p. 607).

He concludes that "no adequate representation of entrepreneurship as a process can be entertained if the intermediate environment is covertly dismissed rather than actively embraced as part of the analysis" (2010, p. 608). In rural contexts, this insight is particularly relevant, for rural jurisdictions have unique advantages, disadvantages, needs and interests, capacities, and interdependencies that affect the "immediate environment." Indeed, this point is a foundation of the asset-based approach to community economic development. As Mathie and Cunningam (2003) describe:

> community-based models: address the economic and social conditions of people's lives; initiate and strengthen the various forms of organizing at a local level for effective control over livelihood; link local initiatives to regional, national, and global

institutions that further local level interests; and lead to a restructuring of economic and political systems that prioritize community interests (p. 3).

Setting this point aside for the moment, I assert that regardless of locale, youth entrepreneurialism can be non-venture specific, and that this is reflective of a specific set of attitudes, skills and behaviours, and contextual influences. The youth entrepreneur is, then, someone who:

1. Holds the individual behaviours for creativity, persistence, resilience, resourcefulness, problem-solving and goal setting;
2. Possesses the ability to take calculated risks and successfully navigate uncertainty;
3. Has access to and actuates specific contextual influences. In particular, youth entrepreneurialism benefits from access to human capital (e.g., enterprising parents or entrepreneurial educators) and social/community capital (e.g., mentorship opportunities, professional experience opportunities, entrepreneurial milieu); and
4. Possesses high levels of intra-individual potential. This manifests as someone who holds a good deal of intrinsic motivation as it results to the broad notion of achievement.

But this definition, as yet, says nothing specific about citizenship. Given the aim of this chapter to advance a concept of youth entrepreneurial citizenship that could be useful in rural education, I turn to T. H. Marshall's (1950) seminal work on social citizenship as a starting point for understanding the interplay between entrepreneurialism and citizenship. In Marshall's (1950) oft-cited quotation, social citizenship emerges when the individual enjoys certain rights, from the "right to a modicum of economic welfare and security to the right to share to the full in the social heritage and to live the life of a civilized being according to the standards prevailing in the society" (p. 12). Thus, economic security is a condition for citizenship. As later scholars have shown repeatedly, limitations on the economic mobility of the individual inevitably lead to limitations on social and/ or cultural capital (Bourdieu, 1997), including the erosion of the more active forms of citizenship (e.g., participation in community clubs, unions, activist organizations). Citizenship demands stability in the basic forms of economics, politics, and culture. Conversely, when citizenship abrades, there are consequences for communal cohesiveness. As Brodie (2002) notes, citizenship evokes the "quality of belonging—the felt aspect of membership in a particular...community" (p. 379), so we may infer that erosion of citizenship may lead to erosion of belonging. Combating this demands a pragmatic strategy, and it is here where entrepreneurialism can earn its stripes.

The Research Setting

This inquiry sought to assess the extent to which participating Nova Scotia public high school students possessed entrepreneurial knowledge, skills, and attitudes (KSA), and if those attributes were linked with citizenship behaviours in selected rural communities. In the earliest form of the research design, I theorized that young people who possessed higher levels of entrepreneurial propensity would actively demonstrate citizenship through community involvement, which, as this chapter has proposed, could translate into population retention and even community stability. Central to this inquiry were public schools, which can play a crucial role in the development and enhancement of entrepreneurial KSAs. To serve this end, I created a mixed-methods study that included survey-driven entrepreneurial self-assessment and in-depth interviewing. These different yet complementary methods were used to measure the many facets of the rural Nova Scotia experience in three communities, resulting in a detailed and elaborated understanding of the interplay between entrepreneurialism and community.

Research participants were drawn from three communities in the province. Each participant was enrolled at the time of the study in senior high school as a Grade 10, Grade 11, or Grade 12 student. The geographic cross-section offered a comparative perspective on the different economic and social realities of contemporary Nova Scotia. Two of the research sites have endured years of notable population decline with the resultant community evolution that often accompanies vast out-migration, while one is the only part of Nova Scotia that has consistently gained, both in terms of economic development and population. A brief description of each, informed by Statistics Canada 2016 census data, proceeds below.

The Three Communities

The first community selected for this research is the most populous county in a region of four mostly rural counties. The region is home to two large employers: a university and a regional hospital. Approximately 60% to 75% of the labour force is employed in the service sector, while the fishing, forestry, and education sectors are significant economic engines.

Community one (C1) has a demographic profile similar to many rural Nova Scotia communities. With a 2016 population of 5,002, C1's median age was 46.2 years. Individual median income, from 2015 data, was $28,359—over $3,000 less than the provincial average. Nearly half (48.8%) of the population in 2016 held a postsecondary certificate, diploma, or degree, and C1's 2016 unemployment rate sat at 9.9%. From 2011 to 2016, C1 lost 3.5% of its population, and it had not seen any significant population growth since 1981.

Community two (C2) was selected for this study due to its declining and aging population, and its well-publicized challenges with out-migration and rapid social change. C2 is expansive and consists of eight former county municipalities that merged in 1995 to create a single municipal unit. There is a small city within C2, and several outlying rural communities. C2's economy has historically been dominated by the natural resources sector. Coal mining, in particular, sustained the area for generations and spawned a variety of spin-off sectors that contributed to a robust economy. Steel-making, fishing, and tourism have also played significant roles in the economic and social development of the region. During the 1990s, C2 experienced substantial economic change when the coal mining and steel-making industries diminished, a transformation that continues to shape the economy and society in C2. According to the 2016 Canadian Census, the region of the province where C2 is situated declined in population by almost 30,000 people between 1991 and 2016. The youth population under the age of 15 declined by 18.1% over the same period. Its population in 2016 was 29,904, marking close to a 1% reduction from 2011 census data. The median household income for C2, as of 2016, was $52,914, and the unemployment rate, as of August 2019, was 13.7%.

Community three (C3) is an outlier compared to the other two regions selected for this study, as it is the only part of Nova Scotia that has experienced consistent population growth in recent years. The regional municipality consists of four former municipalities that were amalgamated in 1996. C3 is a sprawling area that includes two cities and several large suburban communities.

C3 is now in the midst of record population growth. According to the Conference Board of Canada (2019), a population growth of 2% brought the total population to 430,512 in 2018, up from 421,968 in the previous year. The population bump has helped contribute to solid economic growth. The workforce saw a 9% increase in 15 to 24-year-olds, and 6,200 new workers between the ages of 25 and

44 entered the labour force. Both the overall unemployment rate and the unemployment rate for young people ages 15 to 24 fell in 2018, from 6.8% to 5.9%, and from 16.1% to 13.7%, respectively. C3's median age was 41.

Research Design

Data Collection: Phase One

This study began with three research partners, one in each area, administering an entrepreneurial K S A self-assessment survey to participating high school students. This Likert-style self-assessment was specifically designed for this research project, and was adapted from the international 2004 Panel Study on Entrepreneurial Dynamics (Gartner, Shaver, Carter, & Reynold, 2004) and from the work of Lackéus (2013). The research partners were responsible for recruiting student-participants. As each research partner was a practicing high school teacher, they selected participants from one of their class rosters. Minimal parameters were assigned to this process, aside from a request that the sample be composed of a diverse cross-section of students. Ultimately, 200 high school students from three Nova Scotia communities were invited, via an official letter of invitation distributed through the local school board, to complete an online survey related to personal entrepreneurial propensity. In total, 90 students completed the survey, resulting in a response rate of approximately 45%.

The self-assessment used 19 attitudinal Likert scale questions with possible responses spanning from strongly disagree to strongly agree. Each statement in the self-assessment was carefully adapted from both the Panel Study on Entrepreneurial Dynamics (Gartner, Shaver, Carter, & Reynold, 2004) and Lackéus' (2013) "entrepreneurial competencies framework." In basic terms, both frameworks place entrepreneurialism into a series of themes, sub-themes, behaviours, and actions, all informed by leading research in the area. An example of this process is encapsulated in Table 5.1, below.

Data Collection: Phase Two

The second phase of data collection included semi-structured interviews with 12 research participants. Participants were young people currently enrolled as high school students in the three targeted geographic areas (see demographic information in Table 5.2). Interview questions were split into three categories: school experience, community engagement, and perceived entrepreneurialism. The goal of the interview was to understand the extent, if any, that the students held entrepreneurial capacities, how those capacities might influence school and community involvement, and if schools were promoting the development of entrepreneurial KSAS.

TABLE 5.1 Survey development framework

Cognitive characteristic	Knowledge, skills, and attitude assignment	Likert scale statement
Role models and perceived social support	Knowledge and attitude	• "Someone close to me sets a 'good example' in life" • "Someone close to me demonstrates many forms of independence in their life" • "My community supports my ambitions"
Entrepreneurial intensity	Skills	• "When I start working on something, I feel a strong drive it finish it" • "I have a long attention span" • "I prefer not to quit something" • "I am good at blocking out distractions"

Note. Responses to the affirmative generally align with higher levels of entrepreneurial knowledge, skills, and attitudes. Information adapted from Gartner et al. (2004) and Lackéus (2013).

Findings

Survey Data

TABLE 5.2 Participant demographic information

Mean Age	17 years
Gender	63% Female; 37% Male
Percentage of Participants from a Rural Area	40.30%
Percentage of Participants from an Urban Area	59.70%
Average Academic Average	83%

Participants were asked to self-assess the extent to which they held entrepreneurial knowledge, skills, and attitudes. Table 5.3 offers a selected summary of results.

TABLE 5.3 Entrepreneurial knowledge, skills, and attitudes self-assessment results

Question	Strongly disagree (Highly entrepreneurial)	Disagree (Somewhat entrepreneurial)	Agree (Less entrepreneurial)	Strongly agree (Not very entrepreneurial)
If I work hard, I can achieve a goal I set for myself.	0%	2.94%	39.71%	57.35%
I am a creative thinker.	1.47%	14.71%	54.41%	29.41%
My community supports my ambitions.	1.47%	14.71%	54.41%	29.41%
I am persistent when it comes to achieving something.	0%	2.90%	39.13%	57.97%
I am comfortable with uncertainty.	15.94%	40.58%	37.68%	5.80%
I can overcome adversity.	1.45%	8.70%	76.81%	13.04%
I like doing things better than others.	1.45%	27.54%	27.54%	43.48%
I have strong role models.	8.89%	12.05%	46.49%	32.48%
I don't work well with others.	36.23%	46.38%	11.59%	5.80%

Note: Responses from participants were coded using a Likert scale where "strongly agree" was paired with "highly entrepreneurial" through to "strongly disagree," which was paired with "not very entrepreneurial."

Participants were asked to self-assess the extent to which they participated in extra-curricular activities with the question, "How involved are you in extra-curricular activities?" Their answers ranged from very involved (25.71%), to somewhat involved (41.43%), to not at all involved (32.86%).

Interview Data

Twelve current high school students each participated in a 30-minute interview. Nine participants were Grade 12 students, while two were in Grade 11 and one was in Grade 10. The sample was diverse in terms of cultural affiliation, academic achievement, and general life experience. Approximately three quarters of the participants could be described as high achievers, namely, students who obtained exceptional grades and participated in a wide variety of curricular, extra-curricular, and community-based activities. Most participants reported that they enjoyed strong familial support and expressed contentment about their school and community experience. All participants said they intended to pursue a university degree, in disciplines ranging from business and development studies to science and social work. Four participants held a part-time job while attending high school, while one participant was actively maintaining a clothing company as an entrepreneurial venture.

Some participants expressed a measure of discontent with both their school and wider community. Two students had accrued a significant number of school absences resulting in several truancy violations, while one expressed disdain about the social cliques that had come to rule her high school. One student admitted that he was frequently bored in school, while another was burdened by the gossip culture of her hometown. In terms of geography, the participants from rural areas noted that they enjoyed living there, but that they would likely leave to pursue academic or employment opportunities. None of the rural participants, however, ruled out returning to their rural community later in life. All the participants from the urban location hoped to stay in that centre after their formal educational career ended, and none expressed a desire to relocate to a more rural area, even if employment opportunities existed. Each conversation produced some intriguing insights into the complexities of the modern teenage experience and resulted in three distinct themes.

Interview Themes

Entrepreneurial Personalities

Each participant was asked during the interview to offer a self-assessment of their entrepreneurial qualities. A range of choices was provided, including, but not limited to, a propensity for creativity, innovation and resourcefulness, tolerance for risk, organizational capacity, and social and emotional competency. Each participant indicated that, in their opinion, they held many of the entrepreneurial KSAs presented to them. Further, every student could offer examples that demonstrated the degree to which they associated with each KSA. Creativity and persistence were of particular note. Molly, a Grade 12 student from C1, explained that she was comfortable with being creative, and looked for opportunities in school to demonstrate it:

> [Creativity is] something that you have to do yourself. Like...um...which is hard for like, kids who are less creative, or don't know how to be creative. I think you have to be comfortable stepping outside of your comfort zone. You know what I mean? Like, that's...it's important to put yourself in situations where you're going to develop these habits, or attributes, whatever. The teacher has to help, too. Um, so I think

some kids definitely miss the opportunity to, like, grow in that area. I really try though because I think it's important.

Each interview participant self-identified as persistent, a trait associated with entrepreneurialism (Gartner et al., 2004). Persistence had allowed the students to balance their dense academic workload with part-time work commitments and extra-curricular involvement. Persistence also gave each student a pronounced sense of optimism, and a feeling that any challenge could be conquered. Other entrepreneurial traits shared among participants included strong organizational skills, the ability to network, and a competitive spirit. Jack touched on all these ideas:

I think, I think we need...if we could promote more hard workers, and make it competitive academic-wise, and we have these advanced courses, I think we still have students that are willing to go into these advanced courses and work towards each other. Um, I personally think, I know that they're, they're getting rid of advanced courses in high school. I think competition makes people work hard. It does for me.

Many of these KSAS, the participants explained, offered them a series of advantages related to their lived experience. Excellent grades, good organizational skills, and the ability to form strong social networks were mostly attributed to the variety of entrepreneurial KSAS held by each participant.

Community Connection

Regardless of their location, each participant described a fondness for their respective hometown. Emily, who came from a First Nations community in C2, detailed her love for her home, explaining that she "could not imagine growing up in a better place." Evan, whose parents had immigrated to his current hometown (C2), talked affectionately about the warm reception he had received there, while the participants who hailed from urban areas detailed the connection, despite the size of the city, that they felt living there.

The strength of those community connections could have enduring potential. The participants from rural areas all stated that they could envision themselves living in the places of their birth later in life. Many saw great appeal in starting a family in a rural area, and in taking advantage of a perceived slower pace of life. While some participants noted their concern about scant economic opportunities, others were not daunted by this, but saw great opportunity in areas where economic uncertainty was a reality. Mac, a Grade 12 student from C3, captured the spirit of this self-determination:

Well, currently I'm thinking if I do finish design school, I'll find a job where I'm working with businesses...I do want to have my own entrepreneurial business, where people come to me with ideas, and they have no idea how to make these ideas possible. I want to be able to kind of make them possible, in a way. So it's almost like a...guidance counsellor of life. I want to do that here. People have some great ideas in this city.

It is worth noting, however, that all of the participants from rural areas expressed an eagerness to leave, in the short term, to acquire new life experiences or advance their education. After completing university study, the rural participants hoped to spend time in an urban centre before, ultimately, returning home. Emily noted that, "I'm just more about that, like I love [my home] and the community aspect of it, and everybody knows each other, and...but I just feel like there's more opportunities in a bigger city. This place won't give me what I need."

While it remains unseen how many participants will actually return to a rural community in the future, there are a complex set of forces and considerations at play that influence those decisions, and their responses suggest that some of the ingredients of entrepreneurialism—opportunity and creativity—play a role.

Complicated School Experiences

Schools are commonly believed to play a central role in the development of both citizenship behaviours and economic development, but the majority of those interviewed revealed that schools are not adequately supporting the development of the KSAs needed to face the demands of the modern world. These concerns settled in two areas: pedagogical approach by teachers and course programming options. Related to the former, several participants explained that their school experience, to borrow from Freire (1979), was largely transactional. Their teachers, despite very good intentions, had not created the conditions for robust critical thinking, inquiry-based learning, or experiential learning. While this is potentially problematic in its own right, it is of particular concern when we consider the learning style of the student-participants. Almost every student self-assessed as being an active learner, with a strong preference for experimentation, problem-solving, and collaboration. Further, many participants explained that their entrepreneurial KSAs would most certainly benefit from further development in school. Joyce, a Grade 12 student from C3, explained that "school is boring. We do a lot of sitting and listening. I would rather be up and doing things." Mica, from C2, explained that he was "on the fence" about school and frequently felt disengaged while in class. When asked what they would change about school, Jack, Emily, and Fiona all expressed a desire for more experiential learning. According to Fiona, a Grade 12 student from C1:

> Most of my friends like learning hands-on. In biology class we are always given the chance to touch and feel things. We can work through problems and figure things out. All my other classes are discussion only. Um, that can be good, but I would like more than that.

A second area of concern, as it relates to school, emerged primarily from rural participants. This concern manifested in a frustration with the course programming options at their respective schools. More specifically, elective courses in their areas of interest (e.g., business, sociology, technology) were in short supply, limiting the students to the traditional run of high school classes. This is not uncommon, for many rural schools in Nova Scotia operate with a basic number of course options that, as one interviewee noted, could disadvantage students. Henry, from C1, who said he intended to pursue a post-secondary degree in computer engineering, was enrolled in a distance education course in computer programming. While he enjoyed the experience, he noted the difficulty in navigating a robust class in a virtual format. A lack of peer support and delayed access to the course instructor, he explained, made the experience challenging. "Using email as the only means to talk to my teacher has made it tough," he noted, "and there isn't anyone in the school who knows what we are doing in class." Henry's experience might have been different just a year later, when most post-secondary instruction moved online due to COVID-19, forcing an expansion of course offerings and a shift in faculty teaching and communication practices. Nevertheless, many participants from rural areas expressed a desire for more course options that would align with their interests and future career aspirations.

Entrepreneurialism and Community

Considering survey results and interview findings together, this research supports the notion that young people who hold higher levels of entrepreneurial knowledge, skills, and attitudes possess an array of potential social advantages. These advantages seem to include the ability to excel in an academic context, cultivate stable social networks, and engage in robust community involvement.

Furthermore, correlations exist between level of entrepreneurialism and civic virtues, a sense of boosterism, and a willingness to support the mechanisms of the community through volunteerism, economic contributions, and a desire to maintain residence. Selected cross tabulations of the survey and interview data support this point:

- Survey participants with an academic average over 90% self-assessed as highly entrepreneurial;
- Interview participants who self-assessed as highly entrepreneurial were more likely to volunteer in their communities than those who self-assessed as somewhat or less entrepreneurial;
- Survey participants who self-assessed as somewhat or highly entrepreneurial were more likely to be involved in extra-curricular activities; and
- Interview participants who self-assessed as somewhat or highly entrepreneurial possessed a stronger sense of boosterism than those of lesser entrepreneurial propensity.

Each interviewee, regardless of self-assessed KSAs, noted their strong sense of connectedness to their community, rural and urban alike, and the sense of belonging they garnered from their respective hometowns. They described their many volunteer activities as a way of "making a difference" in their community, and expressed that their community reinforced and fulfilled their needs in return, all elements of a classic definition of "sense of community" (McMillan and Chavis, 1986).

Moreover, there appeared to be a strong desire by each participant to use their various entrepreneurial knowledge, skills, and attitudes. For many participants, allowing these traits to lie dormant was, simply, a waste of the meaningful offerings they could make to their community and peers. For these participants, being creative, resourceful, and persistent, for example, emerged as special traits worthy of rendering actionable in a community context.

Conclusion

The findings from this small research study suggest that there is work to be done to help young people acquire and develop entrepreneurial capacity in school. Indeed, if we can come to view these knowledges, skills, and attitudes as important as they relate to personal and professional fulfilment and community vitality, then it may be incumbent upon schools to prioritize them among the demands of curriculum and pedagogy. This does not mean that schools should become business incubators or teach entrepreneurship in a narrow, economic sense. Rather, this is about responding to calls for schools to provide more avenues for creative output, collaboration, and active, experiential learning, which were expressed by student-participants across the province. The results of a shift toward these pedagogical approaches could lead to greater entrepreneurial KSA development and promote the many positive associations linked with them. Interestingly, a shift toward a more entrepreneurial school experience seems not to be an overly onerous request. Several students explained that simple amendments such as more classroom discussion, problem-solving opportunities, and latitude to incorporate more creativity into schoolwork would do much to improve the overall schooling experience, and would allow students to develop, and use, their various entrepreneurial KSAs. Additionally, and as the interview data revealed, there exists the opportunity for a spillover effect. Entrepreneurial KSAs honed in school are both employed and needed outside of the school.

The leap from entrepreneurial KSAs to citizenship is not an obvious one, but it is not that large, and it is well-founded. Turner (2001) argues that "modern society is no longer constituted by a dense network of associations, clubs, fraternities, chapels and communal associations," resulting in the "erosion of citizenship" (p. 198). While this study cannot evaluate whether this thesis applies to rural Nova Scotia, the province's social and economic history reflects the kind of individualization noted by Turner and others, as has been found in other local studies (Wray & Stephenson, 2012). Perhaps ironically, the very people who stand to inherit communities in which citizenship has eroded might have its solution. This research has shown, in part, that rural young people believe that the development and utilization of entrepreneurial KSAs in a rural context could result in more citizenship behaviours. The literature supporting this Nova Scotia study offers good reasons to consider entrepreneurialism broadly, beyond business startups and other fashionable, enterprise-centric definitions and practices, and to appreciate connections between entrepreneurialism's sociological character and the development and strengthening of citizenship. Whether a stronger, more creative, and resourceful citizenship translates into population stability and community vitality is a matter for further research, but this case study has shown that youth entrepreneurialism should be added to the discussion as Canada continues to grapple with an evolving rural experience.

References

Baum, J. R., & Locke, E. A. (2004). The relationship of entrepreneurial traits, skills, and motivation to subsequent venture growth. *Journal of Applied Psychology, 89,* 587-598.

Bourdieu, P. (1997). The forms of capital. In J. Richardson (Ed.), *Handbook of Theory and Research for the Sociology of Education* (pp. 241-285). Greenwood.

Brodie, J. (2002). Citizenship and solidarity: Reflections on the Canadian way. *Citizenship Studies, 6*(4), 377-394.

Burchell, G. (1996). Liberal government and techniques of the self. In A. Barry, T. Osborne, & N. Rose (Eds.), *Foucault and political reason: Liberalism, neoliberalism and rationalities of government* (pp. 19-36). University of Chicago Press.

Conference Board of Canada. (2019). *Municipal population statistics: Atlantic region.* https://www.conferenceboard.ca/e-data/default.aspx

Corbett, M. J. (2007). *Learning to leave: The irony of schooling in a coastal community.* Fernwood Publishing.

Curtin, R. T., & Reynolds, P. D. (2018). *Panel study of entrepreneurial dynamics, PSED I, United States, 1998-2004.* Inter-university Consortium for Political and Social Research. https://doi.org/10.3886/ICPSR37203.v1

Damon, W. (2008). *The path to purpose.* The Free Press.

Damon, W., & Lerner, R. M. (2008). *Entrepreneurship across the life span: A developmental analysis and review of key findings.* The Kauffman Foundation.

Didkowsky, N. K. (2016). *A substantive theory of youth resilience in rural Nova Scotia* [Unpublished doctoral dissertation]. Dalhousie University.

Freire, P. (1979). *Pedagogy of the oppressed.* Sheed and Ward.

Gartner, W. B., Shaver, K. G., Carter, N. M., & Reynold, P. D. (2004). *Handbook of entrepreneurial dynamics: The process of business creation.* Sage Publications.

Geldhof, G., Porter, T., Weiner, M. B., Malin, H., Bronk, K. C., Agans, J. P., & Lerner, R. M. (2014). Fostering youth entrepreneurship: Preliminary findings from the young entrepreneurs study. *Journal of Research on Adolescence, 24*(3), 431-446.

Grant, L. J. (2016, April 12). Cape Breton board to close 17 schools. *Cape Breton Post.* http://www.capebretonpost.com/news/local/cape-breton-board-to-close-17-schools-11678/

Hindle, K. (2010). How community context affects entrepreneurial process: A diagnostic framework. *Entrepreneurship & Regional Development, 22*(7), 599-647.

Lackéus, M. (2013). *Developing entrepreneurial competencies: An action-based approach and classification in entrepreneurial education* [Doctoral dissertation, Chalmers University of Technology]. Chalmers Reproservice. http://vcplist.com/wp-content/uploads/2013/11/Lackeus-Licentiate-Thesis-2013-Developing-Entrepreneurial-Competencies.pdf

Lemke, T. (2001). "The birth of bio-politics": Michel Foucault's lecture at the Collège de France on neo-liberal governmentality. *Economy and Society, 30*(2), 190-207.

MacKinnon, D., & Looker, E. D. (1998, March). Going down the road: Educational and personal impact of leaving home. Paper presented at the Third National Congress on Rural Education, Saskatoon, SK.

Marshall, T. H. (1950). *Citizenship and social class.* Cambridge University Press.

Mathie, A., & Cunningham, G. (2003). *Who is driving development? Reflections on the transformative potential of asset-based community development* (Occasional Paper Series, No. 5). Coady International Institute. https://dspace.library.uvic.ca/bitstream/handle/1828/6802/Mathie_Alison_WhoIsDrivingDevelopment_2003.pdf?sequence=1

McGrath, R. G., & MacMillan, I. (2000). *The entrepreneurial mindset: Strategies for continuously creating opportunity in an age of uncertainty.* Harvard Business School Press.

McMillan, D. W., & Chavis, D. M. (1986). Sense of community: A definition and theory. *Journal of Community Psychology, 14,* 6-23.

Schmitt-Rodermund, E. (2004). Pathways to successful entrepreneurship: Parenting, personality, early entrepreneurial competence, and interests. *Journal of Vocational Behavior, 65,* 498-518.

Statistics Canada. (2011). 2011 Census of Canada topic-based tabulations, immigration and citizenship tables: Immigrant status and place of birth of respondent, sex, and age groups, for population, for census metropolitan areas, tracted census agglomerations and census tracts, 2011 census. https://www12.statcan.gc.ca/nhs-enm/2011/dp-pd/dt-td/Rp-eng.cfm?LANG=E&APATH=3&DETAIL=0&DIM=0&FL=A&FREE=0&GC=0&GI D=0&GK=0&GRP=0&PI D=105411&PRI D=0&PTYPE=105277&S=0&SHOWALL=0&SUB=0&Temporal=2013&THEME=95&V I D=0&VNAMEE=&VNAMEF

Statistics Canada. (2016). Economic indicators, by province and territory (monthly and quarterly) (Nova Scotia). http://www.statcan.gc.ca/tables-tableaux/sum-som/l01/cst01/indio2a-eng.htm

Strait Regional School Board. (2016). *Educational business plan, 2015–2016: Monthly report.* https://srce.ca/sites/default/files//Operations%20Feb%20WC%202016%20(2).pdf

Thornton, P. H. (1999). The sociology of entrepreneurship. *Annual Review of Sociology, 25*(1), 19-46.

Turner, B. S. (2001). The erosion of citizenship. *British Journal of Sociology, 52*(2), 189-209.

Watson, T. J. (2012). Entrepreneurship—a suitable case for sociological treatment. *Sociology Compass, 6*(4), 306-315.

Wray, D., & Stephenson, C. (2012). Standing the gaff: Immiseration and its consequences in the de-industrialised mining communities of Cape Breton Island. *Capital & Class, 36*(2), 323-338.

6

Dispossession, Environmental Degradation, and the Right to be Rural

The Case of Small-Scale Fishers in Chilika Lagoon, India

PALLAVI V. DAS

Introduction

In his "The Right to the City," David Harvey (2008) argues that "Urbanization... has played a crucial role in the absorption of capital surpluses, at ever increasing geographical scales, but at the price of burgeoning processes of creative destruction that have dispossessed the masses of any right to the city whatsoever" (p. 37). It is the capitalists who decide where and how the surplus has to be invested in urban spaces, while the poor and the underprivileged are dispossessed of these spaces. For Harvey (2008), "establishing democratic management over" the deployment of capital surpluses in the city "constitutes the right to the city" (p. 40).

Of course, the process of capital surplus production and absorption is not limited to the city. A large proportion of populations in South Asia and Africa, like a larger proportion of Indigenous people in many advanced countries, lives in rural areas, and rural areas are an important space for capital accumulation. So, apart from the right to the city, it is time to talk about the right to the rural. But what might such a right mean? In order to conceptualize the right to the rural, we need to first understand what constitutes the rural. First, the rural comprises different types of social-ecological spaces: farms and barns, orchards and forests, mountains and hills, playgrounds and grazing land, ponds and lakes, the rural village, markets and roads, buildings for schools and health clinics, places of worship and meeting places, industrial workshops and tourist places, shops, ration centres, etc. Due to capitalist expansion and privatization, the poor are losing access to many of these spaces. Second, the rural, just like the city, is also differentiated along class lines. There are large-scale property owners; petty (small-scale) producers, many of whom are women of an Indigenous background, who sell products of their labour; and men and women of different ethnic identities who sell their labour power for a wage—some of whom may be better off than others. So, the question is: for whom is the right to the rural being curtailed? Generally, it is those in the latter two classes whose right is being curtailed. In the empirical study detailed below, I will focus on small-scale producers.

In this chapter, the main argument is that small-scale producers who depend directly on nature for their subsistence, such as fishers, are the ones who suffer significantly due to the curtailment of their right to access natural resources. The fishers are impacted not only by market forces directly, for example, through fluctuations in the price of fish, but also indirectly when natural resources such as fishing grounds are degraded and/or depleted, thanks to the mechanisms of a competitive market economy. I will illustrate the loss of fishers' rights by briefly examining a fishing community in Chilika Lagoon, India.

Chilika Lagoon, situated on the east coast of India, is the largest brackish water lagoon in Asia. The water-spread area is estimated at 704 square kilometres and 1,020 square kilometres during the summer and monsoon seasons, respectively. However, the lagoon is shrinking gradually and the depth of its water is decreasing because of increasing siltation. Moreover, the nature of the water in Chilika is changing, causing brackish water species, including fish, shrimp, and crabs, to dwindle in number (Samal & Meher, 2003). Chilika's environmental destruction is especially alarming as it is a biodiversity hotspot and has been declared a Ramsar site of international wetland conservation due to its unique mix of freshwater and brackish water that sustains rare flora and fauna (Pattanaik, 2007). Further, this biodiversity supports livelihoods such as fishing, shrimp aquaculture, and tourism (Gönenç & Wolflin, 2005). Nearly 400,000 small-scale fisher families depend on the lagoon for their livelihood (Nayak, 2014). These fishers, because of the natural variability of fish stocks, have a livelihood that is in a state of permanent uncertainty (Faraco et al., 2010). It is these small-scale fishers that are the focus of this study.

Theoretical Framework

Studies on coastal fishing communities such as those of the Chilika have mainly focused on how small-scale fisher families have been experiencing the livelihood crisis (L. K. Das, 2014; Dujovny, 2009; Nayak, 2014; Nayak & Berkes, 2011; Pattanaik, 2007; Samal & Meher, 2003). According to these studies, the threat to the fishers' livelihood is due to many factors such as increased siltation caused by large-scale irrigation projects, the government's dredging of a new sea mouth being an unsuitable solution, and, more importantly, the expansion of illegal shrimp aquaculture (Dujovny, 2009; L. K. Das, 2014). These aquaculture farmers, mostly non-fishers, through their encroachment on fishing grounds and use of violence, engage in illegal shrimp aquaculture, thereby denying the fishers access to their customary fishing grounds. These studies also emphasize the fact that the Indian state, through its inaction against illegal shrimp farmers, pursues neoliberal economic policies that encourage foreign investment and export earnings at the cost of natural resources.

The above accounts of fishers and their livelihood crisis in Chilika tend not to discuss the underlying reasons and mechanisms for the dispossession of the small-scale fishers, when it is a textbook example of a more general mechanism that Marx (1977) called primitive accumulation. In fact, the dispossession of small-scale fishers in Chilika would fit in with what Harvey (2003) calls "accumulation by dispossession," which represents his attempt to update Marx's primitive accumulation. According to Harvey (2007), Marx's concept of primitive accumulation is not a one-off process that happened during the emergence of capitalism, but is an ongoing process. Other theorists like De Angelis (2004) and Patnaik (2008) also argue that land-based practices such as enclosure (i.e., conversion of common, collective, and state land into private property), commodification, and privatization through forceful expulsion of small-scale producers and peasants are contemporary examples of Marx's primitive accumulation. This is because primitive accumulation removes any non-capitalist ownership of property that impedes the development of capitalism or the dominance of market relations.

These obstacles to capitalist development include subsistence-based production using self-employed private property and use of common property resources among direct producers, such as peasants and fishers, who have access to non-capitalist means of production. Therefore, through the process of primitive accumulation, direct producers are coercively dispossessed of their privately or collectively owned means of production and subsistence. These are transferred to the capitalists, in whose hands they are then converted to capital. Thus, primitive accumulation is a series of interrelated processes concerning property where there is: a) separation, alienation, or expropriation of resources from direct producers such as peasants; and b) relocation and concentration or monopolization of those resources in the hands of the capitalist class (Das, in press). However, because capitalism is a historically and geographically uneven process, there are domains (small-scale production such as fisheries or artisan work) in the contemporary world that still exist outside of capitalist production and accumulation. For present-day capitalist accumulation to be constantly maintained and reproduced, there must be pressure on these domains to be brought under the umbrella of capitalist property relations. For that to happen, the direct producers (mainly small-scale property owners) in these domains have to be alienated from their means of production and from their subsistence. Thus, in the contemporary world, the imperative to separate direct producers from their property as a means of production and a means of subsistence continues to exist partly to prevent them from being self-sufficient or continuing to be self-employed or non-wage workers. In addition, present-day capitalism seeks to benefit by converting the resources that were hitherto in the hands of non-capitalist producers into capital, so that capital accumulation will continue and expand. Therefore, as Patnaik (2008) argues, "capitalist accumulation through expansion necessarily has to be complemented by a process of accumulation through encroachment" (p. 111).

The encroachment on or appropriation of physical resources (such as peasants' land, pasture land, water bodies, forests) in rural socio-ecological spaces in the non-capitalist sector can result in direct means of capital accumulation, such as setting up a factory or a commercial enterprise on that land, leading to the transfer of that resource into the hands of private capitalists (Das, in press). This appropriation of resources from small-scale property owners takes place through market mechanisms and through extra-economic mechanisms. Market mechanisms include the rising cost of inputs and stagnant prices for products produced by small-scale producers. These producers also face market competition from big enterprises. Extra-economic mechanisms refer to forcible encroachment on the property and spaces to which they used to have individual or collective access. Primitive accumulation, strictly speaking, refers to the process of dispossession that is more extra-economic than economic.[1] And the state, according to Marx (1977), plays a crucial role in the forcible or extra-economic appropriation of property and resources, so that capitalist expansion and accumulation can take place.

While there have been many studies focusing on the process of appropriation of resources and its direct impact on small-scale producers in rural socio-ecological spaces, not many have examined its indirect impact in terms of resource degradation that affects the livelihood and lives of the dispossessed. Not only are the dispossessed small-scale producers' rights to access their means of production (such as land, ponds, and forests) curtailed, but they are also impacted by pollution and contamination from enterprises/factories/farms established on the appropriated resource. This degradation of resources especially impacts rural small-scale producers such as fishers who directly depend on natural resources like water bodies for their livelihood. Thus, these small-scale producers face a dual loss of rights to the rural: loss of access to natural resources and loss of unpolluted or non-degraded resources. In this chapter, the right to be rural will be discussed in terms of the above dual loss of rights. My third point is that dispossession leads to anti-dispossession politics, whereby small-scale farmers and peasants exercise their agency to not only contest the dispossession, but also to regain their right to the rural.

Through an analysis of interviews, scientific reports, and government publications, the chapter discusses the livelihood challenges facing the small-scale fisher communities in the Chilika Lagoon area in the context of ecological degradation and their response to the resultant unfolding crisis in their lives. While the chapter focuses on the loss of fishing rights experienced by the small-scale fishers in Chilika, it also examines the factors that these fishers perceive as being responsible for and contributing to the ecological degradation of the lagoon. In this preliminary study using semi-structured interviews, 20 people were selected through convenience sampling and interviewed in the summers of 2016 and 2017 in a hamlet on the coast of Chilika Lagoon.[2]

Dispossession and the Loss of the Right to Be Rural

Access rights of small-scale producers to natural resources have varied historically, and this is visible in the case of small-scale fishers in Chilika Lagoon. In the late 1500s, fishing rights were formalized in Chilika Lagoon, with kings, and later landlords, leasing the lagoon to fishers for customary fishing activities in return for tribute or rent (Nayak, 2014). After India's independence, the state took over formal control of the lagoon in 1956. However, the fishers continued to have customary fishing rights, including decision-making powers regarding the accessibility of fishing grounds (Nayak, 2014). Hence, access to fishing grounds under state control was socialized for the fishers, although in a limited sense.

Meanwhile, by the 1970s, shrimp had emerged as one of the most valuable, globally traded seafood products, due to the growing demand of developed countries such as Japan and the United States. Therefore, governments, investors, and international development agencies began promoting shrimp aquaculture as a way to improve rural food security and increase foreign exchange in developing countries (Blythe, Flaherty, & Murray, 2015). Commercial shrimp aquaculture in Chilika was projected as a poverty alleviation measure in Odisha, considered one of the low-income states, and the measure was introduced in the 1980s (L. K. Das, 2014). However, in the 1990s, under economic liberalization policies adopted by the government of India, private investors such as the Tata group were allowed to engage in shrimp aquaculture in the lagoon. This was a classic case of primitive accumulation, with the state engaging in privatizing Chilika Lagoon by transferring resources from the state (and the community of fishers) to private capitalists. The fishers, who had adequate access to the fishing grounds prior to privatization, were now restricted in terms of where in the lake they could practice fishing due to the introduction of market-based shrimp aquaculture by private capitalists. The privatization of the now state-controlled Chilika and the dispossession of fishers was part of the globalization of capitalism, driven by the capitalist market's demand for shrimp in developed countries.

Driven by the imperative of the capitalist market, the state in 1991 for the first time divided the lagoon into areas for shrimp aquaculture (40%) and for capture fishery (60%). The fisheries were further subdivided into two parts at a ratio of 60:40 for fishers and non-fishers (mainly private companies/investors), respectively (L. K. Das, 2014). This allowed non-fishers to engage in shrimp aquaculture for the first time (L. K. Das, 2014). Seeing the lucrativeness of shrimp aquaculture, non-fishers began to spread their farming near the shore beyond the areas allocated to them, and they soon began to encroach on the fishers' traditional fishing areas and dispossess them of their fishing grounds (Dujovny, 2009; Pattanaik, 2007; Samal & Meher, 2003). Thus, the fishers no longer had adequate access to their means of subsistence (fishing grounds), and their access occurred in an undemocratic way, even though they did have some fishing grounds allocated to them.

To explain what happens to the property rights of small-scale producers only in terms of the imperative of the capitalist market would amount to reifying structure (see Callinicos, 2004). People do exercise agency to fight the ways in which structures work. The fishers, through their fishermens' associations, resisted this encroachment and launched a massive social movement that spanned from 1991 up to 2001, and ended with the Supreme Court of India banning illegal shrimp aquaculture (Nayak, 2014). This resistance by the Chilika fishers to gain control over their means of production, their customary fishing areas, is an example of an anti-primitive accumulation movement (Das, in press). The extent to which the fishers regained their rights over their customary fishing grounds depended on the balance of power between them and the state/capitalists. The government, however, tried to sidestep the Supreme Court's ban and legalize shrimp aquaculture in 2002 by passing the Chilika Fishing Regulation Bill, but the fishers mounted a resistance and the bill did not pass in the provincial legislature (L. K. Das, 2014). Although the state stopped leasing out fishing areas for shrimp aquaculture, illegal commercial shrimp aquaculture, leading to the continued dispossession of fishers, has continued in Chilika Lagoon, accounting for almost 60% to 80% of the total lagoon fishing area (Nayak & Berkes, 2011; Samal & Meher, 2003). Thus, the development of commercial shrimp aquaculture has led to the encroachment of the lagoon area by shrimp farmers, reducing the fishing grounds and fish productivity for the small-scale fishers. This is reflected in and confirmed by studies on the impact of shrimp aquaculture on fish productivity in Chilika, which show that the number of fish captured in the lagoon has indeed been decreasing while shrimp production from culture fisheries has increased. At the same time, the quantity of shrimp export has increased (Pattanaik, 2007; Samal & Meher, 2003).

Apart from the illegal encroachment on the lagoon's fishing area by shrimp farmers, fishers in Chilika have experienced restricted access to certain parts of the lagoon, imposed on them by the state for biodiversity conservation. The government has declared Nalabana Island in the lagoon, a bird sanctuary since 1973, a core area of wetland conservation. Therefore, fishers have lost their right to go to Nalabana, a place where, in the past, they often took shelter from storms and other extreme events.

Ecological Degradation and Loss of Rights to the Rural

The above section has highlighted, using the concepts of primitive accumulation or accumulation by dispossession, how the small-scale fishers of Chilika Lagoon have increasingly become alienated from their customary fishing grounds due to encroachment by rich investors. As the interviews with the fishers suggest, apart from their loss of access, the introduction and spread of commercial shrimp aquaculture has led to the ecological deterioration of the lagoon. In interviews, fishers identified the introduction of commercial shrimp aquaculture, increased siltation, and a decrease in salinity due to the lack of a proper sea mouth opening into the Bay of Bengal as the main reasons for the ecological deterioration of Chilika. They stated that illegal shrimp aquaculture, which has caused dispossession, is primarily responsible for the ecological degradation of the lagoon. This in turn has undermined their right to use the lagoon as a means of livelihood, and effectively constitutes an ecologically mediated form of dispossession. Also, they pointed out that the shrimp farm owners use pesticides and chemical feed in their shrimp enclosures (locally known as gheries), which pollute the water, making it poisonous for fish and birds and also destroying some aquatic plants that regulate the water environment of Chilika. Moreover, the fishers noted that the shrimp enclosures block the sea mouth of the lagoon and disrupt tidal flushing and the salinity level of the lagoon. Maintaining the salinity of the lagoon is necessary for the survival of many fish and other aquatic species (Pattanaik, 2007; Samal & Meher, 2003). Because the sea mouth is obstructed by the shrimp enclosures, the fish that typically come into the lagoon from the sea are blocked. Shrimp aquaculture in the region has indeed disrupted the ecosystem, leading to fish stock depletion, and this in turn has compounded the uncertainties of the fishers' livelihood (Pattanaik, 2007).

In 2001, in response to the ecological degradation, the government, through the Chilika Development Authority (CDA),[3] dredged a new sea mouth so that water would circulate properly and siltation would be reduced. However, when interviewed for this research, the fishers reported that the new sea mouth was unable to maintain the salinity of the lagoon. The fishers recalled their elders mentioning that in the past Chilika had seven sea mouths opening into the Bay of Bengal, but over time these mouths have closed. The previous existence of seven sea mouths in Chilika has been confirmed by archaeological and geological studies done in the region (Khandelwal et al., 2008; Tripati & Vora, 2005; Venkatarathnam, 1970). The fishers also reported that 20 years ago, when the two old sea mouths were open, water entered the lagoon through one mouth in one direction and exited in another direction through the other mouth, which maintained the salinity of the lagoon. However, they stated, the new sea mouth is unable to do so. Other studies done among the fishers in this region also support this claim (see Dujovny, 2009; Sahu, Pati, & Panigrahy, 2014). Although the CDA argues that the new sea mouth has improved the quality of the lagoon and hence fish productivity, the fishers said that, on the contrary, it has upset the freshwater and brackish water balance of the lagoon and is thus negatively affecting the fish stocks in the region. In fact, the opening of a new sea mouth has benefitted the non-fishers (those investors who do not belong to the traditional fishing community) in the northern part of the lagoon, who have increasingly expanded their shrimp aquaculture, encroaching on the fishing grounds of the traditional fishers (Dujovny, 2009). Moreover, as noted above, the new sea mouth is obstructed by shrimp enclosures that exacerbate existing ecological degradation and low fish productivity.

The lack of access to and availability of fishing grounds due to the above economic and ecological factors has affected the livelihood of the fishers who are completely and directly dependent on Chilika Lagoon. Highlighting the conditions of scarcity and food insecurity they live with, a fisher noted:

> Previously fishermen were depending on Chilika throughout the year [12 months], but presently, there is no certainty of catching fish. We earn for 3 to 5 days and for the next 5 days we have no earnings. We cannot catch fish due to the non-availability of fish. So, we are living with income scarcity. We are not able to earn even 100 rupees a day.[4]

Other fishers added that due to fish scarcity, they were able to fish for only three months a year (during the rainy season) and that they were spending longer hours a day fishing (12 to 24 hours at a time), compared to 20 years ago when they fished for two to three hours a day to earn their livelihood.

The decreased availability of fish stocks near the shores means the small-scale fishers not only engage in intensive fishing, but also have to go further into the deeper water, and this requires the use of motorboats and improved fishing nets. Given that these inputs in fishing are expensive, and because of the lack of adequate income from fishing and a lack of support from formal credit institutions, the small-scale fishers have to borrow money from the local money-lenders-cum-fish traders at very high interest rates to buy their fishing nets and boats. In order to repay the loans, the fishers sell their catch to the fish traders at a price much lower than the market price. The fish traders in turn sell the fish in the market for a profit. This dependence on moneylenders or informal credit mechanisms has pushed the fishers into indebtedness (L. K. Das, 2014). This indebtedness brings the fishers to bare subsistence living or poverty in many cases, as they are unable to repay the loans and get trapped in a vicious circle. Thus, the fishers are subjected to exploitation on top of their already decreased access to a means of subsistence, caused by modern forms of primitive accumulation.

In order to survive and earn their livelihood, 50% of fishers from Chilika are now migrating to nearby and distant towns and cities in search of work, where they engage in occupations such as construction work and other wage work. Both men and women are resorting to wage work to earn their living due to the decline in fishing income (R. J. Das, 2014). Some are seasonal migrants, while others have sold their boats and have left their home village permanently. Thus, the small-scale fishers of Chilika have been dispossessed of their means of production and subsistence and have had to become wage workers. This is a classic case of Marx's (1977) primitive accumulation and confirms that it is taking place in contemporary times.[5]

Given the above situation, what are the fishers doing about it? For increased access to fishing resources and to prevent further ecological degradation of the lagoon, the fishers have made certain demands of the state. They have insisted that the state should ensure the CDA implements pollution removal in the lagoon. The fishers have argued that for this policy to be implemented properly, illegal shrimp aquaculture should be banned or stopped; they believe it should be considered a criminal activity. In addition, they feel that the government should also take action against the businesses who supply different materials to the shrimp farmers, such as nets for enclosures. Thus, the fishers are aware that both the shrimp farmers and the businessmen supplying inputs to these farmers are profiting from shrimp aquaculture by denying them their rightful access to customary fishing grounds.

According to the fishers, the government officials always promise to break the shrimp enclosures, but they do nothing, as the shrimp farmers often bribe them. Indeed, many of the shrimp farmers have had the support of local politicians, and newspaper reports have attested to the fact that government officials are not demolishing the shrimp enclosures (Express News Service, 2018). Responding to government inaction with acts of desperation, the fishers have often broken the shrimp enclosures on their own,[6] but rather than cooperate with the fishers, the police have arrested them or confiscated their boats and nets. Thus, the fishers hold the elites, especially government officials, responsible for their livelihood deprivation. The state's inaction against the shrimp farm owners is an example of its failure to uphold the fishers' livelihood rights. This is largely because the commercial shrimp farm owners, who are expanding their property rights at the expense of customary rights of fishers, are supported by political leaders and major aquaculture firms (Express News Service, 2018). The aquaculture firms process and sell the shrimp in the rich countries of the Global North, making huge profits while the small-scale fishers are deprived and dispossessed of their means of livelihood (Pattanaik, 2007). Unlike the non-fisher entrepreneurs, the small-scale fishers lack the capital to invest in these farms and therefore are acutely affected by the lack of access to their fishing grounds as the shrimp farms grow (Nayak, Oliveira, & Berkes, 2014). Small-scale fishers justifiably feel threatened as commercial fishers appropriate their fishing grounds while state officials abet what amounts to illegal fishing.

The fishers also pointed out in interviews that, so far, the state has failed in both dredging the old sea mouths and in removing shrimp aquaculture. The fishers have demanded that the government take steps to excavate the increased silt from the lagoon and dredge at least two of the old, closed sea mouths so that there is better circulation of seawater and freshwater in the lagoon, as this, in turn, would increase fish reproduction and availability.

Another major response of the fishers to their livelihood deprivation has been to form a fishermen's association, where members are recruited from each village and the association discusses the livelihood problems facing the fishers. A fisher further explained:

> *We discuss how we will save Chilika from the shrimp gheries [enclosures], from the clutches of ghery owners and non-fishermen. We will take the issue to the government and request the government take suitable action to save our livelihood, otherwise we will strike.*

In the past, for example in the 1990s, as discussed in the previous section, the fishermen's associations were a part of the social movement in Chilika to stop shrimp aquaculture that successfully culminated in the Supreme Court of India's ban on illegal shrimp aquaculture in 2001. They conducted strikes, protests, road blockades, and rallies in front of government offices and the state legislature, demanding government intervention. However, illegal shrimp aquaculture continues. Therefore, the fishers stated that if the government does not take suitable action to stop illegal shrimp aquaculture, they will resort to strikes as they have done in the past, to make the government realize that it is their right to have access to the resources on which their livelihood depends.

Conclusion

This study has shown how small-scale fishers have been, and are being, alienated from their livelihood resources, in this case, fishing grounds, because of the expansion of commercial shrimp aquaculture in the Chilika Lagoon area. The process by which these fishers have lost access or been granted only restricted access to their means of livelihood exemplifies what Marx (1977) termed primitive accumulation and what David Harvey (2003) calls accumulation by dispossession. However, primitive accumulation in the form of expanding commercial shrimp aquaculture in Chilika has resulted not only in restricted access to the means of production and subsistence for the fishers, but also in a degraded ecosystem, namely, the water in which the fish live. Such ecological degradation has in turn effectively resulted in another round of primitive accumulation.

An important conclusion that emerges from this study is that for rural, natural resource-dependent communities such as the fishers in Chilika, their loss of rights entails losing not just their right to access their means of livelihood, but also their right to a healthy, sustainable lagoon ecosystem on which they directly depend for their livelihood. In addition, the lack of fish stocks due to ecological degradation has forced the fishers to engage in intensive and exhaustive fishing, further deteriorating the lagoon ecosystem. To engage in this type of intensive fishing, the fishers use expensive inputs such as motorboats (to go farther into the fishing waters) and fishing nets, and these outlays of resources make them financially dependent on moneylenders and fish traders who exploit them. Yet the state has not intervened to stop the encroachment of the fishers' fishing area by illegal shrimp aquaculture farmers, who the fishers say are in cahoots with local politicians and businessmen. All the above factors have led to the erosion of traditional resource use systems such as customary fishing practices, and marginalized the small-scale fishers who have begun migrating to urban areas as wage workers. This is not a viable solution, as often these migrants (seasonal or permanent) continue to suffer from employment insecurity, poor health, and myriad other negative impacts in the urban areas.

Those fishers who have not migrated continue to try to assert their livelihood right through the fishermen's association. They believe that Chilika is their mother and sustains them, so they want to protect the lagoon from further degradation; at the same time, they want to assert their livelihood right against the process of primitive accumulation. The small-scale fishers of Chilika are demanding their right to be rural, which echoes what the activist group Right to the City Alliance (RTTC) calls rural justice: "The right of rural people to economically healthy and stable communities that are protected from environmental degradation and economic pressures that force migration to urban areas" (RTTC, n.d.). In asserting their right to be rural, the fishers do not want to be alienated from the resources on which their livelihood depends. As this chapter shows, there is an urgent and important need to expand Harvey's right to the city to talk about the right to the rural, as large numbers of people in rural areas, especially small-scale producers, are being dispossessed of their means of livelihood. As these rural areas become important spaces of capital accumulation, small-scale producers are not only losing their access rights to resources, but they are also losing their right to a healthy and sustainable environment. Thus, Laura Barraclough's (2013) call for the right to be rural can be clearly applied to the small-scale fishers of Chilika Lagoon, whose livelihood rights are being denied due to capitalist expansion and a restructuring of the rural economy to meet the needs of global markets.

Notes

1. If the government forces peasants to give up their land for capitalist factories in return for compensation (which is usually a small proportion of what the land is worth), that is still primitive accumulation.
2. The fishers did not want their names and the identity of their village to be revealed. Thus, their names and the name of their village remain anonymous. There were only male fishers in the village, which is typical of small-scale fisher communities in the Chilika area.
3. The government body in charge of implementing actions toward the sustainability of Chilika lagoon.
4. 100 rupees is equal to approximately US $2. Daily wage workers earn more than 100 rupees a day in Odisha.
5. In other words, primitive accumulation is causing slow proletarianization.
6. This is akin to industrial workers breaking machines in England in the nineteenth century as a mark of protest against machines taking their jobs (Luddite movement).

References

Barraclough, L. (2013). Is there also a right to the countryside? *Antipode, 45*(5), 1047-1049.

Blythe, J., Flaherty M., & Murray G. (2015). Vulnerability of coastal livelihoods to shrimp aquaculture: Insights from Mozambique. *Ambio, 44*, 275-284.

Callinicos, A. (2004). *Making history: Agency, structure and change in social theory.* Brill Publishers.

Das, L. K. (2014). Privatisation of CPRs and the informal sector: A case of Chilika Lake. *Economic and Political Weekly, 49*(40). https://www.epw.in/journal/2014/40/reports-states-web-exclusives/privatisation-cprs-and-informal-sector.html

Das, R. J. (in press). *Marx, capital, and capitalism: A global perspective.* Taylor and Francis.

Das, R. J. (2014). Low-wage capitalism, social difference, and nature-dependent production: A study of the conditions of workers in shrimp aquaculture. *Human Geography: A New Radical Journal, 7*(1), 17-34.

De Angelis, M. (2004). Separating the doing and the deed: Capital and the continuous character of enclosures. *Historical Materialism, 12*(2), 57-87.

Dujovny E. (2009). The deepest cut: Political ecology in the dredging of a new sea mouth in Chilika Lake, Orissa, India. *Conservation and Society, 7*, 192-204.

Express News Service. (2018, June 23). Choosing prawn mafia over Chilika? *The New Indian Express*. http://www.newindianexpress.com/specials/2018/jun/23/choosing-prawn-mafia-over-chilika-1832253.html

Faraco, L. F. D., Andriguetto-Filho, J. M., & Lana, P. C. (2010). A methodology for assessing the vulnerability of mangroves and fisherfolk to climate change. *Pan-American Journal of Aquatic Sciences, 5*(2), 208.

Gönenç, I. E., & Wolflin, J. P. (Eds.). (2005). *Coastal lagoons: Ecosystem processes and modeling for sustainable use and development*. CRC Press.

Harvey, D. (2003). *New imperialism*. Oxford University Press.

Harvey, D. (2007). Neoliberalism as creative destruction. *The Annals of the American Academy of Political and Social Science, 610*, 22–44.

Harvey, D. (2008). The right to the city. *New Left Review, 53*, 23–40.

Khandelwal, A., Mohanti, M., García-Rodríguez, F., & Scharf, B. W. (2008). Vegetation history and sea level variations during the last 13,500 years inferred from a pollen record at Chilika Lake, Orissa, India. *Vegetation History and Archaeobotany, 17*(4), 335–344.

Marx, K. (1977). *Capital: A critique of political economy* (Vol. 1). Vintage Books.

Nayak, P. K. (2014). The Chilika Lagoon social-ecological system: An historical analysis. *Ecology and Society, 19*(1), 1. http://dx.doi.org/10.5751/ES-05978-190101

Nayak, P. K., & Berkes, F. (2011). Commonisation and decommonisation: Understanding the processes of change in the Chilika Lagoon, India. *Conservation & Society, 9*, 132–145.

Nayak, P. K., Oliveira, L. E., & Berkes, F. (2014). Resource degradation, marginalization, and poverty in small-scale fisheries: Threats to social-ecological resilience in India and Brazil. *Ecology and Society, 19*(2), 73. http://dx.doi.org/10.5751/ES-06656-190273

Patnaik, P. (2008). The accumulation process in the period of globalisation. *Economic and Political Weekly, 43*(26/27), 108–113.

Pattanaik S. (2007). Conservation of environment and protection of marginalized fishing communities of Lake Chilika in Orissa, India. *Journal of Human Ecology, 22*(4), 292–293.

Right to the City Alliance (RTTC). (n.d.). *Mission, history and platform*. https://righttothecity.org/about/mission-history/

Sahu, B., Pati, P., & Panigrahy, R. C. (2014). Environmental conditions of Chilika Lake during pre and post hydrological intervention: An overview. *Journal of Coastal Conservation, 18*(3), 285–297. https://doi.org/10.1007/s11852-014-0318-z

Samal, K. C., & Meher, S. (2003). Fishing communities on Chilika Lake: Comparative socio-economic study. *Economic and Political Weekly, 38*(31), 3319–3325.

Tripati, S., & Vora, K. H. (2005). Maritime heritage in and around Chilika Lake, Orissa: Geological evidences for its decline. *Current Science, 88*(7), 1175–1181.

Venkatarathnam, K. (1970). Formation of the barrier spit and other sand ridges near Chilika Lake on the east coast of India. *Marine Geology, 9*(2), 101–116.

III
The Right to Rural Health

7

Reproducing the Rural Citizen

Barriers to Rural Birthing and Maternity Care in Canada

SARAH RUDRUM, LESLEY FRANK & KAYLA MCCARNEY

Introduction

Rural communities in Canada suffer from a lack of access to health care and
health care-adjacent services for pregnant and parenting women. As well as
having health consequences, poor access to care significantly shapes social relations and community. While the transition to motherhood is often cited as
a pivotal and joyous moment in women's lives, it is also important to understand pregnancy and birth as potentially vulnerable times. Vulnerability among
any group of birthing women is not inherent; instead, it is connected to a lack
of adequate access to services, including those that are culturally relevant. Just
as vulnerability is contingent, resilience can be fostered through high quality,
culturally appropriate services that connect mothers to each other, to health
services, and to other community supports. Supports for pregnancy and birth
can be designed to facilitate health and material and psycho-social well-being, in
turn fostering the connection and belonging that create resilient rural communities in which families flourish. In fact, ensuring adequate supports inclusive
of midwifery, in opposition to overly medicalized births, has been implicated
in women's collective action for reproductive justice (Shaw, 2013). Without

accessible maternity care in rural areas, women experience the right to be rural as contingent or under threat.

The Canada Health Act (1985) guarantees that essential physician and hospital services are paid for by the government, but there is variation across provinces for what is deemed an "essential health service"—and even in who delivers the care and where care is delivered. Unfortunately, access to midwifery has been framed as non-essential; in rural Canada in particular, where health care access is strained in general, this means women's access to maternity care depends on geography. Research has demonstrated adverse maternal and newborn outcomes occur as a result of reduced access to maternity care in rural Canada (Grzybowski et al., 2015; Lisonkova et al., 2016). Rural women are seen later and less frequently, and at times delay care in order to avoid transfer for delivery, increasing the risk of complications (Grzybowski et al., 2015).

This chapter offers a brief sketch of Canada's unique maternity care contexts with a focus on rural care and introduces findings from our study of maternity care in rural Nova Scotia. During interviews with mothers in communities with and without midwifery services post-regulation, themes including social belonging versus exclusion, community citizenship, and the reproduction of family as core to the sustainability of rural places emerged alongside conversations on care itself.

Background and Contexts

Regionalization/Centralization of Maternity Care Services

For rural communities, the move toward centralization of health care services more broadly has had major impacts on access, with small communities across Canada witnessing the closure of hospitals and health centres. Throughout the 1990s, medical services were centralized in an attempt to concentrate specialized health care in regional centres (de Leeuw, 2016). While the rationale included a desire to have specialist care available in medium-sized regional towns or cities instead of being solely concentrated in major metropolises, rural communities have not benefitted overall, since regionalization also entailed the closure of hospitals in small communities. Maternity care services were not immune to centralization, and as with the centralizing project more broadly, the withdrawal of services was justified by fiscal concerns about providing care in environments low in specialized human resources (Kornelsen et al., 2016, p. 2). For many small communities, centralization has been a solution that creates new problems. Provider shortages persist and patients are left with new costs (Miller et al., 2012);

many rural women experience a tension of growing their families in communities that no longer "do birth," as we encountered in our own study.

The case for centralization has been controversial. Losing maternity care services leads to a "cascade of adverse consequences" for rural women and their babies (Klein et al., 2002, p. 120). The costing argument for centralization often overlooks community and psycho-social factors, as Kornelsen and colleagues (2016) argue, making the case for a "societal approach" to rural maternity care costing (p. 1). In particular, they note that "costs removed from the healthcare system simply do not disappear, but are downloaded onto women and families who have to travel for care" (p. 3). From the perspective of the costs that are introduced via centralization, as a means to reduce health care spending, it is a "false economy" (Klein et al., 2002, p. 120), in keeping with other neoliberal moves in the health care system and with the responsibilization of individuals for their own well-being. Taking the position that equality of access is a necessary precondition for equity in health care, an assessment of the effects of regionalization on non-urban women has found that it undermines equality of access on measures such as choice of care provider, the ability to give birth in one's own community, and quality of care (Benoit et al., 2002). Centralization has been observed to exhibit "a love affair with specialization" (Iglesias, as quoted in de Leeuw, 2016, p. 580), and obstetrics in this context is approached as a specialist service. While, indeed, obstetricians specialize in high-risk deliveries, they are also the backup for others, including midwives, in providing care. Thus, when communities lose a hospital and specialists in high-risk birth, they often also lose their ability to support normal, low-risk birth.

Midwifery: Canadian Contexts and Variance by Province

When birth moved into the hospital in Canada, around the turn of the twentieth century, midwives did not follow, as had been the case in many European settings (Warsh, 2010). Instead, the professionalization of doctors coincided with the institutional sidelining of midwifery. In 1895, midwives were formally excluded from providing care (Born, 2003), pushing them into a precarious space in which they were alegal, unfunded, and unregulated, risking lawsuits in the event of poor outcomes. By the 1990s, campaigns for regulated, publicly funded midwifery, emerging from second wave feminism and the larger women's health movements (MacDonald, 2016), had their first successes. While the introduction of regulated midwifery is significant for its potential to expand women's access to care, and in particular, the choice in provider type and birth location, this potential has only been partially and patchily realized. Ontario and British Columbia were the first to regulate and fund midwives in 1994 and 1998, respectively, with the other provinces and territories following suit. The Atlantic provinces have been among the last to professionalize, with Nova Scotia regulating first in 2009. In Ontario and BC, midwifery has grown slowly but steadily since regulation in 1998 (Stoll & Kornelsen, 2014), and currently, midwives support approximately 16% of births in Ontario and 22% in BC (with a goal of 35% by 2020) (Canadian Midwives Organization, 2021). In these provinces, midwifery services, offered on a fee per course of care basis and dependent on midwives having hospital privileges, tended early on to concentrate in urban centres. Rural midwifery has expanded in provinces with a longer history of midwifery and better numbers, but still faces challenges, especially in remote areas.

Remote and Indigenous Communities

Particular to the Canadian context is the need to serve remote communities as well as diversely situated Indigenous communities. The context of rurality in our Nova Scotia study, discussed below, is not remote. Instead, it is one of the relatively densely populated clusters of small towns with some tertiary care, surrounded by more typically rural "non-town" communities, with relative proximity to Halifax as an urban centre. While this is not atypical of rurality in Canada and especially the Maritimes, the presence of services and proximity to urban centres and their specialists in these communities makes them distinct from remote rurality.

Remote and rural are often paired together rather than clearly disambiguated, but defining the terms is important to advocacy and health care delivery. In Australia, which shares with Canada the contexts of remote communities and Indigenous groups impacted by colonization and poor access to services, a survey found that doctors did distinguish between the rural and remote, viewing remote communities as "smaller, more isolated, and more highly dispersed" than rural communities (Wakerman et al., 2017, p. 6). In Canada, the territories are defined as remote (Zayed et al., 2016), while postal code definitions deal with "remote and rural" rather than making a distinction. An environmental scan of Canadian remote and isolated health care facilities defined communities "located a minimum of four hours away from hospital services by ground transportation, with or without road access" as remote and isolated (Young & Grobelna, 2018, p. 4), but also noted that definitions vary widely.

Rurality or remoteness is not solely about geography or population size; social relations around power and equity are implicated, making an intersectional approach necessary (Rudrum, 2012). Remoteness, perhaps, is also relative: after several decades of declining birth services in many rural areas, places where it was once the norm to birth in community have lost that care option. Without changing their location or their population size, such communities may be seen by their residents as remote when it comes to maternity care. The diversity within rurality contributes to the lack of solid definitions (Miller et al., 2012), but what is clear is that some rural communities have more difficulty accessing maternal health care than others, with geography, transportation, and the absence of local services all playing a role. Women in fly-in communities and those with seasonal road access are still often forced to evacuate to major centres for care, often resulting in significant stress and distress (Lawford et al., 2019). Indigenous people are most affected by poor access in remote communities, due both to the relative prevalence of remote Indigenous communities and to power dynamics in relation to negotiating services and navigating care.

Throughout Canada, Indigenous women live in remote, rural, and urban settings. The relationship between Indigenous communities and the mainstream health care system has been marred by colonial practices, a lack of cultural consideration, and lack of access. Often, Indigenous women have particular health needs, sometimes resulting from social inequities, and relatedly, particular health *care* needs, both biomedical and social. At the population level, outcomes for Indigenous women and their babies are poorer than average on all indicators; these outcomes are rooted in ongoing social inequities, yet are too often addressed through individualized advice targeting behavioural change (Varcoe et al., 2013). In a study of care in four remote coastal First Nations in British Columbia, women emphasized that the impact of evacuating to Vancouver for birth was ongoing, as it was experienced in relation to other sites of poor relationships and experiences. As the authors state, "the erosion of birthing and economic resources fostered negative birth outcomes and experiences. Disconnection from community fractures social supports, including family relationships and cultural practices" (Varcoe et al., 2013, p. 8). This speaks to the relationship between experiences of care and understandings of belonging and citizenship. Health care access, health status, and feelings of belonging or lack of belonging are connected: "Receiving healthcare, not receiving healthcare, and how healthcare is offered all affect physical health and at the same time carry messages about citizenship" (Sinding, 2010, p. 1657). For many remote and rurally situated women, and particularly for Indigenous women in a range of settings, the messages carried via care or its absence feed into social exclusion and lack of belonging.

Some jurisdictions in Canada have introduced maternity care services specifically targeted to meet the needs of Indigenous families. For example, the Six Nations of the Grand River in Ontario and the Innulitsivik Health Centre in Nunavik, Quebec both provide community-oriented midwifery care (Association of Ontario Midwives, 2021; Van Wagner et al., 2012). The National Aboriginal Council of Midwives (NACM) has the goal of re-introducing Indigenous midwives to every Indigenous community, which would support reconciliation efforts more broadly. Non-midwife care practices are also shifting in response to the emerging understanding of health care's place in the reconciliation movement. In British Columbia, Aboriginal Health Improvement Committees have worked to create videos that introduce cultural practices, such as the presence of extended family during birth, to health care providers, in order to shift practices and decrease stigma (Northern Health, 2017). However, other jurisdictions have fewer targeted programs. In provinces where regulated midwifery is recent or slow to reach scale, including Nova Scotia, the focus has been on services and numbers broadly; the targeting of particular sub-groups of women, whether Indigenous women or other groups whose needs are poorly met by mainstream health services, is de-prioritized.

Maternity Care in Rural Nova Scotia

When examining questions related to rural rights, maternity care represents a special case for consideration. This section offers a specific example for thinking through such questions using stories from our qualitative research project, "Pregnancy, Birth, and Parenting Supports as Sites of Rural Resilience." These narratives highlight the importance of local access to comprehensive maternity care that is inclusive of midwifery. Such access is not only important for maternal and family well-being but is also a catalyst in the biological and social reproduction of rural citizens, and an essential ingredient for building and sustaining rural life.

As Taylor (2013) has identified, "while midwifery is thriving in Ontario, British Columbia, and Manitoba, it has stagnated in Nova Scotia" (p. 2). According to the Canadian Association of Midwives (2021), midwives are involved in only 2.9% of births in the province, far below the national average. Midwives only work at three sites in the province, one in Halifax and two in more rural settings; their numbers are similarly insufficient to meet demand (Moulton, 2000; Taylor, 2013).

In this context, we introduced a study that sought to explore the status of rural maternity care, including access to midwifery, since implementation in

Nova Scotia in 2006. Regulated midwifery in Nova Scotia arrived as a response to the long-held demands of birthing women and stakeholders, who had called for a primary care option that met pregnant women's health needs, which included a desire to have choice in provider type and birth location. This was also in response to a general decline of rural maternity services, through the centralization of health care services, which came alongside a move to obstetrical specialization of care and an entrenchment of medicalized birth. The pilot midwifery program in Nova Scotia was introduced in three test sites in the province (Halifax, Lunenburg and the South Shore, and Antigonish) and has yet to expand beyond them; more than a decade later, the majority of communities in Nova Scotia outside of the urban core of Halifax do not have access to a midwifery care provision model. Our research came at an important time to explore rural access to midwifery care, as it remained unclear whether or how a scale-up of midwifery programming would occur, as well as whether and how such a scale-up would meet the needs of diversely situated rural women and their families.

The research plan was to compare two rural areas, one with a provincially funded model midwifery site, Lunenburg and the South Shore, and the other without, the Annapolis Valley. These two were selected as comparable sites; both are small Nova Scotia towns situated amid rural communities, the latter agricultural and home to Acadia University, and the former relying on tourism and home to a UNESCO world heritage site. The two communities are also demographically similar in that both have populations that experience seasonal flux, an aging community that also has draws for younger families, and a similar population size of a little over 100,000 (Statistics Canada, 2016). In both areas, residents are one to two hours away from Halifax by car depending on precise location, with poor mass transit availability.

Despite having a long history of lay midwifery pre-legislation and a hospital that supports birth, the Annapolis Valley was not selected as a pilot site and no midwifery care was available. While we were initially interested in identifying opportunities in and challenges to extending the midwifery care model to unserved rural areas, it quickly became clear that a crisis of sustainability was overshadowing conversations on program expansions. This crisis came to a head when, mid-stream in our research process, the rural midwifery study site in Lunenburg was temporarily suspended due to a staffing shortage. This left only one (equally vulnerable) rural site in operation in the province in Antigonish (which in fact shuttered later that year). In all, thirty interviews and three focus groups were conducted with women and maternity care stakeholders across the two rural areas of Nova Scotia of interest for the study. Qualitative data analysis identified issues pertaining to the failure of upholding rural citizens' rights to universal health care access, and relatedly, feelings of social exclusion among women trying to grow their families within these rural settings. The collapse of the rural model site on the South Shore was evidence of the profound urban–rural divide that characterizes health care access in the province.

What We Heard from Participants

Mothers' stories were marked by a narrative of compromise in the pursuit of a particular quality of life thought to be attainable only in rural communities. What it meant to live in a rural setting was defined in part by what was absent in the community: in mothers' stories, a paucity of public infrastructure in general, as well as of access to amenities, characterized rural in contrast to urban living; rural living also meant both social and geographic isolation, as geographic distance, at times complicated by bad weather and lack of transportation options, made it difficult to foster a community of mothers, though communities, for some mothers, became significant sources of postpartum support. For some of the mothers, these pitfalls were expected compromises of rural family life, made in trade for positive dimensions such as affordability, natural beauty, and a strongly rooted community. It was common for mothers to position themselves along a rural continuum based on distance to services (stores, doctors, hospitals, informal parent groups)—noting that others who lived outside of rural towns "had it worse."

While participants coped with the lack of full-spectrum maternity care services, including postpartum support and specialist services, the loss of primary maternity care was less palatable. Stories of poor access were common from both rural areas studied (one with midwifery and the other without), and focused on various fronts, including access to providers (midwives, doctors, specialists), access to facilities (hospitals), and access to health care and health care-adjacent services (prenatal education, breastfeeding support). For example, many stressed that their community lacked family physicians in general, and particularly doctors and hospitals that "do births and babies." For example, Beatrice lived close to care, but not to delivery care, saying, "the Lunenburg hospital is less than— they don't deliver babies there, but it's less than ten minutes away." In addition to primary care, mothers noted the withdrawal of transitional health care in the postpartum period. For Caroline, this withdrawal of services left a void: "I even wonder if there was, oh, I'm not going to find the word right, a public health nurse? If they were still engaged, if you had a public health nurse who was teaching a prenatal course, whether you would feel, like 'Oh, I could call public health!' But because that ended, that's another level of support that's just gone now."

Without local services, families experienced the burden of long commutes to regional and urban centres (with no public transportation infrastructure) for doctor and obstetrician appointments (typically overbooked), accompanied by long waits at those appointments. As one mother said, "We have access…if we have transportation." But the distance to care incurred financial costs, including the cost of travel itself and lost wages, and caregiving complexities, such as needing to bring children, feeding children outside the home, or arranging child-care. Other factors such as social class, employment, and support were something participants considered when naming themselves lucky despite poor access. For example, Cynthia noted that she was more able than some of her neighbours to manage access challenges, saying, "I'm privileged enough that I can drive into Halifax. I have transportation, I have time, I have means, and I recognize that." Indeed, another participant said, "But I know sometimes if I had an 8:00 appointment, you're leaving at 5:00 in the morning. You can't afford to spend the night, so it can be challenging when we go." Long distance to care also raised safety concerns for some rural women who feared birthing along the highway, mentioned by seven participants and particularly feared among those who tended to have short labours. The desire for homebirth with a midwife was sometimes contextualized within the difficulty of travelling to a facility for delivery. These problems are rarely encountered by urban residents; mothers felt they were not adequately acknowledged and addressed by a government that emphasized urban services, while overlooking the needs of the rural communities that make up the majority of the province.

For some on the South Shore, the relational birth support that mothers sought was brought closer to home with the implementation of midwifery. Several mothers interviewed had in fact moved there from outside the province in pursuit of rural family life. Midwifery access was a pre-condition of choice of residence, indicating that rural birthing has the potential to attract young families as a pathway to rural revitalization. Beth addressed this, telling us:

> There are young families, and young couples, who wanted kids, who moved here knowing that this was the place where they could have midwifery services. I mean, that in itself should be such a large sign that says "Hey! This is a good thing!" If you want to increase your population, if you're afraid of all this brain drain that is

happening on the East Coast—basically you have all of these people moving out
West, all of the young people—then you know, put these things in place that make
the place attractive, and that will flood it with money eventually.

Another mother said, "when we were leaving Alberta, we were travelling a
lot across the country to decide where we wanted to live, and we had a check-
list of things that a new community had to meet, and a midwifery program was
one of them." Lack of access to midwifery can do the opposite; stories were told
of families leaving the Annapolis Valley because "they weren't able to raise their
families, or to birth their children the way they wanted to." Another mother indicated that women were "leaving the province, too...'cause they don't want to be
involved with what's being offered here" and referred to "some women who've
decided, 'I'm not having any more children' under these circumstances." In a
province with an aging population, participants said palliative care was more
available than care for birth, with one participant telling us, "Our communities
are doing more than dying. And I think our health care needs to reflect that." The
draw of rural schools and the threat of school closures were frequently brought
up by participants alongside maternity care. This pairing perhaps reflects a reproductive justice approach in which the right to give birth in community is viewed
as connected with the right to parent in community. Reproductive justice is a
women of colour-centred movement to expand demands for reproductive rights
to include much more than abortion access, and to include access to maternity
care as well as the right to raise children "in safe and sustainable communities"
(SisterSong, n.d.). One focus group participant clearly articulated the uncanny
feeling of social exclusion that resulted from the loss of services including health
care and school, telling us:

All of these people that have moved here, it's because of this reputation of small
school that's thriving, midwifery practice and all this, and if that's gone, I don't
know why people would come here. And it already feels like my kind—young family—
is not wanted here anymore; but I'm here and I don't plan to leave, but it feels like
maybe I'm supposed to. It's a weird feeling.

For many South Shore mothers, there was a fine line between a thriving and
welcoming community and an isolated and inaccessible setting.

Participants recognized that their biological and social reproduction was
necessary to their communities; they were proud of their rural citizenship and
rural reproduction, but recognized it as undervalued. One participant linked

reproduction in the family to the reproduction of rural community, saying, "new children, new citizens need to be born, and they need to be wanted, and they need to be first imagined into life. And if young families can't even imagine having children here, then that's already a death sentence for communities here." Despite an awareness of rural communities as spaces of lack, including lack of access to services, participants also envisioned rural belonging as linking the past with the future, and marking the connection between people and the land. A focus group participant on the South Shore reflected:

One of the things I think of when having a baby rurally for me, especially with midwives, is the empowerment and the connection. My son has a passport that says Pleasantville, and my niece has a passport that says "Bush Island," and she...there's a little museum in the community where I grew up, and it says who the last person was to be born on the island, and my son came home, my older son, with his cousin and he was like "We have to tell them! There's a new birth! In this community!" and it hasn't happened for like, 80 years! And they were so excited. And that's really cool. To think about the anthropology and rural living communities. They were so excited that their little niece was going to go in this museum. It's pretty cool that the first birth in 80 years happened on the LaHave islands, and that they get to hold these passports with these really, remote rural, you know—so that kind of piece is also pretty neat. That's a whole other angle. And the older people in the community talking about it?! One of my sons was born in a house that was probably 200 years old, and the people who were saying "Oh you know who the last person born here..." so it's that whole piece of community to go back to.

For her, birthing and rural connection included connection to the past, to place, and to extended family and neighbours.

In contrast to the South Shore, which had a midwifery site that was briefly shuttered, the Annapolis Valley women completely lacked access to midwifery care and expressed feelings of neglect and unjust discrimination in being denied this option. Some expressed dismay at the criminalization of lay midwifery, which had once been an accessible option with lay midwives well known in their communities. In both study sites, rumours circulated of underground midwifery and of women choosing to birth unattended at home. In the early years of midwifery implementation (prior to long wait lists), Valley women were known to temporarily relocate to the South Shore midwifery project catchment area or to Halifax in pursuit of the care model at the expense of leaving their community. Others noted that doctor shortages meant that finding any maternity care could be a challenge, let alone accessing the preferred model of care. As one mother said, "I feel so passionately about choice, but I feel more passionately about access." In contrast, South Shore women expressed gratitude for living somewhere that had a midwifery program as well as for any care they had received. This was true for mothers who were dropped mid pregnancy from midwifery care due to the closure; despite care delays and a lack of continuity, they were grateful for the care extended by the physicians who had already been oversubscribed pre-closure. Alongside gratitude, participants in both sites expressed concern about the lack of universal access across the province and about the sustainability of a program strained by long waiting lists and overburdened midwives, as well as outrage at the temporary suspension of the program that had occurred.

Feelings about poor maternity care access and the untenable status of rural midwifery in the province were both passive and active. Some passively expressed "feeling lucky" to have had a midwife, or resignation over not having one, demonstrating that some mothers only expressed a weak sense they had a right to services where they lived. Rather, one mother said, "we're going to have to drive, like an hour, but it's our choice for living here. Right?" It was common for mothers to comment that local services would be "helpful," rather than that they were essential. Their rural neglect was normalized in a feeling that, because of where they lived, they had little right to demand services. Others introduced a critique of this way of thinking. As one mother told us:

> It sort of feels like it would be much more convenient for the powers that be if we all just lived in Halifax. And then it would be fine to provide these services. It's like, you shouldn't be asking for anything because you live out in the middle of nowhere. It's very inconvenient to have to provide you with anything.

Her analysis points to how the distance between urban and rural increases when rural needs are overlooked as inessential or inconvenient.

The passive construction of having your needs meet as being lucky was contrasted by the collective action that occurred in the South Shore after the 2018 temporary suspension of the midwifery program. We interviewed eight women affected by the closure, learning that the midwifery crisis in the South Shore became a moment of cohesion and collective feminist resistance around the right to services in rural communities. The service disruption triggered protest for the right to rural midwifery access—protests that were about the right to this care option, and the right to reproduce rurally.

Conclusion

The rollout of midwifery in Nova Scotia constructed geographic divisions between the urban and rural that have continued to this day. Divisions between rural areas were enacted as well, between those with and without pilot sites. The rural midwifery program has been in a pilot stage for over a decade now, with no evidence of expansion to the whole province. In fact, the evidence before us points to neglect for most rural families. In the current state of affairs—a system built to fail—rural women, family, and community are under threat. In response to the closure of the midwifery service in Lunenburg, which occurred because of a staffing crisis resulting from low numbers, community members, among them many study participants, protested by writing letters, meeting their political representatives, and holding a public protest (Devereaux, 2018). The fact that these demonstrations occurred in the area with suspended service, rather than throughout the province, signals the resignation of those who had not had access to midwifery at all since legislation and implementation in 2009. The lack of broad-based protest can be partly explained by the historical absence of midwifery as an option for women in Nova Scotia and the long history of centralized medical services that has dominated birthing.

The Canada Health Act (1985) guarantees that essential physician and hospital services will be paid for by the government, and that Canadians will have reasonable access to insured services. Furthermore, the Act's principle of comprehensiveness means that provincial health insurance programs must include all medically necessary services. Are these principles being upheld with the current arrangement of rural midwifery in Nova Scotia, and in rural Canada as a whole? And who decides the meaning of essential, reasonable, and necessary? If midwifery services are framed as ancillary to the norm of medicalized, obstetrician managed, regional or urban hospital-located birthing, it becomes easier to render them nonessential or unnecessary, particularly when juxtaposed with the broader concerns of health care crises. While what is considered reasonable access to services is open to debate, needing to leave one's community to have a baby at all, or in pursuit of a midwife, has iatrogenic consequences for rural mothers, infants, families, and communities.

Participants' feelings of anger and resignation over the lack of access to midwifery, alongside their framing of access to care as "luck," point to a disinclination to view poor access as an infringement on the right to services enshrined by the Canada Health Act (1985). This is not surprising when services are rendered ancillary or absent. Considering oneself lucky to have midwifery birthing support within one's rural community is a response to knowing other rural women are not served at all. The idea of individual luck depoliticizes health care access and acts as a distraction from sociological explanations as to why some people have access and others do not, and why some services are, or are not, deemed essential by government. Despite framings of luck and a reluctance to ask for more, participants' overall discussions of and approaches to care were engaged, not apathetic. Instead, the presence of those who took to the street when their services were suspended and of others who had collectively advocated for midwifery for decades demonstrates a fight for reproductive justice, and this offers insight on how midwifery can be a pathway to rural revitalization and sustainability and growth. This work fosters the reproduction of families and strengthens the local social bonding at the heart of community.

Pregnancy, birth, and parenting constitute the literal reproduction of society, and, while rural communities can also grow through immigration/migration, when the right to give birth in community with adequate health supports is withdrawn, rural residents feel that their rights as rural citizens are threatened more broadly. Our study demonstrates that beyond the basic question of who will catch their baby, rural women want to feel supported, both via their own informal networks and by the social investments that they know are extended to urban residents. The resurgence of midwifery, including Indigenous midwifery, and movements for reproductive justice are places where the conversation on the right to health care converges with an acknowledgment of the diverse situations and needs of women and their families.

References

Association of Ontario Midwives. (2021). *Indigenous midwifery*. https://www.ontariomidwives.ca/indigenous-midwifery

Benoit, C., Carroll, D., & Millar, A. (2002). But is it good for non-urban women's health? Regionalizing maternity care services in British Columbia. *Canadian Review of Sociology/Revue Canadienne de sociologie, 39*(4), 373-395.

Born, K. (2003). Midwifery in Canada. *McGill Journal of Medicine, 7*(1), 72-77.

Canada. (1985). Canada Health Act. https://laws-lois.justice.gc.ca/eng/acts/c-6/

Canadian Association of Midwives. (2021). *Midwifery across Canada*. https://canadianmidwives.org/midwifery-across-canada

de Leeuw, S. (2016). The missing of mums and babes. *Canadian Family Physician, 62*, 580-583.

Devereaux, A. (2018, January 22). Crowd protests loss of midwives on South Shore. *CBC News*. https://www.cbc.ca/news/canada/nova-scotia/midwives-south-shore-program-suspended-protest-1.4499309

Grzybowski, S., Fahey, J., Lai, B., Zhang, S., Aelicks, N., Leung, B., Stoll, K., & Attenborough, R. (2015). The safety of Canadian rural maternity services: A multi-jurisdictional cohort analysis. *BMC Health Services Research, 15*, 410.

Klein, M., Christilaw, J., & Johnston, S. (2002). Loss of maternity care: The cascade of unforeseen dangers. *Canadian Journal of Rural Medicine, 7*(2), 120-121.

Kornelsen, J., Barclay, L., Grzybowski, S., & Gao, Y. (2016). Rural health service planning: The need for a comprehensive approach to costing. *The International Electronic Journal of Rural and Remote Health Research, Education, Practice and Policy, 7.*

Lawford, K. M., Bourgeault, I. L., & Giles, A. R. (2019). "This policy sucks and it's stupid:" Mapping maternity care for First Nations women on reserves in Manitoba, Canada. *Healthcare for Women International, 40*(12), 1302-1335.

Lisonkova, S., Haslam, M. D., Dahlgren, L., Chen, I., Synnes, A. R., & Lim, K. I. (2016). Maternal morbidity and perinatal outcomes among women in rural versus urban areas. *Canadian Medical Association Journal, 188*(17-18), E456-465.

MacDonald, M. E. (2016). The legacy of midwifery and the women's health movement in contemporary discourses of patient choice and empowerment. *Canadian Journal of Midwifery Research and Practice, 15*(1), 43-50.

Miller, K. J., Couchie, C., Ehman, W., Graves, L., Grzybowski, S., & Medves, J. (2012). Rural maternity care. *Journal of Obstetrics and Gynaecology Canada, 34*(10), 984-991.

Moulton, D. (2000). Birth of Nova Scotia midwifery program delayed. *CMAJ: Canadian Medical Association Journal, 162*(12), 1723.

National Aboriginal Council of Midwives. (n.d.). Indigenous midwifery in Canada. https://indigenousmidwifery.ca/indigenous-midwifery-in-canada/

Northern Health. (2017). Northern Health's Indigenous health program launches new resources and reviews successes. https://stories.northernhealth.ca/news/northern-healths-indigenous-health-program-launches-new-resources-and-reviews-successes

Rudrum, S. (2012). An intersectional critical discourse analysis of maternity care policy recommendations in British Columbia. In O. Hankivsky (Ed.), *An intersectionality-based policy analysis framework* (pp. 47-68). Institute for Intersectionality Research and Policy (IIRP), Simon Fraser University.

Shaw, J. (2013). Full-spectrum reproductive justice: The affinity of abortion rights and birth activism. *Studies in Social Justice, 7*(1), 143-159.

Sinding, C. (2010). Using institutional ethnography to understand the production of health care disparities. *Qualitative Health Research, 20*(12), 1656-1663.

SisterSong. (n.d.). *Reproductive justice.* https://www.sistersong.net/reproductive-justice

Statistics Canada. (2016). Census profile, 2016 census. https://www12.statcan.gc.ca/census-recensement/2016/dp-pd/prof/index.cfm?Lang=E

Stoll, K., & Kornelsen, J. (2014). Midwifery care in rural and remote British Columbia: A retrospective cohort study of perinatal outcomes of rural parturient women with a midwife involved in their care, 2003 to 2008. *Journal of Midwifery & Women's Health, 59*(1), 60-66.

Taylor, B. (2013). Stillborn: Regulated midwifery in Nova Scotia. *Dalhousie Journal of Interdisciplinary Management, 8*(2). http://dx.doi.org/10.5931/djim.v8i2.243

Van Wagner, V., Osepchook, C., Harney, E., Crosbie, C., & Tulugak, M. (2012). Remote midwifery in Nunavik, Québec, Canada: Outcomes of perinatal care for the Inuulitsivik Health Centre, 2000-2007. *Birth, 39*(3), 230-237.

Varcoe, C., Brown, H., Calam, B., Harvey, T., & Tallio, M. (2013). Help bring back the celebration of life: A community-based participatory study of rural Aboriginal women's maternity experience and outcomes. *BMC Pregnancy Childbirth, 13*(1).

Wakerman, J., Bourke, L., Humphreys, J., & Taylor, J. (2017). Is remote health different to rural health? *Rural and Remote Health, 17*(2), 3832. https://doi.org/10.22605/RRH3832

Warsh, C. L. K. (2010). *Prescribed norms: Women and health in Canada and the United States since 1800.* University of Toronto Press.

Young, C., & Grobelna, A. (2018). *Characteristics of remote and isolated healthcare facilities: An environmental scan* [Environmental scan]. CADTH.

Zayed, R., Davidson, B., Nadeau, L., Callanan, T. S., Fleisher, W., Hope-Ross, Espinet, S., Spenser, H., Lipton, H., Srivastaya, A., Lazier, L., Doey, T., Khalid Khan, S., McKerlie, A., Stretch, N., Flynn, R., Abidi, S., St. John, K., Auclair, G., Liashko, V. ...Steele, M. S. (2016). Canadian rural/remote primary care physicians' perspectives on child/adolescent mental healthcare service delivery. *Journal of the American Academy of Child and Adolescent Psychiatry, 25*(1), 24-34.

8

Rural Food

Rights and Remedies for Older Persons in Canada

KATHLEEN KEVANY & AL LAUZON

Introduction

One of the seldom-considered contributing factors to well-being is food security. Canadians may take for granted that all citizens have access to sufficient food if they desire it. Yet, over the last four decades, we have seen increases in food insecurity. Generally, food security has been understood as "the timely availability of food that is safe and nutritious, acquired in ways that are socially acceptable to the individual, without resorting to emergency food supplies, scavenging, or stealing" (Keller et al., 2007, p. 318). Food insecurity is the opposite; as Health Canada defines it, it is "the inability to acquire or consume an adequate diet quality or sufficient quantity of food in socially acceptable ways, or the uncertainty that one will be able to do so" (PROOF, 2018).

In this chapter, we frame food security as a matter of rights—and more specifically, we frame rural older persons' food security and insecurity as components of the right to be rural as it is articulated in this volume. We accept that we are operating within a largely unrecognized, contractual rural citizenship that is governed by unexamined feelings and ideas that make it hard to put the right to be rural into words. For our purposes, the right to be rural is the self-evident right for citizens to live, work, and age in an array of rural and remote geographic settings while retaining full rights of citizenship. Using this perspective to examine food insecurity, we propose that neoliberal policies around agriculture, health care, and social welfare constrain the realization of Canadian citizenship rights, and specifically older persons' right to be rural and right to access sufficient food.

Food (In)security in Canada

Tarasuk, Mitchell, and Dachner (2014) reported that 12% of Canadian households in 2013 experienced some level of food insecurity. This translates into 1.3 million households, or 3.2 million individuals; of the households, 20% or 294,000 were severely food insecure. Nearly 1.1 million Canadians visited a food bank in March 2018, with 5.7 million snacks and meals being served in food banks that month (Sagan, 2019). Food Banks Canada (2016) found that between 2008 and 2016, the use of food banks in Ontario increased by 6.9%. Granted, as Loopstra and Tarasuk (2015) note, food bank usage statistics are an underestimation of food insecurity. They found that between 2007 and 2012, the individuals in Canada experiencing food insecurity increased by 606,500 people, but food bank usage only increased by 130,800 people (Loopstra & Tarasuk, 2015, pp. 446-447). Thus, only about 22% of those people who were newly experiencing food insecurity sought food relief through acquiring food from a food bank. All of this suggests that policy and charitable responses to food insecurity do not fix the inequities that underlie it, nor do they even fix the acute problem of food insecurity for most people who experience it. The insufficiency of responses to food security has major implications, particularly if nutrient-dense, culturally appropriate food is understood as a right and determinant of "life, health, dignity, civil society, progress, justice and sustainable development" (Mcintyre & Rondeau, 2009, p. 188).

This context has spurred considerable research, but there is a dearth of inquiry and interest in the rural context, with most research addressing the issue of food insecurity in larger urban centres (Anderson, 2015; Watson, 2013). Furthermore, there has been little research conducted on rural older persons, a unique population group who may struggle in different ways than their urban counterparts and other rural people (Green et al., 2008). If access to secure forms of nutritious food is a right, then it is imperative to know if food security is truly being addressed for all Canadians, and especially certain populations who may have specific needs arising out of their context.

In this chapter, we begin by providing relevant historical context for the right to be rural, the right to food, and the intersections of these two. We examine some neoliberal economic policies operating in Canada and elsewhere that favour industrial agriculture and reduce protection of land, rural life, and public resources. We end with a case study in four rural counties in Ontario of rural older persons' rights to food and to be rural and expose how global capitalism undermines both.

Neoliberalism and Food Production

To understand food insecurity, it is necessary to understand food production. And in Canada, like in many developed nations, food production policies have shifted. Early twentieth-century policies responded to threats to food security and sovereignty with mobilization around farm labour legislation and agrarian protectionism, among other measures. Yet food production policies and practices over the past 40–50 years can be characterized as neoliberal, insofar as they support the reduction of regulations seen as unfriendly to business, espouse a growing allegiance to free markets (Alvaro et al., 2010; Harvey, 2005), and endorse the "privatisation of public resources, the minimisation of labour costs [and] the dismantling of public programmes" (Levkoe, 2011, p. 690).

The neoliberal model has been found to emphasize the maximization of money and human capital by exploiting natural capital and social resources and disregarding sustainability and social concerns (Brenner et al., 2010; McMichael, 2006; Qualman, 2019). In food production, neoliberal thinking manifests in policies that emphasize reducing impediments and increasing exports to global markets (Harvey, 2016; Qualman, 2019). One result is decades of expansion in industrial agriculture, through farmland consolidation for large-scale production, specialized methods and equipment, and increased reliance on cheap fuel and cheap labour, leading to adverse ecological, socio-political, economic, and equity impacts (Qualman, 2019). Consequently, Canadian agriculture has become a producer of an array of foods largely meant for global consumption (McInnes, 2011), and as Woods (2007) notes, "consumption is distanced from production" (p. 492).

Advances in technologies and processes aided in substantially increasing agricultural production and the ability to feed more people between 1960 and 2015 (Food and Agriculture Organization [FAO], 2017). Yet, the communities where agriculture is located have not seen proportionate gains in employment or prosperity. Consolidation in agriculture means fewer farm employment opportunities, far fewer opportunities for small-scale, owner-operator farms, and shrinking sources of rural livelihoods (Lauzon et al., 2015); foods produced and profits gained in these settings often leave the community (Centre for Local

Prosperity, 2018). For small-scale producers, it becomes increasingly difficult to afford land and equipment, and staying small entails active resistance of discursive and practical pressures to grow through exports.

Moreover, industrial agriculture and farm consolidation today depend on the depletion of natural resources (McMichael, 2006, p. 409; Qualman, 2019, p. 253), and this scenario is projected to get worse. As Wallace-Wells (2019) notes, global climate change will come to have a negative impact on production yields, meaning there will be less available food as the population increases. Furthermore, less food will mean higher prices, which means fewer people will have the financial resources to acquire an adequate supply of nutrition.

When these shifts are viewed alongside the decline of the welfare state and the idea of the public good (Halstrom, 2009; Lauzon et al., 2015), and complicated by the downloading of social responsibilities from federal and provincial governments to municipal governments in Canada, we can assert that rural municipalities and rural people are shouldering increased responsibilities for their own welfare, in a context of diminishing access to the benefits of food production. Rurality exacerbates the challenges that neoliberalism presents for everyday people—a point illustrated well in the case of rural older persons, to which we now turn.

Food Insecurity and Rural Older Persons

Three issues intersect to form the context for rural older persons' food security: poverty, rurality, and health. Below, we address those three issues and their intersections, which are difficult to disentangle and, as such, are not separated in our review.

There were 6 million people aged 65+ in Canada in 2014, representing 15.6% of the population. By 2030, this age group will make up 23% of the population, or 9.5 million people (Government of Canada, 2021). According to the most recent available estimates, approximately 7% of people 65 years and over in Canada have incomes below the after-tax, low-income cut-off; looking only at the individuals who are not married or common-law, 17% of these live below the low-income cut-off (Green et al., 2008; cf. McKay, 2018). At the same time, the cost of a nutritious diet is increasing, and many in Nova Scotia, where our case study took place, cannot afford it and do not have the means to prepare food at home and take advantage of the cost savings that come along with that (Langille et al., 2013; cf. Charlebois et al., 2019).

Looking at health status, while 92% of Canadians over the age of 65 live independently, they may not do so without problems. Within this population, many suffer from chronic diseases: 18.4% have diabetes, 46.8% have arthritis, and 48.7% have high blood pressure, along with a variety of other chronic conditions (Government of Ontario, 2017). These conditions may interfere with older individuals' ability to prepare food, even if they can access it. Moreover, those living on their own may not be motivated to prepare nutritious meals because it is a lot of work for one person, leading to limited food intake and lack of adequate nutrition (Quandt et al., 1998; Quandt et al., 2001). Lauzon (2016) has also noted that education and literacy levels are lower in rural areas than in urban areas, particularly for older individuals. Lower levels of literacy also mean greater challenges in managing one's own care, including managing diet as a strategy for controlling chronic conditions.

The impact that food insecurity in turn has on quality of life and health is well-illustrated by existing studies. Tarasuk and Vogt (2009) found that "food insufficient households" tend to have "higher rates of heart disease, diabetes, high blood pressure, and food allergies compared to those in food-sufficient households," and that food insecurity doubled the risk of diabetes "even after adjusting for socio-demographic factors, physical activity level and body-mass index" (p. 215). The authors connect their findings to numerous other studies that have reported that those in food insecure households are more likely to self-report poor or fair health, have poor functional health, have restricted activity, have multiple chronic health conditions, suffer from major depression and distress, and have poor social support. Food insecurity increases the risk of chronic disease, and this in turn places greater pressure on the health care systems. To wit: we think it is important to note that half of all older persons admitted to hospital during a study period by Allard and colleagues (2016) were considered malnourished upon entry.

Rural older persons in particular may be vulnerable to poor nutritional health due to limited resources, difficulties with transportation, and greater distance to food resources—even if their incomes are not below the low-income cut-off. Indeed, studies have confirmed that older people in rural areas are less likely than those living in urban areas to consume the daily recommended amounts of fruits and vegetables (Sharkey et al., 2010). Quandt and colleagues (1998) observe that older adults have restricted access to health care services in rural settings compared to those living in urban areas, and they identify a deficiency in other services to support nutritional management for the older rural population.

Keating and Eales (2012) argue that rural communities' capacity to meet the needs of older persons in their population is a function of population density and distance from major population centres—an idea Ray D. Bollman explores in this volume as well. Inadequate services in rural communities/areas put the frail and vulnerable at risk (Keating & Eales, 2012), and render them dependent upon the goodwill of family and friends. This is problematic for older adults who may not have family nearby, or have limited social networks they can draw on for assistance (Bitto et al., 2003; Liese et al., 2007).

It is not just access to public services that is compromised in rural places. Bitto and colleagues (2003) note higher grocery prices in rural areas and the concentration of supermarkets in urban zones, leaving residents of rural areas with poor access to an adequate supply of healthy foods (Kaufman, 1999; Liese et al., 2007). The more rural and remote, the greater the access issues (Kelly et al., 2011; Lauzon, 2016).

Granted, remoteness is just one piece of the larger context that enables or limits access to food for older adults (Vilar-Compte et al., 2017). The rural context involves as well the interpersonal, institutional, community, and socio-political factors with which people in this age group interact. These factors all influence food environments and diet-related health outcomes. They intersect with a lack of access to healthy foods, individual behaviours and lifestyles, broader environmental conditions, and levels of education and food literacy, as well as food policies that form the food environment (Palumbo et al., 2019). The upshot of the connections between food security, chronic conditions, health care system costs, and social support coverage is that food security is not just a private trouble; it is a public issue (Mills, 1959) that demands coordinated policy response, whether the goal is improving individual well-being or, to put it crassly, saving taxpayers money. Food insecurity undermines the well-being of rural older persons, as well as their right to food; moreover, it compromises their right to live, work, and age in an array of rural and remote geographic settings while retaining full rights of citizenship.

Stakeholder Perspectives on Rural Food Insecurity and Older Adults

In the summer of 2019, we began a study of rural food insecurity and older adults by interviewing 76 key informants in the counties of Perth, Grey, Bruce, and Huron in Ontario. There are two major urban centres in these four counties: Stratford, with a population of 31,465, and Owen Sound, with a population of 21,341. We interviewed 17 health care professionals, including physicians and nurse practitioners, 19 homecare workers, 20 service providers (e.g., food banks), and 20 public health and municipal staff. Interviews among the four groups of stakeholders were spread evenly across the four counties and focused on factors mediating social and environmental well-being.

Echoing the literature, income was determined to be a driver of food insecurity. As one interviewee noted, "income drives and underpins a lack of access to healthy food," while another interviewee explained that "old age pensions are a fairly limited budget." This is exacerbated, another interviewee noted, by rising "housing, fuel, heating [and] food costs" and pensions not keeping pace with the increases. As noted by another respondent, "older adults are less flexible when it comes to influencing their income." Respondents confirmed that "grocery stores in small towns are often more expensive," and one noted that in rural communities there may be one grocery store, and hence "there is no one for them to compete with." These contributions indicate that the rural older adult's grocery dollar does not go as far as it might in urban centres.

Even assuming that older individuals have adequate incomes, accessing food may still be an issue. Rural older persons may be more challenged when it comes to getting to a grocery store, especially if there is not one nearby. One of the issues unearthed in the interviews, but discussed less in the literature, was the reliance on cars in rural communities. As one respondent explained to us,

> seniors are particularly vulnerable if they do not have a license anymore, or if they have no family in the area to assist them. They often don't have access to services that other patient subgroups do, often because of social isolation. There is no public transportation available in the rural areas and [a] taxi tends to be too expensive for those on a limited income.

Interviewees explained how transportation intersects with health, poverty, and social support to impact the vulnerability of the rural older individual. For example, one stated that "those without family in the area, those with disability and mobility issues, those with cognitive and mental health decline...[and] those without retirement savings who are just living on a Canadian Pension Plan" are vulnerable. A health care professional highlighted this and the challenge of caring for some rural older adults when he stated:

> I have several elderly male patients whose license is gone, who have no kids, who suffer from dementia...understanding these patients do not have the cognition to adequately relay their social situation and also don't have the family support to access nutritional foods is fundamental to establishing care plans.

Some interviewees perceived many older individuals in need as being "too proud" to ask for assistance. Some of this might be attributed to the fact that some of the regions in the study attract many retirees who come with significant financial capital, but little social capital. If they lose a partner or become ill, they can easily become socially isolated, creating challenges, as well as cognitive dissonance, when it comes to finding new ways to access services and food.

Food banks and other social supports come with "a huge stigma," which, according to participants, "is worse in a small town compared to urban areas because there is less anonymity," and many older people "do not want families to know they are struggling with money." Interviewees also pointed out that food banks rely on online publicity, and many in this age group are not technologically adept and hence are not aware of the services. Relatedly, respondents also noted that older individuals often find the divulging of personal information required by social supports like food banks "invasive"; many belong to a generation that values privacy and have come to distrust new technologies as they age. Even if they do access the food bank services, the food acquired is often "carbohydrate heavy," "fast food—preserved, canned or prepackaged because it is cheap and goes a long way." The consensus from interviewees was that "no number of food banks or meal programs are going to be able to lift people out of food insecurity."

One alternative to food banks might be homecare. However, as the government-funded homecare providers highlighted for us, their time with any one individual is limited and there is no time to focus on diet. This is caused and compounded by a chronic shortage of homecare workers, particularly in rural areas. Homecare service providers did note that private homecare is available to assist in meal preparation, but such services can be costly, ranging from $35-80 per hour, a cost many older individuals cannot afford.

Other programs, such as *Meals on Wheels*, cater specifically to older persons with mobility and financial constraints. However, as service providers noted, because of the low population density they are expensive to run. With the 2018 increase in Ontario's minimum wage (to $14 per hour), service providers believed *Meals on Wheels* had become even more expensive, to the point that some older people could no longer afford the service. Moreover, interviewees believed that older individuals living in either Stratford or Owen Sound—the urban centres in the four counties—had access to more diverse services than others in the four counties.

Yet, even if older people have access to food and support services—and can afford them—this does not always mean they will prepare nutritious meals. Echoing the literature summarized earlier, interviewees told us that there can be a lack of motivation to prepare nutritious meals when there is only one person; interviewees' experiences with older individuals had shown them that people in this age group living alone are more vulnerable to malnutrition as a result of not preparing adequate meals.

Some respondents also noted the impact of food literacy. As one observed, "people have heard a lot of different things about what they should or shouldn't be eating. Dr. Oz, the news...It is rare to have someone who has a good understanding of what they should be eating." Furthermore, it was reported that when patients are ill or suffer from chronic conditions, nutrition often becomes a low priority. For these older individuals, they fail to understand the relationship between diet and managing chronic disease or wound healing.

Nutritional well-being can even be compromised by something as simple as poor oral health. As noted by one respondent, those with low-income and poor oral health are unable to chew food and are also unable to have repair work done or get dentures. For example, one respondent told us that dentures can cost up to $3,000, an amount that would be unaffordable for many older persons living on a limited income.

Interestingly, while the health providers we interviewed recognized the importance of diet for older adults, it was not an issue that they addressed in their practices. As one physician explained, "I work independently and it limits the amount of case management I can provide. I don't have a team of professionals to deal with concerns as they come in." Another physician explained: "If I am seeing the person for weight loss or if they are identified as having malnutrition, we would discuss diet...but I probably wouldn't go into 'What are you eating?' unless that was the key original issue or a lot of weight loss happened." This may signal a crucial gap in primary health care, considering that, as noted above, half of all older persons are identified as malnourished upon entry to the hospital (Allard et al., 2016). Part of the gap, according to health care professionals, stems from the lack of affordable dietitians available to rural residents. One health care provider noted that in Canada there is one dietitian for every 20,000 people.

These challenges and their intensity in rural communities struck interviewees as ironic—in terms of having food insecurity become an issue in some of the most productive agricultural land in the country. As one respondent from Bruce County noted, "Bruce County is an agricultural area with an abundance of food produced locally. The problem is harnessing the food to ensure everyone can access what they need. Unfortunately, most of the agriculture in the four counties does not serve local markets, but serves global markets." If food were properly understood to be a human right, more attention would be focused on these various drivers of access to nutritious food. The right to food is indeed delineated in the Universal Declaration of Human Rights (1948). The challenge, which we take up below, is how to put that commitment into practice for rural older persons.

The Right to Food

The Universal Declaration of Human Rights (UDHR) was proclaimed in 1948. Among many other countries, Canada is a signatory. The UDHR seeks to protect the right to food, and the right of all human beings to live in dignity, free from hunger, food insecurity, and malnutrition (United Nations, 1948). The mechanisms to fulfill these rights remain elusive and food insecurity has continued to rise, even though, from 1966 onward, there have been noteworthy steps toward specifying what a right to food means (FAO, 1996; UN Human Rights, 1966; World Commission on Environment and Development, 1987). In the 2015 UN Sustainable Development Goals (SDGS), the right to food is a foundation to advance other goals, as food sufficiency drives and is driven by citizen health, stability in food supply, fair trade, peaceful relations, environmental sustainability, and quality of life for all (United Nations, 2015). While the realization and enforcement of the SDGS is a tall order, their establishment in international law means that citizens are able to call upon their governments to ensure the protection of and access to such resources as water, land, soil, biodiversity, and natural spaces. This might entail ensuring resources and infrastructure are available to enable citizens to produce their own food, and when citizens cannot access adequate food through no fault of their own, governments are obliged to provide food or income to purchase food (Van Esterik, 1999). But like any constitution or law, the SDGS' implementation has been, and will be, unevenly felt (Nash, 2009).

The question of how federal and provincial governments in Canada are addressing the right for rural older citizens to have access to available and affordable food is complex. Civic groups have attempted to hold the Canadian government to task (de Schutter, 2012; Dieticians of Canada, 2017; Finnigan, 2017), but according to Mah, Hamill, Rondeau, and Mcintyre (2014), by 2014 it had not taken much action on food security or food sovereignty. Nevertheless, between signing the UDHR and the start of the twenty-first century, Canada updated and recommitted to its Charter of Rights and Freedoms (Government of Canada, 1982). Officials from Health Canada stated in 1998, as part of Canada's Action Plan for Food Security, that they would "pursue participatory and sustainable food, agriculture, fisheries, forestry and rural development policies and practices in high and low potential areas, which are essential to adequate and reliable food supplies at the household, national, regional and global levels, and combat pests, drought and desertification, considering the multifunctional character of agriculture" (Government of Canada, 1998, p. 35).

Yet, food insecurity is not only targeted by programs specifically meant to deal with food, and indeed, it cannot be treated in isolation from other social determinants of health (Kelly et al., 2011; Yip et al., 2007). Moreover, scholars are increasingly advocating for the recognition of environmental influences, including protecting natural assets and enhancing food environments and amenities to bolster individual and community health (Kelly et al., 2011; Romans et al., 2011). The UN Special Rapporteur on the Right to Food, de Schutter (2012), recommended that Canada focus on democracy itself, including through listening to marginalized voices and food production workers, alongside supplying adequate social assistance; providing a living wage; having more foresight in agricultural policies; and introducing proactive measures to address health, obesity, and chronic disease stemming from poor diets, particularly in rural, northern, and Indigenous communities.

One cannot overlook the mechanisms in place in Canada that do support food security. Programs such as Old Age Security (OAS), the Canada Pension Plan (CPP), and the Guaranteed Income Supplement (GIS) are designed to increase well-being, including food security, in households with older members (Gundersen et al., 2017; Gundersen & Ziliak, 2015; Mcintyre et al., 2016), and they constitute an effective, if not completely sufficient, poverty reduction strategy (Mcintyre et al., 2016; Tarasuk et al., 2014). However, when the discourse and policies focus on the ability of individuals to access, afford, and (to a lesser extent) prepare food, to the exclusion of the way food is produced and distributed in the first place, the imaginable solutions will likewise only tackle half of the problem. In the next section, we suggest that a shift in thinking from food security to food sovereignty—from the consumption of food to its production—may illuminate some of the systemic food security problems and fixes that have thus far eluded Canadian communities.

Food Sovereignty as an Approach to Food Security for Rural Older Persons

Global organizing efforts by La Via Campesina (2018) have raised awareness of food sovereignty, namely, the assertion of peoples' interconnected rights to define their own food and agricultural systems, and to access healthy and culturally appropriate food produced through ecologically sound and sustainable methods. Food sovereignty activism and social movements focus on empowering citizens to control their own food systems and produce more of their own food, positioning people's needs and environmental sustainability before the needs of the market (Chaifetz & Jagger, 2014; Fairbairn, 2012; Trauger, 2014; Vivero Pol, 2013; Watson, 2013).

To put food sovereignty into practice, governments can use mechanisms like municipal level regulations and by-laws, provincial business supports and incentives, as well as federal policies and investments to enable the right to food and the right to be rural through suitable food environments and supported rural regions. Numerous examples of such measures can be found across Canada in regional plans (e.g., Halifax) and community food gardens on municipal land (Halifax Food Policy Alliance, 2018); tax credits for farmers who donate food to eligible food programs such as food banks (Alberta); bills and acts to foster resilient local food economies (Alberta and Ontario); and local food councils comprised of leaders from local food industries that provide advice and recommendations to government (Alberta).

These are important steps, but they tend to underemphasize the importance of small-scale and family-run farms and food production operations, which produce 70% of the world's food and can feed the bulk of the world when supports are available (Nowakowski, 2018). Importantly, small-scale producers have been found to apply practices that support the full life of materials and the bio-economy, while they strive for self-sufficiency, resiliency, and viability (Hamer, 2014). From a sociological perspective, small food-related operations have economic and also social and symbolic functions. Even community gardens and community kitchens, beyond their modest contributions to the availability of fresh, nutritious food, can foster empowering acts of resistance, teach an array of skills, and connect people of all ages (Ecology Action Centre, 2016; Hung, 2017; Upper Grand District School Board, 2018). Such efforts hold the potential to foster greater food literacy, sovereignty, and security.

Conclusion

The persistence of food insecurity and the weak integration of policies around food production and consumption leave us wondering whether Canada's paper commitment to food as a right is genuine. There might be hope, given the fact that a growing number of scholars and political figures have declared the death of the neoliberalism that has delivered the industrialized, global export-oriented food system and its related strain on health care and other government services (Comaroff, 2011; Patience, 2016). Additionally, part of the challenge of food insecurity has been picked up by movements that promote guaranteed incomes and sustainable local food production, such as community gardens and guerilla gardening. Yet much more needs to be done to achieve stability and accessibility around nutritious food, particularly in rural places, and particularly for older individuals. Our interviews highlighted one important fact that is overlooked in most analyses of food insecurity: the potential role of dieticians and other health care providers in improving access to and knowledge about healthy food. As we have demonstrated, issues of the right to be rural and the right to food security and sovereignty are contested, complex, and in constant flux. However, we contend that the right to food, including access to healthy food as consumers and to fair markets as producers, remains a foundational right as articulated in many national and international declarations. Moreover, the right to be rural and the right to food are interconnected: one cannot live where one cannot eat.

References

Allard, J. P., Keller, H., Jeejeebhoy, K. N., Laporte, M., Duerksen, D. R., Gramlich, L., Payette, H., Bernier, P., Vesnaver, E., Davidson, B., & Teterina, A. (2016). Malnutrition at hospital admission—Contributors and effect on length of stay: A prospective cohort study from the Canadian malnutrition task force. *Journal Parenteral and Enteral Nutrition, 40*(4), 487–497.

Alvaro, C., Jackson, L. A., Kirk, S., McHugh, T. L., Hughes, J., Chircop, A., & Lyons, R. F. (2010). Moving Canadian governmental policies beyond a focus on individual lifestyle: Some insights from complexity and critical theories. *Health Promotion International, 26*(1), 91–99.

Anderson, M. D. (2015). Roles of rural areas in sustainable food system transformations. *Development (Basingstoke), 58*(2–3), 256–262. https://doi.org/10.1057/s41301-016-0003-7

Bitto, E. A., Morgan, L. W., Oakland, M. J., & Sand, M. (2003). Grocery store access in rural food deserts. *Journal for the Study of Food and Society, 6*(2), 35–48.

Brenner, N., Peck, J., & Theodore, N. (2010). Variegated neoliberalization: Geographies, modalities, pathways. *Global networks, 10*(2), 182–222.

Centre for Local Prosperity. (2018, February). *Import replacement: Local prosperity for rural Atlantic Canada.* http://centreforlocalprosperity.ca/wp-content/uploads/2018/02/CLP-IR-Study-web-Feb2018-Pages.pdf

Chaifetz, A., & Jagger, P. (2014). 40 years of dialogue on food sovereignty: A review and a look ahead. *Global Food Security, 3*(2), 85–91.

Charlebois, S., Smook, M., Wambui, B. N., Fiander, D., Music, J., & Somogyi, S. (2019). *New Canada's Food Guide offers a more affordable plate, and greater food security—But that may not last* [Press release]. https://www.dal.ca/faculty/management/news-events/news/2019/03/14/release__new_canada___s_food_guide_offers_a_more_affordable_plate__and_greater_food_security____but_that_may_not_last.html

Comaroff, J. (2011). The end of neoliberalism? What is left of the left. *The Annals of the American Academy of Political and Social Science, 637*(1), 141–147.

de Schutter, O. (2012). Special rapporteur on the right to food: Mission to Canada. https://foodsecurecanada.org/sites/foodsecurecanada.org/files/20120321_SRRTF_Aide-mémoire_Canada.pdf

Dietitians of Canada. (2017). Addressing household food insecurity within Canada's poverty reduction strategy. https://www.ourcommons.ca/Content/Committee/421/HUMA/Brief/BR8847313/br-external/DietitiansOfCanada-e.pdf

Ecology Action Centre. (2016). Adventures in local food, gleaning good food [Blog post]. https://adventuresinlocalfood.com/2016/05/10/gleaning-good-food/

Fairbairn, M. (2012). Framing transformation: The counter-hegemonic potential of food sovereignty in the US context. *Agriculture and Human Values, 29*, 217-230. https://doi.org/10.1007/s10460-011-9334-x

Finnigan, P. (2017, December). *A food policy for Canada: Report of the Standing Committee on Agriculture and Agri-Food.* House of Commons, Canada. 42nd parl. 1st sess. https://www.ourcommons.ca/Content/Committee/421/AGRI/Reports/RP9324012/agrirp10/agrirp10-e.pdf

Food and Agriculture Organization (FAO). (1996). *World food summit.* http://www.fao.org/3/w3548e/w3548e00.htm

Food and Agriculture Organization (FAO). (2017). *The state of food and agriculture, 2017: Leveraging food systems for inclusive rural transformation.* http://www.fao.org/3/a-i7658e.pdf

Food Banks Canada. (2016). *Hungercount 2016: A comprehensive report on hunger and food bank use in Canada, and recommendations for change.* https://www.foodbankscanada.ca/getmedia/6173994f-8a25-40d9-acdf-660a28e40f37/HungerCount_2016_final_singlepage.pdf

Government of Canada. (1982). *Canada Charter of Rights and Freedoms.* https://www.canada.ca/en/canadian-heritage/services/download-order-charter-bill.html

Government of Canada. (1998). *Canada's action plan for food security.* https://publications.gc.ca/site/eng/9.647322/publication.html

Government of Canada. (2021). *Food policy.* https://www.canada.ca/en/campaign/food-policy/thefoodpolicy.html

Government of Ontario. (2017, November). *Aging with confidence: Ontario's action plan for seniors.* https://files.ontario.ca/ontarios_seniors_strategy_2017.pdf

Green, R. J., Williams, P. L., Johnson, C. S., & Blum, I. (2008). Can Canadian seniors on a public pension afford a nutritious diet? *Canadian Journal of Aging, 27*(1), 69-79.

Gundersen, C., Kreider, B., Pepper, J., & Tarasuk, V. (2017). Food assistance programs and food insecurity: Implications for Canada in light of the mixing problem. *Empirical Economics, 52*(3), 1065-1087.

Gundersen, C., & Ziliak, J. P. (2015). Food insecurity and health outcomes. *Health affairs, 34*(11), 1830-1839.

Halifax Food Policy Alliance. (2018, March). *HRM food charter* [Draft charter]. https://halifaxfoodpolicy.files.wordpress.com/2018/03/drafthalifaxfoodcharter_march2018.pdf

Halstrom, L. (2009). Public policy and the welfare state. In D. Raphael (Ed.), *Social Determinants of Health* (2nd ed.) (pp. 336-349). Canadian Scholars' Press Inc.

Hamer, E. (2014, April 18). Small scale farmers are feeding our future! *The Ecologist.* https://theecologist.org/2014/apr/18/small-scale-farmers-are-feeding-our-future

Harvey, D. (2005). *A brief history of neoliberalism*. Oxford University Press.

Harvey, D. (2016, July 26). Neoliberalism is a political project. *Jacobin Magazine*.

Hung, H. (2017). Formation of new property rights on government land through informal co-management: Case studies on countryside guerilla gardening. *Land Use Policy, 63*, 381–393.

Kaufman, P. R. (1999). Rural poor have less access to supermarkets, large grocery stores. *Rural Development Perspectives, 13*, 19–26.

Keating, N., & Eales, J. (2012). Diversity among older adults in rural Canada: Health in context. In J. C. Kulig & A. M. Williams (Eds.), *Health in rural Canada* (pp. 427–446). UBC Press.

Keller, H. H., Dwyer, J. J., Edwards, V., Senson, C., & Edward, H. G. (2007). Food security in older adults: Community service provider perceptions of their roles. *Canadian Journal on Aging/La Revue canadienne du vieillissement, 26*(4), 317–328.

Kelly, B. J., Lewin, T. J., Stain, H. J., Coleman, C., Fitzgerald, M., Perkins, D., Carr, V. J., Fragar, L., Fuller, J., Lyle, D., & Beard, J. R. (2011). Determinants of mental health and well-being within rural and remote communities. *Social Psychiatry and Psychiatric Epidemiology, 46*(12), 1331–1342.

Langille, L., Andrée, P., Norgang, E., & Clement, C. (2013). Challenges and opportunities for community food security: The policy landscape in Nova Scotia. https://foodarc.ca/wp-content/uploads/2014/11/ChallengesandOpportunitiesforCFSinNSAugust2013-rev.pdf

Lauzon, A. (2016). The rural learning challenge: Meeting the health needs of rural residents through ICTs. In V. C. X. Wang (Ed.), *Handbook of research on advancing health education through technology* (pp. 1–22). IGI Global.

Lauzon, A., Bollman, R., & Ashton, W. (2015). Introduction. In *State of rural Canada 2015* (pp. 1–8). Canadian Rural Revitalization Foundation. http://sorc.crrf.ca/wp-content/uploads/2015/09/SORC2015.pdf

La Via Campesina. (2018). Globalising the struggle also means globalising solidarity and hope: La Via Campesina, while accepting the XV Navarra International Prize for Solidarity. https://viacampesina.org/en/la-via-campesina-xv-navarra-international-prize-for-solidarity/

Levkoe, C. (2011). Towards a transformative food politics. *Local Environment, 16*(7), 687–705.

Liese, A. D., Weis, K. E., Pluto, D., Smith, E., & Lawson, A. (2007). Food store types, availability, and cost of foods in a rural environment. *Journal of the American Dietetic Association, 107*(11), 1916–1923.

Loopstra, R., & Tarasuk, V. (2015). Food bank usage is a poor indicator of food insecurity: Insights from Canada. *Social Policy and Society, 14*(3), 443–455.

Mah, C. L., Hamill, C., Rondeau, K., & McIntyre, L. (2014). A frame-critical policy analysis of Canada's response to the World Food Summit 1998–2008. *Archives of Public Health, 72*(1), 41.

McInnes, D. (2011, August 1). A new mindset for Canada's agri-food sector. *Policy Options*. https://policyoptions.irpp.org/magazines/agri-food-policy/a-new-mindset-for-canadas-agri-food-sector/

Mcintyre, L., Dutton, D. J., Kwok, C., & Emery, J. H. (2016). Reduction of food insecurity among low-income Canadian seniors as a likely impact of a guaranteed annual income. *Canadian Public Policy, 42*(3), 274–286.

Mcintyre, L., & Rondeau, K. (2009). Food insecurity. In D. Raphael (Ed.) *Social determinants of health* (pp. 188–204). Canadian Scholars' Press Inc.

McKay, M. (2018). *Experiences of food insecurity among older women in rural Nova Scotia* (Master's thesis, Dalhousie University/Dalspace). file:///F:/research/food%2osovereignty/McKay-Madeleine-MA-HPRO-December-2018(1).pdf

McMichael, P. (2006). Peasant prospects in the neoliberal age. *New Political Economy, 11*(3), 407-418.

Mills, C. W. (1959.) *The sociological imagination.* Oxford University Press.

Nash, K. (2009). Between citizenship and human rights. *Sociology, 43*(6), 1067-1083. https://doi.org/10.1177/0038038509345702

Nowakowski, K. (2018, October 12). Why we need small farms. *National Geographic.* https://www.nationalgeographic.com/environment/future-of-food/photos-farms-agriculture-national-farmers-day/

Palumbo, R., Adinolfi, P., Annarumma, C., Catinello, G., Tonelli, M., Troiano, E., Vezzosi, S., & Manna, R. (2019). Unravelling the food literacy puzzle: Evidence from Italy. *Food Policy, 83*, 104-115.

Patience, A. (2016, November 26). What's next after neoliberalism? *Independent Australia.* https://independentaustralia.net/politics/politics-display/allan-patience-whats-next-after-neo-liberalism,9772

PROOF. (2018). *Household food insecurity in Canada.* https://proof.utoronto.ca/food-insecurity/

Qualman, D. (2019). *Civilization critical.* Fernwood Publishing

Quandt, S. A., Acrury, T. A., & Bell, R. A. (1998). Self-management of nutritional risk among older adults: A conceptual model and case studies from rural communities. *Journal of Aging Studies, 12*(4), 351-368.

Quandt, S. A., Arcury, T. A., Bell, R. A., McDonald, J., & Vitolins, M. Z. (2001). The social and nutritional meaning of food sharing among older rural adults. *Journal of Aging Studies, 15*(2), 145-162.

Risager, B. S. (2016, July 23). Neoliberalism is a political project: An interview with David Harvey. *Jacobin Magazine.* https://www.jacobinmag.com/2016/07/david-harvey-neoliberalism-capitalism-labor-crisis-resistance/

Romans, S., Cohen, M., & Forte, T. (2011). Rates of depression and anxiety in urban and rural Canada. *Social Psychiatry and Psychiatric Epidemiology, 46*(7), 567-575.

Sagan, A. (2019, July 7). Little Free Pantries spring up to help tackle food insecurity in Canada. *CityNews.* https://toronto.citynews.ca/2019/07/07/little-free-pantries-spring-up-to-help-tackle-food-insecurity-in-canada-2/

Sharkey, J. R., Johnson, C. M., & Dean, W. R. (2010). Food access and perceptions of the community and household food environment as correlates of fruit and vegetable intake among rural seniors. *BMC geriatrics, 10*(1), 32.

Tarasuk, V., Mitchell, A., & Dachner, N. (2014). *Household food insecurity in Canada, 2012.* https://proof.utoronto.ca/wp-content/uploads/2014/05/Household_Food_Insecurity_in_Canada-2012_ENG.pdf

Tarasuk, V., & Vogt, J. (2009). Household food insecurity in Ontario. *Canadian Journal of Public Health, 100*(3), 184-188.

Trauger, A. (2014). Toward a political geography of food sovereignty: Transforming territory, exchange and power in the liberal sovereign state. *Journal of Peasant Studies, 41*, 1131-1152.

UN Human Rights (1966). *International covenant on economic, social, and cultural rights*. https://www.ohchr.org/en/professionalinterest/pages/cescr.aspx

United Nations. (1948). *Universal declaration of human rights*. https://www.un.org/en/about-us/universal-declaration-of-human-rights

United Nations. (2015). *The 17 goals*. https://sustainabledevelopment.un.org/?menu=1300

Upper Grand District School Board. (2018, May 23). WHSS "Truth About Youth" garden project to connect students and seniors [Blog post]. https://www.ugdsb.ca/blog/whss-truth-about-youth-garden-project-to-connect-students-and-seniors/

Van Esterik, P. (1999). Gender and sustainable food systems: A feminist critique. In M. Koc, R. MacRae, L. Mougeog, & J. Welsh (Eds.), *For hunger-proof cities: Sustainable urban food systems* (pp. 157–161). Ottawa, ON: International Development Research Centre.

Vilar-Compte, M., Gaitán-Rossi, P., & Pérez-Escamilla, R. (2017). Food insecurity measurement among older adults: Implications for policy and food security governance. *Global Food Security, 14*, 87–95.

Vivero Pol, J. L. (2013). Why food should be a commons not a commodity. *Our World, United Nations University*. https://ourworld.unu.edu/en/why-food-should-be-a-commons-not-a-commodity

Wallace-Wells, D. (2019). *The uninhabitable earth: Life after warming*. Tim Duggan Books.

Watson, A. (2013). *Groundswell: A guide to building food security in rural communities*. North Kootenay Lake Community Services Society. http://www.nklcss.org/documents/groundswell/grndswl.pdf

Woods, M. (2007). Engaging the global countryside: Globalization, hybridity and the reconstitution of rural place. *Progress in Human Geography, 31*(4), 485–507.

World Commission on Environment and Development. (1987). *Our common future*. Oxford University Press.

Yip, W., Subramanian, S. V., Mitchell, A. D., Lee, D. T. S., Wang, J., & Kawachi, I. (2007). Does social capital enhance health and well-being? Evidence from rural China. *Social Science & Medicine, 64*(1), 35–49.

9

The Multifaceted Sense of Belonging
Discursive Conceptions of Home by Third Age Residents in Rural Finland

KATJA RINNE-KOSKI & SULEVI RIUKULEHTO

Introduction

In its broadest sense, citizenship is defined as an individual's membership in a nation-state, with rights and duties to follow. This kind of definition is normative in nature, emphasizing rights and duties as cornerstones of contemporary citizenship. Socio-cultural approaches to citizenship highlight the emotional and affective dimensions of citizenship constructed by residents in their daily lives. Another approach to citizenship is understood as being relationally created by mundane actions involving the local community that build citizenship through daily connections with other people and places (Yarwood, 2014, pp. 14, 128, 149).

Citizenship as a relational interaction is strongly connected to neighbourhood and place. We all are citizens of a certain country, living in a certain city or town, in a house or apartment, in a certain neighbourhood. We become an integral part of our local community by attending leisure activities, participating in school parent-teacher associations, interacting with neighbours, and so on. Being a part of one's local social community involves creating a sense of belonging.

The sense of belonging is commonly understood as being part of something. In a way, it is an intuitive criterion for citizenship. Belonging implies more than merely having been born in a place. It suggests that one is an integral piece of the community, that one is a recipient of the culture. This covers both intangible factors (traditions, values, skills, idioms, idiosyncrasies) and material culture (natural resources, buildings, objects) (Cohen, 1982a, p. 21). Home and belonging have much in common. Home is not necessarily a physical place, but where is home? Usually, it is where one is at ease with whom they share their life. At home, one is accepted. This is the sense of belonging (Morley, 2000, p. 17). Based on our feeling of belonging when we are at home, we feel a kind of psychological citizenship: we are part of the community.

Belonging works in two directions at the same time. It has two ends. First, it means that I belong somewhere: to this place, to this community, and so on. Second, it means that something belongs to me: this house, or even the woods behind my village. This is not a question of ownership. The mere belonging makes a person the recipient of both tangible and intangible culture. A sentence such as "This is my school" does not usually mean that I own the school. It means that the school belongs to me because I have spent years in it. It is part of my life, my experiences, and even part of my home. I share this belonging with other members of the community. It belongs to us.

Since 1995, we have had a rich educational and welfare research literature concerning belonging to place and community: belonging to a school (Hoffmann et al., 2002; Hurtado & Carter, 1997; Strayhorn, 2012); belonging to a new homeland (Alghasi, 2016; Chow, 2007); belonging to a sexual community (McLaren, 2009); belonging to a sport team (Adjepong, 2018), to name just a few topics. There are hundreds of publications about the first sort of belonging (I belong somewhere), whereas the second direction (something belongs to me) is almost non-existent in the current research literature. However, the same phenomenon is vividly discussed under other concepts such as psychological ownership (Matilainen et al. 2017; Pierce et al., 2001). The authors assert that there is a difference between judicial and psychological ownership. The last mentioned is a mere feeling, although it is a real motive in society (Matilainen, 2019).

Rural areas usually carry a strong sense of belonging, togetherness, and cohesion that reinforces the rural residents' well-being. Older adults, especially, are strongly attached to their local communities. They may have been living in their community for all their lives or may have moved back to their place of origin to spend their retirement days there. The strong sense of belonging often makes it impossible to think of living somewhere else, and usually many older people wish to live at home for as long as possible (Róin, 2015, p. 27).

At the same time, many rural areas are struggling with the same contemporary challenges, such as a tightening economy and diminishing local services, that are leading to inequality in living conditions compared to urban areas. Many countries are solving this problem by centralizing public services and applying housing policies that direct people to move into more densely populated areas. It is relevant to ask if there is any right to be rural anymore.

In this chapter, we are interested in the ways older people living in their third age are constructing their life in relation to home and housing in rural areas, and as such, producing the elements of citizenship. We consciously return to the concept of belonging in its bi-directional meaning. Both ends of belonging, and what it means to belong, are constantly evoked by whatever means come to hand: language, jokes, aesthetics, the shared knowledge of genealogy or ecology, and the solidarity of sects (Cohen, 1982b, p. 6). These processes occur in everyday life.

Data and Methods

Data collection for the research occurred in 2014 through elicited group discussions with 29 informants living in rural Finland and two written tasks. The "Home Experiences of People at the Third Age in Housing" project was conducted by the University of Helsinki's Ruralia Institute. Our aim was to form an interpretation or a model of homey housing for those in the third age from a multiscalar perspective of home as an experiential space and living community. The research section formed part of a larger research and development project with one target being to develop a participatory design approach to homes for people in the third age (see Riukulehto & Rinne-Koski, 2016).

The concept of a third age is not unambiguous. In many Westernized contexts, the term usually refers to the age range from the 50s through the 60s, when one moves from mid-life to late mid-life (Thelin, 2009, pp. 34-37; Tudor-Sandahl, 2010, p. 14). The third age may also be seen as a more sociologically constructed stage of life that takes place after childhood and during one's active presence in the labour market (cf. Laslett, 1996).

In this research, the opinions of third age people and their thoughts about living, home, and sense of home were explored through elicited group interviews conducted mainly in the subregion of Järviseutu in South Ostrobothnia, Finland. These discussions took place in Vimpeli, Alajärvi, and Lappajärvi. People in the third age were primarily contacted through selected organizations in the target localities. In the selection process, we contacted two retired people's organizations, a home district association, and two projects for which the target groups were local inhabitants in the third age.

The main discussions occurred in rural municipalities. As the data collection advanced, we had the idea of complementing the data with an urban viewpoint and decided to arrange one more group discussion in an urban environment. The Järviseutu connection for the data was not abandoned; to obtain comparison material, we chose South Ostrobothnians living in the metropolitan area and contacted *Helsingin Eteläpohjalaiset ry*, an association of South Ostrobothnian emigrants, to find participants.

A total of 33 participants attended the discussion groups. Of those, 29 matched the criteria of the third age set for the target group of the project. The average age of the participants in the discussions was 71 years. The criteria of the third age in the research project was more sociologically defined than related to age as such. The main precondition was that the respondents were retired and living an active life before being too frail. The target group was reached by contacting organizations and associations with focus groups of older people involved in society actions and associations. The informants thus gathered were presumed to be good examples of people in their third age.

Data Collection

In the collection of data, we used the elicitation interview method, which had been successful in the Ruralia Institute's earlier home studies (Riukulehto & Rinne-Koski, 2013, pp. 13-14; Riukulehto & Rinne-Koski, 2015, 2016; Riukulehto & Suutari, 2012, pp. 6-9). The method is based on elicitation targeted at the participants, which evokes discussion of the topic by participants in a natural and comprehensive way. The advantage is that the conversation proceeds on the participants' own terms, focusing on what they regard as important in relation to each stimulus. In an elicitation interview, the researcher's role is not to steer the conversation, as in a traditional survey or interview. Consequently, the participants emphasized various points, as the same impulses started a conversation on a variety of topics in different discussions. As a result, we obtained a rich data set, which describes the topic in diverse ways and from various perspectives.

The first stimulus was one word: the word "home" written in capital letters in the middle of a slide. Despite the minimal character of the impulse, it evoked lively discussion and even surprising views at the sessions. The expectation was that discussion about the stimulus would expand at some point to concern several homes, and that people might talk about their childhood home, the first home they owned, their moves to different homes, and so on. Consequently, the first stimulus was followed by a question asking the participants to think about which of their homes had been the most important to them and which one the homiest. The third stimulus was about different dwellings. Participants were shown pictures of an igloo, a doghouse, a skyscraper, a futurist house, and a hut. They were asked to study the pictures and to decide which one they felt was the coziest, and why. Likewise, they were asked to give reasons if they felt they could not live in some of the dwellings.

For the fourth stimulus, participants were shown the floor plan of a house. Initially, the picture showed the plan for a common Finnish house, but at the beginning of the second discussion session, it was replaced with the floor plan of a Finnish veteran house (a type of house planned to meet the needs of veterans after World War II). The new picture offered more impetus for discussion: the house model was clearly old-fashioned, and the fact that it was a two-floor solution divided opinions. Also, shortcomings in the floor plan spurred the conversation on. The second floor was left to the participants' imaginations since the plan lacked some doors and windows. The stimulus also included a map, the aim of which was to inspire them to consider the location of the house or home.

Two pictorial collages followed. The first one, the fifth stimulus, led the participants to consider home and hominess with the aid of objects: a coffee maker, a sauna thermometer, a board game, a painting, woolen socks, a coffee set, cleaning equipment, a smartphone, and an easy chair with a dog sitting in it. The sixth stimulus offered a variety of living milieus: the interior of an old farmhouse, the staircase of an apartment building, a hotel room, and dormitory accommodation.

The seventh stimulus was about the importance of nature in housing and to the feeling of coziness. The slide showed two pictures side by side, one of which represented a commercial centre and the other a dirt road in the middle of nature. The title was: "Must there be nature at home?"

Next, two more pictorial collages were shown. First, there was a collection of services people might use connected with housing: massage therapy, a ready-packed shopping bag and spray cleaner, a restaurant at which people were eating, snow removal, and blood sugar testing. This was followed by a pictorial collage of suitcases, a rocking chair, and mailboxes. There were also dancing couples and two small children. The aim of the stimulus was to inspire the participants to discuss their present and future lifestyles.

Each discussion session lasted about 2 to 2.5 hours. All the discussions were recorded and transcribed for analysis. The written material obtained this way totalled about 130 pages.

The elicitation interview framework also included a written elicitation task. At the end of the discussion, each participant was given a pen and paper and asked to write down three important features that made an apartment into a home, and to give their reasons in brief. The aim of the written task was to ensure that all the participants had the opportunity to be heard. It is not as natural for some people to participate in a public and often vivid discussion. Some may not want to say all that springs to mind while other people are listening. They find it easier to articulate their thoughts in writing.

In addition to the use of stimuli, data were produced with a written mental imagery task. Participants were asked to imagine that they had moved to a new apartment from their present home, after which they were offered a positive or negative opportunity to continue the story in their own words. They were told they could imagine the new home as homey or less homey, after which they were asked to describe their new (imagined) home and living environment. The aim of the mental imagery task was to record the participants' opinions about what they considered important for the coziness of the home and the living environment, and what they regarded as push factors.

In previous publications, we have analyzed the data clusters from the written answers and formed a model of a homey home (Riukulehto & Rinne-Koski, 2016). Analyzed as conceptions, the data produces different insights of home, all interconnected with the concept of belonging: home as a building, as emotions, as an interaction, and as places.

Analysis and Results

Discursive content analysis was used to find out, in addition to the model of homey housing, how the representatives of the third age presented their conceptions and expressed their feelings of hominess in relation to their housing experiences. Our previously introduced model of a homey home is based on the structural elements of housing, but it is equally important to examine what elements create the sense of home.

The framework of the analysis was started with content analysis, in which we first categorized the meanings that participants were talking about around homey living and home. These conceptions of home were reflected in the discourse they were interpreted to represent. This was possible because the elicitation interview method allows informants to talk freely about the things that they feel are important or associated with the stimuli presented. By applying this research strategy, the data can be analyzed in more depth, paying attention also to the context and representations involved in addition to the explicit content. The underlying assumption is that social reality is constructed and reproduced by the use of language in social interactions between people. Words are the construction material of our socially created worlds, and therefore it is significant to acknowledge the ways in which words are used while discussing home or describing the elements of third age housing. Chosen words always define given meanings, and these meanings constitute discourses. The interviewees' manners of expressing their thoughts of home and hominess give us a framework through which to analyze the meanings of home (Berger & Luckmann, 1994; Burr, 2015, pp. 10-12, 73-79, 236).

According to this framework, the research question addressed from the data was: in what ways did the informants construct the meaning of home in rural areas? As a result, we identified four conceptions of home:

1. Home as a building.
2. Home as emotions.
3. Home as interaction.
4. Home as places for events.

Home as a Building

The first conception constructs the meaning of home by its physical attributes related to a home as a building. Informants did not emphasize the appearance of the house per se, but focused on using space to support everyday life and housing.

Interior design and the use of space have a strong effect on how a house is experienced. This was revealed when informants were discussing the practicality and functionality of a house. The layout of the house was considered important. As one participant described:

Practicality. When we built, I made a point of not entering the bedroom from the living room. There must be different wings on different sides of the house.

In a deeper consideration, it became clear that when participants were talking about practicality and functionality, they were actually at the core of what makes a house into a home. Practical design and fluent use of space produce safety: the home is bright and easily accessible, and housework is easy when the layout of the house is well designed. The point is understandable if we consider the informants' ages. Good design and use of space create confidence in one's independence in the third age.

One essential part of a Finnish home is the sauna. It is almost a national symbol. In our data, the sauna was seen as a characteristic element of identity: "It's not a Finnish house if there's no sauna. Definitely not." The sauna is an essential part of the family routine. It is used to separate leisure from work, particularly for people in the older age groups: heating up the sauna on a Saturday evening clearly indicates that work is over and it is time to rest. The sauna is still an important part of major holidays such as Christmas and mid-summer. In everyday life, the sauna is seen as a place to reduce stress, to calm down and relax.

The sense of "home" is also created in everyday housing routines. The stimulus of a plain hotel room did not evoke the feeling of being at home. The informants pointed out that they would miss all the equipment that enables housekeeping. The difference between home and a house lies in daily routines: a home is about cooking on a stove, having food in a fridge, and having a vacuum cleaner to maintain the home, and so on.

The picture of a plain hotel room was also revealing in another way: the sense of belonging is not only created in routines, but also in small things. Bric-a-brac acts as an intermediator that produces a feeling of hominess in otherwise plain premises:

> There are no small items at all, no paintings or ornaments, no bowls, flowers, plants. Nothing like that. This is why it felt like a hotel room. There are no signs of living like we have at home. Magazines and handicrafts and everything lying about.

The mundane, daily intermediators of hominess partly create the sense of belonging. To describe it: a house is made to be my home. My possessions, my familiar furniture, my books, and my collections of memories make the place belong to me. The home looks like me and is the home where I enjoy my life. A stage of everyday routines constructs the feeling of hominess. Home is more than walls and a roof. The physical structures of a house are interpreted as a home by representations constructed by safety, independence, and stability. This is where I belong.

Home as Emotions

Along with it being a physical building, informants interpreted the meaning of home as feelings or emotions. They expressed four conceptions of emotions that reflect creating the meaning of home in some way.

First, the informants described the home as the anchor of life (Dovey, 1999). It is a place where they felt rootedness (Tuan, 1977/2011), where they had grown up. The anchor place is not necessarily a childhood home; it may be a later place that one has grown into. Home as an anchor was presented by informants as a bedrock of life, something stable in a changing world. In addition to being a bedrock, it was described as a feeling of acceptance, attachment, and being part of a larger whole.

A person who has lived on a farm for twenty years, in a family homestead; who has worked in the fields through the years, brought the loads of hay from barns; who is so rooted in rural life, giving all his leisure time for the farm. It is very tightly rooted in me, it is the place of my heart even today, it is my home.

In addition to being such an anchor in one's life, the home was also defined as representing security. Security consists of being physically safe and getting to be oneself. No cruel world can harm you at home. A home is a place where one has the feeling that one can let go and relax.

To me, personally, home is a place which is like me, it's my own. Nobody can intrude there in secret or otherwise. I don't let anybody in without an invitation.... Firstly, it is a place where I may be just as I want to be.

My home is my castle. So, I feel my home as being a secure place, easy going, easy to speak about and live with my family. It is an easy place for my grandchildren to come. Now, when I think about this in retrospect, I can say that, in a way, there were three places easy to go: your own home and two other places.

The home is also constructed by memories and the emotions they give rise to. Emotions may concern missing or longing for something that has been left behind, for example, a lost childhood home or the house one lived in as a newlywed. Nostalgic emotions may also concern landscapes. A childhood landscape may have counterparts in one's current housing setup:

When we began to search for a cottage, Ähtäri seemed to be the kind of region...that we got used to in our childhood. So, the cottage was set in Ähtäri.

The fourth and probably the more dominant emotion connected to a home is the feeling of freedom. This is experienced as a blend of pride and ownership, self-determination, and independence of housing: "Nobody dictates [in the single-family house] what your lawn should look like." This experienced feeling of freedom may have its roots in a strong appreciation of home ownership in a single-family house. The desire to own one's house was particularly reflected in the lives of the older people represented in our data.

Home as Action and Interaction

The third conception of the meaning of home was about interaction, which was given several definitions. First, it is important from the third age housing point of view that there is something to do. The importance of doing may occur through the feeling of being useful and occupied, but also in maintaining the home through daily routines. Household chores also structure the day.

> *Even a man or woman in poor condition can make his or her own food. I think it is a deprivation of liberty to have people eat their meals in a communal lunch room.*

Managing everyday chores is also a prerequisite of older people's ability to continue living at home in a rural area where services might be scarce and located far away.

> *However, it certainly occurs to a single person of my age that some other way of housing, easier than a single-family house [should be found]. For there is always mowing, snow clearing, and heating. Even now I have had a fire in the fireplace every day for we have these frosts. It is a fact that something easier should be planned sooner or later. Although this will serve as long as I feel well.*

According to our informants, it is highly important to have something to do at home. A house is not a home if you cannot do anything but sit and look out of the window. This is how the situation was described to be in urban areas. The local pub was claimed to be the only pastime there.

Home is also about social interaction. Being active and accepted as a part of local society gives one the feeling of security and strengthens local ties. However, social interaction is considered to differ depending on the environment:

> *It is an entirely different thing in the city and in the country. The house of a city dweller may really be just a sleeping place but here in the countryside it is something different.*

The discussions about residential area were revealing. The perceived differences between urban and rural showed up in the rural informants' distrust of urban society and the living conditions there. The rural was constructed as a haven, whereas the urban was labelled with loneliness, abandonment, and rootlessness.

In other words, people are watched over here [in the countryside]. Maybe not everyone likes it either. I think it's better that you are watched over to make sure that things don't happen like that one may lie dead in one's own apartment for a long time and nothing happens.

According to our informants, a home seems to have a deeper meaning in rural areas. The urban informants were attached to place as well, but instead of a neighbourhood or locality they were talking about their core family. We saw a clear difference in attitudes.

Home as Places for Particular Events

The idea of home also reveals the significance of place. Place is represented here as a social construction in time, not just by a physical sense of place, but also by the temporal meaning of a place (Cresswell, 2015, pp. 46–51). This became tangible when informants were talking about the roles of their permanent homes and summer houses.

Nearly 819,000 Finns belong to a household that owns a cabin used as a second home. There are over half a million of these summer houses in Finland. In addition to the registered second houses, there are other buildings, such as old farmhouses, that are used as second homes, but that are not counted among the half a million. When these other buildings are taken into account, approximately two million Finns continually use a second house (Finnish Consulting Group Oy, 2016, p. 16, 30; Official Statistics of Finland, 2017). Spending time in a cottage is one of the more treasured leisure-time activities for Finns. The relationship with one's second home, as we can see from the excerpts, is very warm.

We have summer residences. I live in two homes. In the summertime I live in our summer home in Kuopio for about three to four months a year. Then there is my childhood home in Vimpeli, and we should also have enough time to live there, in the childhood home of my soul, and then in Espoo we have this home.

We spend…five months of the year in a summer house in Hollola. And in the fall,
when we had to get it ready for the winter—then we only spent weekends and holi-
days there—I had the feeling that "damn! Is it really over again? We must return
to the city."

Home is a temporal project. It highlights the importance of roots and
memories. This was especially clear when informants were talking about the
milestones of their lives: one's lifetime is demarcated by the homes they have
lived in. Therefore, it is clear that the meaning of home will change over time. For
example, if one's spouse dies, the home is not the same anymore.

I attach both [the most important home and the homiest home] to the moment when
I carried my wife over the threshold to our home. It was the home of my first family
and child.

Yes really, my childhood home is in Alajärvi. As long as [my] father and mother were
alive we visited there, and in fact, it still was our number one home even though we
had lived in Vimpeli for 30 years. This is not the situation any longer now that both
of them are gone. The first home is now here.

In Finland, it is quite normal to have two homes at the same time: one
permanent, often located in an urban environment, the other seasonal, in a
rural environment. One can also have several homes one after another. When
people talk about home, they can easily change the perspective from one place
to another, considering their parallel and successive homes simultaneously. The
whole multi-located set of places is thought of and talked about as their home.

Conclusion

Based on the same research data, we previously introduced a model of homey
housing (see Riukulehto & Rinne-Koski, 2016). We noticed something interesting:
when people are talking about home, they are not talking much about the house
per se. Rather, they talk about elements such as human relations, nature and
environment, independence, and life management. They also talk about functionality and cultural factors, and of course all the objects of daily life. These are the
elements needed to have a house be experienced as a home. In this chapter,
we have taken a new point of view: that of belonging.

The two perspectives (hominess and belonging) have much in common. The sense of belonging to a house is growing stronger in time, and the more important the occupant considers and experiences human relations, the building, and its belongings, the better they can manage their life there. It is the growing sense of belonging that makes a place into a home. The process is deeply experiential. It is temporal and spatial, and it has two ways of being so: this is the place where I belong, and this place belongs to me.

However, it seems that the sense of belonging is constructed slightly differently in each identified conception. Our informants were discussing a house simply as a physical building. But when they talked about the physical reality as a home, the sense of belonging was also there. A house is not a home without all the little things that make it one's own. Adding something personal to an otherwise plain space creates a sense of psychological ownership. In other words, there is a physical factor in the sense of belonging (for buildings, movables, and environment).

The sense of belonging is also present in the second conception, home as emotions, but the tone is slightly different. In this context, a place belongs to me because I have deep emotional roots in it. The place is saturated by emotions, and there is a certain feeling. This emotional factor is expressed by words such as freedom, security, nostalgia, and anchor place. The emotional factor in the sense of belonging creates a strong basis for encountering the outside world. This makes home spread to new places: this is my home landscape because I already have emotions for it.

The third conception, home as interaction, is connected to the social part of the sense of belonging. I become part of the place, and the place will belong to me if I do something there. Interactions with other people and the feeling of being part of the local social community can create a strong sense of belonging. In our data, when people talked about their home, they most often talked about relations with other people (25%). It is in a way a self-fostering circle: the more involved I am, the more attached I become.

And finally, a lot of discussions dealt with the home as a place for events. The most important home for participants was the one where a husband had carried his wife over the threshold. Important events are collected more and more in the course of time. It is easy to see that repetition has a role in the place-based factor in the sense of belonging. A school becomes my school because I have spent many years there. Similarly, we understand, for example, the concept of my workplace, my church, my road, and my berry patch. The formulation has nothing to do with ownership. It has to do with the sense of belonging. I feel that something belongs to me because it plays a certain part in my life. This factor also covers the cases of multi-located parallel and successive homes. In people's minds, they form a common entity. The summer cottage and the city apartment form a whole that can simply and easily be called their home.

In our data, home is a multiscalar process influenced by several ways of belonging. The sense of home is catalyzed by physical elements, emotions, and social involvement, and by important events related to a place. The senses of belonging presented above may overlap. Not all the identified elements need to be present to make one feel at home. The elements may change over time, having different emphasis in different situations in life. Both ends of belonging (this is where I belong; this belongs to me) are at present in the sense of home.

The manifold sense of belonging identified in the elicited group-discussions data of those living in rural third age housing makes an interesting starting point for future research. It is evident that older people living in rural areas are usually strongly connected to and committed to their local community. As such, the sense of belonging is intertwined with a sense of community that is represented not only in feelings of home, but also in feelings of safety and security, as well as in one's contributions to and participation in the local community. These are essential elements of the socio-cultural conception of citizenship that are expressed in everyday life and routines. Encouraging a sense of belonging among residents can be one of the key elements of developing sustainable rural housing to meet future challenges and to foster their right to be rural.

References

Adjepong, A. (2017). "We're, like, a cute rugby team": How whiteness and heterosexuality shape women's sense of belonging in rugby. *International Review for the Sociology of Sport, 52*(2), 209–222.

Alghasi, S. (2016). *Paradoxes of cultural recognition: Perspectives from northern Europe.* Taylor & Francis Group.

Berger, P. L., & Luckmann, T. (1994). *Todellisuuden sosiaalinen rakentuminen* (V. Raiskila, Trans.). Gaudeamus. Also published as: *The Social Construction of Reality* (Bantam Doubleday Dell Publishing Group, 1966).

Burr, V. (2015). *Social Constructionism* (3rd ed.). Routledge.

Chow, H. P. H. (2007). Sense of belonging and life satisfaction among Hong Kong adolescent immigrants in Canada. *Journal of Ethnic and Migration Studies, 33*(3): 511–520.

Cohen, A. P. (1982a). A sense of time, a sense of place: The meaning of close social association in Whalsay, Shetland. In A. P. Cohen (Ed.), *Belonging: Identity and social organisation in British rural cultures* (pp. 21–49). Manchester University Press.

Cohen, A. P. (1982b). Belonging: The experience of culture. In A. P. Cohen (Ed.), *Belonging: Identity and social organisation in British rural cultures* (pp. 1–17). Manchester University Press.

Cresswell, T. (2015). *Place: An introduction* (2nd ed.). Wiley-Blackwell.

Dovey, K. (1999). *Framing places: Mediating power in built form.* Routledge.

Finnish Consulting Group Oy. (2016). *Mökkibarometri 2016* [Finnish free-time residence barometer 2016]. Finland: Saaristoasiain neuvottelukunta, Maa- ja metsätalousministeriö.

Hoffman, M., Richmond, J., Morrow, J., & Salomone, K. (2002). Investigating "sense of belonging" in first-year college students. *Journal of Collage Student Retention, 4*(3), 227–256.

Hurtado, S., & Carter, D. F. (1997). Effects of college transition and perceptions of the campus racial climate on Latino college students' sense of belonging. *Sociology of Education, 70*(4), 324–345.

Laslett, P. (1996). *A fresh map of life: The emergence of third age.* MacMillan.

Matilainen, A. (2019). *Feelings of psychological ownership towards private forests* [Doctoral dissertation, University of Helsinki Ruralia Institute].

Matilainen, A., Pohja-Mykrä, M., Lähdesmäki, M., & Kurki, S. (2017). "I feel it is mine!": Psychological ownership in relation to natural resources. *Journal of Environmental Psychology, 51*, 31–45.

McLaren, S. (2009). Sense of belonging to the general and lesbian communities as predictors of depression among lesbians. *Journal of Homosexuality, 56*(1), 1–13.

Morley, D. (2000). *Home territories: Media, mobility and identity.* Routledge.

Official Statistics of Finland (OSF). (2017). *Free-time residences 2017.* http://www.stat.fi/til/rakke/2017/rakke_2017_2018-05-25_kat_001_en.html

Pierce, J. L., Kostova, T., & Dirks, K. T. (2001). Toward a theory of psychological ownership in organizations. *Academy of Management Review, 26*(2), 298–310.

Riukulehto, S., & Rinne-Koski, K. (2013). *Otta noessa. Kuortaneenjärven kotiseututihentymien syvärakenteita* [Sooty fronts. The deeper structures and accumulations of home in the Lake Kuortane region]. Helsingin yliopisto Ruralia-instituutti.

Riukulehto, S., & Rinne-Koski, K. (2015). Historical consciousness and the experiential idea of home. In S. Riukulehto (Ed.), *Between time and space* (pp. 115–134). Cambridge Scholars Publishing.

Riukulehto, S., & Rinne-Koski, K. (2016). *A house made to be a home.* Cambridge Scholars Publishing.

Riukulehto, S., & Suutari, T. (2012). *Joki on Nurmon äiti. Nurmonjokilaakso kotiseutukuvassa* [River is the mother of Nurmo. Nurmo River Valley in home picture]. Helsingin yliopisto Ruralia-instituutti.

Róin, Á. (2015). The multifaceted notion of home: Exploring the meaning of home among elderly people living in the Faroe Islands. *Journal of Rural Studies, 39*, 22–31.

Strayhorn, T. L. (2012). *College students' sense of belonging: A key to educational success for all students.* Routledge.

Thelin, A. (2009). *Den tredje åldern: en kunskapsöversikt* [The third age: A systematic review]. Institutionen för vårdvetenskap och socialt arbete (Rapportserie i socialt arbete). Växjö universitet.

Tuan, Y. F. (2011). *Space and place: The perspective of experience.* University of Minnesota Press. (Original work published 1977)

Tudor-Sandahl, P. (2010). *Den tredje åldern* [The third age]. Brombergs Bokförlag.

Yarwood, R. (2014). *Citizenship.* Routledge.

IV
The Right to Rural Representation

10
Citizens or Individuals?
Patterns of Local Civic Engagement of Young University Graduates Living in Rural Areas in Poland

ILONA MATYSIAK

Introduction

Referring to Oldfield's (1990) division of citizenship as a status and a practice, Lister (1997) states that not only do people have the status of citizens, but they also need to act as citizens. However, as Bauman (2000) claims, "the individual" is the citizen's worst enemy and individualization, which is characteristic for our times, causes the corrosion and slow disintegration of citizenship (p. 36). People are focused on constructing their own "life policies" and less interested in collective action, because they believe that solving their problems is their own personal responsibility.

In Poland, the systemic transformation of 1989 replaced "real socialism" with democracy and a state-controlled economy with a free market, creating institutional conditions for exercising citizenship. However, at the same time, phenomena well known in Western societies such as consumerism and individualization appeared and spread very quickly. These changes especially affected young generations of Poles who were small children when the transformation occurred or were born in a democratic Poland. This chapter focuses on a particular group of young Polish people: university graduates living in rural areas. In contrast to other countries, about 30% of Polish university graduates of rural origin tend to return to the countryside (Szafraniec & Szymborski, 2016).

The chapter aims to explore whether these young university graduates, as citizens, use their resources in terms of education and skills for the benefit of their villages. Therefore, the patterns of their local civic engagement will be thoroughly explored, with a focus on involvement in local government, local organizations, and informal initiatives addressing the community. These young people's education, in theory, provides them with a good starting point for acting as citizens who have sufficient knowledge, skills, and willingness to make a difference in their local communities. Gregory Hadley's chapter in this collection, for example, builds on the premise that citizenship practices are rooted in education. The issue to be determined is whether they want to act as citizens. The individualization thesis, as proposed by Bauman (2000), suggests that their strong community engagement is not very likely.

The chapter is based on findings from a qualitative study that involved 92 in-depth interviews with university graduates aged 25–34 and living in rural areas (63 women and 29 men), conducted in 10 purposively-selected rural municipalities in Poland.

The subject of this chapter is of crucial importance for Polish and international audiences. Clearly, local civic engagement of young university graduates will help determine the future of the Polish countryside, as graduates will influence the way that rural areas will develop. The significance of the research presented here also goes beyond Poland, as the recent notion of a "right to the countryside" emphasizes the significance of people's participation in shaping the spaces of their everyday lives (Barraclough, 2013).

Context: Rural Areas in Poland

In Poland, a relatively high share of the population resides in the rural areas of the country—39.2% in 2011 (CSO, 2012, p. 47). The Polish agriculture sector is characterized by a large number of small family farms. In 2010, the average area of a farm was 9.6 hectares (Poczta, 2012, p. 84). Another special feature of rural areas in Poland is their spatial diversification. Regional differences pertain to many aspects of life, including the size and productivity of the farms, degree of urbanization, demographic structure, access to communication infrastructure, voting preferences, economic performance, types of local organizations, and even types of social capital (Bartkowski, 2003). This diversification is due to the historical background of the country.[1]

In the last two decades, significant changes in Polish rural areas and their population have been observed. Due to progressive disagrarization of employment, more than 60% of rural residents have nothing to do with agriculture, while the percentage of rural households living on farming alone has dropped below 10% (Wilkin 2018, p. 13). The educational aspirations of the rural population are growing, but at the same time the migration flow from the cities to the countryside—in particular, to the suburbs—is increasing. Halamska (2016) indicates that, as a result of all these changes, "the rural middle class," consisting of white-collar workers and specialists, is emerging. Also, mostly due to EU funds, quality of life, for example in terms of local infrastructure, has been significantly improving (Wilkin, 2018). However, the nature of changes in rural Poland in the last twenty years has not been uniform; dynamics have been different across the country's diverse rural areas, which are developing unevenly.

Citizenship versus Individualization

One view of citizenship—the republican view—sees citizenship as providing the opportunity for political participation via voting, lobbying, and running for office, as well as less formalized activities and political mobilizations within civil society (Nash, 2009, p. 1067). Citizenship in this formulation is a status and a practice; as Lister (1997) points out, it is not enough that people are citizens, they need also to act like ones, using the full potential of this status, i.e., exercising their rights in terms of political and social participation (pp. 35-36). There is good evidence that the enactment of citizenship is affected by structural factors. According to Bosniak (2000), smaller local communities create especially good conditions for putting citizenship into practice by "entailing the face-to-face contact and common experience and interests among community members necessary to enable true collective action" (p. 473). Existing research also finds that university education in particular is positively correlated with civic and political engagement. Highly educated people tend to vote, run for office, get involved in associations, volunteer, and care about public good more frequently than those without university education (e.g., Czapiński, 2015; Halamska, 2016). These findings, at first, suggest that highly educated rural residents might be uniquely engaged in their communities.

However, according to Bauman (2000), republican citizenship has been seriously weakened by individualization—a condition characteristic for our times of "liquid modernity": "The 'citizen' is a person inclined to seek her or his own welfare through the well-being of the city—while the individual tends to be luke-warm, skeptical or wary about 'common cause', 'common good', 'good society' or 'just society'"(p. 36). As Bauman (2000) states, "'individualization' consists of transforming human 'identity' from a 'given' into a 'task' and charging the actors with the responsibility for performing that task and for the conse-quences (also the side-effects) of their performance" (pp. 31–32). Individualization means a process of disembedding without re-embedding, that is, individuals become increasingly detached from collective identities as such categories as class, gender roles, family, and so on disintegrate: the domination of "old ways" is falling apart and a variety of new forms and models are being constructed to choose from. People are focused on constructing their own biographies and are less and less interested in cooperation with others, or in actively supporting the democratic system, because they believe that everyone is responsible for solving their own problems. The public sphere, according to Bauman (2000), is dominated by private affairs and public confessions of private sentiments, which intensifies the feeling that there is no common ground worth taking care of collectively.

In the case of young university graduates living in rural areas in Poland, the small scale of their local communities and their education ostensibly provide them with good grounds for acting as citizens with enough knowledge, skills, and willingness to engage with their villages. On the other hand, they were born around or after the systemic transformation of 1989, when consumerism and individualization arguably took hold, and these have since remained strong in Polish society.

Local Civic Engagement of Young Rural People in Poland:
A Literature Review

Before World War II, the rural areas in Poland gained freedom from the tradi-tional estates system, and a broader assimilation of peasants in Polish society in terms of national and political awareness began. The relatively greater accessi-bility of elementary education and growing acceptance of such education among the peasants increased the life aspirations of the young generation. However, their fulfilment, through further education and professional training, required expenditures available to few. The dynamically developing young peasant movement, with its youth organizations, folk universities, and cultural and self-educational activities, responded to those life aspirations. Young women and men involved in the peasant movement often introduced new agricultural or household management methods, departing from the "ancient traditions" (Chałasiński, 1938).

In the postwar socialist era, centrally controlled and only partially successful modernization projects aimed at urbanizing the rural areas and mechanizing agriculture. The mass character and accessibility of education, mainly on the primary, vocational, and secondary levels, encouraged the young inhabitants of rural areas to aspire to urban standards of living. However, despite the common ideal of migration to cities, some young people stayed in the countryside—due to family reasons, attachment to the place, or being sent to work there by the state. Many of them saw it as a way of giving back—using their education for moving rural communities forward, for instance, by working as teachers, agronomists, or health care assistants, as well as by engaging with their communities (Chałasiński, 1966). However, it has to be noted that in many cases, especially in the early postwar period when the state regime had a more totalitarian character, their activities were subordinated to the goals set by the Communist Party or their engagement was a result of opportunism.

Both in the prewar and postwar periods, relatively few rural youths graduated from universities and other tertiary education institutions. After 1989, the process of massification of higher education in Poland started. Public university education also became widely accessible, as did higher education at numerous private universities and colleges. Rural youth have been taking advantage of these opportunities—currently, they amount to about 30% of all Polish students (CSO, 2017, p. 26). However, rural young people tend to choose higher education institutions located closer to their home villages, which have easier admissions procedures, but are of a lower quality (Szafraniec & Szymborski, 2016). Nonetheless, local tertiary educational institutions could play an important role in providing rural areas with graduates. These young graduates may not be top academic achievers, but they are still skillful and motivated enough to make a difference in their home villages. The question is whether they are willing to do so.

There is no research focused on local civic engagement in Poland among young, highly educated rural residents. However, existing studies covering young generations of Polish people in general provide rather pessimistic conclusions. For example, in analyzing the attitudes of Polish 19-year-olds and 30-year-olds, Szafraniec (2011) distinguished five types of life orientations: "minimalists," "dreamers," "conventionally ambitious," "extremely ambitious," and "ambitious differently" (pp. 44–45). These types cover various attitudes, from passive with rather low life expectations to active, successful, and, last but not least, socially concerned. The analysis shows that attitudes focusing on consumption,

TABLE 10.1 List of rural municipalities selected for the research

Region	Western and northern areas				Former Russian partition	
Province	Dolnośląskie		Warmińsko-Mazurskie		Mazowieckie	
District	głogowski	wałbrzyski	ełcki	szczycieński	pułtuski	siedlecki
Municipality	Pęcław	Walim	Kalinowo	Świętajno	Gzy	Mokobody
Type of municipality	agricultural	tourist	agricultural	tourist	agricultural	tourist
Number of interviews	8	10	9	9	10	9

individual achievements, and family life prevail, especially among the youngest generations. Also, some existing research focused on rural youth points out that their interest in local public affairs is rather low, their community engagement is more declarative than real, and their life aspirations are limited to work and family (e.g., Bartczak, 2016).

Research Design

Below, I explore the local civic engagement patterns of young university graduates in the villages where they live to determine whether this group is willing to use their education and skills to benefit their local communities or is more focused on their personal issues, as the individualization thesis suggests. I adopt a qualitative approach, analyzing interviewees' narratives for detailed information about their subjective perceptions of their local community and their own role in the village (cf. Silverman, 2016).

The analysis covers the young university graduates' involvement in the three most characteristic types of local civic engagement in rural areas in Poland: 1) the local government, 2) local organizations, and 3) informal initiatives (Matysiak, 2014). First, the overall diagnosis of their local civic engagement is formulated. Second, a typology of interviewees identifies whether some types of activities went hand in hand with others, and what kind of characteristics were shared by interviewees belonging to distinguished groups. Third, factors affecting young university graduates' local civic engagement are identified and discussed in detail.

The empirical data analyzed in the text is derived from 92 individual, in-depth interviews with young adults with a BA, BSC, MA, or MSC. The research encompassed young adults who were rural residents and aged 25–34. At this age, people

Former Prussian partition		Former Galicja (Austrian partition)	
Wielkopolskie		Małopolskie	
koniński	leszczyński	gorlicki	nowosądecki
Krzymów	Wijewo	Moszczenica	Gródek nad Dunajcem
agricultural	tourist	agricultural	tourist
9	10	9	10

aim to achieve their aspirations of youth and make decisions of significance for their "life strategies" (family, place of residence, job) (Szafraniec, 2010, pp. 16–17). Young rural residents of urban origin, or not originally from a rural area, were not excluded from the study.

The interviews were carried out in 10 purposively selected rural municipalities in provinces belonging to four historic macro-regions that differ in terms of agriculture, population, and direction of local development. The municipalities were selected according to the following criteria: the share of the population with higher education in the district (*powiat*), characteristics of the local economy, and distance from larger urban centres. Consequently, two municipalities in districts with a relatively high percentage of inhabitants with higher education were selected in each province: an "agricultural" municipality (with more than 60% of the municipality's area being farmland according to the 2010 National Agricultural Census; see Statistics Poland, 2021) and a "tourist" municipality (in the vicinity of nature-related tourist attractions or heritage monuments). To avoid large city suburban populations, each chosen municipality is at least 80 kilometres from a city with a population over 100,000. Between 8 and 10 interviews with university graduates were carried out in each municipality (see Table 10.1).

The initial interviewees were suggested by competent local informants (local authorities, local civil servants, leaders of local social organizations), and others were identified via snowball sampling. The research was carried out between June and September 2016 and in May and June 2017 as part of a research project entitled "The Role of Cultural Capital of Young Rural Inhabitants in the Contemporary Processes of Transformation of Rural Areas in Poland."[2] The interviews were transcribed, coded using MAXQDA 12 software, and subjected to a qualitative analysis.

The typology of the interviewees according to their level of community engagement was created by using fuzzy cluster analysis. The analyzed variables included those related to the three types of local civic engagement distinguished earlier in this section. Unlike regular segmentation methods, which allow the assignment of a respondent to only one cluster, fuzzy clustering enables determination of how well a given respondent fits into all the clusters distinguished. This means that segments should be perceived as ideal types, not disjointed categories (Kaufman & Rousseeuw, 1990).

It must be emphasized that the results of the research are not representative of all rural municipalities in Poland, but the selection of municipalities for research makes it possible to make generalizations limited to particular types of local contexts.

Socio-Demographic Characteristics

The interviewees were 63 women and 29 men, the great majority of whom, particularly the men, originated from the village where they currently lived. In many cases, their parents and grandparents had also come from the area.

A majority of the interviewees held an MA or MSC, with the women more likely to hold these degrees than the men. Some of the most popular areas of study included: education/special education/physical education with a teaching specialization, public administration, management, technical studies such as land management and planning, geodesy, transport, ICT, and production engineering. Only a handful of the interviewees studied disciplines directly related to agriculture. Interestingly, only about one third of the interviewees had moved to a city for the entire duration of their studies or a significant portion of them. The others had typically graduated from local higher education institutions and commuted or had graduated from extension courses (intensive sessions held only on weekends).

A majority of the women participants were married with children, with a few in an informal relationship and ten being single. Half of the men were unmarried or without a partner. Nearly all interviewees were employed. Most of them had found employment in the local labour market (usually no more than 20 kilometres from their place of residence), mostly in local public institutions (municipal public offices, cultural centres, social welfare centres, schools). Only a few interviewees ran their own business or family farm.

The young university graduates interviewed were living in the countryside mostly due to their family relationships and strong attachment to the place. They quite often also spoke about being lucky enough to find a job nearby and good housing opportunities (for example, the possibility of living with their parents or in-laws). Many of the interviewees reported features that positively corre- lated with staying in the countryside: they were often well "rooted" in their local communities (Rérat, 2014); they usually had a working-class or farmer family background (Rye, 2011); and a significant number, particularly women, had a dependent (a parent or a child) at home (Erickson et al., 2018). A great majority of the interviewees planned to continue to live in the countryside. However, some, particularly single and unmarried men, were not sure about their future place of residence.

Interviewees' Overall Local Civic Engagement

Only a handful of the participants, both women and men, fulfilled some func- tion in local government, such as serving as a village representative, member of a village council,[3] or as a municipal or district councillor. A few were consid- ering running for village representative or in a municipal election or had already attempted to do so without success. More than half of the interviewees admitted that they did not take part in village assemblies[4] in their community (more often women than men). About one third of the interviewees participated in such meetings more or less regularly, and the rest only sporadically. Almost one third (more often men than women) participated in local organizations, mostly volun- teer fire brigades (men and women), sports clubs and hobby groups (men), as well as women's organizations and parents' committees at school (women). Some interviewees were involved more intensively, including fulfilling a function in an organization (as president or board member), whereas others were involved only from time to time. Some interviewees, both men and women, and quite often those who were involved in local organizations, pointed out that they took part in, and sometimes led, informal, often *ad hoc* initiatives for their local community. For those who were not involved in a local organization, such initiatives were usually a one-time burst of activity.

The most typical activities mentioned by those who were locally engaged in one form or another included organizing or co-organizing local events and festivals, taking care of the public space in the village, and, less often, taking part in initiatives aimed at improving local infrastructure (e.g., street lighting or a local playground). Many activities in which the interviewees, especially

TABLE 10.2 Basic characteristics of interviewees' local civic engagement in the three distinguished clusters

	Engagement in local government	Participation in local organizations
Regular Activists **N=35**	All interviewees engaged in the local government belonged to this group.	A great majority of interviewees participated in local organizations.
Incidental Activists **N=30**	No one belonged to local government, although a few interviewees had thought about it.	Only very few interviewees participated in local organizations.
Not Active People **N=27**	No one was engaged in local government or had such plans.	No one participated in local organizations.

women, took part were directed at children and youth. Interestingly, a significant number of undertakings were focused on recreation and entertainment, such as winter swimming, running, and organizing amateur car races or video game tournaments.

Considering existing statistics, the interviewees' engagement in local organizations seems to be relatively low in comparison with Poles (40.0%) and rural residents in general (40.0%) (Fedyszak-Radziejowska, 2018, p. 78). It is also worth pointing out that 80.0% of Polish rural residents have been found to express interest in local public affairs, namely, decisions at the level of the village and municipal authorities (Fedyszak-Radziejowska, 2018, p. 82).

Typology of Interviewees According to Their Local Civic Engagement

To create a typology of the interviewees, first hierarchical clustering was conducted. The number of groups (three) was chosen by examining the dendrogram, with the validity of the clustering being tested by crossing it with qualitative material. Fuzzy clustering was then conducted. The intervals between the elements were measured by the squared Euclidean to achieve a clearer segmentation. The Dunn's partition coefficient was 0.981 (the normalized one is 0.971), indicating near-crisp clustering. The average silhouette was 0.33, which showed that some structure was found within the data, although it was not very strong (see Kaufmann & Rousseeuw, 1990).

Informal engagement in local initiatives	Initiating actions on behalf of the community
All interviewees took part in local initiatives on a regular basis.	A great majority of all "initiators" belonged to this group.
Half of interviewees had engaged incidentally, and the rest not at all, although some would have liked to.	Only very few interviewees had initiated local actions by themselves.
The majority of interviewees did not engage at all. Some did incidentally.	Only very few "initiators" belonged to this group.

In terms of the local civic engagement, three types of interviewees were distinguished: "Regular Activists," "Incidental Activists," and "Not Active" (see Table 10.2).

The distinguished groups differed the most in terms of the interviewees' gender, place of origin, family situation, motivations for living in the countryside, family background in terms of local civic engagement, relationships with neighbours, as well as the characteristics of the local context.

The Regular Activists group consisted of 20 women and 15 men (half of all male interviewees), and thus was the most gender-balanced group. This group included relatively fewer people in relationships (slightly more than half of the interviewees) than the other two groups. About two thirds of the interviewees, especially the men, were childless. A great majority currently lived in their home village and had good relationships with their neighbours. Importantly, most of them pointed out that there were thriving local organizations in their community. About half of them had family members who were involved in the local community. This group of interviewees lived in the countryside because they felt strongly attached to their home village and the people. They enjoyed their life there, especially the good housing conditions and work being nearby.

More than two thirds of the Incidental Activists were women (23 versus 7 men). Half of them had continued living in their home village, whereas the rest had moved in from other rural areas or small or medium-sized cities. The latter group was comprised heavily of women who had moved to their husband's home village. The majority of interviewees were married and had one or two children. The dominant motivation behind their decision to live in a rural area was related to family relationships in the village. The interviewees usually had good relationships with their neighbours. About half of them also had family members engaged in the local community. About the same number of interviewees stated that there were active local organizations in their village.

A majority of the Not Active group were women (21 versus 6 men). However, it is important to bear in mind that, in general, most interviewees were women (63 versus 29), resulting in an overall underrepresentation of men among the interviewed individuals. Nevertheless, about two thirds of the Not Active interviewees came from the village where they currently lived. Many of them were married or in a relationship, but only a small group already had children. Interestingly, they often had very limited relationships with their neighbours. Some even felt lonely because they did not have any close friends in the vicinity. Only a small number of them admitted having family members engaged in the local community or said that there were active local organizations in their village. Some of them felt "forced" to live in the countryside due to their husband's preference or the necessity of taking care of elderly parents.

The presented typology shows a tendency toward the accumulation of different types of local civic engagement by the same people. The interviewees differed more in terms of the intensity of their involvement, not in the way they got involved.

Factors Influencing the Interviewees' Local Civic Engagement

There were a few main factors that affected interviewees' involvement with their local communities. First, the research shows that one's family situation matters when it comes to engagement in one's community. It seems that working and having children of a pre-school age hindered the interviewees' local civic engagement, especially in the case of women. As one woman said, "I am busy at home at least till noon. I have to take care of my child, take care of the house...[a] typical mom's life" (5.Pęcław_W.29).[5] Men sometimes also used the "family" argument, but in a slightly different way. For example, one male interviewee justified his absence at the village assemblies by explaining that he preferred to spend that time with his family: "assemblies are organized on Sundays and this is the only day when I have time for my family" (8.Gródek_M.29). In other cases, men usually indicated that they did not have time for community engagement due to their professional obligations. In contrast, not having children or having slightly older children facilitated some interviewees' local civic engagement, especially in initiatives directed at children or youth.

Second, according to the literature, having family members engaged in the local community and serving as role models increases the probability of one's own involvement in similar activities (e.g., Chimiak, 2006). Such tendencies were observed in some interviewees with a high level of local civic engagement. Some had been socialized to take part in this type of activity while helping their active parents or other family members, while others were literally drawn to a local organization, for example, by their siblings. On the other hand, a significant group of interviewees did not want to be involved in the local government precisely because of the discouraging example of a family member: "My father was the village representative. I don't need to do it and I think that it's a really hard task to do. It's really hard, because the people expect too much from you" (2.Gzy_W.29).

Third, the characteristics of the local context and the interviewees' relationships with other village residents also mattered. Greater resources of social capital in the village (Putnam, 2000) appeared to facilitate the interviewees' local civic engagement. Clearly, having more vital and active local organizations means there are more opportunities to get involved and more chances that other young adults also will do so. However, how well the interviewees were embedded in social networks in the local community also seemed to matter. For example, good relationships with neighbours and living in one's own home village facilitated local civic engagement, whereas being an "outsider" and experiencing some exclusion from local networks hindered it. Apart from that, the interviewees who were strongly attached to their local community and happy about living in their home village seemed to be more likely to be civically engaged compared to those who felt "forced" to do so.

Last but not least, a significant group of interviewees indicated that they were simply not interested in getting involved, especially in the local government. For many of them it meant too much responsibility and took too much time if one wanted to fulfill the role properly. Some of them were aware that the older generation expected them to take over and that their reluctance had provoked tensions: "I do not have time for this, because I think that if you do it, you have to be engaged full-time. My father is angry at me and my peers, because he thinks that we should do something for others, get involved in the community and the local government" (8.Walim_M.33). Among those who did not participate in village assemblies, the majority found them unimportant and a waste of time: "I am too lazy for it. When I should go to the village assembly on Sunday around noon, I am usually riding my motorcycle somewhere 300 kilometres from here" (5.Gródek_M.33). For some, the general image of politics visible in mass media was repulsive. Others shared their negative opinions about the local political scene in their communities. They perceived it as dominated by "cliques" of people who always won elections and supported each other. Also, a large proportion of interviewees, mostly women, claimed that they did not have the "right" personality to play the role of a local leader: "I do not like to be a public figure. I prefer to stay in the background, not to be on the front lines and speak publicly" (6.Gzy_W.29). The men who were interviewed never described themselves as "not good enough" for local politics, and as interested in different areas of activity.

Conclusion

The outcomes of the research presented in this chapter suggest that young university graduates living in rural areas in Poland are affected by individualization, which has weakened the status and practice of citizenship in those areas. The majority of interviewees (those who engaged only incidentally or not at all), despite their education and skills, did not seem to see the sense in engaging in their local community, and instead they stayed focused mainly on individual concerns, namely, their work and family life. They preferred to stay away from burden and responsibility, especially as related to any involvement in local government, because they believed very little in the power of collective action. Those who did engage on a regular basis felt strongly attached to their home village, usually cherished their rural life, and were deeply embedded in local formal and informal networks. They often did not have to deal with family responsibilities (yet). However, it is disturbing that, even among this group, there was hardly any interest in getting involved in local government at the village or municipality level.

The presented research outcomes raise several issues important for theoretical debate on citizenship and civic engagement locally. First, following Lister's (1997) line of thought, theories of citizenship should be more sensitive to gender, but should also take into account the life course perspective. Having children or not may not only affect one's life priorities, but it may also affect one's opportunities to get engaged in one's community, especially in the case of women. This important but overlooked point could help identify supports that might help young people with family responsibilities get involved in the political life of their community. Second, the research shows that level of education alone does not

always correlate with local civic engagement. The interviewees' university education alone did not appear to have increased their willingness to get involved
locally. It is possible that, for those who attended a local university, which are
often of a lower quality in comparison with those in larger cities, their education
did not provide cultural capital that was strong enough to create in them the
attitude required to be engaged citizens. On the other hand, the presented
outcomes suggest that, at least in the case of young rural adults, a university
education plays some role in civic engagement only when combined with other
factors, such as an attachment to a place or a position in local social networks.

Finally, this research contributes to the ongoing debate on tensions between
individuality and community (Bauman, 2013). The interviewees characterized
as having the highest level of local civic engagement were well-embedded in
social networks in their village. As a result, they felt more secure and connected
to others, which increased their willingness to get involved. They may also have
felt some pressure or responsibility to get involved if their family members were
involved, too, and if there were active local organizations in their village. On the
other hand, many others felt secure enough to resist pressures related to their
lack of engagement in local politics, and instead got involved in lifestyle or recreation initiatives, which often were not directly aimed at solving problems in their
village. These rather complex results indicate the need for a more in-depth study
of the interplay between individualization, security, and conformity in modern
rural communities.

Notes

1. During the partition period (1795–1918), separate regions of Poland were under the control of
three empires (Russia, Prussia, and the Austro-Hungarian Empire), each of which implemented
different state, social, and cultural policies. Apart from that, Poland's borders were changed
at the end of World War II. The loss of its eastern territories, which were incorporated into
the Ukrainian, Belarusian, and Lithuanian Soviet Republics, was "compensated" for by the
addition of formerly Prussian lands in the west and north.

2. The project was funded by the National Science Centre based on decision no. DEC-2013/11/D/
HS6/04574.

3. The local government institutions operating at the level of the village are rather limited in
terms of power and money in the area. In general, they play an auxiliary role in relation to
the local municipal government.

4. Village assemblies are formal meetings open to all village residents, where important local
affairs are discussed. Often a village representative as well as members of his/her council
are selected to officially represent the residents' interests before municipal authorities.

5. In interview citations, the first number refers to the number of the interview; then the name of the municipality is included; the letters "w" or "м" refer to the interviewee's gender; and the last numbers indicate the age of the interviewee.

References

Barraclough, L. (2013). Is there also a right to the countryside? *Antipode, 45*(5), 1047-1049. https://doi.org/10.1111/anti.12040

Bartczak, J. (2016). Identyfikacja regionalna uczniów gminy Prostki w świetle ich planów i aspiracji życiowych. [Regional identification of pupils from Prostki municipality in the context of their plans and life aspirations]. In T. Herudziński & P. Swacha (Eds.), *Społeczności lokalne wobec wyzwań współczesności [Local communities facing modern challenges]* (pp. 70-81). Wydawnictwo SGGW.

Bartkowski, J. (2003). *Tradycja i polityka. Wpływ tradycji kulturowych polskich regionów na współczesne zachowania społeczne i polityczne. [Tradition and politics. The influence of Polish regions' cultural traditions on contemporary social and political behaviors].* Wydawnictwo Akademickie „Żak".

Bauman, Z. (2000). *Liquid modernity.* Polity Press.

Bauman, Z. (2013). *Community: Seeking safety in an insecure world.* Polity Press.

Bosniak, L. (2000). Citizenship denationalized. *Indiana Journal of Global Legal Studies, 7*(2), 447-509. https://www.jstor.org/stable/20644737

Chałasiński, J. (1938). *Młode pokolenie chłopów. Procesy i zagadnienia kształtowania się warstwy chłopskiej w Polsce. [Young generation of peasants. Processes shaping a social category of peasants in Poland].* Państwowy Instytut Kultury Wsi.

Chałasiński, J. (1966). *Młode pokolenie wsi Polski Ludowej. W poszukiwaniu drogi. Pamiętniki działaczy. [Young generation of the countryside in the postwar Poland. Searching for the right path. Young activists' diaries].* Ludowa Spółdzielnia Wydawnicza.

Chimiak, G. (2006). *How individualists make solidarity work.* Ministerstwo Pracy i Polityki Społecznej.

CSO. (2012). *Report on the results. The national census of population and housing 2011.* Warsaw, Poland: Central Statistical Office.

CSO. (2017). *Higher education institutions and their finances in 2016.* Gdańsk, Poland: CSO Social Surveys and Living Conditions Department.

Czapiński, J. (2015). State of the civil society. In J. Czapiński & T. Panek (Eds.), *Social diagnosis 2015. Objective and subjective quality of life in Poland* (pp. 325-366). The Council for Social Monitoring.

Erickson, D. L., Sanders, R. S., & Cope M. R. (2018). Lifetime stayers in urban, rural, and highly rural communities in Montana. *Population, Space and Place, 24*, 1-12. https://doi.org/10.1002/psp.2133

Fedyszak-Radziejowska, B. (2018). Rural communities: Attitudes, values and socio-economic determinants. In J. Wilkin & I. Nurzyńska (Eds.), *Rural Poland 2018. The report on the state of rural areas* (pp. 69-91). Scholar Publishing House.

Halamska, M. (2016). Struktura społeczna ludności wiejskiej na początku XXI wieku. [Rural population's social structure at the beginning of the 21st century]. In M. Halamska, S. Michalska, & R. Śpiewak (Eds.), *Studia nad strukturą społeczną wiejskiej Polski [Studies on the social structure of the Polish rural population]* (pp. 11-93). Wydawnictwo Naukowe „Scholar".

Kaufman, L., & Rousseeuw, P. J. (1990). *Finding groups in data: An introduction to cluster analysis.* Wiley.

Lister, R. (1997). Citizenship: Towards a feminist synthesis. *Feminist Review, 57*(1), 28-48. https://doi.org/10.1080/014177897339641

Matysiak, I. (2014). *Rola sołtysów we współczesnych społecznościach wiejskich. Płeć jako czynnik różnicujący kapitał społeczny. [Village representatives' role in today's rural communities. Gender as a factor differentiating social capital].* Wydawnictwo Naukowe „Scholar".

Nash, K. (2009). Between citizenship and human rights. *Sociology, 43*(6), 1067-1083. https://doi.org/10.1177/0038038509345702

Oldfield, A. (1990). *Citizenship and community: Civic republicanism and the modern world.* Routledge.

Poczta, W. (2012). Change in agriculture with particular focus on structural transformations. In J. Wilkin & I. Nurzyńska (Eds.), *Rural Poland 2012. Rural development report* (pp. 65-99). Scholar Publishing House.

Putnam, R. D. (2000). *Bowling alone. The collapse and revival of American community.* Simon & Schuster Paperbacks.

Rérat, P. (2014). The selective migration of young graduates: Which of them return to their rural home region and which do not? *Journal of Rural Studies, 35*, 123-132. https://doi.org/10.1016/j.jrurstud.2014.04.009

Rye, J. F. (2011). Youth migration, rurality and class: A Bourdieusian approach. *European Urban and Regional Studies, 18*(2), 170-183. https://doi.org/10.1177/0969776410390747

Silverman, D. (Ed.). (2016). *Qualitative research.* Sage Publications.

Statistics Poland. (2021). *Local data bank* [Database]. https://bdl.stat.gov.pl/BDL/start#

Szafraniec, K. (2010). *Młode pokolenie a nowy ustrój. [Young generation and new systemic changes].* Warszawa, Polska: IRWiR PAN.

Szafraniec, K. (2011). *Młodzi 2011. [Youth 2011].* Kancelaria Prezesa Rady Ministrów.

Szafraniec, K., & Szymborski, P. (2016). Transition from education to employment: A specific character of rural youth of the selected post-communist countries. *Wieś i Rolnictwo, 4*(173), 101-121. https://doi.org/10.7366/wir042016/06

Wilkin, J. (2018). Rural Poland: The present and the past: An overview of the *Report.* In J. Wilkin & I. Nurzyńska (Eds.), *Rural Poland 2018. The report on the state of rural areas* (pp. 11-25). Scholar Publishing House.

11

Beyond the "Rural Problem"

Comparing Urban and Rural Political Citizenship, Values, and Practices in Atlantic Canada

RACHEL MCLAY & HOWARD RAMOS

Introduction

In popular media and policy discourse, rural Canada has been constructed as "a national problem, imagined as a stagnant space of intolerance within a vibrant, multicultural Canada" (Cairns, 2013, p. 624). This is no different for Atlantic Canada, where nearly half the population lives in rural areas. Former Prime Minister Steven Harper, for instance, has blamed the region's economic underdevelopment on a so-called "culture of defeatism" (CBC News, 2002). This critical view of the region's attitudes toward change and its supposed lack of collective will to address economic struggles has been echoed by scholars (McGeorge & Bateman, 2017; Savoie, 2017) and by the Ivany Commission report (Ivany et al., 2014) in Nova Scotia, which focused on a "division between urban and rural perspectives" (p. vii) over the need for economic growth and how best to achieve it.

Attention to the attitudes in rural areas and secondary regions has been increasing since the election of Donald Trump in the US and the rise of right-wing parties in Europe and around the world. More specifically, there has been an increasing focus on the politics of rural regions and what many see as an "urban–rural divide." In that divide, urban cosmopolitanism is seen as foiled by the often-labelled "backward" politics of the rural working class (Cairns, 2013; Cramer, 2016; Hochschild, 2016). Tensions from the perceived divide are exacerbated by what many see as an increase in the power of suburban and rural voters. For some, this is considered to be a "rural problem," where politics of the margins have an outsized effect on electoral outcomes, wresting power from wealthy, educated, progress-driven urbanites. There is a growing concern, therefore, that rural populations are imposing conservative values on the rest of the population (Noack, 2016). In Canada, there is some evidence showing that rural voter turnout remains higher than in cities, and rural populations appear to be highly mobilized (Eneas, 2019; Freeman, 2019). Whether or not the divides seen in the US, Europe, or other parts of the world are also seen in Atlantic Canada is less clear. For this reason, this chapter explores how the research and conclusions drawn from other regions apply to Atlantic Canada.

To explore these issues and understand the underlying mechanisms behind rural political practices and values, this chapter uses data from a 2019 survey of Atlantic Canadians from the Perceptions of Change Project. We begin the chapter by describing the transformation of political citizenship that foregrounds concerns over the "rural problem," as well as how different models of citizenship have been linked to rural and urban areas. Next, we consider whether these assumptions hold for Atlantic Canada. We use tabular analyses on political practices and two simple indexes of political views to analyze whether rural Atlantic Canadians participate more, or differently, in politics than those in urban areas; we assess whether rural residents' political views differ from those of urban residents; and we examine whether and to what degree these differences shape political outcomes in Atlantic Canada.

Changing Political Citizenship

In political economist T. H. Marshall's (1950) classic articulation of citizenship, the right to vote or to hold office comprises its political dimension. In more recent years, however, scholars have also increasingly looked to extra-institutional forms of political action such as protesting, boycotting, or signing petitions as other forms of political expression and political citizenship. Interestingly, this shift in focus was spurred by trends of declining voter turnout across Western democracies. While many scholars have expressed concern over these trends (Howe, 2010; Putnam, 2000; Wattenberg, 2015), others, such as Dalton (2008), frame these changes as part of a generational shift from "duty-based" citizenship to "engaged" citizenship. They argue that younger people favour forms of political participation that are more self-expressive, individualized, and direct than voting.

It is difficult to know at this point in time whether a shift to engaged citizenship norms will ultimately bolster or undermine democracy. Some have lamented that shifting political action to forms of personal development or lifestyle choices obscures the role of larger systems in perpetuating large-scale harm and injustice (Fenton & Barassi, 2011). In this way, an engaged citizenship often frames collective problems in terms of individualized solutions. This individualization of responsibility coincides with the rise of politics and policies that have sought to erode the authority and legitimacy of states and social welfare systems. Such policies seek to limit the role of the state in dispensing social rights and regulations, transferring power to the market (Somers, 2008; Stasiulis, 2002). Thus, the rise of engaged citizenship as well as individualized and extra-institutional political action is linked to the rise of neoliberal politics.

But despite challenges to states' power over time, states continue to exert very real power over people's lives—not least over citizenship rights and status (Lister, 1997, p. 37). If "engaged" citizens are opting out of collective and institutional forms of political participation, such as voting, then politics and power will be disproportionately shaped by those who practice old-fashioned citizenship norms. This has contributed to rising economic inequality since the 1980s and the concentration of wealth among the super-rich, a phenomenon which has been thoroughly documented by economist Thomas Piketty (1997/2015). At the same time, large-scale migration of the economic elite has meant that citizenship has become increasingly "cosmopolitanized," with citizenship rights extended to non-citizen members of political communities (Benhabib, 2007; Fraser, 2008; Nash, 2009). This has led to the rise of elite "super citizens" (Nash 2009), whose wealth enables them to fully reap the rewards of cosmopolitan society. These deepening inequalities have bred resentment among those who have been left out of these transitions, or who view other social groups as benefitting to a greater degree (Cramer, 2016). The rise of right-wing nationalist and populist movements in the West is often cited as a product of these tensions (Inglehart & Norris, 2017). The economic, cultural, and political divide between those who have benefitted from contemporary power structures and those whose communities have stagnated has been inciting pockets of communitarian resistance among those whose status is threatened and who have been denied the spoils of shifting power structures (Harvey, 2008; Inglehart & Norris, 2017). Much of the resistance, according to both popular media and scholarly research, is occurring in rural areas (Cramer, 2016; Hochschild, 2016).

Rural versus Urban

The evolution of citizenship discourse from dutiful and state centred to engaged, neoliberal, or cosmopolitan is often associated with rural and urban areas, respectively. Cities have long been linked to rising individualism and cosmopolitanism (Simmel, 1903/1971) and new forms of politics, while smaller communities are seen as "old-fashioned," more tight knit, and collectivistic (Geys, 2006), as well as slower to change how they practice politics. Voter turnout, for instance, is typically higher among rural populations than urban ones, reflecting the persistence of duty-based citizenship norms in more "bounded" communities (Geys, 2006; Verba & Nie, 1972). Protest, on the other hand, is considered to be an urban phenomenon (Brym et al., 2014; Castells, 2015), and ethical consumption practices have also been linked to the economic prosperity and consumer choice available in cities (Harvey, 2008).

The engaged citizenship of city dwellers has also been associated with progressive or liberal values and cosmopolitanism, while conservative values are more frequently associated with the dutiful citizens of rural regions (Maxwell, 2019). Two explanations are normally provided in support of these associations. The first is economic, and the second is social. Cities are seen as spaces of comparative wealth and economic development, giving rise to what Inglehart (1977) calls post-materialist values. Like engaged citizenship norms, these values emphasize individuals' personal development; however, they emerge only after physiological needs have been met, and safety and security have been ensured (Inglehart, 1977). Rural spaces are often considered relatively poor and underdeveloped (Noack, 2016)—sites for the extraction of resources, not for the accumulation of wealth (Harvey, 2008). Rural populations, therefore, are seen as prioritizing materialist values like economic stability and personal security over loftier post-materialist ideals (Inglehart, 1977). Inglehart and Norris (2017) argue that, in recent years, these values have bent toward xenophobic populism among those who have experienced declining existential security and little economic gain.

However, Inglehart and Norris (2017) also consider backlash against cultural changes as an underlying cause of increasing populist affiliation, bringing us to the second explanation, which addresses the relationships of urban and rural spaces to cultural and ethnic diversity. The economic explanation is insufficient on its own, especially given that geographies of poverty have been changing; increasing numbers of poor immigrants and racialized minorities in cities mean that poverty levels in urban areas are often higher than those in rural areas

(Nolan et al., 2017). Thus, it is crucial to also acknowledge the role of race and ethnicity in the spatial construction of politics.

Rural communities in Canada, as well as in the US and Western Europe, are predominantly white and are stereotyped as resistant to cultural diversity (Cairns, 2013; Noack, 2016). One explanation draws upon Putnam's (2000) concepts of "bridging" versus "bonding" social capital, or the development of in-group bonds compared to those that extend across groups. Sorensen (2014), for instance, finds that rural communities have higher levels of "bonding" social capital, and therefore more tight-knit in-groups, emphasizing a shared history and culture. Urban areas, by contrast, display more "bridging" social capital, which prioritizes loose connections among disparate groups. Racism and xenophobia can result from strong in-group attachments, particularly in the context of declining existential security and economic precarity (Inglehart & Norris, 2017), as well as when cultural changes occur that, in turn, make minority groups and immigrants scapegoats for dissatisfaction with change. Thus, support for right-wing populist leaders in rural areas is a product not only of the resentment felt toward "liberal elites," whose urban progressive values are seen as out of step with rural political consciousness and social identity (Cramer, 2016), but also of fear of minorities and immigrants, whose rising social status under liberal cosmopolitanism is taken as a threat (Hochschild, 2016). What is unclear is whether these observations, largely based on American research, also apply to Atlantic Canada. If analysis shows that they do not, importing them and amplifying them should be avoided; instead, new approaches should be developed to fit the Canadian case.

Atlantic Canada

In the US, election results appear to corroborate the notion of an urban–rural divide (Maxwell, 2019). In Canada, however, they offer a less straightforward picture. For example, the Atlantic provinces—Nova Scotia, New Brunswick, Newfoundland, and Prince Edward Island—have the greatest proportion of rural residents among all the Canadian provinces (Statistics Canada, 2018), and yet, in the 2015 federal election, the Liberal party, which advanced a socially progressive platform, won every riding. Moreover, despite a focus on the region's economic underdevelopment (e.g., Sacouman, 1981; Savoie, 2017), Atlantic Canada has not, thus far, been a major site for far-right politics. Rather, this has been a growing concern in Western Canada, Ontario, and Quebec (Perry & Scrivens, 2016). Atlantic Canada has also faced profound economic, social, and cultural changes in recent years, including an increase in immigration to the area, rapid urbanization, and economic restructuring (Baldacchino, 2012; Gosse et al., 2016; O'Neil & Erikson, 2003); however, despite stereotypes of the region as socially conservative and averse to change, polling data has consistently found its residents to be more progressive and open to diversity than other regions of Canada (e.g., EKOS Politics, 2019; Gunn, 2019). For these reasons, Atlantic Canada serves as an interesting case study for examining rural political views and practices.

Methods

To examine these issues, we draw upon data collected through a telephone survey of 1,072 Atlantic Canadians conducted between January and March 2019. Participants were recruited through a random selection of landline and mobile telephone numbers assigned to the region. Only residents who were 18 years or older when contacted were invited to participate. The survey questions asked participants about their political activities, their views on a variety of political and social issues, and any changes they had noticed in either their political participation or their views over the last few years. Because the survey was voluntary, participants were likely to be more interested and engaged in politics than the average person. Participants reported voting at much higher rates than the actual voter turnout in the region (see Elections Canada, 2016, for estimates on voter turnout). Measures of political action are self-reported, which contributes to the inflation of these rates. Such inflation, however, is common to surveys on political practices (see Karp & Brockington, 2005; Silver et al., 1986). Participants also tended to be older, with an average age of 58 years.

To understand the relationships between region, political values, and practices as a proxy of citizenship, we analyze below three primary forms of political action: whether participants reported voting in the most recent federal election, whether they reported protesting within the last year, and whether they reported boycotting or choosing a product for ethical reasons within the last year. We also consider participants' reported changes in political participation and their changes in political views. We then compare differences between urban and rural residents, as well as participants' views on social and economic issues, including their level of openness to diversity.

To compare urban and rural residents, we assigned participants to each group based on their postal code. Using the Postal Code Conversion File Plus (PCCF+), Version 7A, we considered participants' locations as "urban" when their postal code placed them in either a large (100,000+) or medium-sized (30,000-99,999) population centre, while those living in small (1,000-29,999) population centres or outside of population centres were classified as "rural." Because postal codes outside of cities often cover large geographical areas, the PCCF+ cannot distinguish with certainty those who live within small population centres from those who live outside of them; for this reason, we did not attempt to break down participants' locations into smaller categories.

To understand participants' views on social and economic issues, we asked them to rate their agreement with statements on political and social issues on a scale from 1 to 5, with 1 meaning "strongly disagree" and 5 meaning "strongly agree." To get an overall picture of these differences, we created two indexes: one to measure participants' openness to diversity, focusing on attitudes toward multiculturalism, members of minority groups, immigrants, and refugees, and one to measure participants' views on economic issues. To create these indexes, we added participants' responses (1–5) and sorted these tallies into categories. Most statements were worded favouring the more progressive stance, that is, agreement signified a liberal or progressive view, while disagreement signified a more conservative view. For statements where the opposite was true, we instead added the inverse of participants' responses to the final tally for the index (e.g., if their answer was 1, we added 5; if it was 2, we added 4; etc.). Seven statements were used to create the openness index, which ranges from 7 to 35. Scores from 7 to 14 were coded as "very conservative"; from 15 to 21, as "somewhat conservative"; from 22 to 28, as "somewhat progressive"; and from 29 to 35, they were treated as "very progressive." Five statements were used to create the economic index, ranging from 5 to 25. Scores from 5 to 10 were "very conservative"; from 11 to 15, "somewhat conservative"; from 16 to 20, "somewhat progressive"; and from 21 to 25, "very progressive."

Analysis

We began our analysis by examining political actions by region, and we found that rural participants reported voting in the last federal election at higher rates than city dwellers, at 94.3% compared to 92.2% (see Table 11.1). We also found that rural residents were more likely than city dwellers to have attended a protest in the last year, with 7.6% saying they had, compared to 6.3% in urban areas. Protests are often characterized as urban phenomena, and their successes as dependent on the crowds that can arise, in part, from population density (Castells, 2015). This finding suggests that the subject of rural protest may call for further study, to help us to better understand the role and purpose of demonstrations in the contemporary political repertoire. Urbanites, however, showed substantially higher participation in ethical consumption practices: 45.4% had boycotted or chosen a product for ethical reasons in the last year, compared to 36.2% of rural residents. Some of this difference may be attributed to the wider variety of consumer choices that are available in cities. However, with the increasing prevalence of online shopping, that difference may be less important than it once was.

TABLE 11.1 Forms of political action by region

	Rural	Urban	n	$x^2(1)$	p
Voting	94.3%	92.2%	926	1.427	0.232
Protesting	7.6%	6.3%	951	0.546	0.460
Boycotting & ethical consumerism	36.2%	45.4%	931	7.115	0.008

The differences between urban and rural Atlantic Canadians, particularly in the areas of voting and protesting, were not large; however, when we looked at changes in political participation in the last few years (see Table 11.2), we found that survey participants in rural areas were also more likely than those in urban areas to report that their participation in political activities had increased in the last few years: 19.0% of rural residents reported an increase, compared to 13.5% of urban residents. This may lend partial evidence to findings of a mobilized rural population, which may be increasingly influencing mainstream politics.

TABLE 11.2 Changes in participation by region

	Rural	Urban
Decreased	16.1%	14.2%
Stayed about the same	64.9%	72.3%
Increased	19.0%	13.5%

Note: n=950, $x^2(2)$=5.725, p=0.057

Next, we compared urban and rural survey participants' views on economic and social issues. The largest portion of participants—about half—fell into the "somewhat progressive" category on both the economic and openness indexes. On the economic index, the next largest portion was "somewhat conservative," while "very progressive" and "very conservative" together made up only 16.3% of the sample. On the openness index, both "very progressive" and "somewhat conservative" composed more than 20% of the sample each, compared to only 4.3% for those whose responses were "very conservative." Results in Table 11.3 show that, on economic issues, rural Atlantic Canadians who took part in the survey were slightly more progressive than their urban counterparts. However, the openness index shows that rural Atlantic Canadians were noticeably less likely than their urban counterparts to be "very progressive" on issues of diversity and immigration, by nearly 10 percentage points—and more likely to be "somewhat conservative," by about the same margin. Thus, the stereotype of rural residents as being more conservative and resistant to diversity than urban residents is supported by our data on Atlantic Canada. Because rural residents seem to be participating in politics to a greater degree than those in urban areas, this provides tentative support for the hypothesis that political outcomes may disproportionately reflect this rural conservatism.

TABLE 11.3 Views indexes by region

Economic index*	Rural	Urban
Very conservative	3.5%	6.8%
Somewhat conservative	28.2%	27.4%
Somewhat progressive	55.6%	55.9%
Very progressive	12.8%	10.0%
Socio-cultural index**		
Very conservative	4.3%	4.6%
Somewhat conservative	24.4%	14.5%
Somewhat progressive	49.9%	49.7%
Very progressive	21.4%	31.2%

* $n=884$, $x^2(3)=5.871$, $p=0.118$
** $n=885$, $x^2(3)=16.343$, $p=0.001$

However, these results do not indicate the actual political orientations of those who do choose to participate in politics, or how these may be affected by location in urban or rural spaces. To determine the actual effects that a rural-urban divide could have on political outcomes, we looked at how both participants' openness index level and their region were linked to participation rates, shown in Table 11.4. In the table, we chose to collapse those with "somewhat" and "very" conservative views together, and have done the same with "somewhat" and "very" progressive views, as this offers a cleaner portrait of trends.

TABLE 11.4 Participation rates by region and socio-cultural index category

	Rural		Urban		n	$x^2(3)$	p
	Conservative	Progressive	Conservative	Progressive			
Voting	89.5%	96.4%	86.5%	94.1%	860	15.117	0.002
Protesting	—	8.4%	—	7.5%	883	2.898	0.408
Boycotting	32.4%	38.4%	39.6%	47.0%	866	9.032	0.029

First, we will look at voting. The results show that it is those with more progressive views that were more likely to report having voted in the last election: 96.4% of rural progressives said they did, compared to 89.5% of rural conservatives, and a similar gap exists between the findings for urban progressives and conservatives. Unfortunately, because of the low numbers of conservative protesters from both urban and rural areas, these rates cannot be shown; however, the rate for rural and urban conservatives combined was 6.7%, which is lower than that of both rural and urban progressives, at 8.4% and 7.5%, respectively. Finally, looking at boycotting and ethical consumption, we can see that, while this action was more common among urbanites of either political leaning, there was also a notable gap between progressives and conservatives in both regions. Rural conservatives were the least likely to have boycotted or chosen a product for ethical reasons, at 32.4%, while 38.4% of rural progressives had done so. These results show that, despite the greater political participation in rural areas and the socially conservative leanings of those residents, it has been those with more progressive attitudes toward diversity who have been engaging in political action at the highest rates.

TABLE 11.5 Changes in participation and views by region and socio-cultural index category

	Rural		Urban	
	Conservative	Progressive	Conservative	Progressive
Political participation*				
Decreased	17.4%	14.7%		14.5%
Stayed about the same	58.7%	68.5%	—	75.0%
Increased	23.8%	16.8%		10.5%
Political views**				
Stayed about the same	36.4%	35.7%		34.2%
Changed somewhat	42.2%	49.7%	—	55.3%
Changed a lot	21.4%	14.7%		10.5%

* n=883, x2(6)=17.932, p=0.006

** n=884, x2(6)=11.572, p=0.072

When we considered the possible link between openness to diversity and changes in participation and views over the last few years, however, we found that, at least in rural areas, it was those with more conservative views that were most likely to say their participation had increased: 23.8% of rural conservatives reported an increase in their political participation, compared to 16.8% of rural progressives. Rural conservatives were also the most likely to report that their views had changed "a lot" over the last few years, at 21.4%, compared to 14.7% of rural progressives and 10.5% of urban progressives.

Conclusion

This examination of the urban–rural political divide in Atlantic Canada shows a more nuanced story than is commonly told about rural politics and their effects on political outcomes. We found that rural residents who participated in our survey not only voted at slightly higher rates, but they also protested more. Urban residents, on the other hand, had participated more in consumer politics. These findings align with the popular view of rural areas as more highly mobilized and engaged in group-based forms of political action compared to cities, which may be spaces for individualized political forms that reflect economic advantage. The surprising alignment of protest with rural regions, however, suggests that rural citizens may in fact be both highly engaged and dutiful citizens; the difference lies, more specifically, in their decreased engagement in consumer politics, which is only one form of extra-institutional political action. But the subject of rural protest may call for further research in order to better understand the purpose of demonstrations and their capacity to influence political outcomes more generally.

We also found that rural residents were no more conservative than urban residents on economic issues. Atlantic Canada has a long tradition of "progressive" conservatism and "Red Tories" in power, who were known for being centrist in their policy frameworks and often supported state intervention into the social and economic lives of Canadians. This aligns with Thomas Frank's (2007) observations from the US, where rural regions were the bastion of communism in the 1930s and shifted to conservatism after neoliberal shifts from the 1970s through the 1990s. In many respects, the same can be said for Western Canada's shift from Social Credit, or left-leaning politics of the mid-twentieth century, to core conservativism in the 2000s, to the alt-right politics of the 2010s. In other words, if the political left aims to make inroads in rural areas, the best route may be through economic policies that reduce inequalities. Rural and urban residents have much in common around these issues, and the historical affiliations of rural regions with progressive economic views provide a solid foundation for left-leaning policies to grow.

We observed a substantial divide, however, on matters of openness to cultural diversity and immigration. These findings align with other research that proposes a cultural gap between urban and rural spaces, in which city residents tend to espouse more cosmopolitan values (Speer & Jivani, 2017), as well as with research showing a moral shift among Canadian conservative supporters (Lusztig & Wilson, 2005). Those in rural areas may be more likely to focus on the concerns of in-group members, remaining wary of, or even antagonistic toward, perceived "outsiders." This, too, is a finding that aligns with Frank's (2007) analysis and others from the US, showing that, if progressive parties aim to make inroads in rural areas, it likely will not occur through shared cultural or social values, but rather through economic values, which are less contentious. We also found slightly higher rates of increased participation and extreme changes in political views among rural conservatives in Atlantic Canada, indicating that mobilization of this group has been occurring. However, even in rural areas of Atlantic Canada, those with conservative views on socio-cultural issues remain in the minority, and such changes are not likely to strongly influence political outcomes in the region's near future. Nevertheless, future research should pay attention to the political changes occurring in the region, and to the ongoing effectiveness of right-wing political messaging originating from outside of it that carries anti-immigrant and anti-diversity sentiments. Thus far, observations on urban-rural divides based on the American case do not seem to directly apply to the region, and there is much room to theorize why Atlantic Canada is different.

Overall, findings from the survey offer no evidence to support the idea that social conservatism in Atlantic Canada's rural areas is linked to increased political activity, or that openness to difference results in indifference or decreased political engagement. We found that rural participants with more progressive values reported the highest rates of political participation. These results suggest that it is not very likely that politics in rural Atlantic Canada will be disproportionately shaped by reactionary or populist leanings in the near future; rather, they are being shaped to a greater degree by those with more progressive attitudes toward social issues and cultural diversity. Even among its more conservative residents, the region's long tradition of supporting "progressive" conservatism, which is economically liberal but socially conservative, remains intact.

References

Baldacchino, G. (2012). Come visit, but don't overstay: Critiquing a welcoming society. *International Journal of Culture, Tourism and Hospitality Research, 6*(2), 145-153.

Benhabib, S. (2007). Twilight of sovereignty or the emergence of cosmopolitan norms? Rethinking citizenship in volatile times. *Citizenship Studies, 11*(1), 19-36.

Brym, R., Godbout, M., Hoffbauer, A., Menard, G., & Zhang, T. H. (2014). Social media in the 2011 Egyptian uprising. *The British Journal of Sociology, 65*(2), 266-292. https://doi.org/10.1111/1468-4446.12080

Cairns, K. (2013). Youth, dirt, and the spatialization of subjectivity: An intersectional approach to white rural imaginaries. *Canadian Journal of Sociology/Cahiers canadiens de sociologie, 38*(4), 623-646.

Castells, M. (2015). *Networks of outrage and hope: Social movements in the internet age.* Polity.

CBC News (2002, May 30). Harper plans to battle "culture of defeatism" in Atlantic Canada. https://www.cbc.ca/news/canada/harper-plans-to-battle-culture-of-defeatism-in-atlantic-canada-1.306785

Cramer, K. J. (2016). *The politics of resentment: Rural consciousness in Wisconsin and the rise of Scott Walker.* University of Chicago Press.

Dalton, R. J. (2008). *The good citizen: How a younger generation is reshaping American politics.* CQ Press.

EKOS Politics. (2019). *Increased polarization on attitudes to immigration reshaping the political landscape in Canada.* https://www.ekospolitics.com/index.php/2019/04/increased-polarization-on-attitudes-to-immigration-reshaping-the-political-landscape-in-canada/

Elections Canada. (2016). *Estimation of voter turnout by age group and gender at the 2015 general election.* https://www.elections.ca/res/rec/part/estim/42ge/42_e.pdf

Eneas, B. (2019, May 5). Yellow vest protesters rally in Saskatoon. *CBCNews.* https://www.cbc.ca/news/canada/saskatoon/yellow-vest-protesters-rally-in-saskatoon-1.5123575

Fenton, N., & Barassi, V. (2011). Alternative media and social networking sites: The politics of individuation and political participation. *The Communication Review, 14*, 179-196. https://doi.org/10.1080/10714421.2011.597245

Frank, T. (2007). *What's the matter with Kansas? How conservatives won the heart of America.* Metropolitan Books.

Fraser, N. (2008). Abnormal justice. *Critical Inquiry, 34*(3), 393-422. https://doi.org/10.1086/589478

Freeman, J. (2019, April 10). Analyzing the rural and urban vote in Alberta election 2019. *Global News.* https://globalnews.ca/news/5152772/alberta-election-2019-rural-urban-conservative-ucp-fcp-ndp/

Geys, B. (2006). Explaining voter turnout: A review of aggregate-level research. *Electoral Studies, 25*(4), 637-663. https://doi.org/10.1016/j.electstud.2005.09.002

Gosse, M., Ramos, H., Radice, M., Grant, J. L., & Pritchard, P. (2016). What affects perceptions of neighbourhood change? *The Canadian Geographer, 60*(4): 530-540. https://doi.org/10.1111/cag.12324

Gunn, A. (2019, March 20). Poll shows Atlantic Canadians are less anti-immigrant than national average. *The Chronicle Herald.* https://www.thechronicleherald.ca/news/local/poll-shows-atlantic-canadians-are-less-anti-immigrant-than-national-average-293779/

Harvey, D. (2008). The right to the city. *New Left Review, 53*(September–October), 23–40. https://newleftreview.org/II/53/david-harvey-the-right-to-the-city

Hochschild, A. R. (2016). The ecstatic edge of politics: Sociology and Donald Trump. *Contemporary Sociology, 45*(6), 683–689. https://doi.org/10.1177%2F0094306116671947

Howe, P. (2010). *Citizens adrift: The democratic disengagement of young Canadians.* UBC Press.

Inglehart, R. (1977). *The silent revolution: Changing values and political styles among western publics.* Princeton UP.

Inglehart, R., & Norris, P. (2017). Trump and the populist authoritarian parties: *The Silent Revolution* in reverse. *Perspectives on Politics, 15*(2), 443–454. https://doi.org/10.1017/S1537592717000111

Ivany, R., d'Entremont, I., Christmas, D., Fuller, S., & Bragg, J. (2014). *Now or never: An urgent call to action for Nova Scotia. Nova Scotia commission on building our new economy.* https://www.onens.ca/sites/default/files/editor-uploads/now-or-never.pdf

Karp, J. A., & Brockington, D. (2005). Social desirability and response validity: A comparative analysis of overreporting voter turnout in five countries. *The Journal of Politics, 67*(3), 825–840.

Lister, R. (1997). Citizenship: Towards a feminist synthesis. *Feminist Review, 57*(1), 28–48.

Lusztig, M., & Wilson, J. M. (2005). A new right? Moral issues and partisan change in Canada. *Social Science Quarterly, 86*(1), 109–128.

Marshall, T. H. (1950). Citizenship and social class. In T. H. Marshall (Ed.), *Citizenship and social class and other essays* (pp. 1–85). Cambridge University Press.

Maxwell, R. (2019, March 5). Why are urban and rural areas so politically divided? *The Washington Post.* https://www.washingtonpost.com/politics/2019/03/05/why-are-urban-rural-areas-so-politically-divided/

McGeorge, K., & Bateman, T. M. (2017). Settling for mediocrity: Aging and health care in New Brunswick. *Journal of New Brunswick Studies / Revue d'études Sur Le Nouveau-Brunswick, 8*, 15–31.

Nash, K. (2009). Between citizenship and human rights. *Sociology, 43*(6), 1067–1083.

Noack, R. (2016, November 27). The urban-rural divide that bolstered Trump isn't just an American thing; it's prevalent in Europe, too. *The Washington Post.* https://www.washingtonpost.com/news/worldviews/wp/2016/11/27/the-urban-rural-divide-isnt-just-evident-in-american-politics-its-prevalent-in-europe-too/

Nolan, L., Waldfogel, J., & Wimer, C. (2017). Long-term trends in rural and urban poverty: New insights using a historical supplemental poverty measure. *ANNALS, 672*(1), 123–142. https://doi.org/10.1177%2F0002716217713174

O'Neil, B., & Erikson, L. (2003). Evaluating traditionalism in the Atlantic Provinces: Voting, public opinion and the electoral project. *Atlantis, 27*(2), 113–122.

Perry, B., & Scrivens, R. (2016). Uneasy alliances: A look at the right-wing extremist movement in Canada. *Studies in Conflict & Terrorism, 39*(9), 819–841. https://doi.org/10.1080/1057610X.2016.1139375

Piketty, T. (2015). *The economics of inequality* (A. Goldhammer, Trans.). Belknap Press. (Original work published 1997)

Putnam, R. (2000). *Bowling alone: The collapse and revival of American community.* Simon & Schuster.

Sacouman, R. J. (1981). The "peripheral" Maritimes and Canada-wide Marxist political economy. *Studies in Political Economy, 6*, 135–150.

Savoie, D. (2017). *Looking for bootstraps: Economic development in the Maritimes.* Nimbus Publishing.

Silver, B. D., Anderson, B. A., & Abramson, P. R. (1986). Who overreports voting? *American Political Science Review, 80*(2), 613–624.

Simmel, G. (1903/1971). The metropolis and mental life. In D. N. Levine (Ed.), *On individuality and social forms* (pp. 324–339). Chicago, IL: University of Chicago Press.

Somers, M. R. (2008). *Genealogies of citizenship: Markets, statelessness, and the right to have rights.* Cambridge University Press.

Sorensen, J. F. L. (2014). Rural–urban differences in bonding and bridging social capital. *Regional Studies, 50*(3), 391–410. https://doi.org/10.1080/00343404.2014.918945

Speer, S., & Jivani, J. (2017, June 5). The urban/rural divide and a more inclusive Canada. *Policy Options.* https://policyoptions.irpp.org/magazines/june-2017/the-urbanrural-divide-and-a-more-inclusive-canada/

Stasiulis, D. (2002). Introduction: Reconfiguring Canadian citizenship. *Citizenship studies, 6*(4), 365–375.

Statistics Canada. (2018). *Population and dwelling count highlight tables, 2016 Census.* https://www12.statcan.gc.ca/census-recensement/2016/dp-pd/hlt-fst/pd-pl/Table.cfm?Lang=Eng&T=703&SR=1&S=87&O=A&RPP=25

Verba, S., & Nie, N. H. (1972). *Participation in America: Political democracy and social equality.* Harper & Row.

Wattenberg, M. P. (2015). *Is voting for young people?* Routledge.

12

Defining Indigenous Citizenship

Free, Prior, and Informed Consent (FPIC), the Right to Self-Determination, and Canadian Citizenship

SATENIA ZIMMERMANN, SARA TEITELBAUM, JENNIFER JARMAN
& M. A. (PEGGY) SMITH

Introduction

Citizenship is a right and a responsibility that unifies people in a specific political territory who share common beliefs, customs, values, and desires for the common good.[1] For Indigenous Peoples located within rural regions in geopolitical Canada, Canadian citizenship is in direct contrast with Indigenous aspirations of self-determination. For generations, there has been struggle against successive federal governments' paternalistic control of Indigenous Peoples under the Indian Act (1876) and assimilation policies. These issues have unified Indigenous Peoples who continue to resist Canadian citizenship in favour of Indigenous citizenship. Indigenous Peoples have a constitutional right to self-determination, shared values, customs, traditions, and a strong relationship to rural lands (and in a few cases, land that was once rural and is now either part of rural-urban peripheries or has been engulfed by large urban areas).

Based on data collected in 2006 by Statistics Canada,[2] Ontario is home to approximately 242,495 people with Aboriginal ancestry, the largest Indigenous population in Canada (Government of Canada, 2019). Data collected under the

Registered Indian Population Report indicate that there were 181,524 Registered Indians in 2010 (Government of Canada, 2019). Almost half of Ontario's Registered Indian population live on 207 First Nations reserves and in Aboriginal communities (Government of Canada, 2019). Rural location, First Nations self-determination, and the right to be rural are vital to the ability of Aboriginal peoples to protect their traditional lands and natural resources that they depend on for their very survival.

Indigenous claims to the right to self-determination are not new. When, for example, former Prime Minister Pierre Trudeau's Liberal government presented a White Paper, *Statement of the Government of Canada on Indian Policy*, in 1969, it was viewed by Indigenous Peoples as yet another attempt to assimilate them. In response, the Indian Association of Alberta issued the document *Citizens Plus* (1970)—known as the Red Paper—outlining their right to self-determination, Aboriginal rights and treaty rights, ancestral lands, and the well-being of future generations. More recently, the 2007 United Nations Declaration on the Rights of Indigenous Peoples (UNDRIP) has become an international mechanism used by Indigenous Peoples to affirm their right to self-determination. The UNDRIP emphasizes Indigenous Peoples' right to maintain and strengthen their institutions, traditions, and visions of economic and social institutions (United Nations, n.d.). The principle of free, prior, and informed consent (FPIC) is its most contested principle. Government and industry have taken a linear approach to FPIC focused on natural resources management and view the component of consent as a right to veto (01-NWO, 2017; 03-NWO, 2018; 17-NWO, 2019; 18-NWO, 2019; Papillon & Rodon, 2019).[3] However, FPIC viewed by Indigenous Peoples as both a constitutionally protected Aboriginal right and a discursive tool to increase legitimacy in three overreaching areas: self-determination, Aboriginal identity, and lands and resources (07-NWO, 2018; 08-NWO, 2018; 10-NWO, 2018; 12-NWO, 2018; 15-NWO, 2018; Mitchell et al., 2019; Papillon & Rodon, 2019).

This chapter presents a First Nations perspective on the implications of FPIC in self-governance, Indigenous citizenship, and forestry and natural resources management. Data from interviews conducted in rural Northwest Ontario will show that First Nations interpretation of FPIC reaches far beyond forestry and natural resources management. Free, prior, and informed consent is viewed both as a right and a tool—it is the cornerstone of Indigenous nationhood, especially in rural regions of geopolitical Canada.

The "Right to Be Rural" and Citizenship

The question of whether there is a right to be rural, and furthermore, whether and how the failure to recognize this right manifests in the everyday lives of rural people, are questions that this collection's authors have strived to answer through the many perspectives presented throughout this book. Discourse on the right to be rural focuses on the unequal distribution of citizenship rights and the social inequalities experienced by citizens living in rural areas. Rural citizens often experience limited access to many of the benefits urban citizens take for granted, including healthcare, employment, infrastructure, food, and political representation (Barraclough, 2013; Brenner et al., 2010; Lister, 1997). T. H. Marshall (1950) examined social inequalities through the lens of "citizenship." Marshall (1950) defined citizenship as the relationship between the state and the individuals living within its geopolitical region, a "status bestowed on those who are full members of a community. All who possess the status are equal with respect to the rights and duties with which the status is endowed" (pp. 28-29). Marshall argued that citizenship is not static; instead, it is an evolving relationship composed of civil, political, and social rights. Thus, citizenship goes beyond "liberty of the person, freedom of speech, thought and faith, the right to own property and to conclude valid contracts, the right to justice and the right to participate in the exercise of political power" (1950, pp. 10-11). Citizenship includes

> the whole range from the right to a modicum of economic welfare and security to the right to share to the full in the social heritage and to live the life of a civilized being according to the standards in the prevailing society (Marshall, 1950, p. 11).

By the 1980s, the end of the welfare state, neoliberalism, increased globalization, and the international uncertainty of capitalist economies had brought about a paradigm shift in the conceptualization of citizenship. In most capitalist nations, including Canada, postwar social policies designed to provide every citizen with basic economic security have since eroded and been replaced by a modern citizenship characterized as a contractual agreement between the state and the economically productive citizen (Brodie, 2002; Lister, 1997). The underlying neoliberal shift in modern citizenship has been

> from the right to care determined by inalienable "social rights", to social rights being a reward for "those who deserved it" through their actual and prospective contribution to the economic prosperity of the country (Bauman, 2005, p. 20).

The conceptualization of modern citizenship as a reward for economic productivity creates a great deal of frustration and uncertainty for rural First Nations. These First Nations face many of the same obstacles as non-Indigenous rural communities, including out-migration, a lack of employment opportunities, and unequal access to healthcare, education, food, infrastructure, and political representation. Discourse on modern citizenship is overwhelmingly examined through a colonialist lens and focuses on the relationship between the state and the citizen—in this case, Canada and the individual Canadian citizen. It does not take into account First Nations peoples, the majority of whom are not Canadian citizens and whose rights are not obtained through Canadian citizenship, but through constitutionally protected collective and individual Aboriginal rights and treaty rights. The main contribution of this chapter is to expand the current body of literature on the right to be rural by providing a First Nations perspective based on data collected in a northern Ontario case study.

Case Study

Two First Nations agreed to participate in the case study: Biigtigong Nishnaabeg (formerly the Ojibways of the Pic River) First Nation, and Netmizaaggamig Nishnaabeg (formerly Pic Mobert) First Nation. They are non-signatory First Nations to the Robinson-Superior Treaty (1850) and members of the Anishinabek Nation. They have filed separate comprehensive land claims in the Ontario Superior Court for Aboriginal title over their traditional territory. The Ontario Ministry of Natural Resources and Forestry and the Nawiinginokima Forest Management Corporation have affirmed that both First Nations have a vested interest in the management of the Big Pic, Pic River, Nagagami, and White River forests.

Methods

Eighteen semi-structured interviews were conducted with people active in the Lands, Environmental, Resources Management, and Forestry Departments, and First Nations governance. Initial interviews were conducted in 2017 and 2018. Follow-up interviews took place in 2019, and open communication continues in 2021. Interviews took place in person and by telephone in the Region of Thunder Bay. Participants were selected based on their involvement with: 1) the Nawiinginokima Forest Management Corporation, including First Nations communities directly involved with the Nawiinginokima Forest Management

Corporation; and 2) land tenure modernization in Ontario, First Nations, and Forest Stewardship Council certification.

Participants came from a wide range of backgrounds and ranged in age from 20-80, with the majority being between the ages of 40-70. First Nations participants (except two) representing a First Nation had two years or less experience in the field. The majority had some formal training or college background. They held important positions as community elders, elected band representatives, and higher-level employees in the areas of land, environmental, and resource management, forestry, and First Nations governance. At the time of the study, the majority lived on a reserve. Non-First Nations participants who were working with or acting as a representative for a First Nation were university educated, have had lengthy careers in the forest sector, and lived off reserve. Other Indigenous individuals were interviewed who were not directly connected to the communities involved in the study, but had extensive knowledge of forest certification. They have had extensive careers in forestry, were involved with the Forest Stewardship Council, lived both on and off their respective reserves, and were university educated. Non-Indigenous participants who were not representing a First Nation were all university educated and have had extensive careers in the forest sector; they have worked extensively with First Nations peoples within a forestry context.

Participants were asked questions on two key areas: 1) their perspectives on FPIC, including their experience in applying and understanding the UNDRIP and FPIC; Forest Stewardship Council standards on FPIC: the duty to consult and accommodate; and the expectations, advantages, and barriers to implementing FPIC in forest management; and 2) their perspectives on current practices with regard to Indigenous-corporate-Crown engagement on forest management. For example, who should decide on whether FPIC has been achieved, conditions for withholding consent, the role of certificate holders and government in the certifi-cation and dispute resolution process, the relationship between Indigenous communities and forestry companies, current consultation practices, integration of Indigenous values in forestry planning and operations, and the benefits that accrue to the Indigenous community from forestry activities.

First Nations and the Right to Be Rural

A First Nation, defined as a "band" under the Indian Act (1876), is populated mainly by "status Indians" (Indigenous Foundations, 2009). In northern Ontario, all First Nations except Fort William First Nation are located in rural areas, with many located in remote locations, meaning that there is no road access. Between

1871 and 1921, the Crown entered into treaties with First Nations communities that enabled the Canadian government to actively pursue agriculture, settlement, and resource development in the Canadian West and the North. The treaties are numbered 1 to 11 and are referred to as the "Numbered Treaties." The Numbered Treaties were modeled on the earlier Robinson treaties entered into with First Nations whose ancestral lands were located along the shores of lakes Superior and Huron, negotiated in 1850, and cover northern Ontario, Manitoba, Saskatchewan, Alberta, and parts of the Yukon, the Northwest Territories, and British Columbia. Under these treaties, leaders from First Nations communities who occupied these territories gave up or "ceded" large areas of land to the Crown. In exchange, the treaties provided for such things as reserve lands and other benefits like farm equipment and animals, annual payments, ammunition, clothing, and certain rights to hunt and fish (Crown-Indigenous Relations and Northern Affairs Canada, 2021). The historic treaties also gave the Crown the right to "take up" unoccupied treaty land for mining, lumbering, and other purposes. First Nations dispute that their ancestors ceded the land, arguing that their ancestors only agreed to share the land, nation to nation (Borrows, 1999; Sakej & Henderson, 2002; Fry & Mitchell, 2016). Biigtigong Nishnaabeg and Netmizaaggamig Nishnaabeg First Nations are non-signatories to the Robinson-Superior Treaty of 1850, and therefore neither agreed under treaty to cede or share their traditional lands with the Crown (07-NWO, 2018; 08-NWO, 2018; 09-NWO, 2018; 10-NWO, 2018; 11-NWO, 2018; 12-NWO, 2018; 13-NWO, 2018). Despite being non-signatory First Nations, Biigtigong Nishnaabeg and Netmizaaggamig Nishnaabeg band members are legally treaty peoples with constitutionally protected collective and individual Aboriginal rights and treaty rights. Their unique position as treaty peoples allows First Nations to assert their right to be independent, self-governing, rural nations within geopolitical Canada.

Indigenous Citizenship

According to data published by Statistics Canada in 2006, there were approximately 1,172,785 people with Aboriginal ancestry residing in Canada (Government of Canada, 2019). However, the number of people with Aboriginal identity is likely much higher, as mistrust of the government, residential schools, and the apprehension of First Nations children who were placed into foster care have made it difficult for some individuals to self-identify as Aboriginal (12-NWO, 2018; 15-NWO, 2018; Sakej & Henderson, 2002; Stasiulis, 2002). For Indigenous Peoples living within the geopolitical territory of Canada, the history of Crown and

Indigenous relations has been complicated by Crown betrayals (Manyfingers, 1986; Mitchell et al., 2019; Sakej & Henderson, 2002). The Indian Act (1876) is the legal foundation for the treatment of Indigenous Peoples in Canada. This Act has been amended several times and remains in effect today. Created by colonialists through an act of parliament, it defines how the government of Canada interacts with First Nations bands and their members, defines who is a legal status Indian, and outlines the system of Indian reserves (Belanger, 2014). Importantly, there is no reference to citizenship in the Act (Nishga Tribal Council, 1980). Under the Act, from 1876 to 1951, "the term 'person' meant an individual other than an Indian" (Sakej & Henderson, 2002, p. 435). In 1947, Queen Elizabeth II extended an invitation to Indigenous Peoples to become citizens of the Dominion of Canada. However, Indigenous Peoples were first required to abdicate their Indian status to be legally recognized as a person and then expected to assimilate into dominant Canadian society as citizens (08-NWO, 2018; 10-NWO, 2018; 12-NWO, 2018; Cairns, 2000; Hawthorne, 1966; Sakej & Henderson, 2002). The majority of Indigenous people continue to decline this invitation.

The term "Indigenous citizenship" is precarious at best. It is encased in colonialist ideologies of statehood, nationhood, and citizenship. These are incongruous with Indigenous Peoples' worldviews on self-determination and nationhood (Borrows, 1999; Cairns, 2000; Centre for First Nations Government, n.d.; Indian Association of Alberta, 1970; Manyfingers, 1986; Sakej & Henderson, 2002; United Nations, 2007). Citizenship is based on perceptions of commonality amongst individuals with shared locality, values, histories, laws, politics, and purpose (Brodie, 2002; Cairns, 2000; Cohen, 2010; Galloway, 2017; Manyfingers, 1986; Nash, 2009; Sakej & Henderson, 2002). Colonialist ideals of citizenship as a contractual agreement between the nation-state, which provides citizens with specific benefits, and rights-bearing citizens who are economically "productive" citizens, do not align with Indigenous Peoples' concept of citizenship (08-NWO, 2018; 10-NWO, 2018; 15-NWO, 2018; Ariss & Cutfeet, 2012; Cairns, 2000; Cohen, 2010; Cornet, 2013; Lister, 1997; Nash, 2009; Sakej & Henderson, 2002). For Indigenous Peoples, citizenship is an inherent right based on kinship, tradition, customs, values, laws, and their connection to the land (Manyfingers, 1986; Mitchell et al., 2019; Papillon & Rodon, 2019). All Indigenous participants indicated that their unique connection to the land was the cornerstone of their common identity as stewards of the land for eternity. Today, in the era of twenty-first-century reconciliation, with constitutionally protected Aboriginal rights and treaty rights, and the increased recognition of the UNDRIP, First Nations are focused on protecting their right to self-determination and building vibrant rural communities.

Self-Determination

Indigenous Peoples' Aboriginal rights and treaty rights were protected under the Constitution Act, 1982, sections 25 and 35. Self-determination is not explicitly addressed in the Constitution Act, 1982, but it has become, as a constitutional right, the focus of Indigenous discourse. For example, in the Supreme Court of Canada (s.c.c.) decision in *R. v. Van der Peet* (1996), Justice L'Heureux-Dubé stated:

> It is fair to say that prior to the first contact with Europeans, the Native people of North America were independent nations, occupying and controlling their own territories, with a distinctive culture and their own practices, traditions, and customs (para. 106).

More recently, the U N D R I P is a cumulation of more than two decades of negotiations involving states and Indigenous Peoples. It marks the first time in history that Indigenous Peoples fully participated in the development of an "international legal standard for the protection of their rights" (Muehlebach, 2001, p. 415). Adopted as a Declaration, the U N D R I P is a non-legally-binding resolution that is arguably the most comprehensive international instrument on the rights of Indigenous Peoples (Asia Pacific Forum [A P F] & O H C H R, 2013). It establishes a universal framework of minimum standards for the survival, dignity, and well-being of the Indigenous Peoples of the world, and it elaborates on existing human rights standards and fundamental freedoms as they apply to the specific situation of Indigenous Peoples (A P F & O H C H R, 2013, p. 5).

The United Nations views the right to self-determination as a collective right held by all members of an Indigenous community or nation. Defined as "the right to autonomy and self-government in matters relating to their internal and local affairs...a foundational right, without which the other human rights of Indigenous peoples, both collective and individual, cannot be fully enjoyed" (A P F & O H C H R, 2013, pp. 18–19). The right to self-determination is considered the cornerstone of the U N D R I P.

Prime Minister Justin Trudeau's Liberal government affirmed the U N D R I P on May 10, 2016. In July 2017, the Liberal government published "Principles respecting the Government of Canada's Relationship with Indigenous Peoples." This document promises a "principled foundation for advancing renewed relationships with Indigenous peoples based on the recognition of rights" and to "fulfill [Canada's] commitment to implementing the UN Declaration" (Government of Canada, 2018).

Participants in this study acknowledged that the UNDRIP has the potential to strengthen their fight for self-determination significantly. However, they indicated that there is a lack of understanding among First Nations peoples at the community level about the implications of the UNDRIP. In our interviews, all First Nations participants, except three, indicated that they had little or no prior knowledge of the UNDRIP other than what they had seen sporadically in the news. Implementing the UNDRIP is viewed as a positive step toward reconciliation by Indigenous leaders and governments. If these findings are any indication of the situation as it exists across the country, people at the community level have little or no knowledge of the UNDRIP, and this carries the implication that it will have little or no impact.

The Implications of Free, Prior, and Informed Consent

Despite having limited knowledge of the UNDRIP, the participants in this study had a well-developed understanding of the concept of FPIC, which was discussed at length. Participants understood FPIC as a central tenet for self-determination as recognized in the UNDRIP. The right of FPIC is an "integral element" of the right to self-determination, and obtaining such consent is required in matters of fundamental importance for the rights, survival, dignity, and well-being of Indigenous Peoples (APF & OHCHR, 2013, p. 27).

Participants viewed FPIC as a mechanism through which the immensely unbalanced power between First Nations and the Crown could be realigned, creating a more equal nation-to-nation relationship (07-NWO, 2018; 08-NWO, 2018; 09-NWO, 2018; 10-NWO, 2018; 11-NWO, 2018; 12-NWO, 2018; 13-NWO, 2018; 14-NWO, 2018; 15-NWO, 2018). Free, prior, and informed consent has primarily become the international standard for measuring government legislation and corporate social responsibility, often replacing or expanding the current policies on the "duty to consult" (Fry & Mitchell, 2016; Papillon & Rodon, 2019). However, the interpretation and implementation of FPIC principles remain complicated. Many questions revolve around the meaning of "consent." Defining consent directly relates to the issue of ongoing power struggles between the colonized and the colonizers, who both seek control over natural resource development (10-NWO, 2018; 12-NWO, 2018; 13-NWO, 2018; 15-NWO, 2018; Coates & Favel, 2016; Obed, 2016; Papillon & Rodon, 2019). Participants agreed that the component "consent" is a right to "choice," a right to say "yes," "no," or "not right now." However, in discussions on veto rights, participants felt that the critical term "consent" could be interpreted as a "right to veto." They explained, however, that the idea of a "veto" is not a part of Aboriginal culture, and the idea does not align with Aboriginal values. They suggested that the "right to veto" should be eliminated, or strict guidelines should be developed outlining a veto process that applies to all levels of government.

First Nations' representatives expressed concern regarding the narrow scope of non-Indigenous discourse, which tends to focus on FPIC as a policy that applies solely to natural resources management. From their perspective, FPIC is a discursive tool that can be used to increase legitimacy in three overarching areas: self-determination, Aboriginal identity, and lands and resources. The development of FPIC legislation that adheres to Indigenous Peoples' right to self-determination is instrumental to the protection of Aboriginal identity—described as a system of traditions, beliefs, culture, language, and attachment to the land. Free, prior, and informed consent was viewed to be particularly important as a mechanism to ensure that their people are educated based on traditional Aboriginal ideology, rather than conventional western ideals (08-NWO, 2018; 09-NWO, 2018; 10-NWO, 2018; 12-NWO, 2018; 14-NWO, 2018; 15-NWO, 2018). Additionally, FPIC legislation must recognize Indigenous Peoples' relationship to their traditional lands and their resources (Mitchell et al., 2019; Papillon & Rodon, 2019).

Building Vibrant Rural Communities

Despite the many challenges rural First Nations communities face, Biigtigong Nishnaabeg and Netmizaaggamig Nishnaabeg First Nations are asserting their right to self-determination and growing vibrant, independent, rural communities. Both First Nations groups involved in this study have built extensive economic development portfolios that include interests in hydro, forestry, and mining. Biigtigong Nishnaabeg First Nation has an extensive energy portfolio and an independently owned logging company, while Netmizaaggamig Nishnaabeg First Nation has an extensive forestry portfolio, including an independently owned logging company and a majority stakeholder position in two sawmills located in White River, Ontario and Hornepayne, Ontario. Both First Nations are partners in Supercom Industries LP, a joint venture run by six First Nations communities whose traditional land will be crossed by the East-West Tie hydro expansion. At the time of our study, Supercom Industries LP provided training and "upskilling" for its 172 employees in heavy equipment operation, mechanical harvesting, commercial truck driving, tower assembly, and construction (02-NWO, 2018; 07-NWO, 2018).

Both First Nations provide specialized training for their community members, and participants indicated that an employment opportunity exists for every band member who is able to work regardless of whether if they live on or off the reserve (07-NWO, 2018; 11-NWO, 2018; 12-NWO, 2018). Both First Nations have developed customized education curriculum that incorporates their culture, values, and tradition, as well as the standardized elementary school programming from the Ontario Ministry of Education. Biitigong Nishnaabeg is in the process of building a state-of-the-art education complex. The facility will provide a new education model, developed exclusively around their own culturally appropriate Anishinabek curriculum. The 41,000-square-foot facility will include a daycare, kindergarten, classrooms for grades 1-8, and space for adult education, career training, and conference facilities, as well as a recreation centre. Indigenous and Northern Affairs Canada (INAC) has committed $11.2 million toward the $23 million project (Biigtigong Nishnaabeg, 2016; CBC News, 2018). Both First Nations are focused on retaining their youth through providing a diverse array of recreational programs based on Anishinabek traditions, values, and culture, and ensuring there are opportunities for education and employment security. Both communities have also adopted their own constitutions and laws, banned alcohol and non-prescription drugs on reserve, and developed customized health initiatives designed to improve the daily lives of their community members. For these communities, FPIC is not only viewed as a right, but it is also interpreted as a tool that allows them to utilize their limited resources, assert their right to self-determination, and protect their right to be rural.

Conclusion

The right to be rural is a complex issue with no straightforward solutions for the many rural communities struggling to survive in the twenty-first century. Despite the successes experienced by the Biigtigong Nishnaabeg and Netmizaaggamig Nishnaabeg First Nations, many other rural First Nations in Ontario continue to struggle. One only needs to look at the news to see headlines about First Nations plagued by mercury contamination, boiled water advisories, food shortages, youth suicide, and extreme poverty, and to realize that discussion on the right to be rural needs to expand beyond the lens of modern citizenship and make space for Treaty First Nations, who have a constitutionally protected right to be rural. For Canada to indeed reconcile with Indigenous Peoples, we must take a new approach to citizenship that allows for the recognition of both Canadian citizenship and rural Indigenous citizenship as two distinct but parallel paths to citizenship. Based on Supreme Court of Canada decisions, the Truth and Reconciliation Commission of Canada's (TRC) 94 Calls to Action (TRC, 2015), and UNDRIP's affirming of Indigenous Peoples' right to self-determination, policymakers must strive to adopt the UNDRIP into Canadian legislation in its entirety. This adoption must include a full FPIC policy that reaches beyond natural resources development, supporting all facets of Indigenous governance.

Although our research was limited to participants from a small geographical location within northwest Ontario, they provided a perspective on the UNDRIP and FPIC from a community level of governance, bridging a gap in the rural studies literature regarding the Aboriginal reality. Both the UNDRIP and FPIC are vital mechanisms in attaining self-determination and protection for rural Indigenous communities. Participants in this study were optimistic that the UNDRIP and FPIC could potentially become mechanisms for self-determination. However, the reality is that this will rely on implementing the UNDRIP and FPIC within the framework of Canadian constitutional law. Adopting the UNDRIP and FPIC into Canadian legislation is thus a monumental task. While there is no simple path to follow, Indigenous Peoples must be central figures in the development process. At present, we can conclude that the political rights of Indigenous citizens to consent—meaning to say "yes," "no," or "not now"—are not well known even within the Indigenous community. Much more work needs to be done to ensure Indigenous Peoples are empowered participants in the decision-making process.

Notes

1. All interviews for the research were part of the following study and were conducted by Satenia Zimmermann: "Corporate social responsibility, Aboriginal rights and the principle of free, prior and informed consent (FPIC): Lessons from Canada's forest sector: Northwestern Ontario case study." The case study was funded by the Social Sciences and Humanities Research Council of Canada for 2017-18.

2. Aboriginal demographic data from the 2016 Census was not complete: reserves in Ontario were not adequately enumerated in 2016. See note at the bottom of the Government of Ontario webpage *Indigenous Peoples in Ontario*, at https://www.ontario.ca/document/spirit-reconciliation-ministry-indigenous-relations-and-reconciliation-first-10-years/indigenous-peoples-ontario.

3. In order to protect the anonymity of participants in the study discussed in this chapter, each participant has been assigned an identification code (from 01-NWO through 18-NWO).

Interviews are cited using the assigned participant identification code and the year in which the interview was conducted.

References

Ariss, R., & Cutfeet, J. (2012). *Keeping the land: Kitchenuhmaykoosib Inninuwug, reconciliation and Canadian law.* Fernwood.

Asia Pacific Forum of National Human Rights Institutions (APF), & Office of the United Nations High Commissioner for Human Rights (OHCHR). (2013). *United Nations declaration on the rights of Indigenous peoples: A manual for national human rights institutions.* Sydney and Geneva: APF/OHCHR.

Barraclough, L. (2013). Is there also a right to the countryside? *Antipode, 45*(5), 1047-1049.

Bauman, Z. (2005, December). Freedom from, in and through the state: T. H. Marshall's trinity of rights revisited. *Theoria,* 13-27.

Belanger, Y. D. (2014). *Ways of knowing: An introduction to native studies in Canada.* Nelson.

Borrows, J. (1999). "Landed" citizenship and the multicultural welfare state. In J. C. A. C. Cairns (Ed.), *Citizenship, diversity & pluralism: Canadian and comparative perogatives* (pp. 72-86). McGill-Queen's University Press.

Brenner, N., Peck, J., & Theodore, N. (2010). After neoliberalization? *Globalizations, 7*(3), 327-345.

Brodie, J. (2002). Citizenship and solidarity: Reflections on the Canadian way. *Citizenship Studies, 6*(4), 377-394.

Cairns, A. (2000). *Citizens plus: Aboriginal peoples and the Canadian state.* UBC Press.

Canada, Indian and Northern Affairs. (1969). *Statement of the Government of Canada on Indian policy.* Ottawa: Department of Indian and Northern Affairs. http://epe.lac-bac.gc.ca/100/200/301/inac-ainc/indian_policy-e/cp1969_e.pdf

CBC News. (April 18, 2018). Northwestern Ontario First Nation secures $24 million funding for new education complex. Retrieved July 27, 2021 from https://www.cbc.ca/news/canada/thunder-bay/biigtigong-nishnaabeg-school-funding-1.4619054

Centre for First Nations Government. (n.d.). *Reclaiming our identity: Band membership, citizenship and the inherent right.* Retrieved July 27, 2021 from https://fngovernance.org/wp-content/uploads/2020/06/Reclaiming_Our_Identity.pdf

Coates, K., & Favel, B. (2016). *Understanding FPIC: From assertation and assumption on "free, prior, and informed consent" to a new model for Indigenous engagement on resource development.* MacDonald-Laurier.

Cohen, M. (2010). T. H. Marshall's "Citizenship and social class." *Dissent, Fall,* 81-85.

Cornet, W. (2013). Indian status, band membership, First Nation citizenship, kinship, gender, and race: Reconsidering the role of federal law. In J. P. White, S. Wingert, D. Beavon, & P. Maxim (Eds.), *Moving Forward, Making a Difference: Vol. 5. Aboriginal Policy Research Series* (pp. 145-164). Thompson Educational Publishing Inc.

Crown-Indigenous Relations and Northern Affairs Canada. (2021). *Treaties, agreements and negotiations.* https://www.rcaanc-cirnac.gc.ca/eng/1100100028568/1529354090684

Fry, B., & Mitchell, T. (2016). Towards coexistence: Exploring the differences between Indigenous and non-Indigenous perspectives on land. *Native Studies, 23*(1&2), 35-64.

Galloway, G. (2017, April 2). *Fort William First Nation accepts non-Indigenous man as full member.* https://www.theglobeandmail.com/news/politics/non-indigenous-cousin-in-fort-william-gets-full-first-nation-membership/article34558143/

Government of Canada. (2018). *Principles respecting the Government of Canada's relationship with Indigenous peoples.* http://www.justice.gc.ca/eng/csj-sjc/principles-principes.html

Government of Canada. (2019, November 14). *Indigenous peoples and communities.* Crown-Indigenous Relations and Northern Affairs Canada. Retrieved on July 27, 2021 from https://www.rcaanc-cirnac.gc.ca/eng/1100100013785/1529102490303

Government of Ontario. (2020). *Indigenous Peoples in Ontario.* Retrieved July 20, 2021, from https://www.ontario.ca/document/spirit-reconciliation-ministry-indigenous-relations-and-reconciliation-first-10-years/indigenous-peoples-ontario

Hawthorne, H. (1966). *A survey of the contemporary Indians of Canada: Economic, political needs and policies: Part I.* Government of Canada, Department of Indian Affairs. Queen's Printer.

Indian Association of Alberta. (1970). *Citizens plus: A presentation by the Indian Chiefs of Alberta to Right Honourable P. E. Trudeau, Prime Minister and the Government of Canada.*

Indigenous Foundations. (2009). *Terminology.* https://indigenousfoundations.arts.ubc.ca/terminology/

Lister, R. (1997). Citizenship: Towards a feminist synthesis. *Feminist Review* (57), 28–48.

Manyfingers, M. J. (1986). Determination of Indian band membership: An examination of political will. *The Canadian Journal of Native Studies, 6*(1), 63–75.

Marshall, T. H. (1950). *Citizenship and social class and other essays.* Cambridge University Press.

Mitchell, T., Arseneau, C., Thomas, D., & Smith, P. (2019, October). Towards an Indigenous-informed relational approach to free, prior, and informed consent (FPIC). *The International Indigenous Policy Journal, 10*(4), 1–28.

Muehlebach, A. (2001). "Making place" at the United Nations: Indigenous cultural politics at the UN working group on Indigenous populations. *Cultural Anthropology, 16*(3), 415–448.

Nash, K. (2009, December). Between citizenship and human rights. *Sociology, 43*(6), 1067–1083.

Nishga Tribal Council. (1980). *Citizens plus: The Nishga people of the Naas River in northwestern British Columbia* (2nd ed.).

Obed, N. (2016). Free, prior, and informed consent and the future of Inuit self-determination. *Northern Public Affairs, 4*(2), 38–41.

Papillon, M., & Rodon, T. (2019). From consultation to consent: The politics of Indigenous participatory rights in Canada. In A. Tomaselli & C. W. (Eds.), *The prior consultation of Indigenous peoples in Latin America: Inside the implementation gap* (pp. 261–275). Routledge.

R. v. Van der Peet, 2.S.C.R. 507 (08 21, 1996).

Sakej, J., & Henderson, Y. (2002). Sui Generis and treaty citizenship. *Citizenship Studies, 6*(4), 415–440.

Stasiulis, D. (2002). Introduction: Reconfiguring Canadian citizenship. *Citizenship Studies, 6*(4), 365–375.

Truth and Reconciliation Committee of Canada. (2015). *Truth and Reconciliation Committee of Canada: Calls to action.* http://trc.ca/assets/pdf/Calls_to_Action_English2.pdf

United Nations Declaration on the Rights of Indigenous Peoples (UNDRIP). (September 13, 2007). https://www.un.org/development/desa/indigenouspeoples/declaration-on-the-rights-of-indigenous-peoples.html

United Nations. (n.d.). *Indigenous peoples Indigenous voices: Frequently asked questions: Declaration on the rights of Indigenous peoples.* https://www.un.org/esa/socdev/unpfii/documents/FAQsindigenousdeclaration.pdf

V

The Right to Rural Policy

13

Density Matters and Distance Matters

Canadian Public Policy from a Rural Perspective

RAY D. BOLLMAN

Introduction

Section 6 of Canada's Constitution Act (1982) guarantees the right of mobility across Canada for citizens and permanent residents of Canada. Thus, citizens and permanent residents have, in the most basic sense, the right to be rural, insofar as they are legally accorded the right to move and stay wherever they wish, so long as they abide by certain rules of property and rents and do not infringe on the rights of another. However, as other chapters in this volume show, codified rights do not inherently translate into lived experience. This point is illustrated well by Canada's purportedly "universal" access to health services in rural and urban communities.

This chapter offers a conceptual framework through which to analyze rights, rurality, and access to services, using health policy and the delivery of health services as a case study to demonstrate the framework's utility. I propose that the concept of "differentiated universalism" identifies the key aspects of the right to be rural, and present a geographic or spatial concept of rurality, with two dimensions: low(er) density and/or long(er) distance to density. Together, these two concepts operationalize this discussion of the right to be rural. I bring both the differentiated universalism framework and my spatial concept of rurality to this examination of reasonable access to health care in Canada.

Rights, Reasonable Access, and Differentiated Universalism

As other scholars have noticed, there has been an "astounding" "transformation of Canada's rights culture over the past fifty years (Clément, 2017, p. 15), and a key aspect of that transformation was the articulation of rights and citizenship. Before the 1960s, demands for free speech and responsible government and integrated schools were premised on citizenship, rather than humanity. But, according to Clément (2017),

> by 1967, human rights had become the common vernacular for framing grievances... The pervasiveness of "rights talk" has since become manifest in almost every aspect of Canadian life...For many, this is a cause for celebration [but] there are implications to framing a broader range of grievances as human rights. Human rights is a discourse of absolutes: they are non-negotiable principals. Framing grievances as human rights places them above the pragmatic considerations of policy-making (pp. 16–18).

I believe it is possible to reconcile the notion of the right to be rural with the "pragmatic considerations of policy-making." I note that while the "absolutes" of the discourse of rights might well conflict with the pragmatics of policy, rights can exist only within a nation state that enforces them through law and policy, and (some) rights have demonstrably eroded over time as nation states have ceded (some) sovereignty to international markets (Bauman, 2005; Harvey, 2008).

The erosion of rights is perhaps most evident, in Canada, in the realm of what T. H. Marshall (1950) called "social rights": "the whole range from the right to a modicum of economic welfare and security to the right to share to the full in the social heritage and to live the life of a civilized being according to the standards prevailing in the society" (p. 11). Looking at urban and rural experiences of social rights, I note that residents in both types of communities are technically granted universal access to social programs, but in the implementation of these policies and programs, it is quietly stated that the policy/program ensures "reasonable" access. This is not a new modification of policy, but I propose that the hedging of an absolute right by promising a right to reasonable access has facilitated the erosion of social rights, and this invites a discussion of differentiated universalism.

The concept of differentiated universalism, derived from the influential work of Ruth Lister (1997), conveys the view that differentiated delivery mechanisms are required to deliver equal/universal access to a given service. For example, they are required to deliver equal/universal access to schooling to children with disabilities and to ensure equal/universal access to the workplace to women who bear children (Lister, 1997). Simply put, this is a recognition that equity does not always mean the same delivery mechanism for everyone.

In general, and notwithstanding the intense pull of family, finances, and place attachment (Alton & Low, 1992), individuals can choose whether to live urban or rural in a way that one does not really choose to be disabled or a woman capable of childbearing. However, differentiated universalism can be applied to the right to be rural, because, for one thing, urban society benefits from or needs the resources produced by rural society (such as lumber, oil, food, ski hills, canoe expeditions, etc.), and thus the rurality of some people serves an indispensable function for the rest of society. But the rationale goes beyond rural workers who provide goods and services (e.g., raw and manufactured goods, fly-in fishing excursions, etc.). For example, the forced relocation of (some) Inuit in the north was due, in part, to the desire to establish sovereignty in Canada's northern territories (Madwar, 2018). Given the lack of choice of the Inuit in this situation, differentiated universalism seems to be justified in this case in the argument for a differentiated mechanism to deliver universal access to social services (health, education, etc.). Generally, differentiated universalism justifies, in my view, a differentiated approach to delivering public services to the rural residents of Canada. But how does a policymaker begin? A first step, in my view, is adopting a suitably nuanced but precise operational definition of rurality.

The Spatial Dimensions of Rurality: Density and Distance-to-Density

Rural is a spatial concept (Bollman & Ashton, 2018; Bollman & Reimer, 2018, 2019; Reimer & Bollman, 2010; World Bank, 2009). Whether it is used for statistical, analytical, personal, or polemical objectives, "rural" implies something about the geographical location of its object. Even where rural is used in a metaphorical sense, or as a facet of identity, it implies actors in localities with low density and/or a longer distance away from higher density localities.

Thus, conceptually, rurality refers to individuals residing in geographical localities as specified by two dimensions: their density and their distance-to-density. Typically, density is indicated by the population size of a locality, and distance-to-density is indicated as the physical distance or the resources (time

FIGURE 13.1 The two dimensions of the rurality of localities: density and distance-to-density

	Index of rurality in the *density* dimension									
	(from lower rurality [i.e., higher density] to higher rurality [i.e. lower density])									
Index of rurality in the *distance* dimension	10	20	30	40	50	60	70	80	90	100
(from lower rurality [i.e., shorter distance] to higher rurality [i.e. longer distance])	(low rurality, high density)									(high rurality, low density)
10 (low rurality, short distance)										
20										
30										
40										
50										
60										
70										
80										
90										
100 (high rurality, long distance)										

and money) expended to travel to a locality of higher density. Adopting these indicators, it can be accepted that individuals are more rural if they reside in localities with a relatively low population and/or in localities with a relatively longer distance to higher density localities.

The relationship between the two is most usefully represented as a continuum—as illustrated in Figure 13.1. Individuals residing in a locality that falls into the upper-right-hand part of this diagram are residing in a smaller town (i.e., higher rurality in the density dimension) that is adjacent to an urban or metro centre (i.e., lower rurality in the distance-to-density dimension). Metro-adjacent individuals have easier access to urban or metro jobs and services (e.g., hospitals[1]) and to a larger market to sell their goods and services. At the same time, they are living in a small-town locality (i.e., higher rurality in the density dimension). These individuals likely experience a small town "way-of-living" (perhaps less air pollution, less crime, fewer traffic jams, etc.), but are able to access a metro market and metro services.

Individuals residing in a locality that falls into the lower-left-hand part of Figure 13.1 cannot (easily) access the market or services of an urban or metro centre (i.e., high rurality in the distance dimension), but are residing in a larger town (i.e., lower rurality in the density dimension). These individuals are constrained to "small-town" or "small-city" opportunities (e.g., employment or services), but are living in a locality with a higher population density that will support the availability of many services, such as those found in a regional service centre. In order to further illustrate the implications of this continuum-based definition of rurality, I apply it next to the context of health outcomes and services delivery in Canada.

Rurality and Health Outcomes

In the Constitution Act of 1982, one may not discriminate against a person based on their geospatial location (Deber, 2014, p. 12). However, I contend that the dimensions of rurality (density and distance-to-density) should be considered for each and every public policy or program. At one time this was attempted in Canada via a rural lens (Clemenson, 1994; Organisation for Economic Co-operation and Development [OECD], 2002, pp. 171–180; OECD, 2010, Box 4.2), managed by the federal Rural Secretariat, which was dissolved in 2013 after fifteen years of operation (Hall & Gibson, 2016).

The loss of the rural lens in Canada's parliament is significant, even if it achieved very little and was barely used during its short life. Policy is experienced differently for rural residents, and, arguably, policy should be adjusted and differentially implemented to try to ensure a common policy outcome for urban and rural residents. Health services are a prime example of how geospatial location— operationalized as a function of density and distance-to-density—limits the universality of purportedly universal public programs (Deber, 2014, p. 60, 117). Geospatial location affects people's health outcomes, their access to health services, and their community's ability to attract and retain health professionals.

Canada's health care system is known worldwide as an example of a universal, publicly funded system. But its definition of universality is actually that every Canadian should have "reasonable access to health services without financial or other barriers" (Government of Canada, 1985), and reasonable access has been interpreted with considerable elasticity. Two examples highlight this issue: first, individuals in Canada have the right under Canadian law to obtain an abortion, but the provincial health care system in Prince Edward Island did not provide this service up to 2017. Before that, individuals in Prince Edward Island who needed an abortion had to pay the transportation and accommodation costs to access an abortion in a different province (Cadloff, 2019). Second, residents of Nova Scotia who require a lung transplant are placed in a queue at a hospital in Toronto. CBC News reported that some individuals chose palliative care and an earlier death as they did not have the funds to travel to Toronto and to pay for accommodation (about $2,500 per month, less the $1,500 per month stipend offered by the Nova Scotia government) (Ray, 2019a). The provincial minister of health was embarrassed by this situation and subsequently increased the monthly stipend to $2,500 (Ray, 2019b). The main point in these two examples is that distance matters—not rurality, per se—and reasonable access does not tie, and has not tied, the government or service delivery partners to any concrete definition of a reasonable travel cost.

Fittingly, rural health care delivery has been a political issue in Canada for some time. In a report prepared by the Library of Parliament, John Wooton, at the time the special advisor on rural health to the federal minister of health, is quoted as saying, "if there is two-tiered medicine in Canada, it's not rich and poor, it's urban versus rural" (Laurent, 2002). Indeed, rurality has been found to impact health outcomes (among many others, see DesMeules & Pong, 2006; Mitura & Bollman, 2004). Some of the difference is simply that, in rural communities, there are relatively more children and seniors, lower incomes, seasonal employment, and thus higher unemployment rates over a given year, and occupations in resource sectors (agriculture, fishing, logging, mining) with a higher incidence of injuries. As a result of such social determinants, life expectancies are lower and self-reported health status is lower. However, Kapral et al. (2019) warn that "risk factor modification is a *necessary but insufficient* target for future interventions in rural areas" (p. 2; emphasis added).

Indeed, much of the research on rural–urban health differences identifies access to care, whether measured as proximity to a doctor or a hospital, as a primary differentiator—not disease prevalence or risk factors (cf. Ng, Wilkins, & Perras, 1993; Ng, Wilkins, Poole, & Adams, 1997, 1999; Oluwole et al., 2018; Pitblado & Pong, 1999; Pong & DesMeules, 2011; Pong & Pitblado, 2005). Access is especially difficult when it comes to medical specialists, such as perinatal services and newborn intensive care (Centre for Rural Health Research, 2012), and mental health professionals (Michelin, 2019; Uibu, 2019), and when access is constrained by rurality, the results, not surprisingly, can be life-threatening. As others in this volume, such as Kevany and Lauzon, illustrate, access to sufficient food can be more difficult in rural places, and this impacts people's health (see also Deber, 2014, p. 136). The examples are seemingly endless; rurality has also been found to increase the difficulty of escaping domestic abuse (Dawson et al., 2019, p. 22; Heck, 2019), the incidence of diabetes (Arnason et al., 2019), limited access to continuing care services (Brassolotto et al., 2018, p. 7), and a lower capacity to ensure safe drinking water (Deber, 2014, p. 147). Finally, density and/or distance-to-density impact a community's ability to attract and retain doctors and other health practitioners (Hallstrom et al., 2018, p. 79), despite rural living's advantages, such as easy access to nature, a safe(r) environment within which to raise family, etc. (Dhillon, 2016).

Optimistically, some communities have proactively overcome the rural disadvantage, investing in facility upgrades and direct recruitment (Ray, 2018; Robinson, 2019; Toth, 2018). Even these (sparse) examples of community success illustrate and emphasize the point that policy discussions should focus on a precise understanding of "reasonable" and "access" and associated costs faced by rural residents.

Implementing a Statistical Classification of Density and Distance-to-Density

In this analysis, density is represented as the population size of the locality where one resides. As discussed below, the measure of distance-to-density is a remoteness index of the cost to travel to a population centre of 1,000 or more inhabitants (Alasia et al., 2017), which I have selected from among many various approaches to measuring "distance"[2] (e.g., World Bank, 2016; Australian Institute of Health and Welfare, 2004; Cromartie & Nulph, 2019; Cromartie et al., 2012; Alasia et al., 2017).

Alasia et al.'s (2017) model, adopted here, is premised on the argument that the "cost of travel" provides a better continuous index of the degree of remoteness for each given locality, compared to the calculations used in other studies, because it recognizes the differing cost of toll roads, trains, ferries, and air flights to travel a given distance. For each geographic unit in Canada, they use:

- a gravity model that calculates the cost of travel to each population centre (of 1,000 or more residents) within a 2.5 hour time to travel; and
- the population size of each population centre, to calculate a population-weighted index of remoteness from each locality to a population centre. The use of the population of each population centre to weight the cost of travel is based on the expectation that a larger population centre would have a greater range of services and/or provide a wider range of market options for goods and services that could be provided by a given locality.

The resulting remoteness index is scaled from 0 to 1, where 1 is assigned to the locality with the highest calculated cost of travel.[3] The index for each other locality is the cost of travel for the given locality as a percent of the cost of travel for the most remote locality.

Similarly, Alasia et al. (2017) also calculated an accessibility index for selected services using the same general methodology. Rather than a population centre as the destination (and where the population size is used for weighting), each available destination is a census subdivision (CSD)[4] for the simple reason that data are available for each CSD for generating the weight for each CSD in providing a given service. The weight is the total revenue generated in a CSD by all enterprises providing a given service. Again, the CSD with the highest cost of travel is assigned an index value of 1, and then the index value for each other CSD is the cost of travel as a percent of the cost of travel for the CSD with a value of 1.

The Demographic Weight of Canadian Residents at Each Level of Density and Distance-to-Density

To divide Canada's population into a grid of density and distance-to-density (see Figure 13.1), I have classified individuals according to the population size (density) and remoteness index (distance-to-density, as per Alasia et al., 2017) of the CSD where they reside.

In 2011 (the year for which the remoteness index was delineated), there were 5,253 CSDs in Canada (see Table 13.1).[5] The modal group was 1,366 CSDs (26% of all CSDs) with a population of 100 to 499 inhabitants. There were 11 CSDs with a population of 500,000 or more.

Perhaps not surprisingly, most CSDs had a relatively lower remoteness index because the cost of transportation for each locality was calculated as a percent of the cost of travel for the highest-cost locality. The modal group was 1,438 CSDs (27% of all CSDs) with a remoteness index of 0.3 to 0.39 (i.e., their cost of travel to access a population centre, weighted by the size of the population centre, was 30–39% of the cost of travel for the highest-cost locality).

Looking at the number of "small" and "remote" communities, there were 1,877 CSDs (36% of all CSDs) with a population of less than 25,000 and a remoteness index of 0.4 or more (Group A in Table 13.1). In terms of the number of "smaller" and "more remote" communities, there were 527 CSDs (10% of all CSDs) with a population of less than 5,000 and a remoteness index of 0.6 or more (Group B in Table 13.1).

However, the demographic weight (i.e., the distribution of the population) gives a much different perspective. In 2011, the number of residents in CSDs with a population of 500,000 or more was 10.6 million (32% of all Canadians) (see Table 13.2). The population residing in a CSD with a remoteness index of less than 0.09 was 14 million (42% of all Canadian residents). In "small" and "remote" communities, there were 1.6 million residents (5% of all Canadian residents) residing in CSDs with a population of less than 25,000 and a remoteness index of 0.4 or more

TABLE 13.1 Distribution of census subdivisions by density and by distance-to-density

	Population size of census subdivision												
Remoteness Index (RI)	500,000 and over	100,000 to 499,999	50,000 to 99,999	25,000 to 49,999	10,000 to 24,999	5,000 to 9,999	2,500 to 5,000	1,000 to 2,499	750 to 999	500 to 749	100 to 499	Less than 100	All census subdivisions
	Number of census subdivisions												
Less than 0.09	6	19	15	24	49	30	19	13	3	3	3	2	186
0.1 to 0.19	5	13	18	24	79	106	114	202	64	65	99	40	829
0.2 to 0.29		7	9	9	60	96	124	204	63	94	168	89	923
0.3 to 0.39			5	11	34	39	82	269	131	176	462	229	1,438
0.4 to 0.49					10	39	68	137	78	115	311	158	916
0.5 to 0.59					3	2	25	60	20	41	166	117	434
0.6 to 0.69							4	21	15	19	77	112	248
0.7 to 0.79			GROUP A				1	14	12	17	53	59	156
0.8 to 0.89							1	9	13	11	22	10	66
0.9 to 1.0					GROUP B		1	4	3	2	5		15
No population												42	42
All census subdivisions	11	39	47	68	235	312	439	933	402	543	1,366	858	5,253
	Percent distribution of number of census subdivisions												
Less than 0.09	0	0	0	0	1	1	0	0	0	0	0	0	4
0.1 to 0.19	0	0	0	0	2	2	2	4	1	1	2	1	16
0.2 to 0.29		0	0	0	1	2	2	4	1	2	3	2	18
0.3 to 0.39			0	0	1	1	2	5	2	3	9	4	27
0.4 to 0.49					0	1	1	3	1	2	6	3	17
0.5 to 0.59					0	0	0	1	0	1	3	2	8
0.6 to 0.69							0	0	0	0	1	2	5
0.7 to 0.79			GROUP A				0	0	0	0	1	1	3
0.8 to 0.89							0	0	0	0	0	0	1
0.9 to 1.0					GROUP B		0	0	0	0	0		0
No population												1	1
All census subdivisions	0	1	1	1	4	6	8	18	8	10	26	16	100

Note: Adapted from "Census of Population: 2011," by Statistics Canada (Table 98-311-XCB2011006), 2012 (https://www12.statcan.gc.ca/datasets/Index-eng.cfm?Temporal=2011).

TABLE 13.2 Distribution of population of census subdivisions by density and by distance-to-density

Remoteness index (RI)	500,000 and over	100,000 to 499,999	50,000 to 99,999	25,000 to 49,999	10,000 to 24,999	5,000 to 9,999	2,500 to 5,000	1,000 to 2,499	750 to 999	500 to 749	100 to 499	Less than 100	All census subdivisions
					Population (× 1,000)								
Less than 0.09	6,905	4,047	1,134	822	828	209	66	25	3	2	0	0	14,041
0.1 to 0.19	3,693	2,182	1,308	866	1,165	760	394	332	56	41	33	1	10,832
0.2 to 0.29		1,052	642	292	895	679	450	317	55	59	49	4	4,493
0.3 to 0.39			365	378	499	254	290	425	113	108	137	8	2,578
0.4 to 0.49					123	258	227	209	68	71	90	5	1,050
0.5 to 0.59					38	13	87	99	17	26	45	3	329
0.6 to 0.69							13	30	13	12	20	2	91
0.7 to 0.79			GROUP A				3	21	10	10	14	1	59
0.8 to 0.89							3	13	11	7	7	0	41
0.9 to 1.0					GROUP B		3	6	3	1	1		14
No population													0
All census subdivisions	10,598	7,281	3,449	2,358	3,548	2,173	1,538	1,477	348	336	397	24	33,528
				Percent distribution of number of census subdivisions									
Less than 0.09	21	12	3	2	2	1	0	0	0	0	0	0	42
0.1 to 0.19	11	7	4	3	3	2	1	1	0	0	0	0	32
0.2 to 0.29		3	2	1	3	2	1	1	0	0	0	0	13
0.3 to 0.39			1	1	1	1	1	1	0	0	0	0	8
0.4 to 0.49					0	1	1	1	0	0	0	0	3
0.5 to 0.59					0	0	0	0	0	0	0	0	1
0.6 to 0.69							0	0	0	0	0	0	0
0.7 to 0.79			GROUP A				0	0	0	0	0	0	0
0.8 to 0.89							0	0	0	0	0	0	0
0.9 to 1.0					GROUP B		0	0	0	0	0		0
No population													0
All census subdivisions	32	22	10	7	11	6	5	4	1	1	1	0	100

Note: Adapted from "Census of Population: 2011," by Statistics Canada (Table 98-311-XCB2011006), 2012 (https://www12.statcan.gc.ca/datasets/Index-eng.cfm?Temporal=2011).

(Group A in Table 13.2). And in "smaller" and "more remote" communities, there were 205,000 residents (1% of all Canadian residents) residing in communities with a population of less than 5,000 and a remoteness index of 0.6 or more (Group B in Table 13.2).

Thus, in 2011, 36% of Canadian communities (i.e., CSDs) were "small" and "remote," accounting for 5% of all residents. "Smaller" and "more remote" communities accounted for 10% of all CSDs in Canada, and for 1% of all Canadian residents. Perhaps obviously, the thresholds used for classifying "small" and "remote" depend upon the issue under consideration. These thresholds are merely illustrative.

Population Size and Accessibility to Health Services

To classify Canada's population into a grid (see Figure 13.1) of density and accessibility to health services in particular, I have classified the population according to the population size of the CSD where they reside. To classify individuals according their accessibility to health services, I have used the index of accessibility to any health care or social assistance facility, as calculated by Alasia et al. (2017) and as described above. Each type of health facility has a specific industry classification code as defined by the North American Industry Classification system (Statistics Canada, 2017). Facilities defined as health care and social assistance enterprises are classified as NAICS 62.[6]

In 2011 (the year for which the accessibility index was delineated), there were, as before, 5,253 CSDs in Canada (see Table 13.3). Most CSDs had a relatively high accessibility to a health care service. In terms of the number of "small" and "low accessibility" communities, there were 2,945 CSDs (56% of all CSDs) with a population of less than 25,000 and an accessibility index of less than 0.81 (Group A in Table 13.3). And, for the "smaller" and "lower accessibility" communities, there were 701 CSDs (13% of all CSDs) with a population of less than 5,000 and an accessibility index of less than 0.70 (Group B in Table 13.3).

However, again, the demographic weight (i.e., the distribution of the population) gives a much different perspective. For "small" and "low accessibility" communities, there were 2.6 million residents (8% of all Canadian residents) residing in CSDs with a population of less than 25,000 and with an accessibility index of less than 0.81 (Group A in Table 13.4). And for "smaller" and "lower accessibility" communities, there were 284,000 residents (1% of all Canadian residents) residing in communities with a population of less than 5,000 and an accessibility index of less than 0.70 (Group B in Table 13.4).

TABLE 13.3 Distribution of census subdivisions by density and by accessibility to any health care or social assistance facility (NAICS 62)

	population size												
	Population size of census subdivision												
	500,000 and over	100,000 to 499,999	50,000 to 99,999	25,000 to 49,999	10,000 to 24,999	5,000 to 9,999	2,500 to 5,000	1,000 to 2,499	750 to 999	500 to 749	100 to 499	Less than 100	All census subdivisions
Index of accessibility to any health care or social assistance facility (NAICS 62)	**Number of census subdivisions**												
0.926 and over	11	19	12	13	12	8	3	1					79
0.9 to 0.925		10	15	24	80	62	51	65	14	11	14	4	350
0.875 to 0.89		10	10	9	21	50	67	120	48	49	67	25	476
0.850 to 0.874			7	12	46	51	51	88	26	27	47	29	384
0.81 to 0.84			3	10	54	85	113	216	76	110	234	118	1,019
0.77 to 0.80					19	43	89	227	114	154	373	176	1,195
0.73 to 0.76			GROUP A		2	12	41	120	59	94	291	148	767
0.70 to 0.72					1	1	13	29	14	43	112	69	282
0.60 to 0.69							9	55	32	42	168	143	449
Less than 0.60					GROUP B		2	12	19	13	60	146	252
All census subdivisions	11	39	47	68	235	312	439	933	402	543	1,366	858	5,253
	Percent distribution of number of census subdivisions												
0.926 and over	0	0	0	0	0	0	0	0					2
0.9 to 0.925		0	0	0	2	1	1	1	0	0	0	0	7
0.875 to 0.89		0	0	0	0	1	1	2	1	1	1	0	9
0.850 to 0.874			0	0	1	1	1	2	0	1	1	1	7
0.81 to 0.84			0	0	1	2	2	4	1	2	4	2	19
0.77 to 0.80					0	1	2	4	2	3	7	3	23
0.73 to 0.76			GROUP A		0	0	1	2	1	2	6	3	15
0.70 to 0.72					0	0	0	1	0	1	2	1	5
0.60 to 0.69							0	1	1	1	3	3	9
Less than 0.60					GROUP B		0	0	0	0	1	3	5
All census subdivisions	0	1	1	1	4	6	8	18	8	10	26	16	100

Note: Adapted from "Census of Population: 2011," by Statistics Canada (Table 98-311-XCB2011006), 2012 (https://www12.statcan.gc.ca/datasets/Index-eng.cfm?Temporal=2011).

TABLE 13.4 Distribution of population of census subdivisions by density and by accessibility to any health care or social assistance facility (NAICS 62)

	Population size of census subdivision												
	500,000 and over	100,000 to 499,999	50,000 to 99,999	25,000 to 49,999	10,000 to 24,999	5,000 to 9,999	2,500 to 5,000	1,000 to 2,499	750 to 999	500 to 749	100 to 499	Less than 100	All census subdivisions
Index of accessibility to any health care or social assistance facility (NAICS 62)	Population (× 1,000)												
.926 and over	10,598	4,047	916	452	232	56	10	2					16,314
.9 to 0.925		1,842	1,081	863	1,209	453	177	114	12	6	4	0	5,760
.875 to 0.89		1,393	720	309	322	344	232	193	43	30	23	1	3,611
.850 to 0.874			551	404	706	370	183	144	22	17	13	1	2,412
.81 to 0.84			181	329	784	575	409	340	67	69	69	5	2,827
.77 to 0.80					260	295	312	352	98	94	111	6	1,528
.73 to 0.76					24	75	137	184	51	57	85	4	618
.70 to 0.72			GROUP A		11	6	42	44	12	27	31	2	174
.60 to 0.69							29	88	27	26	45	4	219
ess than 0.60					GROUP B		6	17	16	8	16	2	65
ll census subdivisions	10,598	7,281	3,449	2,358	3,548	2,173	1,538	1,477	348	336	397	24	33,528
	Percent distribution of number of census subdivisions												
.926 and over	32	12	3	1	1	0	0	0					49
.9 to 0.925		5	3	3	4	1	1	0	0	0	0	0	17
.875 to 0.89		4	2	1	1	1	1	1	0	0	0	0	11
.850 to 0.874			2	1	2	1	1	0	0	0	0	0	7
.81 to 0.84			1	1	2	2	1	1	0	0	0	0	8
.77 to 0.80					1	1	1	1	0	0	0	0	5
.73 to 0.76					0	0	0	1	0	0	0	0	2
.70 to 0.72			GROUP A		0	0	0	0	0	0	0	0	1
.60 to 0.69							0	0	0	0	0	0	1
ess than 0.60					GROUP B		0	0	0	0	0	0	0
ll census subdivisions	10,598	7,281	3,449	2,358	3,548	2,173	1,538	1,477	348	336	397	24	33,528

Note: Adapted from "Census of Population: 2011," by Statistics Canada (Table 98-311-XCB2011006), 2012 (https://www12.statcan.gc.ca/datasets/Index-eng.cfm?Temporal=2011).

Thus, 8% of Canadian residents were living in "small" communities with "low" accessibility to health services. And 1% of Canadian residents resided in "smaller" communities with "lower" accessibility to health services. Please note that, importantly, these thresholds are merely illustrative.

Not surprisingly, the distribution of the population in terms of their accessibility to health services is shown to differ by province. For Canada as a whole, in 2011, 16.3 million residents had a high accessibility (index of 0.926 and higher) to health care and social assistance facilities (see Table 13.5). This represented 49% of all Canadians in that year. However, only five provinces had any individuals residing in CSDs with a health care accessibility index of 0.926 or higher (Quebec, Ontario, Manitoba, Alberta, and British Columbia).

The numbers in bold in the top panel of Table 13.5 shows the province/territory with the largest number of residents living at each level of accessibility to health care services. For example, the province with the most residents with an accessibility index of less than 0.60 was Manitoba, with 20,000 residents residing at this lower level of health care accessibility. For residents with a health care accessibility index of 0.60 to 0.69, the province with the largest number of residents in this category was Quebec (39,000 residents).

The numbers in bold in the middle panel of Table 13.5 shows the province/territory with the largest share of its population in a given accessibility index group. In the group of lowest accessibility (accessibility index less than 0.60) was 10% of the population of Yukon. In the accessibility group of 0.60 to 0.69 was 62% of the population of Nunavut. In the category with the highest level of accessibility (an index of 0.926 and higher) was 68% of Ontario's population.

To summarize the difference across the provinces/territories, provinces/territories were ranked by the share of their population with an accessibility index of less than 0.81. In 2011, all (100%) of the communities in each of the Territories had a health care accessibility index of less than 0.81 (see Figure 13.2). Prince Edward Island ranked 4th, with 54% of their population in this category, and Newfoundland and Labrador ranked 5th, with 48% of their population in this category.

However, the ranking of the provinces/territories is very different when looking at the absolute number of residents in communities with a health care accessibility index of less than 0.81. The province with the most residents (as opposed to the highest percentage) with a health care accessibility index of less than 0.81 was British Columbia, with 471,000 residents in this category (see Figure 13.3). This was followed by Quebec with 428,000 residents and Saskatchewan with 347,000 residents in this category.

TABLE 13.5 Distribution of population by accessibility to any health care or social assistance facility (NAICS 62)

Province/Territory	Index of accessibility to any health care or social assistance facility (NAICS 62)										
	0.926 and over	0.9 to 0.925	0.875 to 0.89	0.850 to 0.874	0.81 to 0.84	0.77 to 0.80	0.73 to 0.76	0.70 to 0.72	0.60 to 0.69	Less than 0.60	All census subdivisions
	Population (× 1,000)										
	(bold font shows largest absolute number in each column)										
Newfoundland & Labrador	0	0	106	24	139	93	86	**35**	29	2	515
Prince Edward Island	0	0	0	0	64	54	22	0	0	0	140
Nova Scotia	0	390	0	254	207	66	5	0	0	0	922
New Brunswick	0	0	195	94	303	152	6	0	1	0	751
Quebec	3,698	**2,054**	1,035	305	400	**290**	88	8	**39**	3	7,918
Ontario	**8,749**	1,948	**1,137**	472	321	135	55	18	26	18	12,879
Manitoba	664	0	5	217	142	68	45	22	26	**20**	1,209
Saskatchewan	0	222	193	47	225	197	94	29	23	5	1,034
Alberta	1,909	2	474	470	**530**	146	84	25	7	5	3,651
British Columbia	1,295	1,144	465	**529**	497	284	**117**	33	31	5	4,400
Yukon	0	0	0	0	0	23	2	1	4	3	34
Northwest Territories	0	0	0	0	0	19	7	1	13	1	41
Nunavut	0	0	0	0	0	0	7	2	20	3	32
Canada	16,314	5,760	3,611	2,412	2,827	1,528	618	174	219	65	33,528
	Percent distribution of population within each province/territory										
	(bold font shows largest percent in each column)										
Newfoundland & Labrador	0.0	0.0	20.6	4.7	26.9	18.1	16.6	6.8	5.7	0.4	100.0
Prince Edward Island	0.0	0.0	0.0	0.0	**45.5**	38.8	15.7	0.0	0.0	0.0	100.0
Nova Scotia	0.0	**42.3**	0.0	**27.6**	22.4	7.1	0.6	0.0	0.0	0.0	100.0
New Brunswick	0.0	0.0	**26.0**	12.5	40.3	20.3	0.8	0.0	0.1	0.0	100.0
Quebec	46.7	25.9	13.1	3.9	5.0	3.7	1.1	0.1	0.5	0.0	100.0
Ontario	**67.9**	15.1	8.8	3.7	2.5	1.0	0.4	0.1	0.2	0.1	100.0
Manitoba	54.9	0.0	0.5	17.9	11.8	5.7	3.8	1.8	2.1	1.6	100.0
Saskatchewan	0.0	21.5	18.7	4.6	21.7	19.0	9.1	2.8	2.3	0.5	100.0
Alberta	52.3	0.0	13.0	12.9	14.5	4.0	2.3	0.7	0.2	0.1	100.0
British Columbia	29.4	26.0	10.6	12.0	11.3	6.5	2.7	0.8	0.7	0.1	100.0
Yukon	0.0	0.0	0.0	0.0	0.0	68.7	5.2	2.9	13.0	**10.3**	100.0
Northwest Territories	0.0	0.0	0.0	0.0	0.0	46.4	17.0	2.6	31.1	2.9	100.0
Nunavut	0.0	0.0	0.0	0.0	0.0	0.0	21.0	**7.1**	62.0	9.9	100.0
Canada	**48.7**	**17.2**	**10.8**	**7.2**	**8.4**	**4.6**	**1.8**	**0.5**	**0.7**	**0.2**	100.0

TABLE 13.5 (CONT.) Distribution of population by accessibility to any health care or social assistance facility (NAICS 62)

Province/Territory	0.926 and over	0.9 to 0.925	0.875 to 0.89	0.850 to 0.874	0.81 to 0.84	0.77 to 0.80	0.73 to 0.76	0.70 to 0.72	0.60 to 0.69	Less than 0.60	All census subdivisions
	Location quotient: intensity of population share relative to Canada-level population share (bold font shows location quotients greater than 1)										
Newfoundland & Labrador	0.0	0.0	1.9	0.7	3.2	4.0	9.0	13.1	8.7	2.2	1.0
Prince Edward Island	0.0	0.0	0.0	0.0	5.4	8.5	8.5	0.0	0.0	0.0	1.0
Nova Scotia	0.0	2.5	0.0	3.8	2.7	1.6	0.3	0.0	0.0	0.0	1.0
New Brunswick	0.0	0.0	2.4	1.7	4.8	4.4	0.4	0.0	0.2	0.0	1.0
Quebec	1.0	1.5	1.2	0.5	0.6	0.8	0.6	0.2	0.8	0.2	1.0
Ontario	1.4	0.9	0.8	0.5	0.3	0.2	0.2	0.3	0.3	0.7	1.0
Manitoba	1.1	0.0	0.0	2.5	1.4	1.2	2.0	3.4	3.3	8.4	1.0
Saskatchewan	0.0	1.3	1.7	0.6	2.6	4.2	4.9	5.4	3.5	2.3	1.0
Alberta	1.1	0.0	1.2	1.8	1.7	0.9	1.3	1.3	0.3	0.6	1.0
British Columbia	0.6	1.5	1.0	1.7	1.3	1.4	1.4	1.5	1.1	0.6	1.0
Yukon	0.0	0.0	0.0	0.0	0.0	15.1	2.8	5.6	19.9	53.0	1.0
Northwest Territories	0.0	0.0	0.0	0.0	0.0	10.2	9.2	5.1	47.6	14.8	1.0
Nunavut	0.0	0.0	0.0	0.0	0.0	0.0	11.4	13.7	95.1	51.0	1.0
Canada	1.0	1.0	1.0	1.0	1.0	1.0	1.0	1.0	1.0	1.0	1.0

Note: Adapted from "Census of Population: 2011," by Statistics Canada (Table 98-311-XCB2011006), 2012 (https://www12.statcan.gc.ca/datasets/Index-eng.cfm?Temporal=2011).

In the Territories in 2011, 100% of the population resided in a community with an index of accessibility of less than 0.81 to any health care or social assistance facility.

In 2011, British Columbia had 470,000 residents residing a community with an index of accessibility less than 0.81 to any health care or social assistance facility.

Conclusion

To wrap up, I would like to review the policy approach to reconcile the policy objective of reasonable access and the rurality dimensions of low(er) density and long(er) distance-to-density. If one accepts that the dimensions of rurality are density and distance-to-density, and that every policy and program applies across the spatial dimensions of density and distance-to-density, it follows that crafting

FIGURE 13.2 Percent of population in low-accessibility index census subdivisions by province

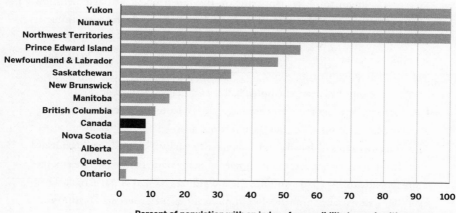

Percent of population with an index of accessibility to any health care or social assistance facility (NAICS 62) of less than 0.81

Note : Adapted from "Census of Population: 2011," by Statistics Canada (Table 98–311-XCB2011006), 2012 (https://www12.statcan.gc.ca/datasets/Index-eng.cfm?Temporal=2011).

FIGURE 13.3 Population (× 1,000) in low-accessibility index census subdivisions by province

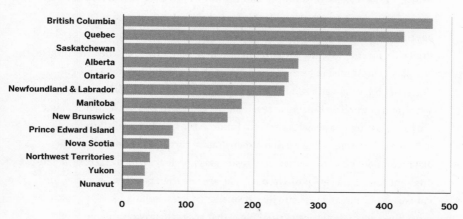

Population (× 1,000) residing in a census subdivision with an index of accessibility to any health care or social assistance facility (NAICS 62) of less than 0.81

Note : Adapted from "Census of Population: 2011," by Statistics Canada (Table 98–311-XCB2011006), 2012 (https://www12.statcan.gc.ca/datasets/Index-eng.cfm?Temporal=2011).

rural policy for any purpose requires an assessment of the implications of density and distance-to-density (Bollman & Ashton, 2018; Bollman & Reimer, 2018; Reimer & Bollman, 2010). By identifying the two independent spatial dimensions of rurality, this analysis has offered a practical, pragmatic rural lens for seeing the costs and benefits of different service delivery models for health care, and for evaluating the "reasonableness" of the right to access health care in Canada across the urban-rural continuum.

The rural lens has been attempted before in Canada (Clemenson, 1994; Organisation for Economic Co-operation and Development [OECD], 2002, pp. 171–180; OECD, 2010, Box 4.2), but the effort was abandoned (Hall & Gibson, 2016). Providing measures of density and distance-to-density is a necessary step toward recovering the rural lens, but action is needed. Some novel proposals have emerged more recently that seek to minimize the individual's burden of travel costs wherever they live, namely, through telecommunications (Blackberry et al., 2018) and even drones in emergency responses (Smee, 2019), and some have shown promise in reducing the cost of distance. Even Canada's own "telehealth" initiatives were developed not only to "share health-related information among various health care providers and health care settings," but also to "deliver services over large and small distances" (Laurent, 2002, pp. 19–20).

Another proposal would invite urban dwellers to travel to rural specialists instead of the reverse (or simply rewarding or incentivizing such a reversal with shorter wait times for care) (see Centre for Rural Health Research, 2017, 2018), but this would depend on the "willingness of urban surgical patients to travel to rural sites for care" (Centre for Rural Health Research, 2017, p. 3), when the reverse is typically presumed to be the option. Yet, such a proposal denotes a recognition that both urban and rural residents of Canada contribute to the economic, social, and cultural well-being of residents of Canada. In this sense, all residents are participating in a social contract to improve the well-being of all residents of Canada. However, the geospatial dimensions of rurality (i.e., density and/or distance-to-density) mean that rural residents experience this social contract in different ways. Some are positive, but many are less than positive. Generally, individuals would actually prefer to live in smaller centres (Bollman & Biggs, 1992, p. 14), but a major drawback of rural life is that access to private amenities (e.g., grocery stores) and to public services (e.g., education services, health services, etc.) is constrained (Rural Secretariat, 1999).

This discussion of health care shows that density and distance-to-density have important implications for the well-being of rural residents, compared to those living urban. Rural policy, by the very definition of rurality, should entail attention to density and distance-to-density for each and every policy proposal. None of this argument should imply that "the social and the market are separate spheres of activity, and that the constitution of the former is dependent [on] the level of development of the latter" (Siltanen, 2002, pp. 410–411). In other words, if differentiated universalism is predicated on the idea that individuals and communities' entitlements to rights depend on their contributions to the market, it will reproduce and intensify existing inequalities in access. Nevertheless, the dimensions of rurality operationalized in this chapter provide an empirical scaffolding on which to craft a plan for differentiated universalism for rural residents to receive reasonable access to public services.

Appendix

TABLE 13.A Examples of census subdivisions with an Index of Remoteness greater than 0.60

Name of census subdivision	2011 Population	2011 Remoteness index (RI)
Attawapiskat, ON	3,417	0.945
Pond Inlet, NU	1,549	0.850
Kuujjuaq, QC	2,375	0.828
Nain, NL	1,188	0.822
La Romaine, QC	1,016	0.790
Fort Simpson, NT	1,238	0.770
Shamattawa, MB	998	0.750
Blanc-Sablon, QC	1,118	0.728
Lac La Hache, SK	1,251	0.709
Buffalo Narrows, SK	1,153	0.683
Bella Bella, BC	1,095	0.670
Norway House, MB	4,758	0.646
Kugluktuk, NU	1,450	0.603

Note: Adapted from "Census of Population: 2011," by Statistics Canada (Table 98-311-XCB2011006), 2012 (https://www12.statcan.gc.ca/datasets/Index-eng.cfm?Temporal=2011).

TABLE 13.B Examples of census subdivisions with an Index of Remoteness of 0.4 to 0.59

Name of census subdivision	2011 Population	2011 Remoteness index (RI)
Bakers Lake, NU	1,822	0.597
Les Iles-de-la-Madeleine, QC	12,291	0.574
Arviat, NU	2,318	0.566
Mackenzie County, AB	10,927	0.550
Red Lake, ON	4,366	0.544
Hay River, NT	3,606	0.536
Havre-Saint-Pierre, QC	3,418	0.531
Wawa, ON	2,975	0.523
Guysborough, NS	4,189	0.519
Sioux Lookout, ON	5,037	0.510
La Loche, SK	2,611	0.508
Gaspé, QC	15,633	0.505
Channel-Port aux Basques, NL	4,170	0.500
Barrington, NS	6,994	0.492
Iqaluit, NU	6,699	0.480
The Pas, MB	5,513	0.479
Chibougamau, QC	7,541	0.466
Fort Frances, ON	7,952	0.461
Thompson, MB	12,829	0.429
Kapuskasing, ON	8,196	0.427
Prince Rupert, BC	12,508	0.424
Dauphin, MB	8,251	0.411
Gander, NL	11,054	0.409
Kimberley, BC	6,652	0.407
Powell River, BC	13,165	0.402
Eskasoni, NS	3,309	0.402
Boissevain, MB	1,572	0.401

Note: Adapted from "Census of Population: 2011," by Statistics Canada (Table 98-311-XCB2011006), 2012 (https://www12.statcan.gc.ca/datasets/Index-eng.cfm?Temporal=2011).

Notes

1. The characteristics of a locality do not define the rurality of a locality. Here, examples are used to illustrate the point. Although larger hospitals may be associated with larger localities, one would not expect a one-to-one relationship between a larger hospital and a larger locality.

2. The World Bank (2009, Chapter 9) acknowledged a third "D," namely "Division," which includes: a) the thickness of borders (e.g., tariffs, non-tariff barriers) for the transfer of goods, services, and people from one jurisdiction to another; and b) ethnic/cultural/language differences ("divisions") that sometimes constrain the transfer of goods, services, and people from one jurisdiction to another. Thus, access to services (or access to a market for one's goods or services) is often determined by more than density and distance-to-density.

3. Localities with the highest calculated cost of travel were typically in Nunavut (such as Grise Fiord), but the locality with the highest cost of travel (and thus assigned a remoteness index = 1) was the Weenusk First Nation (also known as Peawanuck), which is maybe 40 kilometres up the Winisk River from the community of Winisk on Hudson Bay in northern Ontario.

4. A census subdivision (CSD) is the general term for incorporated towns and incorporated municipalities, or areas treated as municipal equivalents for statistical purposes (e.g., Indian reserves, Indian settlements, and unorganized territories) (Statistics Canada, 2016).

5. Table 13.1 shows the count of CSDs for each size class of the index of remoteness. For examples of CSDs with a remoteness index greater than 0.6, see Table 13.A in the Appendix. Examples of CSDs with an index of remoteness of 0.4 to 0.59 are shown in Table 13.B, in the Appendix.

6. Enterprises classified as NAICS 62 include offices of physicians (6211), dentists (6212), other health practitioners (6213) (e.g., chiropractors, optometrists, etc.), out-patient care centres (6214) (e.g., family planning centres, community health centres, etc.), medical and diagnostic laboratories (6215), home health care services (6216), other ambulatory health care services (6219) (e.g., ambulance services, etc.), hospitals (622), nursing and residential care facilities (623), and social assistance (624) (e.g., child and youth services, individual and family services, community food services, vocational rehabilitation services, child daycare services, etc.). See Statistics Canada, 2017, "North American Industry Classification System: 2017," Ottawa: Statistics Canada, Catalogue no. 12-501, http://www5.statcan.gc.ca/olc-cel/olc.action?objId=12-501-X&objType=2&lang=en&limit=0.

References

Alasia, A., Bédard, F., Bélanger, J., Guimond, E., & Penney, C. (2017, May 9). *Measuring remoteness and accessibility: A set of indices for Canadian communities* (Catalogue no. 18-001). https://www150.statcan.gc.ca/n1/pub/18-001-x/18-001-x2017002-eng.htm

Alton, I., & Low, S. (1992). *Place attachment*. Plenum Press.

Arnason, T., Tanuseputro, P., Tuna, M., & Manuel, D. G. (2019). Municipal transportation policy as a population health intervention: Estimating the impact of the *City of Ottawa Transportation*

Master Plan on diabetes incidence. *Canadian Journal of Public Health, 110*(3), 285–293. https://doi. org/10.17269/s41997-018-0168-9

Australian Institute of Health and Welfare. (2004, March). *Rural, regional and remote health: A guide to remoteness classifications* (A I H W Catalogue Number P H E 53). http://ruralhealth.org.au/sites/ default/files/other-bodies/other-bodies-04-03-01.pdf

Bauman, Z. (2005). Freedom from, in and through the state: Marshall's trinity of right revisited. *Theoria* (December), 13–27.

Blackberry, I. D., Wilding, C. B., Perkins, D., Greenhill, J., Farmer, J., Bauer, M., Winbolt, M., Morely, C., O'Connell, M., & Morgan, D. (2018). Virtual dementia-friendly rural communities. *Australian Journal of Dementia Care, 7*(6), 11–13.

Bollman, R. D., & Ashton, W. (2018). Rural policy in Canada. In W. Meyers & T. Johnson (Eds.), *Handbook of international food and agricultural policies: Vol. 1. Policies for agricultural markets and rural economic activity* (pp. 149–180). Hackensack, NJ: World Scientific Publishing. https://doi. org/10.1142/10606-vol1

Bollman, R. D., & Biggs, B. (1992). Rural and small town Canada: An overview. In R. D. Bollman (Ed.), *Rural and small town Canada* (pp. 3–44). Thompson Educational Publishing.

Bollman, R. D., & Reimer, B. (2018, July 28 to August 2). The dimensions of rurality: Implications for classifying inhabitants as "rural", implications for rural policy and implications for rural indicators. Paper presented at the 30th International Conference of Agricultural Economists, Vancouver, BC. https://ageconsearch.umn.edu/record/277251/files/1467.pdf

Bollman, R. D., & Reimer, B. (2019). What is rural? What is rural policy? What is rural development policy? In M. Vittuari, J. Devlin, M. Pagani, & T. G. Johnson (Eds.), *The Routledge handbook of comparative rural policy.* Routledge.

Brassolotto, J., Haney, C.-A., Hallstrom, L., & Scott, D. (2018). Continuing care in rural Alberta: A scoping review. *The Canadian Geographer, 63*(1), 159–170. https://doi.org/10.1111/cag.12487

Cadloff, E. B. (2019, November 20). How PEI became one of the most accessible places for women's health care in Canada. *Chateleine.* https://www.chatelaine.com/health/pei-abortion-access/

Centre for Rural Health Research. (2012, May). *Access to maternity care: Distance matters* [Policy brief: Monitoring and maintaining quality of care series]. https://med-fom-crhr.sites.olt.ubc.ca/ files/2012/12/3-1-distance-matters.pdf

Centre for Rural Health Research. (2017, November). *Patients travelling from urban geographies to rural hospitals for procedural care: A realist consideration.* https://med-fom-crhr.sites.olt.ubc.ca/ files/2018/07/RER-Scoping-Review-Final.pdf

Centre for Rural Health Research. (2018, May). Urban to rural travel for surgical care [RER policy brief]. https://med-fom-crhr.sites.olt.ubc.ca/files/2018/07/RER-Policy-Brief-Final.pdf

Clemenson, H. (1994). Mandate for small communities and rural areas. In B. Reimer & G. Young (Eds.), *Development strategies for rural Canada: Evaluating partnerships, jobs and communities* (pp. 3–6). Rural Development Institute for the Agriculture and Rural Restructuring Group.

Clément, D. (2017). Canada's rights culture: Fifty years later. *C I T C Canadian Issues: 1967 to 2017: Canada transformed*, pp. 15–19. https://acs-aec.ca/wp-content/uploads/2019/05/CITC-2017-Fall-Winter.pdf

Cromartie, J., & Nulph, D. (2019). *Documentation: USDA 2010 frontier and remote (FAR) area codes.* Economic Research Service, U.S. Department of Agriculture. https://www.ers.usda.gov/data-products/frontier-and-remote-area-codes/documentation/

Cromartie, J., Nulph, D., & Hart, G. (2012, December 3). *Mapping frontier and remote areas in the U.S.* Economic Research Service, U.S. Department of Agriculture. https://www.ers.usda.gov/amber-waves/2012/december/data-feature-mapping-frontier-and-remote-areas-in-the-us/

Dawson, M., Sutton, D., Carrigan, M., & Grand'Maison, V. (2019). *#CallItFemicide: Understanding gender-related killings of women and girls in Canada.* Canadian Femicide Observatory for Justice and Accountability (CFOJA) and the Centre for the Study of Social and Legal Responses to Violence (CSSLRV), University of Guelph. https://femicideincanada.ca/callitfemicide.pdf

Deber, R. B. (2014). Concepts for the policy analyst. In R. B. Deber & C. L. Mah (Eds.), *Case studies in Canadian health policy and management* (pp. 1–93). University of Toronto Press.

DesMeules, M., & Pong, R. (2006, September). *How healthy are rural Canadians? An assessment of their health status and health determinants.* Canadian Institute for Health Information (CIHI). https://secure.cihi.ca/free_products/rural_canadians_2006_report_e.pdf

Dhillon, P. (2016). *The surprising lives of small town doctors: Practising medicine in rural Canada.* University of Regina Press.

Government of Canada. (1982). Constitution Act. https://laws-lois.justice.gc.ca/eng/const/page-15.html#h-43

Government of Canada. (1985). Canada Health Act. https://laws-lois.justice.gc.ca/eng/acts/c-6/

Hall, H., & Gibson, R. (2016, August). *Rural proofing in Canada: An examination of the Rural Secretariat and the rural lens.* http://ruraldev.ca/wp-content/uploads/2018/12/RuralProofinginCanada-HallGibson.pdf

Hallstrom, L. K., Dymchuk, E., & Woodhead-Lyons, S. (2018). Continuing care in northern Alberta: Capacity and collaboration. *Journal of Rural and Community Development, 13*(4), 66–86.

Harvey, D. (2008). The right to the city. *New Left Review, 53*(September–October), 23–40. https://newleftreview.org/II/53/david-harvey-the-right-to-the-city

Heck, A. (2019, February 19). Analysis: Isolated, abused, nowhere to go: The barriers rural women face leaving abusive relationships. *Orangeville Banner.* https://www.orangeville.com/news-story/9181979-analysis-isolated-abused-nowhere-to-go-the-barriers-rural-women-face-leaving-abusive-relationships/

Kapral, M. K., Austin, P. C., Jeyakumar, G., Hall, R., Chu, A., Khan, A. M., Jin, A. J., Martin, C., Manuel, D., Silver, F. L., Swartz, R. H., & Tu, J. V. (2019). Rural-urban differences in stroke risk factors, incidence and mortality in people with and without prior stroke. *Cardiovascular Quality and Outcomes, 12*(2), 1–10. https://pubmed.ncbi.nlm.nih.gov/30760007/

Laurent, S. (2002). *Rural Canada: Access to health care.* Ottawa: Library of Parliament, Parliamentary Research Division, Economics Division. Report PRB 02-45E.

Lister, R. (1997). Citizenship: Towards a feminist synthesis. *Feminist Review, 57*(1), 28–48.

Madwar, S. (2018, July 25). Inuit High Artic relocations in Canada. *The Canadian Encyclopedia.* https://www.thecanadianencyclopedia.ca/en/article/inuit-high-arctic-relocations

Marshall, T. H. (1950). *Citizenship and social class.* Cambridge University Press.

Michelin, O. (2019, February 10). "The hardest part of being in a Northern Indigenous community is all the deaths": Grieving becomes part of our culture as we face tragedies head on, again and again. *CBC News.* https://www.cbc.ca/news/indigenous/opinion-death-grieving-indigenous-labrador-1.5011436

Mitura, V., & Bollman, R. D. (2004, March 23). *Health status and behaviours of Canada's youth: A rural-urban comparison* (Catalogue number 21-006-X I E). https://www150.statcan.gc.ca/n1/en/catalogue/21-006-X2003003

Ng, E., Wilkins, R., & Perras, A. (1993). *How far is it to the nearest hospital? Calculating distances using the Statistics Canada Postal Code Conversion File* (Catalogue no. 82-003). Statistics Canada.

Ng, E., Wilkins, R., Poole, J., & Adams, O. B. (1997). *How far to the nearest physician?* (Catalogue number 82-003). Statistics Canada.

Ng, E., Wilkins, R., Poole, J., & Adams, O. B. (1999). *How far to the nearest physician?* (Catalogue number 21-006-X I E). Statistics Canada. https://www150.statcan.gc.ca/n1/en/pub/21-006-x/21-006-x1998005-eng.pdf?st=0RMZvCSJ

Oluwole, O., Rennie, D. C., Senthilselvan, A., Dyck, R., Afanasieva, A., Adamko, D. J., & Lawson, J. A. (2018). Asthma diagnosis among children along an urban-rural gradient. *Journal of Asthma, 55*(11), 1242-1252.

Organisation for Economic Co-operation and Development (O E C D). (2002). *O E C D territorial reviews: Canada.*

Organisation for Economic Co-operation and Development (O E C D). (2010). *O E C D rural policy reviews: Quebec, Canada.*

Pitblado, J. R., & Pong, R. W. (1999). *Geographic distribution of physicians in Canada.* Centre for Rural and Northern Health, Research Laurentian University. http://documents.cranhr.ca/pdf/distrib/GEOREPORT.pdf

Pong, R. W., & DesMeules, M. (2011). Patterns of health services utilization in rural Canada. *Chronic Diseases and Injuries in Canada, 31,* 1-36. http://www.phac-aspc.gc.ca/publicat/cdic-mcbc/31-1-supp/pdf/31supp1-eng.pdf

Pong, R. W., & Pitblado, J. R. (2005). *Geographic distribution of physicians in Canada: Beyond how many and where.* Canadian Institute for Health Information. https://secure.cihi.ca/free_products/Geographic_Distribution_of_Physicians_FINAL_e.pdf

Ray, C. (2018, February 20). This Ontario town is home to 8,000 residents—and 18 family doctors. *C B C News.* https://www.cbc.ca/news/canada/nova-scotia/physician-recruitment-goderich-ontario-success-1.4538925

Ray, C. (2019a, March 13). They face financial ruin to get a new lung. Some are choosing to die instead. *C B C News.* https://www.cbc.ca/news/canada/nova-scotia/lung-transplants-atlantic-canada-toronto-financial-cost-1.5047818.

Ray, C. (2019b, April 26). Lung transplant patients among those to benefit from travel allowance boost. *C B C News.* https://www.cbc.ca/news/canada/nova-scotia/health-care-lung-transplants-travel-allowance-1.5111969

Reimer, B., & Bollman, R. D. (2010). Understanding rural Canada: Implications for rural development policy and rural planning policy. In D. J. A. Douglas (Ed.), *Rural planning and development in Canada* (pp. 10-52). Nelson Education Ltd.

Robinson, A. (2019, January 27). Carbonear has a new research hub for rural health care. *The Compass*. https://www.cbncompass.ca/news/local/carbonear-has-a-new-research-hub-for-rural-health-care-278979/

Rural Secretariat. (1999). *Federal framework for action*. Agriculture and Agri-Food Canada.

Siltanen, J. (2002). Paradise paved? Reflections on the fate of social citizenship in Canada. *Citizenship Studies, 6*(4), 395-414.

Smee, M. (2019, March 28). Peel Region ponders adding drone-mounted, talking defibrillator to its EMS fleet. *CBC News*. https://www.cbc.ca/news/canada/toronto/peel-region-ponders-adding-drone-mounted-talking-defibrillators-to-its-ems-fleet-1.5074441

Statistics Canada. (2012). Census of population: 2011. Ottawa: Statistics Canada. (Table 98-311-XCB2011006). https://www12.statcan.gc.ca/datasets/Index-eng.cfm?Temporal=2011.

Statistics Canada. (2016). Dictionary: 2016 census of population. Ottawa: Statistics Canada. (Cat no. 98-301X-2016001). https://www12.statcan.gc.ca/census-recensement/2016/ref/dict/geo012-eng.cfm.

Statistics Canada. (2017). *North American industry classification system: 2017* (Catalogue no. 12-501). http://www5.statcan.gc.ca/olc-cel/olc.action?objId=12-501-X&objType=2&lang=en&limit=0

Toth, K. (2018, August 8). How the town of Inuvik, N.W.T., went from 1 doctor to 11, in just 6 years. *CBC News*. https://www.cbc.ca/news/canada/north/doctors-inuvik-shortage-1.4768986

Uibu, K. (2019, January 20). Mental health patients in rural Australia feel "forgotten", despite billions in funding. *ABC Wide Bay*. https://www.abc.net.au/news/2019-01-21/treating-mental-health-in-the-bush/10705826

World Bank. (2009). *Reshaping economic geography*. http://documents.worldbank.org/curated/en/730971468139804495/pdf/437380REVISED01BLIC1097808213760720.pdf

World Bank. (2016). *Measuring rural access using new technologies*. http://documents.worldbank.org/curated/en/367391472117815229/pdf/107996-REVISED-PUBLIC-MeasuringRuralAccessweb.pdf

14

Rural Citizenship Under the Impact of Rural Transformation

Unpacking the Role of Spatial Planning in Protecting the Right to Be Rural in Zimbabwe

JEOFREY MATAI & INNOCENT CHIRISA

Introduction

Rural transformation is a reaction to the forces of change exerted by the combined forces of globalization (Afshar, 1994), unequal spatial development (Unwin, 2017), as well as changes in political and administrative systems that impact on governance. This, in turn, affects rural citizens. Rural transformation impacts the relationship between individuals and the state, principally their rights, as espoused by Smith (2000, as cited in Yarwood, 2017). Rural citizens' ways of life, rights, and obligations, among other citizenship elements, are, in most cases, compromised. The aim of this chapter is to unpack the role of spatial planning in addressing rural citizenship challenges in the face of transforming rural places. The chapter argues that rural citizenship is under threat from rural transformation. The transformations are the resultant effect of, inter alia, urban bias and globalization. Spatial planning as a tool that transcends rural and urban administrative boundaries, coordinates and integrates development, and promotes equal spatial development can provide a lasting solution in guiding rural transformation in a manner that enhances the rights of rural citizens.

Background of the Study

One of the major characteristics of the twentieth century is the growing inter-connectedness between the global and local levels as well as between people and places (Afshar, 1994). Migration, politics, communication, technology, and environmental issues are increasingly becoming globalized. While globalization has positive aspects such as removing barriers to development, rural areas have struggled as businesses, even those based on resource extraction, have become more mobile and flexible. This pushes rural people to migrate to large urban centres (Unwin, 2007), and governments respond to the pressure of urbanization by concentrating their efforts on urban areas while paying little regard to rural areas, creating what Lipton (1977) termed "the urban bias." Urban bias then leads to spatial inequalities between rural and urban areas.

Political economy plays a critical role in the transformation of rural areas through the erosion of social systems (Brodie, 2002). In Zimbabwe, for example, the capitalist economic system and the segregation of society along racial lines had serious negative impacts on the rights of some groups of society to carry out their obligations as members of the Zimbabwean nation. Policies and laws were promulgated that limited the rights of the Black majority to access and perform certain economic activities. The Land Apportionment Act of 1930, for example, included a provision for the allocation of land on the basis of race (Chirisa & Dumba, 2012). The National Registration and Native Passes Act of 1936 and 1937, the Native Land Husbandry Act of 1951, and the Tribal Trust Lands Act of 1965, among other acts, had negative effects on the citizenship of the African nationals of Zimbabwe (Chirisa & Dumba, 2012), as these acts limited or totally removed their rights to perform certain duties and to access certain resources equally.

At independence in 1980, the new government's thrust was to redress the irregularities created by the colonial government through the adoption of a socialist approach (Rambanapasi, 1989). The government adopted policies that aimed at creating equal opportunities for all citizens by addressing the social and economic disparities created by the colonial government. However, the government moved from the socialist approach to a neoliberal governance system in the 1990s (Rambanapasi, 1989). Although this change was seen as a positive development from the economic perspective, the ideology resulted in a reduced role for the government in development programs and in the provision of social infrastructure in rural areas. Little attention was paid to citizenship rights. It is against this background that this study was conducted to unpack the role of spatial planning in addressing the challenges facing rural citizenship in the face of transforming rural spaces. Spatial planning affects the physical, social, and economic development of both rural and urban areas, can provide lasting solutions to the citizenship problems that the people in rural areas are facing. Thus, the study answers the question: can spatial planning improve the rights of rural citizens in the face of the changing realities of rural spaces?

Conceptualizing Citizenship, Rural Transformation, and Spatial Planning

The conceptual framework of the study is premised on the relationship between citizenship as a concept, rural transformation as a process, and spatial planning as a process and tool that is used to guide spatial development and governance. Citizenship, according to Brodie (2002), means membership within a bordered territory. It also defines the relationship between individuals and the state as well as the relationship between individuals through the lens of rights. Turner (1993, p. 2, as cited in Brodie, 2002) defines citizenship as practices that define a person as a competent member of society, and that shape the flow of resources to persons and social groups. Based on the characteristics of citizenship, it can be deduced that rural transformation is linked to citizenship in two ways, either as a factor influencing the transformation of rural spaces or as a product of the process of transformation. For example, changes in the economic systems of rural societies influence the flow of goods and services between rural and urban places. This relationship has the effect of either enfranchising or disenfranchising rural people.

Rural transformation also involves the reorganization of society in a given space (Berdegué et al., 2013). This reorganization can influence the production of the rural space, for example, in terms of who is involved in what and how, as well as how the various facets of citizenship, including the rights of the people, are affected by the reorganization of society in that rural space. Spatial planning, being a tool that shapes and makes places (Morphet, 2011) through the coordination and integration of activities in space, can influence the location of various activities and subsequently the flow of activities between places, that is, within rural places and between rural and urban places in a participatory manner (Nadin, 2007). Thus, spatial planning has the capacity to influence the nature of transformation in rural spaces in a participatory and sustainable manner, which in turn enhances rural citizenship and subsequently protects the rights of rural people. In a broader perspective, spatial planning has been adopted in the European Union to address imbalances between states. It has been adopted by countries such as Germany to address imbalances between rural and urban regions. Such adoption of spatial planning protects and enhances the rights of rural citizens by not only ensuring that there is minimum bias toward urban areas, but also by ensuring the equal distribution of resources between urban and rural places.

Theoretical Framework

The study is informed by two theories: the right to the city and Lipton's urban bias theory. The choice of theories is based on the prescriptive and explanatory capacity of the two theories in the context of the study, in which there is a need to explain the nature of rural transformation, particularly as a product of the urbanization process (Chung, 2013), and to give direction on the way forward through a guiding framework that ensures the production of rural spaces that enhance rural citizenship rights.

The Right to the City

Propounded by Henri Lefebvre in 1996, this theory explains how space in the city is created (Wilson, 2011). It identifies three dimensions of space, namely, the perceived space, the conceived space, and the lived space. Production of urban space, therefore, equates to the production of all the aspects of urban life as defined by the three dimensions of urban space (Munya et al., 2015). The theory states that the production of urban space is underpinned by the principles of participation and appropriation. The participation principle gives a central role in the production of urban space to the citizens, while the principle of appropriation advocates that citizens should access, occupy, and use that urban space. Although this theory focuses on urban space production, its relevance to this study cannot be overlooked. The production of urban space relates to the process of urbanization, and urbanization is directly and indirectly linked to the transformation of rural areas (Isserman, 2001; H. Long et al., 2011). Munya et al. (2015), for example, posit that urbanization is driven by energy that is mostly generated or obtained in rural areas, often at the expense of the rural area with little or no recompense.

Barraclough (2013), on the other hand, argues that although the theory is about the right to the city, Lefebvre did not define a city as a central place nor as urban, but rather as a space of use-value where people meet, confront their differences, reciprocate knowledge, and acknowledge ideological and political confrontation as well as ways of living. This perspective indicates that the right to the city can be "created anywhere and everywhere, including in the places we imagine as rural" (Barraclough, 2013, p. 1047). In the context of this study, the theory enfranchises rural citizens to participate in the creation of their spaces, and in indicating the potential role of both rural and urban citizens, to take part in the shaping of spaces in rural areas. It also emphasizes the rights of rural citizens to access, occupy, and use space as members of the community. However, the theory does not acknowledge the role of exogenous forces in influencing the production of space, for example, the influence of globalization on local activities that shape space production.

Lipton's Urban Bias Theory

The main thrust of urban bias theory is to illustrate that the most important class conflict in poor countries is between the rural and urban classes (Lipton, 1977). The main argument put forward by the theory is that people in the urban areas are powerful such that they have the capacity to direct a lopsided share of resources for their own interests and away from the rural population, thus creating an urban bias. This not only makes the rural people poor, but it creates inequalities within rural areas due to the biased nature of development policies (Lipton, 1982, as cited in Unwin, 2017). According to the theory, the town benefits from cheap surpluses in the form of food and other exportable goods. In the process, some rural elites benefit from a perceived unholy alliance with urban elites, as espoused in the cumulative causation hypothesis introduced by Gunnar Myrdal (Fujita, 2007). It is this kind of relationship that makes rural areas poorer while urban areas generally develop. Although the theory is not exhaustive in its explanation of these inequalities, it goes a long way in explaining the unbalanced relationship between rural and urban areas, which in turn disenfranchises rural people's rights, in some ways, to equal opportunities for social and economic activities. It also explains the unequal distribution of resources between rural and urban areas, which again challenges the rights of rural citizens.

Literature Review

Citizenship can be described in different ways, and the emphasis given to the various elements of citizenship influences how citizenship can be defined in a specific context. According to Smith (2000, as cited in Yarwood, 2017), citizenship describes a person's relationship with the state, particularly through the lens of rights and duties that are associated with the relationship. This concurs with Lister's (1997) definition, which relates citizenship to a set of rules that govern how individuals relate to the state and how individuals relate among themselves.

This includes what individuals are entitled to and what they are obliged to do as members of a community.

Marshall's ground-breaking achievement expands citizenship beyond the concept of individual freedom to one that embraces social and economic rights (Marshall, 1950, as discussed in Somers, 1994). Following Marshall's work, citizenship can be viewed from three perspectives that include legal (civil), political, and social rights. Civil rights are associated with an individual's formal liberties, for example, the right to associate, the right to justice, and the right to be freely employed for payment, while political rights connote one's ability to vote or participate in political offices. Social rights go beyond legal and political rights to include access to a minimum level of security in economic terms for every member of the national state (Brodie, 2002). In line with the right to rurality, despite the importance of all the elements of citizenship, the social component of citizenship is of critical importance to this study, as it provides avenues for popular participation in social and economic activities (Turner, 2001). These avenues are critical in shaping the flow of resources to individuals and social groups (Brodie, 2002), as well as in shaping rural spaces, as espoused by Cloke, Marsden, and Mooney (2006), as it is through working, acting, and living in space that rural space is shaped.

Yarwood (2017) adds the spatial dimension to the description of citizenship and argues that space is critical because it determines one's belongingness to a given locality and also what they are entitled to and obliged to do. For example, local spaces offer crucial settings for engagement in activities and/or events such as voting in local elections, volunteering in service provision, and simply staying there as a local citizen. Such activities and engagements can be carried out within defined localities. Besides being exercised in defined territories, they also shape the spaces within such territories; for example, participating in elections will result in the selection of a representative who can work toward enfranchising or disenfranchising the local people's citizenship rights. However, Nash (2009) is of the view that the relationship between citizenship and nationality is challenged by the processes and discourses of globalization, which question the relevance of political participation in cases where issues are framed in terms of the interests and values of citizens whose states are separate and distinct. Although the overview of citizenship given above is not complete, it fulfills the purpose of this chapter in that it clearly indicates the dimensions of citizenship that can influence or be influenced by rural transformation processes that warrant intervention through spatial planning.

Rural transformation is a process of complete change in society in which rural societies diversify their livelihood activities, reducing their dependence on agriculture (Berdegué et al., 2013). Unwin (2017) argues that although rural transformation can be seen as a process, it is also a product of deeper structural transformations of society. Using the definition of structural transformation by Herrendorf, Rogerson, and Valentinyi (2014), rural transformation is a product of the "reallocation of economic activity across the broad sectors of agriculture, manufacturing and services" (p. 3). Therefore, rural transformation is caused by social, cultural, political, and economic activities that drive changes in the agricultural, manufacturing, and services sectors.

One of the factors driving rural transformation is the diversification of rural economies (Berdegué et al., 2013). Diversification influences the transformation of rural areas through an increase in agricultural labour productivity. Increased labour productivity in agriculture drives some rural people from agricultural employment to non-farm employment; the result of this is increased disposable income and, consequently, the investment of surplus income in non-farm activities. However, there are instances where the surplus is invested in urban areas. This situation results in disinvestment in rural areas and promotes further exploitation of rural resources.

The urbanization of rural areas (Berdegué et al., 2013; Chung, 2013; Johnson, 2001; N. Long et al., 2010) is another way in which rural spaces are transformed. This has consequential effects on the rights of rural citizens. Kuhn (2008) argues that most of the people who are becoming urbanized are not migrating into urban areas, but rather are living an urban life in areas that were formally classified as rural areas. While these forces of transformation cannot be directly linked to citizenship, the literature shows that there is an existing relationship. For example, if rural areas increasingly become urbanized, there is an accompanying provision of services such as health facilities, improved educational facilities, transport infrastructure, and shopping facilities, which, according to Cresswell (2009), are critical in achieving social welfare rights; thus, their provision in rural places enhances rural citizenship rights. However, rural transformation through urbanization can have negative effects on the rural areas' economies, sustainability, and inclusivity. For example, urbanization of rural areas consumes valuable agricultural land and ecological resources such as waterways and forests (Kuhn, 2008).

Rural transformation can therefore be seen as a function of the double effect of the cumulative growth of existing cities and the urbanization of rural areas. Since cities grow by exploiting rural resources (Munya et al., 2015; Schaeffer et al., 2013; Unwin, 2017), Barraclough (2013) argues that the lives of people in rural areas are overwhelmingly influenced by decision-making in the city. Although Barraclough (2013) goes on to state that this entails rural people being linked and entitled to the right to the city, it can be argued that it also limits the rural people's rights as their role and sense of being are no longer endogenous, but instead are a product of the interaction of exogenous forces.

Considering that there are inequalities between rural and urban areas (Unwin, 2007) that result in the disenfranchisement of, or that at least compromise, rural people's citizenship rights, Kuhn (2008) suggests that there is a need to develop policy interventions that are integrative and complementary to avoid the dichotomy between rural and urban areas. Spatial planning, described by Waterhout (2008) as methods that are largely used by the government to guide the spatial distribution of activities in order to create a rational organization of land uses and linkages between those land uses, can be used to influence the relationship between rural and urban areas and the flows that accompany the rural–urban relationship.

In summary, rural transformation is a product of the interaction of social, physical, political, cultural, and economic processes. The nature of this interaction can have positive or negative effects on rural citizenship. While rural transformation has been studied extensively (Berdegué et al., 2013; Chung, 2013; Cloke et al., 2006; N. Long et al., 2010), as has citizenship (Barraclough, 2013; Bauman, 2005; Turner, 2001; Yarwood, 2017), no study has been conducted to unpack the relationship between the processes of transformation that rural areas are undergoing and their consequential effects on rural citizenship rights. It is, therefore, the objective of this study to unravel this relationship. The following section outlines the methodology that was used to uncover what is happening on the ground.

Methodology

The aim of this research is to examine the role of spatial planning in addressing rural citizenship challenges in the face of continuously changing rural places. To achieve this objective, we adopted an exploratory approach, conducting a desk review and key informant interviews with purposefully selected persons in relevant central government departments and local authorities. In undertaking the study, a number of ethical considerations were adopted. Consent was sought before the interviews were conducted and information from the respondents was treated with high levels of confidentiality. Anonymity was ensured by withholding the names of the participants. The collection of data was focused on rural citizenship in the face of transforming rural places, and on exploring the potential of spatial planning in addressing the consequential effects of rural transformation on rural citizenship rights. The desktop review, based on an analysis of existing literature and of relevant government policy documents influencing rural transformation and citizenship, began the data collection process. Interviews with key informants played a complementary role, ensuring that the collected data was reliable and valid. Thus, interviews were conducted with provincial heads of government departments specializing in spatial planning and rural development. Officials from local planning authorities were also interviewed to provide data on how transformations in rural areas were impacting on rural citizenship. While the review may not be exhaustive, it provides adequate information to give insights and lessons about the role of spatial planning in responding to the effects of urbanization and rural transformation on rural citizenship.

Results

This section presents the findings in line with the study objectives. The findings focus on the nature of rural transformation taking place in Zimbabwe and its effect on the citizenship of people living in rural communities. A section on citizenship in Zimbabwe will be presented first for context.

Citizenship in Zimbabwe

Citizenship in Zimbabwe is about belonging, identity, and access to rights, benefits, and privileges. The Zimbabwe Citizenship Bill (2018) states that a Zimbabwean citizen is entitled to the rights, privileges, and benefits of citizenship and is equally subjected to the duties and obligations of citizenship. Among the rights that are pertinent to this research are: the right to have access to basic health care services, including reproductive health care services, the right to have access to education, and the rights to vote and to access information. These rights have spatial implications in that, for them to be exercised in an equal manner, there is a need for spatial distribution that enhances access. If, for example, there is a need to ensure that everyone has access to education, information, and health care, certain types of infrastructure should be distributed across the nation in a manner that ensures that every citizen can access them. Similarly, if one is to participate in local elections, they should have a defined geographic location where they can participate in making decisions. This contextualized overview of citizenship in Zimbabwe enables analysis of the effects of rural transformation on citizenship and of how spatial planning can be integrated into a rural citizenship and rural transformation system.

Characterizing Rural Transformation in Zimbabwe

Rural transformation is taking various pathways, either confirming or disproving some of the theoretical and conceptual explanations of rural transformation espoused in the preceding sections. Urbanization is among the main factors influencing the transformation of rural places. Diversification of economic activities is also evident in most parts of rural Zimbabwe, while unevenness, poverty traps, and inequality traps also characterize transformation in the country.

Urbanization is one of the prominent features of Zimbabwe's space. Infrastructure and Cities for Economic Development (ICED) (2017) states that there is rapid urban growth in some cities and towns, urban sprawl, and provincial variations. In 2002, Zimbabwe's urban population was 4,029,707, which grew by 6.31% to 4,284,145 in 2012, an increase of 0.63% per year (Mbiba, 2017). The Zimbabwe National Statistics Agency and United Nations Population Fund (2015) projects this urban population will reach 5,826,082 by 2025, up from 4,284,145 in 2012. The movement is propelled by a general decline in agricultural production in rural areas owing to an increase in the price of agricultural inputs, unreliable rainfall patterns due to climate change, and discouraging market prices for agricultural products. The poor state and lack of social and economic infrastructure in rural places are also encouraging the increased rate of population movement to urban areas as people seek better educational and health facilities. Besides the increase in the number of people in existing urban centres, Zimbabwe is also experiencing an increase in the number of urban centres. To date, there are 472 small urban centres (ICED, 2017). This means that Zimbabwe's rural areas are also urbanizing, a feature that explains the transformation of rural places in the country. Thus, besides the changes in rural places through the sprawl of existing urban centres, there is an increase in the number of urban centres as the population increases. Scoones (2016) notes that there are many more retail outlets—shops, bars, butchers, and various sorts of service providers ranging from tailors to hairdressers.

Besides these urbanization processes, rural inhabitants in Zimbabwe are transforming economically. The rural populations in most parts of the country have incorporated non-farm activities, and in some instances have completely shifted from agricultural activities to other economic activities. Data gathered from interviews shows that rural households have a diversified income portfolio. There has been a general reduction in agricultural activities in favour of non-farming activities in rural Zimbabwe despite the increased access to land through the Fast Track Land Reform Programme. However, contrary to the view that diversification is a product of increased agricultural production (Berdegué et al., 2013), Zimbabwe's rural diversification is a response to the structural transformation and shocks that the rural people are exposed to (Ersado, 2000; Herrendorf et al., 2014; Hoddinott, 2006; Mutenje et al., 2010). Thus, the increase in the prices of agricultural inputs due to economic instability, the unreliable rainfall patterns, and the associated droughts have pushed people to resort to non-farm activities, including mat weaving in low veld areas such as Nyanyadzi and Birchnough Bridge, timber production using mobile sawmills in the eastern regions, carpentry, welding, and vending, among multiple other non-farm activities. However, there are diversifications emanating from improved agricultural activities and infrastructural investment programs such as rural electrification programmes.

In Zimbabwe, the majority of rural citizens are trapped in poverty. The percentage of rural people living below the poverty line in Zimbabwe was reported at 84.3 % in 2011, according to the Zimbabwe Poverty Report of 2017 (ZimStat, 2017). A study of three districts covering rural areas by Chiripanhura (2010) outlines that Zimbabwe has been trapped in poverty since the year 1997. The most severe form of poverty that people in rural Zimbabwe are experiencing is income poverty, which makes it difficult for people to invest in assets that enable them to diversify their income generation activities. Although asset poverty is one of the poverty traps affecting rural citizens, Chiripanhura (2010) argues that it is less severe than income poverty. Zimbabwe is also characterized by inequalities spatially, economically, and socially. The high proportion of poverty rates prevalent in the country today are deeply rooted in these inequalities, some of which were introduced through colonialism (Mupetesi et al., 2017). Rambanapasi (1989) indicates that there are some regional inequalities, as the levels of development between the rural and urban regions are different. Although the government has tried to address the unevenness through adopting various policies such as the Growth with Equity (GWE) and decentralization, the differences persist. This unevenness has trapped rural citizens as it prevents them from growing economically, forcing them to remain behind while the developed urban regions continue to grow.

Discussion

The previous section provided a general overview of citizenship and the transformations taking place in Zimbabwe's rural places. The findings show that Zimbabwe's rural places are going through transformations that are manifesting in various ways, such as through urbanization and diversification. Unevenness, poverty, and inequality traps are also a common feature of Zimbabwe's rural landscape. The question is: how do these transformations impact on the citizenship of rural people? This section provides a discussion on how the various forms of transformation in rural places in Zimbabwe are affecting rural citizenship.

The increased number of urban inhabitants due to rural–urban migration is one of the characteristic features of urbanization in Zimbabwe. This increase accompanied by a general decline in the rural population can force the government to shift its focus to the urban areas in trying to address urbanization problems such as housing needs, informality, water supply problems, infrastructure upgrading and installation to keep up with the swelling urban population, and urban food security, among other issues. Similarly, policymakers being politicians, they are likely to concentrate on impressing the urban population, which can determine their return to office through elections because of their voting power.

In terms of industry, industrial operations find it profitable to locate their activities in large cities because the large population provides suitable opportunities for industrial growth. For example, cities provide more labour at a lower cost due to the increased concentration of unemployed people, as well as a ready market for industrial outputs. However, the growth of industry in urban areas does hold negative externalities for the rural areas, such as the overexploitation of natural resources and pollution, among others. These urbanization-related problems affect rural citizenship in a number of ways. First, the shift of focus to urban centres means that infrastructural (both social and economic) investment in rural areas is reduced. This affects rural people's access to some social services such as quality education and health. However, it should be noted that the urbanization of rural areas does hold some advantages for rural citizens. Development of urban settlements attracts investment in infrastructure, which is very useful in the protection and enhancement of rural citizenship.

Diversification of livelihood strategies, on the other hand, explains transformation in the economic systems of the rural communities. Although diversification is generally good for protecting rural people from shocks and disasters, most of the alternatives employed are environmentally destructive. Tree cutting for timber production, mining, and rudimentary industrial activities all contribute to the degradation of the natural environment. This affects rural people's access to the environment, particularly in the time to come. Unevenness, inequality traps, and poverty traps are also influencing the nature and rate of transformations taking place in rural areas. Uneven development is one of the factors driving rural–urban migration as people seek residency in developed places where access to quality education and health facilities and economic opportunities is easy. This further reinforces unevenness and impacts on rural citizens' access to basic facilities and employment opportunities. Poverty traps further make the poor people poorer as they cannot find alternatives to make ends meet. Ultimately, they remain poor and unable to exercise their rights as citizens. The integration of spatial planning in policy formulation and the planning of rural and urban areas can address the problems accompanying rural transformation in Zimbabwe. Spatial planning allows for the coordination and integration of policies and programs that affect rural and urban development. In this way, urban bias is eliminated from the investment framework and substituted with equity. Spatial planning can also influence the location of land use activities in space. As such, it can be a suitable tool to address the problem of the cumulative location of economic activities in developed places and distribute them across space.

Conclusion

The study has revealed four main issues. First, citizenship is tied to the spatial configuration of activities. That is to say, citizenship is enhanced by certain facilities that can effectively work if they are spatially distributed in a manner that allows them to be accessed and used with ease by the citizens. Examples are education and health facilities, whose location relative to the citizens determines the extent to which an individual's right to access them is met. Therefore, the use of spatial planning to influence the location of such facilities will, in some way, enhance rural citizenship.

Second, it was also revealed that rural transformation is taking place in Zimbabwe and that it is taking place in various forms: in the physical space, economic activities, and social organizations. Urbanization is the chief driver of rural transformation, with its various effects affecting rural citizenship differently—positively or negatively. On the other hand, rural inhabitants are diversifying their economic activities and, in the process, shaping rural spaces and consequently improving or compromising rural citizenship.

Third, unevenness, poverty traps, and inequality traps are also influential factors in the transformation of rural areas in Zimbabwe. Unevenness is manifesting mostly in the context of the rural–urban dichotomy, reinforcing the differences between urban and rural areas. Poverty traps are also contributing to the transformation of urban space in a negative way. Poor people are turning to natural resources as a source of livelihood, degrading the natural environment, further trapping themselves in poverty, and contributing to climate-related problems. This affects citizenship in rural areas negatively, as they may lose their sense of being citizens and compromise on some of their obligations to protect the environment.

Finally, rural transformation has a spatial component, that is, the changes that are taking place are influencing rural spaces. As such, spatial planning as a tool that adds space as a component in policies can be very useful in ensuring that the process of rural transformation benefits rural citizens and effectively protects and enhances their citizenship. Hence, it is concluded that spatial planning can address rural citizenship issues in a number of ways.

Based on these conclusions, we propose that spatial planning should be adopted in the planning and guiding of development in rural and urban areas. A comprehensive approach that looks at development as a way to holistically join the rural and urban spaces is required so as to ensure that bias in development is eliminated. This will safeguard and enhance the citizenship of people in rural communities. We also recommend that rural citizenship be considered in the same way that urban citizenship is considered. The production of rural space should be a product of local people's participation in decision-making, rather than an accidental result of urbanization and diversification. As such, a spatial planning approach can serve to ensure that rural areas are not recipients of urbanization externalities, but a result of reciprocity between urban and rural places. Rural citizenship will be enhanced this way.

References

Afshar, F. (1994). Globalization: The persisting rural-urban question and the response of planning education. *Journal of Planning Education and Research*, 13(4), 271–283.

Barraclough, L. (2013). Is there also a right to the countryside? *Antipode*, 45(5), 1047–1049. https://doi.org/10.1111/anti.12040

Bauman, Z. (2005). Freedom from, in and through the state: T. H. Marshall's trinity of rights revisited. *Theoria*, 52(108), 13–27.

Berdegué, J. A., Rosada, T., & Bebbington, A. J. (2013). *Rural transformation*. https://idl-bnc-idrc.dspacedirect.org/handle/10625/51569

Brodie, J. (2002). Citizenship and solidarity: Reflections on the Canadian way. *Citizenship Studies*, 6(4), 377–394.

Chiripanhura, B. M. (2010). Evidence from three districts: BWPI working paper 121. *Journal of Development Studies* (June), 1-32.

Chung, H. (2013). Rural transformation and the persistence of rurality in China. *Eurasian Geography and Economics*, 54(5-6), 594-610.

Cloke, P. J., Marsden, T., & Mooney, P. H. (2006). *Handbook of rural studies*. Sage Publications.

Cresswell, T. (2009). The prosthetic citizen: New geographies of citizenship. In *Political power and social theory* (pp. 259-273). Emerald Group Publishing Limited.

Ersado, L. (2000). *Income diversification in Zimbabwe: Welfare implication from urban and rural areas*. World Bank.

Fujita, N. (2007). Myrdal's theory of cumulative causation. *Evolutionary and Institutional Economics Review*, 3(2), 275-284.

Herrendorf, B., Rogerson, R., & Valentinyi, Á. (2014). Growth and structural transformation. *Handbook of Economic Growth*, 2, 855-941.

Hoddinott, J. (2006). Shocks and their consequences across and within households in rural Zimbabwe. *Journal of Development Studies*, 42(2), 301-321.

Infrastructure and Cities for Economic Development (ICED). (2017). *Briefing: Zimbabwe's changing urban landscape: Evidence and insights on Zimbabwe's urban trends.* Zimbabwe.

Isserman, A. M. (2001). Competitive advantages of rural America in the next century. *International Regional Science Review*, 24(1), 38-58.

Johnson, T. G. (2001). The rural economy in a new century. *International Regional Science Review*, 24(1), 21-37.

Kuhn, S. (2008). Urban-rural linkages. *Governance: An International Journal Of Policy And Administration*, 2000-2011.

Lipton, M. (1977). *Why poor people stay poor: A study of urban bias in world development*. ANU Press. https://openresearch-repository.anu.edu.au/handle/1885/114902

Lister, R. (1997). Citizenship: Towards a feminist synthesis. *Feminist review*, 57(1), 28-48.

Long, H., Zou, J., Pykett, J., & Li, Y. (2011). Analysis of rural transformation development in China since the turn of the new millennium. *Applied Geography*, 31(3), 1094-1105.

Long, N., Jingzhong, Y., & Yihuan, W. (2010). *Rural transformations and development: China in context*. Edward Elger Publishing, Inc.

Mbiba, B. (2017). On the periphery: Missing urbanisation in Zimbabwe. *Africa Research Institute*. https://www.africaresearchinstitute.org/newsite/publications/periphery-missing-urbanisation-zimbabwe/

Morphet, J. (2011). *Effective practice in spatial planning*. Routledge.

Munya, A., Hussain, N. H. M., & Njuguna, M. B. (2015). Can devolution and rural capacity trigger de-urbanization? Case studies in Kenya and Malaysia respectively. *GeoJournal*, 80(3), 427-443.

Mupetesi, T., Francis, J., & Gomo, R. (2017). Poverty rates in a rural district of Zimbabwe: A case study of the Guruve district. *Journal of Social Sciences*, 43(1), 25-37.

Mutenje, M. J., Ortmann, G. F., Ferrer, S. R. D., & Darroch, M. A. G. (2010). Rural livelihood diversity to manage economic shocks: Evidence from south-east Zimbabwe. *Agrekon*, 49(3), 338-357.

Nadin, V. (2007). The emergence of the spatial planning approach in England. *Planning Practice and Research*, 22(1), 43-62.

Nash, K. (2009). Between citizenship and human rights. *Sociology, 43*(6), 1067-1083.

Rambanapasi, C. O. (1989). Regional development policy and its impact on regional planning practice in Zimbabwe. *Planning Perspectives, 4*(3), 271-294.

Schaeffer, P. V., Kahsai, M. S., & Jackson, R. W. (2013). Beyond the rural-urban dichotomy. *International Regional Science Review, 36*(1), 81-96.

Scoones, I. (2016, May 1). Small towns in Zimbabwe are booming thanks to land reform. *Zimbabweland.* https://zimbabweland.wordpress.com/2016/05/01/small-towns-in-zimbabwe-are-booming-thanks-to-land-reform/

Scoones, I., & Murimbarimba, F. (2020). Small towns and land reform in Zimbabwe. *The European Journal of Development Research,* 1-23.

Somers, M. R. (1994). Rights, relationality, and membership: Rethinking the making and meaning of citizenship. *Law & Social Inquiry, 19*(1), 63-114.

Turner, B. S. (2001). The erosion of citizenship. *British Journal of Sociology, 52*(2), 189-209.

Unwin, T. (2017). Urban-rural interaction in developing countries: A theoretical perspective. In *The geography of urban-rural interaction in developing countries* (pp. 11-32). Routledge.

Waterhout, B. (2008). *The institutionalisation of European spatial planning.* IOS Press.

Wilson, J. (2011). Notes on the rural city: Henri Lefebvre and the transformation of everyday life in Chiapas, Mexico. *Environment and Planning D: Society and Space, 29*(6), 993-1009.

Yarwood, R. (2017, March 6). Rural citizenship. *International Encyclopedia of Geography: People, The Earth, Environment and Technology* (October), 1-8. https://pearl.plymouth.ac.uk/bitstream/handle/10026.1/8685/rural%20citizenship3.pdf?sequence=1

The Zimbabwe Citizenship Bill (2018). *Citizenship Rights in Africa Initiative.* https://citizenshiprightsafrica.org/zimbabwe-citizenship-bill-2018/

ZimStats (2017). *Zimbabwe poverty report 2017.* https://www.zimstat.co.zw/wp-content/uploads/publications/Income/Finance/Poverty-Report-2017.pdf

The Zimbabwe National Statistics Agency and United Nations Population Fund (UNFPA). (2015, August). *2012 Zimbabwe population census: Population projections thematic report.*

15

The Right to Multiple Futures in the Shadow of Canada's Smart City Movement

S. ASHLEIGH WEEDEN

RURAL AREAS ARE AT A PRECIPICE—sitting at the nexus of significant local and global transformations that will be shaped both by formal policies and the informal mechanisms by which we negotiate what it means to be connected in the contemporary context.[1] In the wake of global restructuring and the neoliberalization of public policy and placemaking, communities of all types are increasingly responsible for their own development. Current rural realities have outgrown many previous assumptions used to support rural development and new critically oriented frameworks are required (cf. Bryden et al., 2011; Copus & de Lima, 2015; Douglas, 2005; Hallstrom et al., 2015; Halseth, 2015; Markey et al., 2015; Organisation for Economic Co-operation and Development [OECD], 2018; Pezzini, 2001). In this vein, the implications of the varying capacities of rural communities to evaluate and respond to the rapid pace of technological change is becoming an area of increased tension and attention.

The perspective presented in this chapter is that rural areas have an important opportunity to be thoughtful about the way technology is invited into the public domain. Central to this undertaking is challenging the unquestioned urbanism at the core of most discussions about civic technology while learning from challenges at the urban frontier. While the language of "smart cities" presents challenges for addressing contemporary rural realities, questions about what these initiatives mean for contemporary citizenship transcend any rural/urban divide. As rural communities look to partner with technology companies to modernize service delivery, important questions must be asked about the compromises that rural citizens may feel compelled to make in the absence of the benefits of density (cf. Clancy, 2019; Bollman, this volume). This chapter will explore how citizen resistance to smart city projects represents an ongoing struggle for the right to the city and will reflect on the important implications smart projects raise for the right to be rural.

Smart Cities?

The smart city represents "a series of new urban uses [employing] information and communication technology" (Picon, 2015, p. 9), with the central focus being on digital tools that use data collection and monitoring to promote more efficient economic management of the day-to-day functioning of the urban environment. Smart initiatives are most frequently promoted by large, multinational technology companies (such as Cisco Systems Inc., Google's parent company Alphabet Inc., Microsoft, IBM, and others). Cardullo and Kitchin (2018) argue that most smart city projects promote "pragmatic, instrumental, and paternalistic discourses and practices rather than those of social rights, political citizenship, and the common good" (p. 813). Such projects are "much less concerned with user-experience and are driven instead by the potential for data collection and optimized consumerism" (Morozov, 2018, p. v), and they tend to treat citizens as "nodes of socio-technical networks under corporate or government control" (Zandbergen & Uitermark, 2020, p. 1733). This remains true across many contexts and is not merely a question of infrastructure or architecture (cf. Cardullo & Kitchin, 2018; Zandbergen & Uitermark, 2020). As these developments gain traction around the world, the increasing influence (even dominance) of such technology in daily life, and the uneven nature of its distribution, is producing serious debates about digital access and adoption, data ownership and governance, consent, privacy, and citizenship in the digital era.

New technology companies have often argued that they are too innovative to be regulated (Friesen & Owen, 2019). As these companies commercialize once-public services and spaces through smart city projects, they directly challenge the ways people experience their public lives and negotiate their rights as citizens by introducing surveillance, decreasing anonymity, and commercializing individual data—usually within a policy framework that does not appropriately or adequately govern these activities. Exploring resistance to smart cities speaks to Harvey's (2003) argument that the only way to challenge the pressures of privatization is through active democratic participation (Cardullo & Kitchen, 2018).

Rural Futures in the Shadow of the Smart City

The struggle to reconcile rural realities with the language and ethos of smart cities frameworks echoes Barraclough's (2013) struggle to reconcile Lefebvre's (1996) concept of the right to the city with an interpretation that preserves a right to the countryside. Further, the persistent rural/urban divide in both the availability of technological infrastructure and the capacity to effectively manage it often obscures or ignores the different experiences of rural people as smart cities expand their reach into the countryside.

Twenty years ago, the OECD (2001) defined the "digital divide" as "the gap between individuals, households, businesses and geographic areas at different socioeconomic levels with regard to both their opportunities to access information and communication technologies (ICTs) and to their use of the Internet for a wide variety of activities" (p. 5). Over time, recognition that pre-existing, persistent, and systemic geographic and socioeconomic inequalities produce multiple digital divides has added complexity to the way these edges perpetuate old hierarchies through digital inclusion/exclusion, digital inequity, and digital inequality (cf. Philip et al., 2017; Roberts, Anderson et al., 2017; Roberts, Beel et al., 2017; Weeden, 2019). However, most scholarship and public policy on the role of technology in rural development emphasizes the importance of "catching up" rural areas in terms of access, availability, and adoption (cf. Kandilov & Renkow, 2010; OECD, 2001; Philip et al., 2017; Prieger, 2002, 2013; Roberts, Anderson et al., 2017; Salemink, Strijker, & Bosworth, 2017). The directive seems to be that rural areas should welcome investment in technological infrastructure, no matter the source. For example, some rural communities are partnering with Huawei to build broadband infrastructure, despite serious concerns about the company's connections to the Chinese government and its notorious record of mass surveillance (Jung, 2019). Other communities continue to seek partnerships with Google Fiber, despite the company's history of abandoning community projects even after receiving significant public investment (Raymond, 2019). The assumption seems to be that technology is inherently a progressive force for positive change (at best) or neutral (at worst), that its widescale adoption in both the public and private spheres is inevitable, and that the need to overcome the digital infrastructure divide is so great that rural communities cannot afford for governance and regulatory implications to slow any promised progress.

We are only just starting to see investigations into the ways this approach to technological diffusion is changing the way we think about placemaking, democracy, and citizenship—particularly when it comes to the implications of the collection, commodification, and commercialization of individuals' data in public spaces. While such data has been characterized as "the new oil" (cf. Dance, LaForgia, & Confessore, 2018; The Economist, 2017; Matsakis, 2019), some have argued that it may be more like uranium—something dangerous, with long-lasting implications if it leaks (Doctorow, 2008). No matter whether we focus on the benefits of civic technology or the dangers of poor data governance, decisions about these strategies will have serious implications in a world where algorithms, not humans, are increasingly making decisions about everything from transit to policing. While this information might be useful for planning transportation routes or addressing public safety, it also raises issues of reinforcing human biases in racial profiling (Vincent, 2019) and could expose personal data that puts individuals at risk (e.g., someone secretly visiting an HIV clinic; see Doctorow, 2008). Policymakers must wrestle with the mechanics of whether individuals can meaningfully consent to having their information collected and stored, appropriate mechanisms for opting out when these collection mechanisms are in the public sphere, and questions about the storage and long-term use of that information. Beyond logistics, we must also recognize the ways that smart technology might serve to deepen systemic social, economic, and geographic inequities.

Despite the difficulty of reconciling urbanist smart city language with the rural experience and a general lack of recognition of the intersection of technology and rural realities, the smart city phenomenon will inevitably have rural implications as technological infrastructure diffuses from urban centres to the rural and remote periphery. Moreover, as rural-based industries become more technological (e.g., agricultural technology poses similar surveillance and identification risks, as well as risks for food security), there is notable silence on what the spread of smart city technology might look and feel like for rural people and places. This lacuna is fertile ground for exploring the ways in which technology is influencing the rights of citizens to participate in both decision-making frameworks and the actual decisions that shape the places where they live their lives, whether urban or rural. While there appears to be little rural resistance to smart city-style projects (yet), perhaps due to the desire to catch up noted above, the resistance to smart city projects in some of the world's largest metropolises offers a window into the ways rural communities should be deliberate about deciding whether and how to adapt the smart city to the smart countryside. This window for thoughtful decision-making is perhaps the only benefit for rural communities that lack the technical infrastructure required to immediately implement smart civic initiatives.

Power, Resistance, and Negotiating Digital Democracy

The layered interactions of social justice, community planning, and design, and the constitution of citizenship as a lived experience mediated by technology, present new territory for examining the socio-technical systems that shape the complex interactions between humans and technology, including the design and planning of urban environments (Patorniti et al., 2017). In practice, these issues have surfaced most dramatically in major metropolitan areas in the last five years. Smart city projects in New York (Amazon), Berlin (Google/Alphabet), and Toronto (Alphabet/Sidewalk Labs[2]) have faced growing criticism (Harris, 2019). In contrast, Barcelona has shifted toward combining "a digital revolution with a democratic revolution" grounded in a right to the city that emphasizes technological sovereignty and public stewardship (Cardullo & Kitchin, 2018, p. 826; cf. Bria, 2017; Foth et al., 2015; Galdon, 2017; March & Ribera-Fumaz, 2018). Marshall's (1964) seminal explorations of the politics of citizenship, rights, and social change are being played out in real time as societies are being reconstructed through the tensions between capitalism, neoliberalism, citizenship rights, and arguments of "tech for good."

In Toronto, the now-cancelled Sidewalk Labs smart city project, proposed by Alphabet Inc. (the parent company of Google) in partnership with Waterfront Toronto, had promised to be the world's first sensor-integrated neighbourhood built "from the internet up" (Barth, 2018). The project was ostensibly cancelled due to the economic uncertainties presented by the COVID-19 pandemic (Warburton, 2020). However, the cancellation should be contextualized by the increasing public coverage of criticisms and calls for the project to be cancelled by citizens and organizations, both local to Toronto and around the world, which predates the pandemic. Sustained public backlash to the project focused largely on the proposed unilateral transfer of a large tract of public land to Alphabet Inc. for a private development and the lack of transparency about who would ultimately be accountable for the ongoing governance of the Sidewalk Labs project (The Globe and Mail, 2019; Bliss, 2018). This transfer was marketed as being for the public good, despite the obvious corporate capture of public assets. Ceding control of public spaces to private corporations compromises the value of community spaces as "locations of the exercise and fulfillment of collective rights as a way of assuring equitable, universal, just, democratic, and sustainable distribution and enjoyment of the resources, wealth, services, goods, and opportunities" (Habitat International Coalition, 2005, as cited in Soja, 2010, p. 106). The spectre of smart city surveillance capitalism is increasingly perceived as especially threatening in the wake of scandal after scandal where technology companies keep getting it wrong in managing people's data at both the micro and macro scales (cf. Beretta, 2019). Objections to the Orwellian potential of the Sidewalk Labs project escalated to the point where the Canadian Civil Liberties Association (CCLA) filed a lawsuit against the City of Toronto, the Government of Ontario, and the Government of Canada over constitutional challenges related to "[outsourcing] the public interest to a private company without democratic or legal authorities," and it "worrie[d] the project [had] opened the door to a 'non-consensual, state-authorized mass capture of Canadians' personal information'" (Deschamps, 2019; Kirkwood, 2020). This reaction reinforces Somers' (1994) argument that social change is "made by those whose sense of who they *are* has been violated fundamentally" (p. 65). Thus, the constitution of citizenship in the shadow of the smart city creates a dynamic relationship of justice and enforcement in which citizens are simultaneously powerful and vulnerable.

These challenges highlight the way contemporary society is constructed via the power dynamics of social and technological networks (Castells, 2011). Ursula M. Franklin (1999) urged us to take a closer look at these dynamics, as "technology changes the social and individual relationships between us. It has forced us to examine and redefine our notions of power and of accountability" (p. 2). Twenty years later, Megan Beretta (2019) echoed Franklin in her argument that "decisions around regulation in the digital realm are actually defining our rights as citizens" (p. 4). As such, technology cannot be treated as an externality in the ongoing negotiation of identity and citizenship.

Smart Challenges from Skeptical Citizens

To explore and address the noted lack of discussions about the constitution of citizenship as a lived experience mediated by technology, the remainder of this chapter leverages a qualitative exploration of approximately two years of public, written engagement by Bianca Wylie[3] with the Sidewalk Labs project in Toronto. This exploration of new terrain in the landscape of digital justice is leveraged to reflect on key questions for rural communities as they look to define their own digital destinies.

Wylie's ongoing series of blog posts on Medium.com[4] about the Sidewalk Labs project constitute a public journal of her engagement with the concept of the smart city and what it means for her identity and experience as a citizen of Toronto. Wylie's public commentary was selected for analysis because: she is widely referenced as a major public advocate for digital democracy; she is perhaps the most publicly recognized and closely associated individual actor, outside of government or a corporate position, engaging with this issue as a citizen in the Canadian landscape (cf. Barth, 2018); and she has consistently publicly documented her evolving relationship to this process in writing. Because existing literature focuses on smart city proponents (cf. Patorniti et al., 2017), analyzing a singular and vocal citizen opponent is intended to address underexplored narratives attached to the smart city phenomenon. In using a collaborative, feminist approach that seeks to centre the research subject in the research process, Wylie's experience serves not only as source material but also as a critical and reflexive lens for questions about the way technology is shaping the experience and exercise of citizenship.

Jones and Alony (2008) argue that blogs like Wylie's provide "rich and deep personal accounts" (p. 440). They are typically written to gain recognition, develop social contact, fulfill a need for documentation or introspection, and/or enable information and skill development (cf. Clyde, 2006; Graham, 2002; Meyer & Allen, 1991; Nardi et al., 2004; Pedersen & Macafee, 2007; Rosenbloom, 2004; Turgeon, 2004; Williams & Jacobs, 2004). As such, they are valuable, reliable data sources that lend themselves particularly well to content analysis of writers' personal experiences and narratives. Further, because they are written independently of the research process, blogs may not be as vulnerable to the researcher's influence as other forms of data collection (Hartley, 2001). All 42 of Wylie's smart city and Sidewalk Labs related posts published on Medium.com at the time of writing this chapter (April 2019) were imported into NVivio[5] for analysis. Wylie's extensive catalogue of writing on the Sidewalk Labs project in other publications or with co-authors and her numerous media interviews on the subject have been excluded from analysis, as her writing on Medium.com represents her first-hand account of her evolving engagement with the Sidewalk Labs project, unfiltered and unfettered from any potential editorial input by formal media outlets, co-authors, or the research process for this chapter.

From December 2017 through the project's cancellation, Bianca actively wrote about what smart city projects meant for her experience of citizenship vis-à-vis the Sidewalk Labs project. The result is a compelling narrative of her engagement with what Franklin (1999) identified as the reconstruction of power and account-ability through technology. This practice underscores Somers' (1994) argument that our concepts of what it means to be a citizen are most strongly shaped through threats or violations by external forces. Wylie quite clearly saw Sidewalk Labs as a threat to her rights to informed participation, consent, and privacy (cf. Barth, 2018). Wylie's posts start out as mostly skeptical-but-still-curious reflections from public meetings held by Sidewalk Labs in Toronto. Her writing escalates in emotionality over time, with urgent appeals to reconsider key aspects of the project. Her later writing demands that the project be stopped entirely, as she argues that it is gaslighting citizens, "hijacking" the democratic process, and ultimately, producing a "civic tragedy" that presents a "looming threat" to local democratic participation (Wylie, 2018a, 2018b, 2018c, 2018e, 2018f, 2019a , 2019b). The titles of her posts reflect this shift. For example, "Sidewalk Toronto: A Hubristic, Insulting, Incoherent Civic Tragedy—Part I" (Wylie, 2019a), which indicates her sharp disappointment and an urgent sense of betrayal.

FIGURE 15.1 Nvivo generated word cloud analysis of Bianca Wylie's 42 Medium.com posts about smart cities and the Sidewalk Lab project in Toronto, Ontario

Thematically, the word "public" features heavily in Wylie's posts, with ideas of public process, public ownership, and public oversight figuring prominently throughout the entire arc of her writing. In some posts, it represents nearly 60% of the coded content (such as in "Sidewalk Toronto: An Open Letter to the New Sidewalk Labs Advisory Council," Wylie, 2018d) (see Figure 15.1 for a visual representation of the coded data). This emphasizes how a right to the commons shapes Bianca's identity as a citizen—and how she views Sidewalk Labs as responsible *to* the "public" while not necessarily being *of* the public.

The concept of "process" also appears as a strong theme. Questions about governance, democratic participation, and the process (or lack thereof) of citizen engagement in the development and execution of the Sidewalk Labs project sometimes represent as much as 50% of the coded content in a post. Closely related is the concept of "consultation," which highlights Wylie's consistent requests for more and higher quality public participation in the proposed project plan. These eventually become calls for the project to be stopped entirely. From Wylie's perspective, if the public is not involved in determining the scope of the Sidewalk Labs project, that project becomes a direct threat to civil rights. This perception reflects increasing concerns about the way neoliberal approaches to placemaking shift power dynamics in favour of private enterprises and echoes the influence of Michael Gurstein's writing on Wylie's views about technology and social justice. In 2015, Gurnstein argued it was time to

> drop the Digital Divide posturing and...address the real issues of social justice that are emerging in, on and through the Internet or be transparent with the obvious reality that the Internet overlords and their academic, technical community and civil society hirelings want nothing more...than to get on with the business of figuring out how to make the rich richer and the rest of us grin and bear it.

As such, Wylie's growing sensitivity to the influence of private interests in the public sphere mirrors David Harvey's (2003) assertion that the "creation of a new urban commons, a public sphere of active democratic participation, requires that we roll back that huge wave of privatization that has been the mantra of a destructive neoliberalism" (p. 941). Wylie's active democratic participation also underscores Henri Lefebvre's (1996) hope that ordinary people will become the site of resistance against neoliberal restructuring (Barraclough, 2013). Wylie notes this in her post "Sidewalk Toronto, the City of Toronto, and Our Right to Multiple Futures":

Some think that tech companies already have everything they need from us to make data products for cities. They don't. They need our mass consent to exist in public spaces...There are fundamental reasons why the public service is in charge of caring for humans. The legitimacy of this charge is already suffering at all levels of government. Eroding it further in the name of innovation and co-design is a big step and not one to take without expansive and inclusive city-wide conversation (2018g).

This argument that the private sector should return to its realm (i.e., real estate development and product innovation) while the public sector reclaims ownership over digital governance and democratic placemaking mirrors Barcelona's democratic digital revolution (noted earlier in this chapter; cf. Cardullo & Kitchin, 2018; Wylie, 2019c) and frames resistance to smart cities as an opportunity for civic renewal and restoring citizens' right to the city.

Exploring the Interval

Observing the largest city in Canada struggle to navigate the relationship between technology and the right to the commons raises important questions for rural communities. As rural dynamics change, local governments are often at the forefront of rural policy discussions (Markey et al., 2015). However, they may face far more limited capacity—technological or administrative—when faced with determining their own digital futures. And while there is seemingly no rural equivalent to Bianca Wylie whose experience we can examine, it is only a matter of time. The Sidewalk Labs example raises important questions related to community capacity to critically evaluate the terms of engagement when technology companies seek to enter the public sphere.

Crucially, this is an area in which rural citizens may actually benefit from being on the lagging side of the digital divide—in the absence of enabling infrastructure, rural communities may have the opportunity to more carefully consider whether and how they will invite these technologies into the public sphere. If we are to maintain a right to the rural in the shadow of the smart city, governments across all jurisdictions must not abdicate or allow a co-optation of public planning processes by private interests in trade for, as yet, unsubstantiated claims at economic development. However, this may be a naïve position, as rural examples of the opposite have begun to take shape. For example, the Town of Innisfil, Ontario, partnered with Uber instead of building public transit and quickly encountered challenges in scalability, financial sustainability, and data privacy (Bliss, 2019).

A glimmer of hope is appearing through regional approaches, where mid-sized cities are partnering with rural communities and working together to build digital capacity. For example, senior officials involved in Guelph-Wellington's exploration of what it might mean to be a smart region appear to be centring the social values of public stewardship. This seems to be the result of a nearly direct lesson-learned-style response to Wylie's public documentation of her experience with Sidewalk Labs. This Twitter exchange between Wylie and Barbara Swartzentruber[6] is one indication of this response:

> Bianca Wylie
> @biancawylie
> New short paper on confidence intervals + data policy, from me and @seanmmc-donald for @OurFoodFuture cc: @trubesb Do chime in if you have thoughts!...
> 12:19 PM, 27 Mar 2019

> Barb Swartzentruber
> @trubesb
> Smart cities place data, and the potential value it unlocks, at the center of public investments. We're starting slow to be inclusive and thoughtful, so we can go fast once we hit our stride. Guelph's smart city is also a just city.

Guelph-Wellington's partnership (called "Our Food Future"[7]) is working to make explicit connections to public values. By focusing on themes related to food and sustainability, the Guelph-Wellington approach hints at an understanding that rural regions provide an impressive array of unmonetized services to urban populations, including food security, energy security, water purification, ecosystem diversity, and natural amenities. These benefits will play an increasingly important role as the layered effects of late-stage capitalism, neoliberal restructuring, and climate change force new negotiations of both the right to the city and the right to the countryside.

The diverging paths of Sidewalk Labs and the Guelph-Wellington approach to the smart city appear to lead to very different futures. The Guelph-Wellington approach appears to seek to leverage both the agglomeration effects of urbanization and the sector-based advantages of rurality in a way that reaffirms a sense of inclusion, justice, and equality. It is a project that responds to Matt Clancy's (2019) argument that a successful reimagining of contemporary rural and regional development will depend on "using information technology to push agglomeration benefits out of the physical sphere and into the digital realm." The Guelph-Wellington partnership warrants deeper future exploration to examine if the rhetoric bears out in practice and enables the type of digital inclusion agenda set out in the 2017 Special Issue of the *Journal of Rural Studies*: one that is based on a "flexible, responsive and inclusive (participatory and equal opportunity) policy" that addresses "uneven digital geographies of place" (Roberts, Beel et al., 2017, p. 358). If we are to be intentional about the right to rurality today and in the future, such agendas must recognize that there is nothing inherently progressive, positive, or even neutral about the way technology is shaping citizenship.

Conclusion

Resistance to smart city projects demonstrates that any potential smart country-side projects must reflect cognizance of how they affect citizenship rights. As other chapters in this volume have detailed, technology is frequently offered as a sensible solution to the challenges of service delivery in sparsely populated areas. However, this chapter illuminates the potential for digital technologies to generate new risks to citizenship rights in the process of trying to expand access to other rights. Governments must engage meaningfully with the risks and benefits that come with digital infrastructure—and this struggle will continue to provide fertile ground for addressing a broad variety of challenges to the right to be rural today and well into the future. For example, if connectivity allows us to be in multiple spaces at once, whether physically or virtually, and the right to be rural is conceptualized as claiming rural spaces, how will rural communities negotiate this networked future? If digital infrastructure is required to meet the demands of the contemporary economy, but rural people must trade their privacy and right to consent to corporate capture of their communities for access to it, what does this mean for the weight of rural citizenship rights?

This chapter has explored the growing public debate regarding the role of digital technologies in our private and public lives and the ongoing negotiation of the rights and obligations associated with both the conceptualization and lived experience of citizenship in the smart city. It has raised more questions than answers. Issues raised here are only the beginning of a difficult and important confrontation between the shifting and expansive pervasiveness of technology in our civic, social, and economic lives and the conscious conversations we must have about what this means for both formal constitutional rights and the informal experiences of citizenship in our contemporary world. Policymakers and researchers alike would be well served to make digital literacy their top priority as they seek to balance the benefits of connectivity with the enormous risks of handing responsibility for investing in the digital future to private interests. Both academics and practitioners must engage in critical examinations of the capacity of governments (particularly local governments) to effectively navigate the murky implications of our current trajectory toward the latter. If we are to advance ideas around what the right to be rural means in an increasingly digitally-mediated world, our next steps must be to question who that right belongs to—people or private interests—and shift our attention toward citizens and communities, civic technology for the commons, and the right to multiple futures.

Notes

1. The time and resources required to write this chapter were supported with funding from the Digital Rights Community Grants Program, a partnership between Digital Justice Lab, Tech Reset Canada, and the Centre for Digital Rights. The author would like to offer her sincere gratitude to Bianca Wylie for her important contributions to the development of this chapter.

2. The official website for the Sidewalk Labs/Sidewalk Toronto projects can be accessed at the following links: https://sidewalktoronto.ca/ and https://www.sidewalklabs.com/.

3. Bianca Wylie is widely recognized as a key voice in the opposition to the Sidewalk Labs project. She has been interviewed by news outlets around the world, including *The Washington Post* and *The Guardian*. In 2018, Bloomberg's CityLab dubbed her the "Jane Jacobs of the Smart Cities Age" (Bliss, 2018).

4. Bianca's writing on Medium.com can be accessed publicly at www.medium.com/@biancawylie.

5. NVivo is a qualitative data analysis computer software package produced by QSR International. It has been designed for qualitative researchers working with very rich text-based and/or multimedia information.

6. Barbara Swartzentruber is the Executive Director of Strategy, Innovation and Intergovernmental Services for the City of Guelph. This tweet was captured from her public Twitter account. The City of Guelph has partnered with the County of Wellington to pursue a regionally networked smart-cities project based on developing a circular food economy through both social and technological innovation. More information can be found at City of Gueph, "Guelph-Wellington Awarded Smart Cities Challenge Prize," May 14, 2019, https://guelph.ca/2019/05/guelph-wellington-awarded-smart-cities-challenge-prize/.
   Note that Bianca Wylie has worked with the City of Guelph on previous open government initiatives and has contributed to developing critical frameworks for the "Our Food Future" initiative.

7. The City of Guelph's description of the Our Food Future project can be found at https://web. archive.org/web/20200403020757/https://guelph.ca/city-hall/city-administrators-office/ smart-cities-challenge/foodinnovation/.

References

Barraclough, L. (2013). Is there also a right to the countryside? *Antipode, 45*(5), 1047–1049. https://doi. org/10.1111/anti.12040

Barth, B. (2018, August 8). The fight against Google's smart city. *The Washington Post*. https://www. washingtonpost.com/news/theworldpost/wp/2018/08/08/sidewalk-labs/

Beretta, M. (2019, February 5). How is tech lobbying shaping federal policy? *Policy Options*. http:// policyoptions.irpp.org/magazines/february-2019/how-is-tech-lobbying-shaping-federal-policy/

Bliss, L. (2019, April 29). Uber was supposed to be our public transit. *CityLab*. https://www.citylab. com/transportation/2019/04/innisfil-transit-ride-hailing-bus-public-transportation- uber/588154/

Bliss, L. (2018, September 7). How smart should a city be? Toronto is finding out. *CityLab*. https:// www.citylab.com/design/2018/09/how-smart-should-a-city-be-toronto-is-finding-out/569116/

Bria, F. (2017, October 25). Reclaiming Europe's digital sovereignty. *Financial Times*. https://www. ft.com/content/f096bcf6-87d5-4023-a9b5-73ae847076b2

Bryden, J., Efstratoglou, S., Ferenczi, T., Johnson, T., Knickel, K., Refsgaard, K., & Thomson, K. (2011). *Towards sustainable rural regions in Europe: Exploring inter-relationships between rural policies, farming, environment, demographics, regional economies and quality of life using system dynamics*. Routledge.

Cardullo, P., & Kitchin, R. (2018). Smart urbanism and smart citizenship: The neoliberal logic of "citizen-focused" smart cities in Europe. *EPC: Politics and Space, 37*(5), 813–830.

Castells, M. (2011). A network theory of power. *International Journal of Communication, 5*, 773–787.

Clancy, M. (2019, March 29). Rehabilitating the death of distance to revitalize rural economies. Retrieved April 8, 2019, from https://medium.com/@mattclancy/ rehabilitating-the-death-of-distance-to-revitalize-rural-economies-a975788824e

Clyde, L. A. (2006). Teacher librarian. *Infotech, 32*(3), 43–45.

Copus, A., & de Lima, P. (2015). *Territorial cohesion in rural Europe: The relational turn in rural development*. Routledge.

Dance, G. J. X., LaForgia, M., & Confessore, N. (2018, December 18). As Facebook raised a privacy wall, it carved an opening for tech giants. *The New York Times*. https://www.nytimes. com/2018/12/18/technology/facebook-privacy.html

Deschamps, T. (2019, March 5). Canadian Civil Liberties Association threatens lawsuit over Sidewalk Labs project. *CTV News*. https://www.ctvnews.ca/business/ canadian-civil-liberties-association-threatens-lawsuit-over-sidewalk-labs-project-1.4322909

Doctorow, C. (2008, January 15). Personal data is as hot as nuclear waste. *The Guardian*. https://www. theguardian.com/technology/2008/jan/15/data.security

Douglas, D. (2005). The restructuring of local government in rural regions: A rural development perspective. *Journal of Rural Studies, 21*(2), 231–246.

The Economist. (2017, May 6). Regulating the internet giants: The world's most valuable resource is no longer oil, but data. https://www.economist.com/leaders/2017/05/06/the-worlds-most-valuable-resource-is-no-longer-oil-but-data

Foth, M., Brynskov, M., & Ojala, T. (2015). *Citizen's right to the digital city: Urban interfaces, activism, and placemaking.* Springer.

Franklin, U. M. (1999). *The real world of technology.* House of Anansi Press.

Friesen, D., & Owen, T. (2019, April 8). Why are governments slow to regulate social media? *Global National.* https://globalnews.ca/video/5144195/why-are-governments-slow-to-regulate-social-media

Galdon, G. (2017). Technological sovereignty? Democracy, data, and governance in the digital era. *CCCB Lab.* https://lab.cccb.org/en/technological-sovereignty-democracy-data-and-governance-in-the-digital-era/

The Globe and Mail. (2019, June 24). Sidewalk Lab's vision and your data privacy: A guide to the saga on Toronto's waterfront. https://www.theglobeandmail.com/canada/toronto/article-sidewalk-labs-quayside-toronto-waterfront-explainer/

Graham, B. L. (2002). Why I weblog: A rumination on where the hell I'm going with this website. In J. Rodzvilla (Ed.), *We've got blog: How weblogs are changing our culture* (p. 242). Perseus.

Gurstein, M. (2015, April 15). Why I'm giving up on the digital divide [Blog]. https://gurstein.wordpress.com/2015/04/15/why-im-giving-up-on-the-digital-divide/

Hallstrom, L., Ashton, W., Bollman, R., Gibson, R., & Johnson, T. (2015). Policy designs in rural Manitoba: Alternatives and opportunities in the midst of change. *Manitoba Law Journal, 38*(2), 185–219.

Halseth, G. (2015). *Transformation of resource towns and peripheries: Political economy perspectives.* Routledge.

Harris, J. (2019, April 3). Street battle: The activists fighting to save their neighbourhood from the tech giants. *The Guardian.* https://www.theguardian.com/technology/2019/apr/03/facebook-amazon-google-big-tech-activists-new-york-berlin-toronto-

Hartley, J. (2001). Employee surveys: Strategic air or hand-grenade for organisational and cultural change? *The International Journal of Public Sector Management, 13*(3), 184–204.

Harvey, D. (2003). Debates and developments: The right to the city. *International Journal of Urban and Regional Research, 27*(4), 939–941.

Jones, M., & Alony, I. (2008). Blogs: The new source of data analysis. *Journal of Issues in Informing Science and Information Technology, 5,* 433–446.

Jung, C. (2019, February 28). Huawei's security risks outweigh its investment in Canada. *The Huffington Post.* https://www.huffingtonpost.ca/chauncey-jung/huawei-canada-national-security-risks_a_23677820/

Kandilov, I. T., & Renkow, M. (2010). Infrastructure investment and rural economic development. *Growth and Change, 41*(2), 165–191.

Kirkwood, I. (2020, January 31). Waterfront Toronto pushes back Sidewalk Labs deadline, responds to CCLA lawsuit. *BetaKit.* https://betakit.com/waterfront-toronto-pushes-back-sidewalk-labs-deadline-responds-to-ccla-lawsuit/

Lefebvre, H. (1996). *Writings on cities* (E. Kofman & E. Lebas, Trans.). Blackwell.

March, H., & Ribera-Fumaz, R. (2018). Barcelona: From corporate smart city to technological sovereignty. In A. Karvonen, F. Cugurullo, & F. Caprotti (Eds.), *Inside smart cities: Place, politics and urban innovation* (pp. 229-242). Routledge.

Markey, S., Breen, S., Gibson, R., Lauzon, A., Mealy, R., & Ryser, L. (Eds.). (2015). *The state of rural Canada: 2015.* Canadian Rural Revitalization Foundation.

Marshall, T. H. (1964). *Class citizenship and social development.* Heinemann.

Matsakis, L. (2019, February 15). The W I R E D guide to your personal data (and who is using it). *W I R E D.* https://www.wired.com/story/wired-guide-personal-data-collection/

Meyer, J. P., & Allen, N. J. (1991). A three-component conceptualization of organizational commitment. *Human Resource Management Review, 1,* 69-98.

Morozov, E. (2018). *Rethinking the smart city* [Unpublished master's thesis]. University of Waterloo. Waterloo, Canada.

Nardi, B. A., Schiano, D. J., Gumbrecht, M., & Swartz, M. (2004). Why we blog. *Communications of the ACM, 47*(12), 41-46.

Organisation for Economic Co-operation and Development (O E C D). (2001) *Understanding the digital divide.* https://www.oecd.org/sti/1888451.pdf

Organisation for Economic Co-operation and Development (O E C D). (2018). *Rural 3.0: A framework for rural development.*

Patorniti, N. P., Stevens, N. J., & Salmon, P. M. (2017). A systems approach to city design: Exploring the compatibility of sociotechnical systems. *Habitat International, 66,* 42-48.

Pedersen, S., & Macafee, C. (2007). Gender differences in British blogging. *Journal of Computer-Mediated Communication, 12,* 1472-1492.

Pezzini, M. (2001). Rural policy lessons from O E C D countries. *International Regional Science Review, 24*(1), 134-145.

Philip, L., Cottrill, C., Farrington, J., Williams, F., & Ashmore, F. (2017). The digital divide: Patterns, policy and scenarios for connecting the "final few" in rural communities across Great Britain. *Journal of Rural Studies, 54,* 386-398.

Picon, A. (2015). *Smart cities: A spatialized intelligence.* Wiley.

Prieger, J. E. (2002). The supply side of the digital divide: Is there redlining in the broadband internet access market? *S S R N, 41*(2), 346-363. https://doi.org/10.2139/ssrn.297499

Prieger, J. E. (2013). The broadband digital divide and the economic benefits of mobile broadband for rural areas. *Telecommunications Policy, 37*(6-7), 483-502.

Raymond, A. K. (2019, March 14). When Google Fiber abandons your city as a failed experiment. *Gizmodo.* https://gizmodo.com/when-google-fiber-abandons-your-city-as-a-failed-experi-1833244198

Roberts, E., Anderson, B. A., Skerratt, S., & Farrington, J. (2017). A review of the rural-digital policy agenda from a community resilience perspective. *Journal of Rural Studies, 54,* 372-385.

Roberts, E., Beel, D., Philip, L., & Townsend, L. (2017). Rural resilience in a digital society: Editorial. *Journal of Rural Studies, 54,* 355-359.

Rosenbloom, A. (2004). The blogopshere. *Communications of the ACM, 47*(12), 30-33.

Salemink, K., Strijker, D., & Bosworth, G. (2017). Rural development in the digital age: A systematic literature review on unequal ICT availability, adoption, and use in rural areas. *Journal of Rural Studies, 54*, 360–371.

Soja, E. W. (2010). *Seeking spatial justice.* University of Minnesota Press.

Somers, M. R. (1994). Rights, relationality, and membership: Rethinking the making and meaning of citizenship. *Law & Social Inquiry, 19*(1), 63–114.

Turgeon, M. C. (2004). *10 reasons why blogging is good for you* [Blog]. https://web.archive.org/web/20140104164711/http://mcturgeon.com/blog/2004/11/24/10reasonstoblog/

Vincent, J. (2019, April 3). AI researchers tell Amazon to stop selling "flawed" facial recognition to the police. *The Verge.* https://www.theverge.com/2019/4/3/18291995/amazon-facial-recognition-technology-rekognition-police-ai-researchers-ban-flawed

Warburton, M. (2020, May 7). Alphabet's Sidewalk Labs cancels Toronto "smart city" project. *Reuters.* https://www.reuters.com/article/us-canada-sidewalk-idUSKBN22J2FN

Weeden, S. A. (2019). Radical rurality: Imagining multiple futures beyond the city limits. *Some Thoughts.* https://some-thoughts.org/weeden.html

Williams, J. B., & Jacobs, J. (2004). Exploring the use of blogs as learning space in the higher education sector. *Australasian Journal of Educational Technology, 20*(2), 232–247.

Wylie, B. (2018a). Debrief on Sidewalk Toronto public meeting #3: A master class in gaslighting and arrogance. https://medium.com/@biancawylie/debrief-on-sidewalk-toronto-public-meeting-3-a-master-class-in-gaslighting-and-arrogance-c1c5dd918c16

Wylie, B. (2018b). Sidewalk Toronto: Amnesia, willful ignorance, and the beautiful anti-democratic neighbourhood of the future. https://medium.com/@biancawylie/sidewalk-toronto-amnesia-wilful-blindness-and-the-beautiful-anti-democratic-neighbourhood-of-32341737a4dc

Wylie, B. (2018c). Sidewalk Toronto: A brazen and ongoing corporate hijack of democratic process. https://medium.com/@biancawylie/sidewalk-toronto-a-brazen-and-ongoing-corporate-hijack-of-democratic-process-a96a1253fb2b

Wylie, B. (2018d). Sidewalk Toronto: An open letter to the New Sidewalk Labs Advisory Council. https://medium.com/@biancawylie/sidewalk-toronto-an-open-letter-to-the-new-sidewalk-labs-advisory-council-8f521e633c92

Wylie, B. (2018e). Sidewalk Toronto: Democratic deception, smart city doublespeak, and the long game. https://medium.com/@biancawylie/sidewalk-toronto-democratic-deception-smart-city-doublespeak-and-the-long-game-11759670d734

Wylie, B. (2018f). Sidewalk Toronto: The anti-democratic power of alphabet's patient capital. https://medium.com/@biancawylie/sidewalk-toronto-the-anti-democratic-power-of-alphabets-patient-capital-e07e0d660a21

Wylie, B. (2018g). Sidewalk Toronto—"Sold out" public meetings and Sidewalk Labs' sole source contract in Illinois. https://medium.com/@biancawylie/sidewalk-toronto-sold-out-public-meetings-and-sidewalk-labs-sole-source-contract-in-illinois-a4ba34ba7593

Wylie, B. (2019a). Sidewalk Toronto: A hubristic, insulting, incoherent civic tragedy—Part I. https://medium.com/@biancawylie/sidewalk-toronto-a-hubristic-insulting-incoherent-civic-tragedy-part-i-ae1e71ed6940

Wylie, B. (2019b). Sidewalk Toronto: A hubristic, insulting, incoherent civic tragedy—Part II. https://medium.com/@biancawylie/sidewalk-toronto-a-hubristic-insulting-incoherent-civic-tragedy-part-ii-334129560cb1

Wylie, B. (2019c). Sidewalk Toronto: It's time for waterfront Toronto 3.0—Onward and upward. https://medium.com/@biancawylie/sidewalk-toronto-its-time-for-waterfront-toronto-3-0-onward-and-upward-245a99729c6a

Zandbergen, D., & Uitermark, J. (2020). In search of the smart citizen: Republican and cybernetic citizenship in the smart city. *Urban Studies, 57(8)*, 1733-1748. https://doi.org/10.1177%2F0042098019847410

16

"What Makes Our Land Illegal?"

Regularization and the Urbanization of Rural Land in Ethiopia

ESHETAYEHU KINFU & LOGAN COCHRANE

Introduction

Ethiopia is one of the world's least urbanized nations, with less than a fifth of the population being classified as urban. However, the country is rapidly urbanizing. The current urbanization rate (2.2% for the 2010-2030 period) is greater than the global, continental, and regional average growth rates (United Nations Department of Economic and Social Affairs [UN DESA], 2018). Ethiopian urban population growth is not only attributed to the classical causes (i.e., natural population growth and migration), but also to annexation (Kinfu et al., 2019). A longitudinal study of 20 rural areas in Ethiopia has shown that these areas have been urbanizing, as reflected by their changing socioeconomic and spatial characteristics (A. Pankhurst, 2017). This chapter explores how these processes impact rural residents and their rights. This question is particularly important for Ethiopia, as the majority of its population consists of smallholder farmers who only have usufruct land rights (user rights), not ownership rights. Since the state owns all the land, and the governance system has restricted individual freedoms under the guise of development (Dejene & Cochrane, 2019), questions have been raised about who benefits from the political and legal decisions regarding rural land, and what implications these decisions have for the rights of rural residents.

Urbanization tends to be framed as a movement of people. However, expanding urban populations frequently appear alongside the expansion of urban jurisdictions. This type of expansion is termed "horizontal" growth, and this has occurred at significant rates in recent decades in Ethiopian cities: from 1986 to 2010, Addis Ababa expanded by 180%; from 1986 to 2011, Bahir Dar expanded by 168%, and over the same time period, Gondar expanded by 374% (Wubneh, 2018). Hawassa, the city of focus in this chapter, expanded by 235% between 1987 and 2011 (Wondrade, Dick, & Tveite, 2014). As the land jurisdictions change, rural land becomes urban, without any person necessarily moving their residence. In the Ethiopian context, this shift is also a formal one, as the country has a tenure system that governs rural land and another that governs urban land. Notably, there is no tenure system to govern the land that falls in between: peri-urban land (found between the urban and rural within the urban-rural region, which functions as a transition zone and holds mixed land uses despite the nature of its holders and residents, who are mainly rural), and transforming land. Rather, land is simply classified as either rural or urban.

Land is dichotomized as rural or urban in Ethiopia based on its administrative location: the land found within the administrative boundary of urban areas is urban land and the rest is classified as rural land. The dichotomy radiates into all land development, governance, and planning systems (Kinfu et al., 2019). The two types of land classifications are different in terms of the type of occupation, holding, use, development, and governance systems. These further determine the nature and characteristics of the settlements growing in the areas and the planning responses (for details, see Kinfu et al., 2019).

To facilitate the transfer of land from the rural to the urban, Ethiopian cities have had two options. The first option is expropriation. Under the principles of eminent domain, which delimit the government's power to take private property and convert it to public use, the state is permitted to take any land for public purposes, including urban development. This option forces those using the land outside the urban boundary to wait until "development reaches their area." Rural villages and their respective farmlands have no right to transform or change the land until urban plans and the expansion of cities reach them. Development is associated with urban growth, and this association of development with urban areas denies rural residents' rights of development. Any changes to land use and land development actions are strictly subject to the laws of the development permit. The laws technically limit the rights of rural residents to transform their settlements by stating the need to get development permits, which are practically impossible to obtain. As a result, development permits are associated with the existence of urban plans. The second option available to Ethiopian cities is to make rural land urban through the process of regularization. This process involves the incorporation of land and various developments as zoning expands and the tenure system shifts from rural to urban. Often this regularization process has been used to address challenges emerging from the immediate and short-term changes that follow shifts in tenure (Federal Democratic Republic of Ethiopia [FDRE], 2011, 2013).

The rapid urbanization of Ethiopian cities, the consequent horizontal growth, and the annexation of rural residents and land into the urban territory, as well as the lack of transition and governance mechanisms have made the rural land within urban peripheries into areas of contention and contestation. Governance structures within the city have primarily focused on obtaining rural land and using that land within city development plans. This includes leasing newly obtained land, often at high rates, providing new forms of revenue for the city. However, in the process, rural residents lose their land, often being granted very low rates of compensation and with little to no options for refusing or negotiating these processes. The extent of these processes is significant. As will be discussed, in the Hawassa municipality alone, nearly 18,000 plots found within the annexed rural land were deemed "illegal" land holdings. Effectively, through such processes, the rights of rural citizens are being denied, their livelihoods are being lost, and the rural wealth held by rural residents is being transferred to the government.

Methods and Situating Theory

This chapter draws upon a 2016–2018 study in which we collected mixed methods data in Hawassa, specifically focusing upon two peri-urban areas, Datto-Odahe and Tullo-Argo. An exploratory research design informed the design of the study, with primary data being collected in 34 key informant interviews, field observations, and 400 household surveys. Secondary data, particularly government reports and policy documents, were also used to validate the findings and deepen the research. The study explored multiple dimensions of peri-urban areas and the issues experienced therein. This chapter focuses upon one component: regularization. Additional information on the methods, methodology, and other components of the study are available in Kinfu (2019). We have approached theoretical questions of rural rights by analyzing the findings, following Fukuyama (2011), rather than having theory drive our research and analyses.

Our findings highlight processes of accumulation by dispossession at the micro scale (Harvey, 2003), however, in this case, the imperial actor is a socialist-oriented state. While Harvey (2003) focused attention on neoliberalism and capitalism as mechanisms that drive accumulation by dispossession, in the Ethiopian context, state capture is the focal mechanism. In some instances, the minority elite or foreign investors lease the accumulated land, but it remains held by the state after being acquired. This suggests that within developmental state contexts, the processes of dispossession and the outcomes of accumulation by a minority are similarly occurring, but with unique mechanisms and by different actors. In Ethiopia, expropriated rural land does not become privatized, but remains under public ownership (effectively, owned by the state). In this regard, land tenure in Ethiopia complicates narratives of neoliberal and post-neoliberal policies (Brenner, Peck, & Theodore, 2010), as it does not embrace a neoliberal privatization of land. Nor have the Marxist-inspired policies of public ownership of all land remained static. Instead, the country has created its own pathway of tenure, with land certification in the rural system and lease holding in the urban system. Yet, these systems operate within a socio-political environment wherein constitutional equality does not equate with equality in reality. Inequalities of social citizenship, to draw upon Marshall (1950) via Turner (2003), mean that not all people have equal opportunity. This study highlights how the rights of urbanites supersede those of the rural, with the latter even having their multigenerational-held land deemed illegal for political and economic purposes.

Contextualizing Land and Rights

For millennia, Ethiopian land has been held by a minority (R. Pankhurst, 1966). In many parts of the country, the system operated in a feudal form, where those who tilled the land obtained limited benefit from their labour and were vulnerable to the whims of large landowners. Demands for change began in the early 1900s, but took concrete form in the 1960s, with the "land to tiller" movement, which called for the land to be given to those who used it (Zewde, 2014). Following the fall of the imperial regime (1974) and the rise of the military one (1974–1991), the government introduced radical land reform. All tenure agreements were nullified, the state took ownership of all land, land was redistributed to people throughout the country with holding size limits, and the sale of the newly redistributed land was prohibited (see Cochrane, 2017). When the current government came to power (1991–present), it drafted a new constitution (approved in 1995), which re-affirmed state ownership of all land and usufruct rights for individuals (FDRE, 1995). In doing so, the state maintained its control over how land is used, developed, and transferred (e.g., as inheritance to children). The state also outlined that it can take land if it is unused, or if users do not abide by the land tenure regulations, in which case it will be redistributed. The Government of Ethiopia has long viewed land as its critical political and economic resource and as a main national development tool (FDRE, 2011). In particular, rural land has been viewed as a critical input for economic development (FDRE, 2002), and it remains the case that land management is focal for the government in its management of the country (Ministry of Urban Development and Housing Construction [MODHCO], 2015).

One of the largest political changes that occurred with the coming of the current government (1991–present) was the introduction of what is called ethnic federalism. This approach to governance involves creating borders that largely align with ethno-linguistic boundaries, granting each region a degree of autonomy for decision-making. A strong federal government and its development of long-term plans and granting of limited political freedoms drove this change. Using this model, national economic growth has been among the highest in the world and has been sustained at a high rate for over a decade (Cochrane & Bekele, 2018). In the process of implementing this vision, however, a wide range of freedoms were restricted, contributing to frustration and protest, which would force significant political change in 2018 (Dejene & Cochrane, 2019). The details of the recent political changes are beyond the scope of this chapter. As of the time of writing, the changes have not resulted in any major shifts to the land tenure systems.

With regard to land tenure changes, the regulatory system has not evolved progressively over time; rather, it has been impacted by specific political and legal junctures. Albeit summarized, the following offers one example regarding this in Hawassa: in 2005, shifts in urban governance policy were undertaken, which resulted in the annexation of large amounts of rural areas into the city boundary. This change, however, was not simply a legal one related to tenure, but was strongly linked to political changes as well (for additional details, see Kinfu et al., 2019). For the 2005 election, eleven rural areas and one urban area were annexed into Hawassa, resulting in a population increase of 35% and a land area increase of 76% for the city (Kinfu et al., 2019). Political negotiations at the time allowed rural areas to keep the land operating under the rural tenure system, even though it was within the jurisdiction of the city and should have been under the urban tenure system. It is notable that during the 2005 election, many cities voted for the opposition, and the city boundary changes were linked with processes of maintaining political power for the ruling government. The negotiations were political in that the city administration and the regional state compromised the provisions of the urban land law, which stated that land within the administrative boundary of the city was meant to be urban land. Such a status would have prohibited the private transfer of urban land prior to urban planning and development permitting (FDRE, 2011). The compromise was surfaced by the superseding political ideology of ethnic federalism alongside the intention of the ruling party to change the heterogeneous demographic characteristics of urban areas by increasing the number of inhabitants indigenous to the area that the ruling party thought were its constituencies and political partisans (Kinfu et al., 2019). Following these politico-legal changes, people who had their lands annexed into the city boundary found many new opportunities, such as developing their land as multi-unit rental spaces or selling their land to developers. Given that the land was within the city, these were expected outcomes; however, as the land was classified as rural, the uses of this land were restricted. As a result, rural residents found themselves in the middle of these decisions—although without a voice and entirely forgotten. Later, in 2015, their land was deemed "illegal" and they were charged with illegally using their land.

Urbanizing Rural Rights through Regularization

Regularization was a legal process established by the government to legitimize the peri-urban land held by rural residents that had been annexed (reclassified as urban land) into urban areas. This was meant to address a widely recognized problem of rural land holdings in an urban area, where the land was supposed to have urban status and function under the urban tenure system. Unless the land was regularized, these holdings were deemed to be illegal landholdings. The legal process stated the modalities through which old possessions and so-called illegal landholdings were to be planned, registered, and certified. From an administrative point of view, the process focused on the formalization of the transition of rural land into urban land. Further, the process was aimed at establishing a land development and management system to accommodate and incorporate these lands so they would be accounted for and considered when the city made investments, such as in new infrastructure (Southern Nations, Nationalities and Peoples Regional State [SNNPRS], 2015b, 2015c, 2016). The regularization program was also seen as a policy instrument aimed at abolishing rent-seeking tendencies of those holding urban land (deemed as a deficiency of the developmental state political economy pursued by the state) and at freeing the peripheral land from rent seekers (SNNPRS, 2016). Essentially, this was viewed as a process of urbanizing rural land and property rights.

The regularization policy categorized the different types of landholdings based on the ways the land was acquired. These categories included old (generationally held) holdings and illegal landholdings. Old possessions were landholdings legally acquired but not registered, such as those acquired before the lease system was introduced, land delivered as a replacement for land expropriated for public interest, and land that had legal permission for acquisition but remained under the rent hold system. The illegal landholdings were landholdings deemed as illegally acquired by new landholders, including farmers changing their farmland into built-up areas, and not recognized by an authorized body (SNNPRS, 2015a, 2015b). The policy recommendations differentiated the land holding types in order to justify the policy presumptions and to inform policy directions (see Table 16.1).

TABLE 16.1 Comparison of land hold types in 2017

	Old possessions	Illegal possessions
Locations	Inner city	Peripheries (rural land)
Modes of occupation	Legal and not registered	Illegal and not registered
Average area	More than 200m²	200–300m²
Occupants	Residents	Squatters and speculators
Plan	Within plan boundary	Unplanned annexed areas
Effects	Urban design and standard	Urban form and development
Landholding system	Rent	Lease
Dates of occupation	Not specified	Strictly defined
Fees of registration	Rent	Fines, fees, and lease
Extra land	Given priority	Expropriation

Note: Adapted from Federal Democratic Republic of Ethiopia (FDRE), 2011, Urban lands lease holding proclamation (Proclamation no. 721/2011) (http://admin.theiguides.org/Media/Documents/Urban-land-lease-proclamation-no-721-20111.pdf); Southern Nations, Nationalities and Peoples' Regional State (SNNPRS), 2015, የተሻሻለው የደቡብ ብሔሮች፣ ብሔረሰቦች እና ሕዝቦች ክልል መንግስት የከተማ መሬት ሊዝ ደንብ ቁጥር ፭፻፹፬/፪ሺ፯. ሀዋሣ, ኢትዮጵያ [Improved Southern Nations, Nations, Nationalities and Peoples' Regional State Urban Land Lease Regulation No. Hawassa, Ethiopia]; and SNNPRS, 2015, የከተማ መሬት በሊዝ ስለመፍቀድ የወጣ ደንብ ቁጥር 123/2007 ለማስፈጸም ተሻሽሎ የወጣ መመሪያ ቁጥር 8/07. ሀዋሣ, ኢትዮጵያ [Urban Land Lease Permitting Regulation No. 123/2007 Amended Directive No. 8/07. Hawassa, Ethiopia]. In the public domain.

While the policy presumed that old possessions were located within the city's municipal boundary, not easy or expensive to expropriate, and slated for urban renewal projects, it presumed that the illegal land holdings were at the peripheries. Old possessions were presumed to be legally occupied, but not registered, and illegal landholdings were presumed to be illegally occupied and not registered. The old possessions were viewed as being occupied by urban residents who were integrated into the urban economy and as already located within the established socioeconomic fabric of the city, while the informal landholdings were seen as being occupied by squatters or speculators. Due to these reasons, regularization was deemed the most suitable for old possessions, while expropriation was used for the illegal possessions. However, the government adapted regularization to legitimize the illegal landholdings found at the peripheries, "just to be tolerant of the already established investment" (Interviews conducted in 2016). The policy focused on the new landholders and overlooked the rural population and farmers within the villages, and thus it denied their rights.

The law provided the right to develop and transfer urban plots categorized as old possessions at any time the holder demanded, and no strict prohibitions were stated. However, the farmland or rural landholders living on land annexed into the city administration were prohibited by the law from transferring their land to third parties. The law not only nullified rural landholders' right to construct, it also announced the possibility that rural landholders could lose their landholding rights and that the municipality could expropriate the land without any compensation. In addition, the new regulations made it a crime to broker or sell farmland or other "illegal" landholdings (SNNPRS, 2015b). The land could be expropriated when "the development reaches the area" based on the expropriation laws and procedures (SNNPRS, 2015b). The farmers were obliged to pay the rural land use tax and were strictly prohibited from making any changes after the annexation, as well as from rejecting any efforts to utilize land transfer attempts prior to the usufruct rights being labelled as illegal (SNNPRS, 2015b).

There were different processes proposed as solutions to the complexities emerging from the land tenure changes. Without delving into great detail, these included the following two pathways: (1) possessions that were classified as old were allowed to continue into the urban leasehold tenure system; and (2) possessions of land that were viewed as illegal had to be changed to the urban tenure system, which included the payment of fees and fines as a condition of registration and as a form of punishment for holding land deemed illegal. Those holding old possessions were recommended to pay for the land use lease because it was presumed that the old possessions were legitimate, but the occupants had just failed to register. On the other hand, the so-called illegal landholders were subjected to paying the lease price and a fine per metre squared (25 ETB) for their "illegal" acts.

The Rights of Holders

The two types of land holdings were treated differently in terms of the conditions set for determining the plot size, as well as the land holding system, lease price, and expropriation of land. As a result, the registration and planning recommendations varied. The regulations and processes were broadly and clearly defined for the old possessions, while the illegal ones were narrowly defined and largely disregarded in favour of pro-urban rights. The regularization program thus provided ample rights to the holders of old possessions and fell short of recognizing the rights of the annexed rural residents and their land rights, as summarized in Table 16.1 and Table 16.2. The differences of the holders can be summarized as follows.

1. The presumptions of the law failed to recognize rural citizens' constitutional rights to development, including housing construction. Instead, they were labelled as illegals. The regularization law was intended to partially punish and partially tolerate them. Yet, the categorization between the old possessions and illegal land was based on the ways the landholders acquired the land. The rural landholders claimed that they were not illegal holders on the basis of how they acquired the land, as they had acquired it legally through the provisions of the rural land law. Thus, it was unclear why the land was labelled as illegal.

2. Rural landowners within the annexed areas were restricted in their use of the land if it had been labelled or identified for development or planned for development, regardless of the timeline or status of that development. These landholders were subjected to a waiting period until the development reached them, while the holders of old possessions were free to transfer and develop their land.

3. The rights to develop and to transfer rural land for rural landholders (constitutional property rights and the right to use rural land as per the rural land tenure system of Ethiopia) were transformed into crimes and violators were subjected to criminal punishment.

4. The law provided the right to replacement land with compensation for the properties deemed old possessions, and only provided a conditional right for replacement land and no compensation for the illegal landholders.

5. The law provided wide opportunities to accommodate and maintain the landholding of the old possessors through co-ownership, if the

plots were sub-standard and adjacent to each other. It provided opportunities for old possessors to retain lands over 500 metres squared, as
leaseholds, and to negotiate and adjust with adjacent land in order to
maintain a regular shape for the 500+ metres squared of land. These
rights were denied or overlooked for the illegal landholders.

6. The land required for infrastructure and services was expropriated with
   compensations for the old possessions and without compensation for
   the illegal landholders.

7. The payment modalities for registration of the old possessions were of
   the freehold mode, but the illegal landholders were subjected to lease
   prices and fines for their illegal acts.

The Regularization Campaign

In 2015, the regional state within which Hawassa is located launched a regularization campaign and mobilized the political leaders to execute it. The regional
assembly was responsible for launching the campaign, and local taskforces were
established to commence the regularization so as to "close the cases once and for
all." The taskforces were expected to coordinate all stakeholders and local authorities, prohibit illegal practices, and establish transparent land development and
management systems. The campaign aimed to regularize old possessions and
illegal landholdings as well as establish a sustainable preventive system to prohibit
the illegal holding of land. It was intended to create consensus among stakeholders
about the negative impacts of illegal settlements, demark a city/town and district
boundary, and maintain healthy urban-rural linkages (Interviews conducted in
2016; SNNPRS, 2015c).

In May 2015, Hawassa City Administration organized a taskforce that led the
program, and three technical teams, comprised of urban planners and surveyors,
undertook the regularization activities. The city administration prepared an
action plan that paralleled the regional campaign (Interviews conducted in 2016
and 2017). The taskforce conducted a meeting with the residents of peri-urban
settlements to inform them about the modalities of the process and identified
elected community representatives who were to be responsible for working with
the taskforce and representing the voice of the residents. Massive regularization
of old possessions and illegal landholding plots ensued (Interviews conducted in
2016). In 2016, 583 plots of land were identified as old possessions in Hawassa city,
and 570 of those plots were regularized in 2016. A total of 17,916 plots of land were
identified as illegal land holdings in Hawassa city (SNNPRS, 2016), and of those

TABLE 16.2 Recommended modes of handling land holdings based on classification

Plot standards	Plot size	Recommended modes of registration for old possessions	Recommended modes of registration for illegal landholdings
Sub-standard (< 150m²)	< 150m²	Replacement of 200m² with compensation	Replacement of 200m²
	Two adjacent plots and each < 150m²	Co-ownership with agreements, and maintenance of regular shapes	Merging and common use merging, and regularization
To the standard (200–500m²)	150–200m², irregular in shape and difficult to maintain with regular shapes because of the nature of constructions	200m² replacement with compensation	None
	150–200m² with some regular shape: the front and back sides not < 7m²	Registration, with regular shape	Regularization, with regular shape
	Two adjacent plots of 150–200m² each	Agreement, with regular shape and co-ownership	None
	Residential, up to 500m², with rent price	Registration of the 500m² and expropriation of extra land, if extra land has a built structure registered with a base lease price; if unwilling to pay lease price, expropriation with compensation	Reduction in size for services and infrastructure, and with a lease price per m²
Super-standard (> 500m²)	If extra /500+m² is not adequate, to be developed as an individual plot	Registration, with rent price	None
	For irregular adjacent plots	Maintenance of regularity with "give and take" principle through negotiations	None
	If extra /500+m² is adequate, to be developed as an individual plot	Priority of leasehold given to current landholder	Demolition of any > 500m² and banking of land without any compensation
		If landholder is incapable or unwilling, expropriation with compensation	If all 500m² totally occupied with built structure, regularization with maximum lease

Note. Adapted from Southern Nations, Nationalities and Peoples' Regional State (SNNPRS), *2015,* የከተማ መሬት በሊዝ ስለመፍቀድ የወጣ ደንብ ቁጥር 123/2007 ለማስፈጸም ተሻሽሎ የወጣ መመሪያ ቁጥር 8/07. ሀዋሳ, ኢትዮጵያ *[Urban Land Lease Permitting Regulation No. 123/2007 Amended Directive No. 8/07. Hawassa, Ethiopia].*

plots of land, only 2,014 (5.3%) were regularized in 2016. Conversely, in the same year, 4,138 houses were built on new plots, while 2,458 were demolished in the regional state (SNNPR), and 599 were demolished in Hawassa (SNNPRS, 2016).

Maintaining Rural Rights through Resistance of Regularization Process

The so-called illegal landholders resisted registering. Indeed, only 5.3% were registered up until 2017. Even though more than 16,000 title deeds were prepared in Hawassa city, the landholders delayed registration, asking instead: "What makes our land illegal?" Rural residents felt this was unjust and that it denied their right to be rural (Interviews conducted in 2017). As a result, two important resistances began.

The first form of resistance was against the mode of registering the landholdings in the annexed peripheral areas, and the second was against the land being classified in the illegal landholding category. The residents had three meetings and told the city and the regional administration to revise their proposals. Rural residents argued that their land was legally held on the basis of the rural land law that governed their landholding before the annexation, and hence the law should not work retroactively. They also claimed that the modes of registration clearly privileged the old possessions found in the inner city and harmed the rural residents. An elder asked the officials, "tell me what made a land of my ancestors, transferred across the generations that I am transferring to the next generation, illegal, which I must pay the fees and fines for!" The elder further argued that "the city administration needs our land not us!"—pointing out the efforts of the city to extract the wealth of rural areas for the city's benefit, while neglecting the rights of rural residents. As a result, the city administration delayed registration and was forced to revise the modalities. The new proposals were to consider the rural land as old possessions as well. This worked because the administrators demanded political support from the rural community, mainly during elections (see Kinfu et al., 2019). The changes that included the illegal land further encouraged land transfer and, as a result, new developments (i.e., transfers of land to others and changes in land use). This in turn challenged the effectiveness of the regularization policy. In this regard, the rural resistance was effective, and these holdings were thereafter equated with the old holdings.

The second form of resistance began as the preparation of the city's new urban plan launched in August 2018. The residents of the rural sub-city called for public demonstrations and massive social media agitations to advocate a "Say no to the master plan!" movement. This was similar to the movement that had taken place in Addis Ababa two years before, regarding the rural areas adjacent to the capital city. In 2018, the youth living in the peripheries of Hawassa demonstrated near the city administration building, calling for an immediate public response to stop the plan. A public consultation meeting was called to explain the plan, which ended without consensus. According to the rural residents interviewed in 2018, the resistance to the new plan emanated from three main issues: (1) the unresolved partiality of the regularization that treated the rural landholders as illegal, which remained contentious; (2) the suspicions of the community toward the lawmakers' hidden "political agendas that have been affecting the rights of the rural and the native inhabitants"; and (3) the recent undertakings on the issues of the new regional state and the ownership of the city. In response, the mayor publicly banned the preparation of the new plan and admitted to the failure to adequately include the community members. The planning process has officially been stopped since then.

This experience sheds light on two important issues. First, the accumulation by dispossession activities of the state did not consider the rights of rural residents. Indeed, it seems wealth and power accumulation on the part of the government, as well as political maneuvers, were the driving motivations. Second, rural residents have effective tools—at least in these instances—to resist and counteract these processes. In these two examples, both resistance strategies driven by rural residents were successful in halting the policy changes that were to impact them negatively. The former was successful in deterring the urbanized policy and the punishing of rural residents for their so-called illegal holdings. This was achieved because it helped to acknowledge the legality of rural landholding rights, and as ways were found to accommodate the transition of rural rights into urban ones without punishment. This further supported the efficacy of urban land production and rural-urban linkages. The latter resistance halted the development of new planning documents altogether.

Conclusion

Drawing upon the politico-legal contexts and land governance systems of Ethiopia, this chapter has examined how the urbanization and annexation processes around rural land are occurring within the city of Hawassa. In so doing, it has highlighted how the rights of rural citizens have been neglected, often for the benefit of the municipal government and urban dwellers. We scrutinized the land governance system in terms of the regularization of rural land and explored its implications for the rights of rural residents. Ethiopia's urban land policy has affected rural citizens in ways that have prohibited their rights of development and neglected their property rights. The development permit technically limits the rural residents in terms of their constitutional rights, and it makes them wait for urban development to reach them and their geographic area before they can transfer or develop their land. This highlights the underlying policy failure in that the policy only associates development with urbanization. Regularization was introduced to urbanize the annexed rural areas, and this denied citizens' right to be rural and the rights of landholders in rural areas in the following ways:

- The policy wrongly proclaimed the rural landholders to be illegal, while the rural residents had acquired and developed the land as per the rural land laws.
- The regularization process denied rural citizens their right to development and property rights, despite these being constitutional rights.
- The various modes of regularization tolerated old possessions found inside the city limits and overlooked various other modes of landholdings in the annexed rural areas.
- The provisions of the regularization policy prohibited and punished the so-called illegal acts, which went against the legitimate rights of rural residents.
- The regularization policy resulted in resistance and violence, which escalated to the point of affecting urban growth and development as well as urban-rural linkages in the long term.

The denial and neglect of rural residents' rights demonstrates how land policy tools like regularization in Ethiopia work to negatively impact the rights of rural citizens. Furthermore, this case study demonstrates how governance tendencies favour urban areas and urbanization, which are associated with development. However, much of the wealth obtained by urban residents and urban government administrations is being drawn from the rural areas and rural residents. This case is also instructive in how, at least in some instances, people have the power to negotiate and navigate changes. This is not always the case, as has been demonstrated in other parts of the country. One factor that could enable a more positive relationship is that the urban centre and the surrounding rural areas share an ethno-linguistic identity, a factor relating to aspects of social citizenship (Marshall, 1950; Turner, 2003). In other instances, such as the resistance to the Addis Ababa Master Plan, resistance has been much more confrontational and violent. In many ways, the neglect of rural residents' rights in Hawassa is extremely problematic, and the issues remain unresolved. In other ways, the case of Hawassa provides an example for other cities regarding how to engage in dialogue and be responsive to rural residents, as opposed to imposing directives that result in conflict and violence.

References

Brenner, N., Peck, J., & Theodore, N. (2010). After neoliberalization? *Globalizations, 7*(3), 327–345.

Cochrane, L. (2017). *Strengthening food security in rural Ethiopia* [Doctoral dissertation]. University of British Columbia, Vancouver, BC.

Cochrane, L., & Bekele, Y. (2018). Contextualizing narratives of economic growth and navigating problematic data: Economic trends in Ethiopia (1999-2017). *Economies, 6*(4), 1–16.

Dejene, M., & Cochrane, L. (2019). Ethiopia's developmental state: A building stability framework assessment. *Development Policy Review, 37*(S2), 161–178.

Federal Democratic Republic of Ethiopia (FDRE). (1995). *Constitution of the Federal Democratic Republic of Ethiopia* (Proclamation number 1/1995). http://library.stic.et/documents/30479/593917/Proclamation+number+1-1995-Constitution+of+the+Federal+Democratic+Republic+of+Ethiopia.pdf/5e3bcdb1-b22e-4c63-ef12-46567d0be00b?version=1.0

Federal Democratic Republic of Ethiopia (FDRE). (2002). የኢፌዴሪ የገጠርና ግብርና ልማት ፖሊሲና ስትራቴጂ. የኢትዮጵያ ፌዴራላዊ ዴሞክራሲያዊ ሪፐብሊክ መንግስት. አዲስ አበባ. ሜጋ ማተሚያ ቤት [FDRE rural and agricultural development policy and strategy. Mega Printing House].

Federal Democratic Republic of Ethiopia (FDRE). (2011). *Urban lands lease holding proclamation* (Proclamation no. 721/2011). http://admin.theiguides.org/Media/Documents/Urban-land-lease-proclamation-no-721-20111.pdf

Federal Democratic Republic of Ethiopia (FDRE). (2013). አደጋን የሚቋቋም፣ አረንጓዴና ተደራሽ የከተሞች ልማት ፖሊሲ. በከተማ ልማትና ኮንስትራክሽን ሚኒስቴር, የኢትዮጵያ ፌዴራላዊ ዴሞክራሲያዊ ሪፐብሊክ መንግስት, አዲስአበባ [*Risk, green and accessible urban development policy*. Ministry of Urban Development and Construction, Government of the Federal Democratic Republic of Ethiopia, Addis Ababa].

Fukuyama, F. (2011). *The origins of political order: From prehuman times to the French revolution*. Farrar, Straus and Giroux.

Harvey, D. (2003). *The new imperialism*. Oxford University Press.

Kinfu, E., Bombeck, H., Nigussie, A., & Wegayehu, F. (2019). The genesis of peri-urban Ethiopia: The case of Hawassa City. *Journal of Land and Rural Studies, 7*(1), 71–95.

Marshall, T. H. (1950). *Citizenship and social class and other essays*. University of Cambridge Press.

Ministry of Urban Development and Housing Construction (MODHCO). (2015). *The state of Ethiopian cities*. Mega Printing.

Pankhurst, A. (Ed.). (2017). *Change and transformation in 20 rural communities in Ethiopia: Selected aspects and implications for policy*. Tsehai Publishers.

Pankhurst, R. (1966). *State and land in Ethiopian history*. Institute of Ethiopian Studies.

Southern Nations, Nationalities and Peoples' Regional State (SNNPRS). (2015a). የተሻሻለው ደቡብ ብሔሮች፣ ብሔረሰቦች እና ሕዝቦች ክልል መንግስት የከተማ መሬት ሊዝ ደንብ ቁጥር ፳፻፰፲/፪ሺ፯.

ሀዋሳ, ኢትዮጵያ [Improved Southern Nations, Nations, Nationalities and Peoples' Regional State Urban Land Lease Regulation No. Hawassa, Ethiopia].

Southern Nations, Nationalities and Peoples' Regional State (SNNPRS). (2015b). የከተማ መሬት በሊዝ ስለመፍቀድ የወጣ ደንብ ቁጥር 123/2007 ለማስፈጸም ተሻሽሎ የወጣ መመሪያ ቁጥር 8/07. ሀዋሳ, ኢትዮጵያ [Urban Land Lease Permitting Regulation No. 123/2007 Amended Directive No. 8/07. Hawassa, Ethiopia].

Southern Nations, Nationalities and Peoples' Regional State (SNNPRS). (2015c). የከተሞች ማስፋፊያ አከባቢ የህገወጥ ግንባታን ለመከላከል የተዘጋጀ የንቅናቄ ሰነድ. ሀዋሳ, ኢትዮጵያ [Motion document to prevent illegal construction of urban expansion areas. Hawassa, Ethiopia] (Unpublished).

Southern Nations, Nationalities and Peoples' Regional State (SNNPRS). (2016). የከተሞች ማስፋፊያ አከባቢ የህገወጥ ግንባታን ለመከላከል የስራ አፈጻጸም ሪፖርት. ሀዋሳ, ኢትዮጵያ [Performance report to prevent illegal construction in urban expansion area. Hawassa, Ethiopia] (Unpublished).

Turner, B. S. (2003). The erosion of citizenship. *British Journal of Sociology, 52*(2), 189–209.

United Nations Department of Economic and Social Affairs (UN DESA). (2018). *World urbanization prospects 2018: Highlights.* https://population.un.org/wup/Publications/Files/WUP2018-Highlights.pdf

Wondrade, N., Dick, Ø. B., & Tveite, H. (2014). Landscape mapping to quantify degree-of-freedom, degree-of-sprawl, and degree-of-goodness of urban growth in Hawassa, Ethiopia. *Environment and Natural Resources Research, 4*(4), 223–237. https://doi.org/10.5539/enrr.v4n4p223

Wubneh, M. (2018). Policies and praxis of land acquisition, use, and development in Ethiopia. *Land Use Policy, 73*, 170–183.

Zewde, B. (2014). *The quest for socialist utopia: The Ethiopian student movement c. 1960–1974.* Addis Ababa University Press.

VI
The Right to Rural Mobility

17

Exploring Rural Citizenship through Displacement

An Analysis of Citizenship in the Context of Refugee Resettlement and Integration in Rural Canada

STACEY HAUGEN

Introduction

The increasing number of forcibly displaced persons worldwide has raised questions of citizenship, belonging, and integration. In particular, the ongoing Syrian conflict has contributed significantly to the unprecedented 70.8 million persons experiencing displacement today (UNHCR, 2019). In the fall of 2015, the newly elected Canadian government committed to resettling thousands of Syrian refugees in a matter of months. By the beginning of 2017, more than 40,000 Syrians had been resettled to over 350 communities across Canada, including many smaller and rural places (Government of Canada, 2017a). And yet, despite the growing number of refugees being resettled into diverse communities across the country, little research has been done on integration in rural regions (Haugen, 2019).

In this chapter, I specifically address the right of refugees to rural spaces, and how understandings of rural citizenship are shaped by the rural newcomer and impacted by the larger, bureaucratic system of resettlement. Throughout the chapter I ask: what does rural citizenship and the right to be rural mean for displaced persons who find themselves in rural and smaller communities in

Canada? For refugees in Canada, I argue that the right to be rural is not clearly evident nor easily obtained. Refugees do not choose if they will be resettled to a rural or urban area. If they end up in a rural place, they face numerous challenges and must rely on local volunteers to help them find services and integrate into the community. Thus, local volunteers become gatekeepers to their community, and how they understand citizenship and integration impacts the lives of resettled refugees. In this resettlement system, rurally resettled refugees are not granted the same citizenship rights as those living in urban areas where newcomers have access to government supports. In this chapter, I address questions of rural citizenship through a theoretical analysis of social and market citizenship in rural spaces, alongside the lived experiences of refugees and rural community members.

Citizenship and Displacement

For refugees who have been displaced from their home country, citizenship, in terms of belonging to a state with defined borders, can be a fraught concept. Citizenship is intrinsically tied to the existence of the state and the defense of a set of artificially defined borders that represent the inclusion of those who belong and exclusion of anyone understood as "other" or "undesirable." Janine Brodie (2002) explains citizenship as an individual's membership within, and relationship to, a bordered territory that is recognized as a state within the international community. For Brodie, "citizenship has little meaning, conceptually or empirically, outside of the context of the modern national state" (p. 379). In an increasingly globalized world, the connection between citizenship and the state has come under increasing scrutiny. As Kate Nash (2009) contends, "processes and discourses of globalization mean that questions of political participation which are framed in terms of the interests and values of citizens within separate and distinct nation-states are inappropriate where issues and events are not contained within national territories" (p. 1068). Armed conflict, environmental degradation, natural disasters, and civil unrest are all events that can and often do spill over borders. Citizens forcibly displaced from their homes can face numerous challenges in accessing their rights and finding a sense of belonging in a world defined by a state-centric system of citizenship.

Other scholars of citizenship have argued that neoliberalism—as a policy regime, economic theory, and even a "worldview" (Kotsko, 2018) that imposes market rationality on spheres that have traditionally been outside the market— has transformed understandings of citizenship. In neoliberal regimes, social citizenship, which involves holding a sense of belonging to a state and having the right to access state resources, is being overshadowed by market citizenship. In Nawyn's (2011) formulation, market citizenship is defined by a person's economic productivity, and excludes those who are poor or rely on government assistance (pp. 679-680). It does so by transforming things that were once citizenship rights or entitlements by default into things that citizens earn through employment or must actually pay for from private providers. As Bauman (2005) puts it:

> the wellbeing of a country tends to be measured these days by the amount of money changing hands and by the speed with which the changing is done...It should not therefore come as a surprise that the underlying shift, seldom articulated explicitly and yet easy to spot between the lines of official speeches, is from the right to care determined by inalienable "social rights", to social rights being a reward for "those who've deserved it" through their actual and prospective contribution to the economic prosperity of the country, measured primarily by the viability and vigour of the consumer markets (pp. 19-20).

While market citizenship makes consumerism and the ability to generate wealth the most important criteria for belonging, for T. H. Marshall, social rights are inalienable and should not be determined by a citizen's economic status. For Marshall (1950), "citizenship is a status bestowed on those who are full members of a community. All who possess the status are equal with respect to the rights and duties with which the status is endowed" (pp. 28-29). Somers (2008) agrees, arguing that social inclusion is the most important aspect of citizenship, as "the first right to political membership must equally include the *de facto* right to *social* inclusion in civil society. By social inclusion I mean the right to *recognition* by others as a moral equal treated by the same standards and values and due the same level of respect and dignity as all other members" (p. 6). For T. H. Marshall (1950), the existence of a welfare state offers protections for all citizens and works to mitigate the inequalities created and perpetuated within a capitalist system. In Western nations where neoliberalism is understood to be the hegemonic (if receding) policy framework, many have documented a shift from understanding social rights as undeniable to contingent on economic factors (Somers, 2008; Stasiulus, 2002).

As non-citizen newcomers, refugees find themselves in the middle of this struggle between market and social citizenship. Nawyn (2011) argues that refugees can stand at the intersection of the "market/social citizenship conflict" as they are foreigners—outsiders—and often arrive with few material resources (p.

680). Complicating this struggle is the way in which many countries position refugees as beneficial to their market economies. Heins and Unrau (2018) contend that in an effort to reject understandings of refugees as "dark" and "dangerous," many academics, politicians, and governments emphasize the economic value that newcomers bring to the state. Leaders in receiving countries call upon their citizens to see refugees not only as persecuted individuals but also as consumers and "workers who address the shortage of labor in many industries" (Heins & Unrau, 2018, p. 227). Thus, in a neoliberal, capitalist society, refugees are not offered a sense of belonging based on their humanity, but on their ability to contribute economically to society. Bauman (2005) states that belonging and "social rights are now to be offered selectively. They ought to be given if and only if the givers decide that giving them would accord with their interest; not on the strength of humanity of the recipients" (p. 21). This narrative is also used by Canadian politicians and international organizations to make refugees more appealing to provincial governments and the public by positioning refugees as economic contributors to society and not only passive recipients of aid (UNHCR Canada, 2019; Wright, 2019).

In the Canadian context, the way in which refugees experience this "market/social citizenship conflict" is in part influenced by the program through which they arrive in this country. Canadian resettlement takes place through two streams: government assistance and private sponsorship. For refugees resettled through government assistance, resettlement services, including income support, are provided through the Resettlement Assistance Program (RAP). In the RAP, representatives welcome refugees at the airport, help refugees find a place to live, and refer refugees to other federal and provincial settlement and newcomer services that can help them with language training, employment, and other services (Government of Canada, 2017b). Government-assisted refugees can only be resettled in communities with a RAP, which are almost exclusively located in urban centres (Government of Canada, 2018a). Refugees can also be resettled through private sponsorship, where Canadians come together to raise funds and commit to socially and economically supporting a refugee for their first year in Canada (Government of Canada, 2017b). The Blended Visa Office-Referred resettlement program is another type of private sponsorship. Through this program, the UNHCR refers refugees for resettlement and the Canadian government contributes a portion of the funds needed for resettlement, while the private sponsorship group takes care of the rest (Government of Canada, 2017b). Through private sponsorship, refugees can be resettled anywhere a group has formed, and thus many refugees have been resettled in rural Canada through this program (Government of Canada, 2017a).

Methods

In an effort to understand resettlement in rural places, I undertook a research project with funding from the International Development Research Centre (IDRC) in the spring and summer of 2017. I travelled to four smaller communities across four provinces, talking to refugees and community members about their experiences. The first community I visited was in southwestern Ontario. It has a population of 8,000 people and is 150 kilometres from the nearest urban centre. One Syrian family had been sponsored into this community. Next, I travelled to a rural region in Nova Scotia where a coalition of individuals was supporting three Syrian refugee families. Two of the families lived in a community of 3,000 people that is 20 kilometres from the nearest urban centre. The other family lived in a neighbouring community of 500 people that is 50 kilometres from the nearest urban centre. The third community was in southern Alberta. It has a population of 800 and is 100 kilometres from the nearest urban centre. One intergenerational Syrian family had been sponsored into this community. Lastly, I visited a community of 6,000 people in central Saskatchewan in which one Syrian family was sponsored. The community is 110 kilometres from the nearest urban centre. Of the six refugee families that I spoke with, three were privately sponsored families, two were Blended Visa Office-Referred families, and one was a government sponsored family that had moved out of the city with the support of a rural sponsorship group. Three of the families had arrived in the winter of 2016 and the other three had arrived in the fall of 2016. In total, I conducted formal interviews with 45 rural refugee sponsors, community members, and service providers, and 10 Syrian refugees. I also met and spoke informally with additional community members and newcomers at social gatherings and other events in each community. I learned what rural resettlement looks like in Canada, and about the benefits, challenges, and concerns that refugees and rural Canadians confront along the resettlement journey (Haugen, 2019).

Findings

Through my research I found that private sponsorship can be further wrought with the social/market citizenship dilemma, as citizens become the gatekeepers for refugees accessing community supports and services, especially in rural and smaller communities. Many smaller communities do not have access to the same settlement services, public transport, or other amenities that urban places offer, and thus the connections and relationships that the refugee maintains with the private sponsorship group and other community members are particularly important. In this situation, my data demonstrates that private sponsors are put in a position of power and their own personal understanding of citizenship rights can impact the refugee family they are supporting. In rural places, personal contacts are particularly important and lead to employment opportunities, access to informal services, and ultimately belongingness within a community. The need to make connections within the community is structured within a power relationship between the rural citizen, most significantly the private sponsors, and the newcomer. When they first arrive, refugees rely heavily on private sponsors, especially if they do not have easy access to many, if any, other settlement services in the community. Private sponsors hold their own personal understandings of belonging and have their own socially constructed conception of citizenship and the rights and responsibilities that go along with that status.

When sponsors and/or community members understand citizenship and belonging through a market framework, challenges can arise when the refugee family does not ascribe to the same ideas and accesses government supports. For one of the sponsorship groups I met with, differing ideas of what the refugee family should have the right to access led to dysfunction within the group, disappointment on both sides of the sponsorship, and conflict with the refugee family. The refugee family reinforced this, saying that for them, cultural differences did not present a challenge to belonging within the community, but tensions around money and budgeting did arise. A few sponsorship members were upset that the refugee father wanted to stay in English school instead of going to work. They felt they had received conflicting information on what was best for refugees from their Sponsorship Agreement Holder (s A H)[1] regarding employment, and they wanted the family to take employment opportunities found for them and avoid government assistance. While there was some recognition that expecting the family to be self-sufficient by the end of their first year in Canada may have been unrealistic, a few members of the group expressed the sentiment that they may have chosen not to be involved in sponsorship at all if they had known the refugee family would be accessing government assistance. One sponsor member stated "our group was really hopefully that they [the refugee family] would be able to be supporting themselves by the end of the year, and I think they don't feel like that's important to them...we knew going in that there were all of these [employment] opportunities for them, and we felt like it would be a real benefit at the end of the year if they wouldn't have to be supported by the government." For these sponsors, well integrated and fully functioning members of society are economically self-sufficient.

The sponsors who had such feelings also felt like the sponsorship group, and ultimately the refugee family, had disappointed and failed the community because the family was accessing government supports. These sponsors were offended that privately sponsored refugees were entitled to a variety of economic supports. One sponsor who valued paid employment over other types of assistance stated: "I'm offended that they [the refugee family] took my volunteer money, and my time, and now my tax money as well through welfare. They are getting so many services." They felt that the refugee family should not have the right to access additional services, and their definition of success and ultimately belonging hinged on the refugee family being economically self-sufficient. In this context, understandings of belonging and citizenship were situated within a market framework that placed value on paid work and devalued individuals on government assistance, regardless of the right of the recipient to this type of assistance. While the sponsors recognized that the family had different goals and understandings of success, the power imbalance between the family and the sponsorship group meant that what the sponsors understood as success and their view on the refugees' right to access services impacted the family.

Others with close connections to the same refugee family did not hold similar views. Community members stated that expecting the family to be self-sustaining within a year was just not realistic. They did not view accessing government supports as a failure, saying that the government committed to supporting the newcomers, and those supporting the refugees should make it easy for the family to access services available to help them settle. One person said that the group discouraging government supports only disadvantaged the refugee family, who could have been signed up for waitlists for services like housing and daycare earlier if some in the group had not actively discouraged it. They contended that the Canadian government had said: "they would support these people just like Canadians." Another individual agreed, saying that signing the family up for government assistance was positive because "they are trying to improve themselves...and those benefits are there to help people that are in that situation." They thought it was especially positive for the adults in the family, who wanted to continue to go to English classes and improve their language skills.

In other communities, the sponsorship groups I spoke with did not explicitly hold the same strong opinions regarding the right to access social services and other forms of assistance, although similar sentiments related to market citizenship were present in a few individual interviews. Most knew that the refugee family might be accessing government assistance after the sponsorship was over, and they were prepared to help them do that. While all groups were concerned with finding the sponsored family appropriate employment opportunities, the majority were aware of the need to balance their own expectations of economic self-sufficiency with the needs and desires of the family. One sponsor said they had expected the family to be more anxious to start working, but for a few reasons that had not been the case. While the group was concerned about the well-being of the family, they respected the family and worked to inform them of their options after the year of sponsorship was over.

Because of the power dynamics inherent in the private sponsorship model, the refugees I spoke with were sometimes hesitant to say anything negative about their sponsors or other community members. While they were honest about the challenges they faced, including difficulties with transportation, the language barrier, missing family and friends back home, and lacking certain services and amenities only available in the city, they were understandably less eager to discuss any tensions or conflicts that had arisen with private sponsors, whether these were big or small concerns. All the refugee families spoke of tight finances and having difficulties making ends meet at different points within their first year. One refugee commented that while they were very grateful to be in Canada, they were frustrated by the economic challenges they faced, specifically a lack of clarity and certainty from their sponsorship group regarding their budget, access to private sponsorship funds, and government supports. Speaking about their frustrations with differing economic expectations from the sponsorship group, this refugee stated, "The moment I'm in Canada I should be equal to you so why would I be treated differently?" There was an understanding that they had been accepted into Canada as resettled refugees, and should thus be offered the same resources and access to services and opportunities as Canadian citizens, regardless of the expectations of individual sponsorship members.

Claiming social rights to essential services can be a challenge for refugees living in rural areas, and a newcomer's sense of belonging can be impacted by a lack of resettlement funding for rural places. While rural communities are not excluded from participating in the private sponsorship program, the refugees they sponsor are not necessarily supported through the same newcomer and resettlement services as those available in urban spaces. Decisions regarding service delivery are made in cities, and thus, for a number of reasons such as population density, cost, and governance structures, government-funded services are largely urban. The services that the sponsorship groups and refugees I met with were able to access depended largely on the province in which they lived, and on the ability of the community to meet gaps in service provision with volunteers and other informal methods. Of course, a lack of rural services impacts local residents as well, but this can be more pronounced for refugee families. The resettlement process can cause rural residents to ask questions about the right to be rural in their communities, as they become more aware of the lack of available services.

When trying to find information on resettlement and newcomer services in their region, many sponsors found that existing government-funded services were often urban, and thus inaccessible or irrelevant to their sponsored refugees. One sponsor in Ontario said that they had attended a workshop on resettlement in a nearby city and received some information concerning programming from their SAH, but many of the services were only available in the closest urban centre, which is two hours away. Another sponsor, who was assisting a government-assisted refugee family in their move from the city into a rural area, said that there were long waitlists to access urban services, even for government-assisted refugees. This sponsor said that the Immigrant Service Centre where they sought resettlement assistance only thought of the government-funded refugee family as urban and did not have much to offer regarding resettlement services outside of the city. In another interview, a service provider and SAH in an urban centre near one of my study's sponsorship groups stated that they did not work in rural areas outside of the city and were hesitant to sponsor refugees in rural areas. Another sponsorship group in Alberta did not even access the resettlement office in their nearest urban centre, as they did not think the information would be relevant. In another rural community in Saskatchewan, there was an Immigrant Service Centre in the community, which was helpful, but the centre did not often deal with refugees, and thus they did not have the same knowledge base as urban resettlement centres. Another sponsor in the same community said that they went to the nearest urban resettlement centre, but the resources were all based out of the city and the staff did not travel, so it was not very helpful.

Even when critical capacity and population density make it possible for more services to be provided in rural areas, service delivery is still often left in the hands of the community and volunteers. In one region that I visited, the need for an English language school was so great that a community church started a school in their basement with the help of two community members that spoke Arabic and had English language training. In a few months, the school went from serving 4 to 30 students, most of whom were Syrian refugees privately sponsored into the region in early 2016. However, there were also a few immigrants and other newcomers accessing the centre. At the time of my research, over 40 volunteers were helping to run the program. The classes are accessed by a variety of students, ranging from those who do not know how to read or write to university graduates. Students at the school not only learn English, but they also meet and socialize with other refugees in the region and integrate into the community. Yet, this school is entirely funded by the community church and supported by a large group of volunteers. While this is a great success for this community, as the English language school is providing an important service for newcomers and private sponsors in the region, it is not necessarily the solution. Efforts like these require an immense amount of volunteer labour, adequate space, and the right combination of social capital and community resources, which do not exist in every community. Without this service, the family I visited, and many of the other students, would not have had access to appropriate English language training in the region despite the demand for such a program.

A Right to Be Rural?

In the context of declining rural rights and services, combined with sentiments of market-based citizenship, what does the right to be rural mean for resettled refugees? First, while all refugees are granted permanent residence when they come to Canada (Government of Canada, 2017c), they do not have an explicit or legal right to live in a rural area. Government-assisted refugees are resettled to urban centres with the required services, and privately sponsored refugees are for the most part sent to the community in which their sponsors live, whether it be rural or urban. As permanent residents, resettled refugees have the right to live and work anywhere in the country (Government of Canada, 2019); however, it is difficult for refugees to live outside of an area in which they are receiving either government or private supports. My findings reflect this difficult reality. The government-sponsored family that I spoke with did not want to live in the city they had been resettled to. They had come from a smaller community in Syria and didn't want to live in an apartment. They wanted a house and a garden. Only with the help of a local, rural private sponsorship group, who was waiting for two other refugee families to arrive, was the family able to resettle into a rural area. After several months of struggling to find work and access language services, and of feeling isolated, there was a discussion about whether the family wanted to move back into the city. However, after much deliberation, the family made it clear why they wanted to stay in the rural community. They had made friends, their children liked the school, and after moving into the centre of town, they did not feel as isolated and enjoyed their life in the community. While the father had to commute into the city for work, and driving to language classes was still a challenge, the family decided that the benefits of rural living outweighed the other complications. For this family, their desire to live rurally was evident, despite the very real resettlement barriers. Many of the private sponsors I spoke with also recognized that some refugee families, including those who are government-funded, may want to live in rural areas.

In Canada's resettlement system, smaller communities cannot resettle government-assisted refugees regardless of what the community has to offer or what the refugee would prefer. For example, community members I spoke with in Saskatchewan indicated that their small community had many available services for refugees looking to live in a smaller place. Government RAP funding could be facilitated through their existing newcomer centre, and government-assisted refugees could access an English language school hosted in the local college as well as some affordable housing options in the community. Yet, the government had not looked to leverage those existing rural services, nor considered that some refugees might want the choice of living in a rural setting. For example, two privately sponsored families I spoke with made it very clear that they enjoyed living in a rural setting. They have each now purchased a home in their new community and have no intentions of leaving anytime soon. Both families cited the quiet, safety, and space as the reasons they wanted to stay in rural Canada. Of course, there are still others who move on to urban spaces after they complete their first year of support. I spoke with two refugee families who had decided to move into the city because they wanted to be closer to a larger Arab community and education opportunities.

Second, for refugees resettled to rural places, the social/market citizenship dilemma is further wrought with power structures inherent in the private sponsorship model and the informal networks that exist in smaller places in general. Regardless of residency status, citizenship rights are uneven and limited to those who have access to legal rights and moral or material resources (Nash, 2009, p. 1079). In Nash's (2009) words, "the enjoyment of rights is never a simple matter of legal entitlement; it also depends on social structures through which power, material resources and meanings are created and circulated" (p. 1069). By relying on social capital to accomplish resettlement and integration, the government passes the social right of citizenship on to the private citizen and their rural community. Somers (2008) explains that neoliberal governments are then able to claim that gaps in social rights and access to essential services are not the fault of a decline in funds to rural communities, but are instead the fault of private citizens and communities who lack social capital.

> *Clearly, the appeal of the social capital concept for the neoliberals and conservatives is in its indictment of public sector investment. It vindicates antistatism by blaming civic decline on the usual sociological suspects of the welfare state and its public services. Most conveniently, it explains the intractability of market failures and externalities not by neoliberalism's starvation of the public sector or its policies of privatization and structural readjustment, but by inadequate quantities of social capital (Somers, 2008, p. 253).*

Third, a system that relies on the social capital of communities to fill gaps in essential services means that rural refugees do not have the same right to access services as refugees living in urban spaces. Somers (2008) recognizes this, contending that: "the concept of social capital is grounded on the imperatives of duty, responsibility, coerced cooperation, moral and religious values, voluntary labor, and absolute trust in the market—but is devoid of rights" (p. 248). When housed within the language of social capital, the right of the rural refugee to social citizenship is entirely based on the ability of a rural community to provide the service in the absence of government investment. In this system, the burden of essential service delivery in rural communities is placed on the private sponsor and community, instead of with urban decision-makers, who often make decisions on behalf of rural peoples. As Laura Barraclough (2013) contends more generally, the "lives of people in the countryside are overwhelmingly structured by decision-making in the cities" (p. 1048).

Conclusion

For refugees in rural areas, citizenship means finding a new place to call home despite the barriers and challenges present in rural and smaller Canada. It can mean choosing to commute into work and to language classes in order to own a house and have a garden. Living outside of an urban centre can mean having access to fewer resources and feeling excluded from settlement programming that does not consider the rural refugee. For government-assisted refugees, the right to be rural is even more distant and unrealistic as there is no way to express a desire to live rurally when funding does not often flow outside of urban centres. Unfortunately, many of the challenges and barriers that newcomers face when attempting to access their social citizenship rights in rural and smaller communities are inherent to life in rural Canada today. A neoliberal and market system as well as international pressures combined with a lack of recognition at the decision-making table of government have contributed to the overall decline of rural communities. In this reality, rural success stories that are contingent on social capital and volunteer networks cannot be held up as the only way for rural citizens and newcomers to achieve their social rights. Access to essential services must be understood as a right that rural citizens are entitled to because they are citizens. Without this understanding, rural communities will continue to decline and underfunded and disappearing services will remain a fact of life in rural Canada for both newcomers and the citizens who already call rural Canada home.

Note

1. A Sponsorship Agreement Holder is an organization that holds a special agreement with the Government of Canada to help resettle refugees in Canada (Government of Canada, 2018b).

References

Barraclough, L. (2013). Is there also a right to the countryside? *Antipode, 45*(5), 1047–1049. https://doi.org/10.1111/anti.12040

Bauman, Z. (2005). Freedom from, in and through the state. *Theoria, 52*(108), 13–27.

Brodie, J. (2002). Citizenship and solidarity: Reflections on the Canadian way. *Citizenship Studies, 6*(4), 377–394.

Government of Canada. (2017a). *#WelcomeRefugees: Key figures.* http://www.cic.gc.ca/english/refugees/welcome/milestones.asp

Government of Canada. (2017b). *How Canada's refugee system works.* https://www.canada.ca/en/immigration-refugees-citizenship/services/refugees/canada-role.html

Government of Canada. (2017c). *After you apply: Get next steps—Refugee status from outside Canada.* https://www.canada.ca/en/immigration-refugees-citizenship/services/refugees/help-outside-canada/after-apply-next-steps.html

Government of Canada. (2018a). *Find help to adjust as a refugee in Canada.* https://www.canada.ca/en/immigration-refugees-citizenship/services/refugees/help-within-canada/government-assisted-refugee-program/providers.html

Government of Canada. (2018b). *Sponsorship agreement holders: About the program.* https://www.canada.ca/en/immigration-refugees-citizenship/services/refugees/help-outside-canada/private-sponsorship-program/agreement-holders.html

Government of Canada. (2019). *Understand permanent resident status.* https://www.canada.ca/en/immigration-refugees-citizenship/services/new-immigrants/pr-card/understand-pr-status.html

Haugen, S. (2019). "We feel like we're home": The resettlement and integration of Syrian refugees in smaller and rural Canadian communities. *Refuge, 35*(2), 53-63.

Heins, V. M., & Unrau, C. (2018). Refugees welcome: Arrival gifts, reciprocity, and the integration of forced migrants. *Journal of International Political Theory, 14*(2), 223-239.

Kotsko, A. (2018). *Neoliberalism's demons: On the political theology of late capital.* Stanford University Press.

Marshall, T. H. (1950). *Citizenship and social class and other essays.* Cambridge University Press.

Nash, K. (2009). Between citizenship and human rights. *Sociology, 43*(6), 1067-1083.

Nawyn, S. (2011). "I have so many successful stories": Framing social citizenship for refugees. *Citizenship Studies, 15*(6-7), 679-693.

Somers, M. R. (2008). *Genealogies of citizenship: Markets, statelessness, and the right to have rights.* Cambridge University Press.

Stasiulus, D. (2002). Introduction: Reconfiguring Canadian citizenship. *Citizenship studies, 6*(4), 365-375.

UNHCR (United Nations High Commissioner for Refugees). (2019). *Figures at a glance.* https://www.unhcr.org/figures-at-a-glance.html

UNHCR Canada. (2019, June 20). *Refugees are good for Canada.* https://www.unhcr.ca/news/refugees-good-canada/

Wright, T. (2019, June 23). Hussen says he wants Canada to accept more refugees as economic immigrants. *Canada's National Observer.* https://www.nationalobserver.com/2019/06/21/news/hussen-says-he-wants-canada-accept-more-refugees-economic-immigrants

18

Local Politics of Inclusion and Exclusion

Exploring the Situation of Migrant Labourers and their Descendants after Land Reform in Rural Zimbabwe

CLEMENT CHIPENDA & TOM TOM

Introduction

Citizenship and rights are central to development and governance discourses (see e.g., Barraclough, 2013; Bauman, 2005; Brodie, 2002; Harvey, 2008; Lister, 1997; Marshall, 1950, 2005, 2009; Nash, 2009; Somers, 2008; Stasiulis, 2002; Turner, 2001). Enhancing the participation of and benefits to excluded groups is increasingly becoming a key principle in development. At the international level, inclusive development is enshrined in the United Nations' Sustainable Development Goals. In this chapter, we will examine Zimbabwe's Fast Track Land Reform Programme (FTLRP), which has been hailed for having major redistributive outcomes (Binswanger-Mkhize & Moyo, 2012; Chibwana, 2016; Chipenda 2018, 2019; James, 2015; Mazhawidza & Manjengwa, 2011; Mkodzongi, 2013; Moyo, 2013; Scoones, 2015; Tekwa & Adesina, 2018). The program led to the resettlement of 180,000 families (170,000 under A1 scheme and 10,000 under A2 scheme[1]) on 13 million hectares. However, not much is known about the lives of migrant labourers and their descendants in the aftermath of the land reform. We will use Marshall's (1950) conceptual lenses of social citizenship (civil, political, and economic) to frame our analysis of the consequences of the FTLRP for the lives of these migrant workers.

Migrant Labour System, Land Reform, and the Migrant Question in Contemporary Zimbabwe

The history of migrant labour in Southern Africa is well documented (see Amanor-Wilks & Moyo, 1996; Arrighi, 1970; Clarke, 1977; Chambati & Moyo, 2004; Palmer, 1977). The rise of the capitalist economy and emergence of farms and mines saw the creation of a labour migrant system during colonialism. This emergent labour relations system was based on a labour reserve comprising mainly of migrants from neighbouring countries. Most of the labourers were from Zambia, Malawi, and Mozambique. The imposition of taxes on Indigenous populations by the colonial administration was aimed at raising funds and compelling this large human resource to partake in the emerging capitalist economy. In order to meet their tax obligations, the Indigenous population had to provide labour on the farms and in mines. Due to incentives provided to migrant labourers, some opted to migrate to neighbouring countries to work on farms and in mines. Consequently, in the latter part of the twentieth century, the labour regime consisted of a combination of migrant and domestic labourers who serviced the colonial capitalist economy. Colonialism saw the emergence of a semi-proletarianized African labour force that was economically and extra-economically subordinated to the labour markets of mines, farms, and industries in urban areas (Mafeje, 2003; Palmer, 1977).

Relics of the migrant labour system remain today. Examples are the labour arrangements and farm compound system, which formed (and still form) a labour tenancy arrangement, in which a certain portion of land was set aside for the residence of both migrants and domestic labourers. It was a system of control and regulation. Labourers resided on the farms and worked in return for residency rights (Clark, 1977). This labour regime was insecure, exploitative, and aimed at extracting surplus value while creating a cyclical and exploitative system geared toward the reproduction of farm workers (Chipenda, 2019).

With the FTLRP, approximately 200,000 jobs were lost on acquired farms and 30,000 to 45,000 workers were displaced to urban and communal areas as well as informal settlements and towns (Chambati, 2017; Chambati & Moyo, 2004; Chambati & Magaramombe, 2008). Although the exact number is not known, some farm workers migrated to neighbouring countries, with Mozambique and South Africa being dominant destinations (Hammar, Raftopoulos, & Jensen,

2010; Rutherford & Addison, 2007). Approximately, over two thirds of the former farm workers remained on the former large-scale commercial farms (LSCFs) (Chambati & Moyo, 2004; Magaramombe, 2010). The FTLRP led to a net gain in livelihoods as 45,000 farm workers and 4,000 LSCFs were replaced by 180,000 farm households who now engaged in farming and diversified livelihood activities. This reconfiguration created employment opportunities that catered to the new communities (see Chambati, 2017; Mkodzongi, 2016; Moyo, 2011).

However, the FTLRP marginalized farm workers. Only 8.1% were allocated land (Alexander, 2003; Moyo et al., 2009). Farm workers were accused of supporting the opposition political party (Movement for Democratic Change, or MDC) and for being anti-land reform. Consequently, they were excluded from allocation processes and were not given special recognition as a group requiring resettlement, like war veterans and women. Furthermore, this period saw the amendment of citizenship laws. This was interpreted as a way of disenfranchising farm workers to weaken the opposition.

At independence in 1980, the Lancaster House Constitution had allowed for dual citizenship. This had protected the rights of migrant workers and their descendants. However, the new Citizenship of Zimbabwe Act (1984) stated that no Zimbabwean citizen was allowed to hold dual citizenship. This was a result of a constitutional amendment in 1983, which removed the provision of dual citizenship that had been contained in the constitution to protect white interests. The requirement was to a large extent politically driven, and those with dual citizenship were required to renounce it. Despite this law, dual citizenship persisted. In 2001, the government introduced the Citizenship Amendment Act (No. 12). It was also politically driven as the ruling party was under threat and it tightened citizenship, making it mandatory for those with foreign citizenship to renounce it. In addition, the country's registrar general ordered that any Zimbabwean with a possible claim to foreign citizenship had to renounce it in order to remain a citizen (Lourenco, 2012). This affected thousands of Zimbabweans. They were prevented from obtaining identity and travel documents with the condition that they had to sort out their citizenship status first. Voting and other rights were curtailed during this time (which was deliberate), and Lourenco (2012) calls this a condition of denationalization. These statutory requirements saw a large number of citizens with a claim to foreign citizenship renouncing it to retain their Zimbabwean citizenship. The 2013 Zimbabwean Constitution created moves for resolving contentious citizenship issues, but a lot remains unresolved. While the constitution recognizes citizenship by birth for those whose parents were born outside of Zimbabwe, people of foreign descent continue to experience challenges.

Conceptual Aspects, Research Area, and Methods

T. H. *Marshall and the Theory of Citizenship*

Thomas Humphrey Marshall's (1893–1982) famous essay "Citizenship and Social Class" (1950) can be located within a British historical context primarily aimed at presenting a theory of social as opposed to individual rights. Turner (2001, 2009) argues that Marshall was interested in the sociology of social rights with a focus on social class, the welfare state, and the transformation of postwar capitalism. Citizenship is full membership in a community, with those who attain this status being equal in all rights and duties associated with it (Marshall, 1963, p. 72). This implies that the individual, by virtue of being a citizen, is entitled to certain rights, and in turn, the state is also duty bound to meet certain standards for citizens. Marshall (1950) developed a typology of citizenship, arguing that citizenship is divided into three parts: civil, political, and social rights. The civil component touches on individual freedoms, and includes the right to justice, property, and freedom of speech. Marshall (1963) sums up civil rights as "the rights necessary for individual freedom, liberty of the person, freedom of speech, thought and faith and the right to own property and to conclude valid contracts and the right to justice" (p. 74). The political component focuses on the right to exercise political power, for example, rights to a secret ballot and to free and fair elections. The social is a right to "a modicum of economic welfare and security [and] the right to share to the full in the social heritage and to live the life of a civilized being" (Marshall, 1964, p. 69). Social rights gained much prominence after World War II.

In societies there exist institutions, namely, the judiciary, legislature, local government, and educational and social services, through which the three sets of rights are articulated, and the institutions give them expression (Marshall, 1950). From this, welfare services emerge as an amelioration of the condition of the working class (Turner, 2001). In addition, citizenship can be seen as modifying the negative impact of the market by redistributing resources on the basis of rights. A consequence of this is the emergence of tension between the principles of equality underpinning democracy and the actual inequalities of opportunity, wealth, and income that are a characteristic of capitalist society. In this context, a contradiction exists between citizenship and capitalism. Citizenship is a status position that mitigates the negative effects of economic class within capitalist society (Turner, 2001, p. 190).

Marshall's concept of social rights has been important in providing us "with substance to the liberal-democratic promise of equality by integrating the economically and socially-marginalized into the broader community of rights-bearing citizens" (Brodie, 2002, p. 377). He was able to bring to the fore the idea that, while there are citizenship rights, there are also discernible challenges. This is exemplified by the right to participate in public life, which he saw as meaning little in a context where citizens face the challenges of poverty and powerlessness. His proposal, while acknowledging this and the inequalities brought on by modern capitalism, was aimed at building social solidarity beyond the limitations and conflicts posed by ethnic and class peculiarities.

Marshall's theory has had its fair share of criticism. While it is beyond the scope of this chapter to fully present the interrogation, it is important to highlight the critiques. Given that Marshall theorized over half a century ago in a different historical context, it is not surprising that some of his ideas are no longer relevant to the contemporary context. Marshall's analysis was to a large extent informed by the postwar state (of Britain), with citizenship rights being seen as integral in building social solidarity and advanced capitalist societies entrenched in values of citizen equality and social progress. Marshall developed his theory in a context of fusion of citizenship rights and welfare state formations, with their full range of social policies aimed at providing citizens with social security and opportunities for social mobility. This has changed, making some basic tenets of Marshall's theory inapplicable to contemporary society (Brodie, 1997). Erosion of social citizenship in the contemporary neoliberal state has been witnessed due to the rise of neoliberalism, which has reversed the redistributive effects of postwar social policies and increased economic insecurity and social isolation, impacting especially those in the wage economy (Brodie, 1997, 2002). States have put in place different measures aimed at catering to all social strata, while promoting good governance premised on the principles of solidarity, planning, and progress (Brodie, 1997, p. 232). This illustrates the changes occurring after Marshall developed his theory.

The Marshallian framework has been criticized for restricting itself to men, or more specifically, to a white male working-class perspective, and for failing to acknowledge the social rights of women (Held & Thompson, 1989; Lister 2003). The framework sees citizenship as a form of liberal reformism—offered rights rather than substantial benefits. In this context, it can be seen as a strategy undertaken by the ruling class through promises, rather than as the enactment of citizenship (Mann, 1987). Marshall has been criticized for ignoring gender, ethnic, and racial divisions (Crowley, 1998; Tully, 1996). He also made an assumption that society was heterogeneous, with the concept of citizenship being seen as uniform. Marshall fails to distinguish active from passive citizens in a context of distinct historical trajectories (Turner, 1990).

In contemporary times, criticisms against the Marshallian framework have increased, given the challenges that have arisen with the emergence of contemporary social forces. Turner (2009) highlights challenges posed by European integration, the politics of emergent lesbian, gay, bisexual, transgender, and intersex (LGBTI) communities, the rise of environmental movements, the emergence of new medical technologies, and the neoliberal transformation of the welfare state, among other new contexts that cannot be comprehended using the framework. Against this background, Turner (2009) considers the need for a post-Marshallian framework on citizenship.

Despite these criticisms, we argue that the framework is still very much applicable in interrogating the current situation of first, second, and third generation migrants in rural Zimbabwe. While Marshall's context of postwar Britain is very much different from contemporary rural Zimbabwe, we argue that, socially and economically, there are some similarities. His typology is vital in exploring outcomes of the FTLRP pertaining to migrants. The typologies facilitate understanding of social citizenship from a political, economic, and civil rights point of view, as will be presented in later sections. We next provide a brief background on the study area and research methods.

Research Area

The study was undertaken in two rural districts in Zimbabwe, namely, Goromonzi (Mashonaland East Province) and Zvimba (Mashonaland West Province) in 2018. Goromonzi district is located approximately 32 kilometres east of Harare, while Zvimba is located approximately 85 kilometres northwest of Harare. Both districts lie in Natural Region II, one of the best agro-ecological regions in the country, with favourable climatic conditions and soils as well as high annual average rainfalls. Prior to and after the FTLRP, in both districts, several agricultural activities were, and have been, undertaken, with major crops for food and export being produced. These have included maize, flue-cured tobacco, wheat, tomatoes, carrots, potatoes, peas, onions, cabbages, and soya beans, among others, as well as livestock production. Due to the FTLRP, both districts now have a tri-modal agrarian structure. Goromonzi now has 2,822 A1 farms from 71 former LSCFS (on 32,628 hectares) and 846 A2 farms from 51 former LSCFS (84,456 hectares). The number of households across all the sectors increased from 20,253 to 23,921 after the FTLRP. Zvimba, on the other hand, prior to the FTLRP, had 718 LSCFS and approximately 150,000 households within the customary tenure regime.

Concrete, field-based evidence was considered integral to informing this study on the current situation of migrants after land reform in rural Zimbabwe.

To this end, the study was field-based and empirically grounded, and applied an interpretive research paradigm and qualitative research approach. Input for the study was sought from respondents in both districts. In Goromonzi, input was sought from participants from Manor Estate, Brunton, Bains Hope, Warrendale, and Mashonganyika farms, as well as the communal area of Chinyika. In Zvimba, respondents were drawn from Fennmerre, Sutton B, and St Lucia farms, and from Chirau and Kasanze communal areas.

In all, 30 former farm workers and 20 community farm members participated in interviews for the study. In addition, 12 in-depth interviews with key informants, mainly from government departments and local authority structures, were conducted. All of the respondents were useful in providing insights on the situation of persons of foreign descent after redistributive land reform in rural Zimbabwe.

Social Citizenship: The Political

Marshall (1950) presented the political dimension as one of the important pillars of citizenship. Through the political, he argued, one can understand the exercise of political power and citizenship participation (for example, in elections). The history of farm workers in Zimbabwe as well as their contemporary situation provides interesting insights on the relationship between citizenship and politics in a rural context. Literature on the situation of farm workers in colonial and post-colonial Zimbabwe portrays them as invisible, voiceless, illiterate, powerless, bound, in most instances, within a quasi-feudal relationship with their employers, and trapped in exploitative socioeconomic and political processes. The post-2000 period in the aftermath of land reform provides critical insights on the nexus between citizenship and political processes. '

During this period, disenfranchisement, marginalization, and denial of socio-economic rights, as well as intimidation and violence against persons of foreign descent were experienced (Daimon, 2016). The ruling ZANU (PF) party was accused of perpetrating these acts in the face of growing opposition. As indicated earlier, a series of politically driven legislative reforms in the post-2000 era saw a number of persons of foreign descent losing their citizenship rights. The ZANU (PF) government reconstructed identity and citizenship. The situation was exacerbated by bureaucratic processes, which made the citizenship renunciation processes cumbersome and expensive. During the land reform process, national identity became defined through a narrow ZANU (PF) chauvinistic particularism that was inspired by xenophobic tendencies. The national

discourse was redefined, and farm workers were portrayed as serving the interests of white farmers and opposition political parties (Hartnack, 2009; Mlambo,
2010; Pilosoff, 2012). For this reason, they were targets of violence and were seen as
not deserving the same rights and entitlements as other citizens.

For the ZANU (PF) government, persons of foreign descent (labelled "aliens")
provided an important swing vote, hence the numerous legislation amendments to disenfranchise them (Raftopoulos & Phimister, 1997). The Citizenship
of Zimbabwe Amendment Act (1/2002) resulted in the renunciation period of
foreign citizenship being reduced to only six months and in aliens failing to vote
in the presidential election of that year. A bureaucratic and expensive renunciation process saw aliens failing to vote in the 2005 parliamentary as well as the
2008 harmonized elections. Amendments made to citizenship laws were aimed
at creating numerous coercion technicalities, so as to either withdraw or extend
alien voting rights. The ruling party was seen as selectively denying or allowing
alien voting rights to their advantage (Nugent et al., 2007). Citizenship, in this
context, became redefined and used as an instrument to retain political power
and control.

As indicated above, aliens were in some instances disenfranchised from participating in voting processes due to legislative amendments. This study sought to
interrogate the participation of respondents in political processes at local and
national levels. The study looked at their participation in elections since 2000,
political party belonging, and freedom to choose political leaders. The nexus
between citizenship and the political was prioritized.

Choice of Political Leaders and Participation in Electoral Processes
In both Goromonzi and Zvimba, most respondents (90%) indicated that, in their
areas, they were free to choose a political leader of their choice. A respondent at
Manor Estate in Goromonzi said: "There is no infringement on our political choice.
In this area, for the councillor, member of parliament and president, we always
choose a person of our choice. However, we are guided by the political environment." This was echoed by another respondent at St Lucia farm in Zvimba, who
said: "There is rarely any intimidation or violence these days. We are not forced to
vote anyone into office. Everyone is free but, in some cases, there are contextual
hurdles."

These sentiments mark a shift from what is portrayed in mainstream literature—the view that aliens were subjected to gross intimidation and violence
and were not allowed to exercise their voting rights. Respondents indicated that

democratic space had increased with time and that intimidation had dwindled. For this reason, 24 respondents (13 in Goromonzi and 11 in Zvimba) indicated that they voluntarily belonged to a political party as active members, with only two in Goromonzi and four in Zvimba not belonging to any party. In Goromonzi, three held positions in the party as secretary, treasurer, and committee member, while in Zvimba, two were members of the Ward Development Committee (WADCO), one was a local representative of the Women's League, and one was a local representative for the Youth League's organizing committee.

Respondents reported actively participating in elections. A comparative approach to participation in the 2000 and 2018 elections shows a significant increase in participation. During the height of legislative amendments in the mid-2000s, participation in elections significantly decreased. More recently, in the 2018 elections, the number of respondents who participated in the elections increased, with only one respondent not participating due to not having a national identity card. Voting trends from 2000, captured during our fieldwork, are presented in Figure 18.1 below, which pertains to Goromonzi district.

FIGURE 18.1 Participation in elections since 2000 in Goromonzi (N=15)

2000	5
2002	0
2006	2
2008	6
2013	4
2018	14

Local and National Politics: Access to Land under the FTLRP and in Communal Areas

Mainstream literature on farm workers and land reform depicts former farm workers as having failed to access land due to their perceived support for former white farmers and opposition political parties (Daimon, 2016). The foreigner tag is seen as having automatically excluded them from accessing land (Chipenda, 2019). Against this background, we explored the realities of aliens and land access during and after land reform processes. These have implications on livelihoods and citizenship rights.

Participants in our study indicated that not having Zimbabwean citizenship had been a major impediment to accessing land during and after the FTLRP. One respondent at Warrendale farm in Goromonzi district said: "I failed to access land because I am not a citizen. My wife is an alien as well. Chances of us owning land were drastically reduced."

A female respondent at Fennmerre farm in Zvimba district indicated that she and other women had experienced a "double tragedy" of being aliens and experiencing gender bias in informal land invasions and formal allocation.

Lack of access to land was a challenge during the FTLRP and remains so in contemporary times. Some respondents indicated that they were denied access to land because they were viewed as "outsiders" (despite some of them being born in Zimbabwe). Due to a lack of access, some respondents had cultivated very small pieces of land, usually on state land (usually less than two acres). Even when land becomes available on fast-track farms and in communal areas, aliens are not considered. A respondent in Goromonzi summed this up by saying:

> As aliens there is an unwritten rule that we should not own land because we do not belong. We do not enjoy the same rights as natives. Even if you are a citizen, just having a foreign name puts you at a disadvantage.

In Zvimba, some headmen in the Chirau and Kasanze communal areas indicated that they were reluctant to allocate land to the former farm workers who had been evicted from the neighbouring large-scale commercial farms. A headman in Kasanze area boldly indicated his position:

> In my view, the former farm workers of alien origin are the same as the former white owners of the farms. They are all foreigners. I rejected their request for land after they were evicted from large-scale commercial farms.

Former farm workers' failure to access land after losing employment in LSCF increased their vulnerability to poverty and other socioeconomic vagaries. Such vulnerability was higher for aliens who neither had a home nor a means for survival in either Zimbabwe or their country of origin. However, some women of foreign origin indicated that they had indirect access to land through being married to local men.

Local Authority Structures

An important outcome of the FTLRP was the transformation and reconfiguration of rural authority structures, with the emergence of traditional leaders and a Committee of Seven (Co7)[2] on A1 farms being the major highlight. Traditional leadership whose jurisdiction had been confined to the communal areas was extended to the farming areas. Chiefs under whose jurisdiction A1 farms fell appointed their village heads (*masabhuku*) to serve these areas. The C07 and traditional leaders now play numerous roles on the farms, including day-to-day administration, managing common resources (farm infrastructure and grazing land), settling disputes, and spearheading development and natural resource conservation (see Chipenda, 2018; Murisa, 2009; Sadomba, 2008).

For the respondents, traditional leaders and the C07 posed major challenges influencing their exercise of citizenship rights. They indicated that these institutions were, to a large extent, a political creation and over the years had served the interests of farmers and not the alien communities. The C07 was accused of actively coercing persons of foreign descent to provide their labour on farms in return for residency rights. This was reported to be continuing despite the designation of farm compounds on A1 farms to be on state land, with farmers not having the power to evict residents from these areas. The C07 and traditional leaders were also accused of supporting A1 farmers who wanted to occupy houses owned by former farm workers, politicizing food and inputs distribution, and supporting A1 farmers who demanded rent from former farm workers. Traditional leaders were accused of usurping the powers of the police and the courts by exercising powers and authority for which they had no legal mandate.

Traditional leaders in Goromonzi and Zvimba provided contrary views. For example, at Dunstan farm in Goromonzi, *sabhuku* Choto refuted these allegations and argued that they were an authority established by the government and had legal authority to exercise their roles on the farms. He indicated that they were an integral part of the farming communities in ensuring social cohesion. In Zvimba, *sabhuku* Muza of St Lucia farm explained that they presided over cases of petty criminality, settled disputes, and ensured the enforcement of traditional laws and customs. He said that they worked in conjunction with the C07 and the government, and that only those who did not appreciate their roles would speak negatively about them.

Social Citizenship: The Social

On social rights, Marshall (1964, p. 69) focused on the realization of economic rights and welfare security for citizens. Social rights include the redistribution of resources, amelioration of conditions of the working class through welfare services, and protection of citizens from vagaries of the market.

We sought with this study to consider the state of social rights for those living in the resettlement areas. For some, the land reform program created economic opportunities, while others missed out. In both districts, all participants indicated that the FTLRP opened up access to natural resources in areas that were hitherto a preserve for white large-scale commercial farmers. Natural resources are now available mainly for household use and for commercial purposes. Available natural resources include firewood, minerals (mostly gold), wild animals, fish, honey, thatch grass, sand, and granite (used for construction), among other resources.

Despite the opening up of broad opportunities for complementary sources of social reproduction and social protection for the majority, aliens are sometimes excluded. Beyond the exclusion of some groups, overexploitation of forests and sands is a major environmental threat. In Zvimba, an Environmental Management Agency (EMA) officer reiterated the following: "Environmental degradation particularly the massive cutting down of trees for curing tobacco and for sale, are major problems EMA is grappling with in this area and other new farm communities."

The possession and use of skills are essential in realizing socioeconomic well-being. In Goromonzi, nine of the alien farm workers were skilled and six were unskilled, while in Zvimba, seven were skilled and eight were unskilled. Available skills included tobacco farming, driving, horticulture production, and animal husbandry. These skills had been acquired from previous white employers. The economic value of these skills was locked in due to the low number of opportunities to access land.

Social Citizenship: The Civil

Civil rights also occupy the core of Marshall's (1950, 1963) conceptualization of social rights. Under this category, Marshall prioritizes natural justice in its diversity, entitlement to participate in civil activities, protection from discrimination, and rights that protect individuals' freedom from infringement, among other civil essentials. All participants in both districts emphasized the expansion of participation opportunities in associational life and local farm groups after the FTLRP. Generally, everyone was free to participate in community activities and practice accepted religions. Issues existed pertaining to migrant labour and their descendants.

Covert and overt marginalization or exclusion on the basis of citizenship were observed. At Sutton B farm in Zvimba, for instance, only one of the farm workers of Malawi origin belonged to a burial society, while one descendant of a farm worker of Zambian origin belonged to a microfinance association. Migrant farm workers and their descendants reiterated being reminded that they had "come from elsewhere" and were thus not allowed to contribute to the agenda of civil gatherings or make crucial community decisions. Some locals were also opposed to intermarriages. Given the importance of associational life to well-being, we can conclude that most former farm workers and their descendants are disadvantaged.

A home is an essential need, yet most of these aliens are landless and thus do not have a permanent home. Most aliens have nowhere to go after retirement, so farm workers are forced to work until their death, and while they may access land in communal areas, may have to negotiate with locals. Views of participants were crystallized on failing to enjoy full rights due to alien status. Difficulties in accessing registry documents due to alien status were widely emphasized. In Goromonzi, 14 participants had a birth certificate, 10 had a national ID, and 4 had a passport (out of 15). In Zvimba, the numbers were 10, 11, and 1 out of 15, respectively. Challenges in accessing documents are due to a lack of documentation by parents; the cumbersome and costly process of obtaining documents due to procedures that need to be fulfilled; the travel that is necessary; and low cooperation by staff at the registrar general's office.

Government welfare schemes are essential in providing for civilians in Zimbabwe. Between 2006 and 2018, these schemes included the provision of rice, maize, seed, sugar beans, and fertilizer. In Goromonzi and Zvimba, nine and six aliens, respectively, had benefitted from the program. However, this civil right was not realized by some aliens because local leaders deliberately excluded them in compiling lists of beneficiaries or in distributing food and agricultural inputs. However, a nuanced interrogation is vital because civil rights are not restricted to the contexts of membership in local associations, marriage, registry documents, and social welfare schemes.

Migrants and the Right to be Rural in Zimbabwe

Migrants have rights that include the right to live and work in Zimbabwe, and the right to be to be rural. Zimbabwe is a signatory to various UN conventions and protocols including the International Convention on the Protection of the Rights of All Migrant Workers and Members of their Families (1990), International Labour Migration (ILO) Migration for Employment Convention Number 97 (1949), and ILO Migrant Workers Convention Number 143 (1975). These provisions focus on various aspects of migrant labour in member states. In addition, the rural areas where fast-track farms are located have the right to development and to good governance that maximizes and sustains the well-being of everyone, including aliens. However, while these legal rights exist on paper, the reality is that many migrants are not presently able to exercise them.

Conclusion

The indestructibility of land provides a basis for production, reproduction and social protection, short and long-term insurance and accumulation, and sustained well-being. Drawing on the concepts of local politics of inclusion and exclusion and Marshall's articulation of citizenship, this chapter has explored the situation of migrant labourers and their descendants after the FTLRP in Zimbabwe. The analysis points to several issues of citizenship in relation to political, civil, and social facets. However, migrant farm labourers and their descendants have recently realized increased participation in political processes due to revised electoral provisions and enhanced civil rights, particularly participation in associational life. Still, owning and using land as a key socioeconomic resource has not improved for aliens in the aftermath of the FTLRP. In most cases, they lost their employment and were not allocated land within farms and in communal areas. Moreover, members of this group are barred from holding essential leadership positions and their membership in local associations is low. Access to legal documents, loans, and other economic opportunities is low due to their alien citizenship status. Politics of inclusion and exclusion are covertly or overtly applied against this group in ways that reduce social, political, and civil rights and benefits. However, a nuanced approach that focuses on achievements, opportunities, challenges, and prospects is essential.

Notes

1. A1 farms are small-scale farming models created by the land reform program, while A2 farms are middle-scale farms, which are much larger than A1 farms.
2. These were put in place at the height of the farm invasions and were a replica of similar structures that existed at the height of the war of liberation. They are comprised usually of at least seven elected members who have different responsibilities.

References

Alexander, J. (2003). "Squatters", veterans and the state in Zimbabwe. In A. Hammar., B. Raftopoulos, & S. Jensen (Eds.), *Zimbabwe's unfinished business: Rethinking land, state and nation in the context of crisis* (pp. 83-117). Weaver Press.

Amanor-Wilks, D., & Moyo, S. (1996). *Labour migration to South Africa during the 1990s*. ILO/SAMAT.

Arrighi, G. (1970). Labour supplies in historical perspective: A study of the proletarianization of the African peasantry in Rhodesia. *Journal of Development Studies, 6*(3), 197-234.

Barraclough, L. (2013). Is there also a right to the countryside? *Antipode, 45*(5), 1047-1049. https://doi.org/10.1111/anti.12040

Bauman, Z. (2005). Freedom from, in and through the state. *Theoria, 52*(108), 13-27.

Binswanger-Mkhize, H., & Moyo, S. (2012). Zimbabwe: From economic rebound to sustained growth—Note II: Recovery and growth of Zimbabwe agriculture. World Bank.

Brodie, J. (1997). Restructuring and the new citizenship. In P. Evans & G. Wekerle (Eds.), *Women and the Canadian welfare state: Challenges and change* (pp. 126-140). Toronto University Press.

Brodie, J. (2002). Citizenship and solidarity: Reflections on the Canadian way. *Citizenship Studies, 6*(4), 337-394.

Chambati, W. (2017). Changing forms of wage labour in Zimbabwe's new agrarian structure. *Agrarian South: Journal of Political Economy, 6*(1), 1-34.

Chambati, W., & Moyo, S. (2004). *Impacts of land reform on farm workers and farm labour process: Review of the agricultural sector following the implementation of land reform*. SMAIAS.

Chambati, W., & Magaramombe, G. (2008). An abandoned question: Farm workers. In S. Moyo, K. Helliker, & T. Murisa (Eds.), *Contested terrain: Civil society and land reform in contemporary Zimbabwe*. SS Publishing.

Chibwana, M. W. T. (2016). *Social policy outcomes of Zimbabwe's Fast Track Land Reform Programme (FTLRP): A case of Kwekwe district* [Doctoral dissertation, University of South Africa].

Chipenda, C. (2018). *After land reform: What about the youth?* Proceedings of the International Conference on Authoritarian Populism and the Rural World of the Emancipatory Rural Politics Initiative (ERPI), International Institute of Social Studies (ISS), The Hague, Netherlands, 17-18 March 2018.

Chipenda, C. (2019). Redistributive land reform as a social policy instrument: An alternative strategy for women empowerment in the Global South. In M. S. Raste & B. Bhattacharya (Eds.), *Strategies and dimensions for women empowerment* (pp. 307-330). Central West Publishing.

Clarke, D. (1977). *Agricultural and plantation workers in Rhodesia*. Mambo Press.

Crowley, J. (1998). The national dimension of citizenship. In T. H. Marshall (Ed.), *Citizenship studies 2* (pp. 165-178). Cambridge University Press.

Daimon, A. (2016). ZANU (PF)'s Manipulation of the "alien" vote in Zimbabwean elections: 1980-2013. *South African Historical Journal, 68*(1), 112-131.

Government of Zimbabwe. (1984). Citizenship of Zimbabwe Act No 23, Chapter 4:01 of 1 December 1984. Government Printers.

Government of Zimbabwe. (2002). Citizenship of Zimbabwe Act No 23, Chapter 4:01, 1/2002 (s. 43). Government Printers.

Government of Zimbabwe. (2013). Constitution of Zimbabwe. Government Printers.

Hammar, A., Raftopoulos, B., & Jensen, S. (Eds.). (2010). *Zimbabwe's unfinished business: Rethinking land, state and nation in the context of crises.* Weaver Press.

Hartnack, A. (2009). Transcending global and national (mis)representations through local responses to displacement: The case of Zimbabwean (ex-)farm workers. *Journal of Refugee Studies, 22*(3), 351–377.

Harvey, D. (2008, September–October). The right to the city. *New Left Review,* 53. https://newleftreview.org/II/53/david-harvey-the-right-to-the-city

Held, D., & Thompson, J. B. (Eds.). (1989). *Social theory of modern societies: Anthony Giddens and his critics.* Cambridge University Press.

International Labour Migration (ILO). (1949). C097 - Migration for Employment Convention (Revised) Number 97. https://www.ilo.org/dyn/normlex/en/f?p=NORMLEXPUB:12100:0::NO::p12100_instrument_id:312242

International Labour Migration (ILO). (1975). C143 - Migrant Workers (Supplementary Provisions) Convention Number 143. https://www.ilo.org/dyn/normlex/en/f?p=NORMLEXPUB:12100:0::NO::P12100_ILO_CODE:C143

James, G. (2015). *Transforming rural livelihoods in Zimbabwe: Experiences of fast track land reform 2000–2012* [Doctoral dissertation, The University of Edinburgh].

Lister, R. (1997). Citizenship: Towards a feminist synthesis. *Feminist Review, 57*(1), 28–48.

Lister, R. (2003). *Citizenship: Feminist perspectives* (2nd ed.). Macmillan.

Lourenco, N. (2012). *Denationalisation and the politics of citizenship in Zimbabwe.* European Network on Statelessness.

Mafeje, A. (2003). The agrarian question: Access and peasant responses in Sub-Saharan Africa. *Civil Society and Social Movements Programme, Paper No. 6.* UNRISD.

Magaramombe, G. (2010). Displaced in place: Agrarian displacements, replacements and resettlement among workers in Mazowe district. *Journal of Southern African Studies, 36*(2), 361–375.

Mann, M. (1987). Ruling class strategies and citizenship. *Sociology, 21*(3), 339–354.

Marshall, T. H. (1950). *Citizenship and social class and other essays.* Cambridge University Press.

Marshall, T. H. (1963). *Sociology at the crossroads.* Heinemann Educational Books.

Marshall, T. H. (1964). *Welfare in the context of social policy.* Cambridge University Press.

Marshall, T. H. (2005). Developing the global gaze in citizenship education: Exploring the perspectives of global education NGO workers in England. *International Journal of Citizenship and Teacher Education, 1*(2), 76–91.

Marshall, T. H. (2009). *Inequality and society* (J. Manza & M. Sauder, Eds.). Norton and Company.

Mazhawidza, P., & Manjengwa, J. (2011). *Women's access to land after fast track land reform in Vungu district, Gweru.* International Land Coalition.

Mkodzongi, G. (2013). *Fast tracking land reform and rural livelihoods in Mashonaland West Province of Zimbabwe: Opportunities and constraints. 2000–2013* [Unpublished doctoral dissertation]. The University of Edinburgh.

Mkodzongi, G. (2016). "I am a paramount chief; this land belongs to my ancestors": The reconfiguration of rural authority after Zimbabwe's land reforms. *Review of African Political Economy, 43*(1), 99–114.

Mlambo, A. S. (2010). From an industrial powerhouse to a nation of vendors: Over two decades of decline and deindustrialisation in Zimbabwe 1990–2015. *Journal of Developing Societies*, *33*(1), 99–125.

Moyo, S. (2011). Three decades of agrarian reform in Zimbabwe. *Journal of Peasant Studies*, *38*(3), 493–531.

Moyo, S. (2013). Land reform and redistribution in Zimbabwe since 1980. In S. Moyo & W. Chambati (Eds.), *Land and agrarian reform in Zimbabwe: Beyond white-settler capitalism* (pp. 29–78). CODESRIA.

Moyo, S., Chambati, W., Murisa, T., Siziba, D., Dangwa, C., & Nyoni, N. (2009). *Fast track land reform baseline survey in Zimbabwe: Trends and tendencies, 2005/06*. AIAS.

Murisa, T. (2009). *An analysis of emerging forms of social organisation and agency in the aftermath of Fast Track Land Reform in Zimbabwe* [Unpublished doctoral dissertation]. Rhodes University, South Africa.

Nash, K. (2009). Between citizenship and human rights. *Sociology*, *43*(6), 1067–1083.

Nugent, P., Dorman, S. R., & Hammett, D. (2007). *Making nations, creating strangers: States and citizenship in Africa*. Sage Publications.

Palmer, R. (1977). *Land and racial domination in Rhodesia*. Heinemann Educational Books.

Pilosoff, R. (2012). *The unbearable whiteness of being: Farmers' voices from Zimbabwe*. Weaver Press.

Raftopoulos, B., & Phimister, I. (Eds.). (1997). *Keep on knocking: A history of the labour movement in Zimbabwe, 1900–97*. Zimbabwe Congress of Trade Unions.

Rutherford, B., & Addison, L. (2007). Zimbabwean farm workers in northern South Africa. *Review of African Political Economy*, *34*(1), 619–635.

Sadomba, W. Z. (2008). *War veterans in Zimbabwe: Complexities of a liberation movement in an African post-colonial settler society* [Unpublished doctoral dissertation]. Wageningin University, The Netherlands.

Scoones, I. (2015). Zimbabwe's land reform: New political dynamics of the countryside. *Review of African Political Economy*, *42*(144), 190–205.

Somers, M. R. (2008). *Genealogies of citizenship: Markets, statelessness, and the right to have rights*. Cambridge University Press.

Stasiulis, D. (2002). Introduction: Reconfiguring Canadian citizenship. *Citizenship Studies*, *6*(4), 365–375.

Tekwa, N., & Adesina, J. (2018). Gender, poverty and inequality in the aftermath of Zimbabwe's land reform: A transformative social policy perspective. *Journal of International Women's Studies*, *19*(5), 45–62.

Tully, J. (1996). *The crisis of global citizenship*. Newcastle University.

Turner, B. S. (1990). Outline of a theory of citizenship. *Sociology*, *24*(2), 189–217.

Turner, B. S. (2001). The erosion of citizenship. *British Journal of Sociology*, *52*(2), 189–209.

Turner, B. S. (2009). *Rights and virtues*. Bardwell Press.

United Nations. (2015). *Sustainable Development Goals*.

United Nations High Commissioner for Human Rights. (1990). International Convention on the Protection of the Rights of All Migrant Workers and Members of their Families. https://www.ohchr.org/EN/ProfessionalInterest/Pages/CMW.aspx

19

Rural Redlining in the Danish Housing Market

Toward an Analytical Framework for Understanding Spatial (In)justice

JENS KAAE FISKER, ANNETTE AAGAARD THUESEN &
EGON BJØRNSHAVE NOE

Something Wicked this Way Comes

The universal Nordic welfare model has been known to provide a high level of equality in services and rights across populations, in spite of uneven geographies, due in large measure to a very low degree of commodification (Esping-Andersen, 1990) and a high degree of resilience toward idiosyncratic income shocks (Dercon, 2002). Over the last decade, however, public sector structural reforms in Denmark have disproportionately affected the rural population (Svendsen, 2013). Both discursively and in concrete policies, it has become common practice to deteriorate conditions for the rural population, referring to a lack of viability and efficiency considerations. These changes have also made themselves felt in the rural housing market. On the one hand, people who want to move to a rural area run into difficulties when trying to secure a mortgage, while on the other hand, people who want to move away find themselves stuck in place with an unsellable home. This chapter hones in on the first of these experiences as it exemplifies a denial of the right, not only to be, but to become rural.

Changes in mortgage lending practices have effectively redlined—that is, "a mortgage lenders' practice of mapping high-risk neighbourhoods by encircling them with red lines" (McCann, 2009, p. 626)—parts of the Danish countryside, even though homeownership is expected to have "important economic impacts on individual consumers and the macroeconomic environment" (Letkiewicz & Heckmann, 2018, p. 89). Potential house buyers are seemingly being rejected based entirely on the location of the place in which they wish to reside, not on an assessment of their personal financial situation. Given that affected areas are already challenged by out-migration and loss of services, the new situation risks exacerbating already existing patterns of uneven development in ways that are detrimental to the continued viability of local communities as places of settlement. Arguably, it also engenders a substantial curtailment of the rights of citizens to decide where to live. Moreover, these dire circumstances have come about in a country otherwise well known for possessing one of the best mortgage systems in the world (Lunde, 2016).

In pointing out and analyzing this issue, we are not claiming that such developments have resulted from any kind of ill-will or malicious intent directed against rural areas and those who live there. Rather, we are identifying a wicked problem[1] (Rittel & Webber, 1973) and proposing an analytical framework that can help us gain a multiperspective understanding of it. To develop and test the framework, we have used initial findings from an ongoing project, while conceptually drawing together Nancy Fraser's (1997, 2009) work on justice and Edward Soja's (2010) work on spatial justice to generate a schematic outline of the seemingly vicious circle of spatial injustice in the Danish rural housing market. Our mission here is only to develop better ways of understanding the issue at hand and how it came into being, not to chart and evaluate the various responses it has engendered. The most notable response can be described as "community-based risk management arrangements" (Bhattamishra & Barrett, 2010), where communities join forces to provide loans or buy houses (Hørve, 2018) to support the local real estate market; this is a practice that has, however, mostly been confined to so-called "strong" villages (Gunn et al., 2015). While these and other responses[2] are no doubt important, they nevertheless lie beyond the scope of the current chapter.

Conceptualizing Spatial Justice

The hallmark of Fraser's (1997, 2009) work on justice is her insistent search for the often multifaceted roots of injustice. Refusing to dwell only on the apparent forms of oppression, she makes a threefold distinction between oppressions rooted in political economy, oppressions that are culturally rooted, and finally, those that are rooted in political systems. These, then, are her three dimensions of justice: redistribution (relating to the economic), recognition (relating to the cultural), and representation (relating to the political). When we ask how redlining injustices came into being in the Danish countryside, Fraser's three-fold distinction helps to qualify the question, by splitting it into three: what are the roles of (re)distribution, recognition, and representation in the emergence of rural redlining in Denmark?

Fraser's concept of justice, however, is not spatial by design, although her use of it has often been highly sensitive to spatial issues (e.g., globalization). By drawing on Soja's (2010) attempt to construct a theory of spatial justice, we can begin to remedy this by intersecting the three aspects of justice with a spatial schematic. More precisely, what Soja brings into the equation is a scalar trialectic, explained further below, consisting of exogenous geographies, endogenous geographies, and mesogeographies. What gets to count as exogenous, endogenous, or meso depends on the scale at which spatial injustices are observed. In our case, the "base scale" is national and the injustice of redlining is primarily distributional in terms of its outcome. A disentanglement of its roots, however, needs to be sought across issues of redistribution, recognition, and representation, as well as through a mix of exogenous, endogenous, and mesogeographical processes and relations (as schematized in Figure 19.1). The following subsections provide a more thorough introduction, first, to Fraser's three-dimensional concept of justice, and second, to its spatialization through Soja's trialectics.

FIGURE 19.1 Analytical framework

Soja (2010)	Fraser (2009)		
Spatial	Justice		
	Redistribution	Recognition	Representation
Exogenous geographies			
Endogenous geographies			
Mesogeographies			

Note: Based on Fraser's (2009) three-dimensional conception of justice and spatialized through Soja's (2010) scalar trialectic of spatial justice.

A Three-Dimensional Concept of Justice

The three dimensions of justice promoted by Fraser flow directly from the history of second wave feminism as it has unfolded since the post-World War II period.

In the initial phase, injustices were conceived of primarily in terms of distributional issues, and feminist thought and activism were, on the whole, closely aligned with social democratic and Marxian principles of egalitarian redistribution. In other words, injustice was seen as rooted in political economy. With the onset of the post-socialist era and the surge of neoliberalization from the 1980s onwards, this focus on redistribution was broadly forsaken in favour of a renewed focus on various forms of identity politics in which injustice was seen primarily through the prism of recognition, i.e., focusing on injustices of a cultural origin. Fraser's (1997) intervention in this debate was an attempt to reconcile between the two perspectives of distribution and recognition. She critiqued the identitarian version of the latter, while acknowledging that it was indeed necessary to include cultural issues of recognition alongside economic issues of distribution in any adequate conceptualization of justice. But the two had to be seen as deeply intertwined.

Fraser (2009) later supplemented the resulting dual perspective with a third dimension: political issues of representation. In this move, she was compelled by the growing perception that many subjects are denied even the possibility of having claims to justice heard. Political representation can no longer be assumed, if ever it truly could, and justice is often denied even before injustices of distribution or recognition come into play. They are rendered invisible in advance by various forms of misframing or misrepresentation. In this sense, representation should not be seen simply as an extra dimension lashed on as an afterthought. Without political representation there simply cannot be any claim to redistributive or recognitional justice: "The political in this sense furnishes the stage on which struggles over distribution and recognition are played out" (Fraser, 2013, p. 195).

The identification of these dimensions alone, however, does not tell us what justice is; it only conveys the various guises in which (in)justice may confront us. The what of justice for Fraser (2013) "centers on the principle of *parity of participation*. According to this principle, justice requires social arrangements that permit all (adult) members of society to interact with one another *as peers*" (p. 164). Thus, "justice requires participatory parity across all major axes of social differentiation" (p. 167). Parity of participation, then, is what brings together the three dimensions in a common framework. The inclusion of representation, in particular, highlights how "contests that used to focus chiefly on the question of *what* is owed as a matter of justice to members of political communities now turn quickly into disputes about *who* should count as a member and *which* is the relevant community. Not only the substance of justice but also the *frame* is in dispute" (Fraser, 2013, p. 13).

With this in mind, we conceptualize denials of the right to be rural as spatial injustices produced through a complex interplay between (economic) maldistribution, (cultural) misrecognition, and (political) misframing. Seeking spatial justice—the affirmation and realization of a right to be rural—requires an analytical approach that takes into account all three dimensions and a political praxis that is not confined to act only in the economic, the cultural, or the political sphere. The symptoms of the particular spatial injustice that we analyze—that of rural redlining—appear in the distributive dimension as unequal geographical access to mortgages and thereby to the housing market. Rather than confine the analysis to the economic dimension, we use Fraser's conceptualization to initiate a multidimensional analysis that traces the roots of injustice—and seeks ways of achieving participatory parity—across all three dimensions. But, in order to do this, we need to complement Fraser's framework with an explicit spatialization of the justice concept.

Spatializing (In)justice

We find the entry point for such an exercise in Soja's *Seeking Spatial Justice*, in which he identifies three geographies that act as sources of spatial injustice: endogenous geographies, exogenous geographies, and mesogeographies. These geographies, much like the three dimensions of justice, are seen as tightly interwoven, but not as reducible to one another. In Soja's (2010) view, exogenous geographies are associated with "thick layers of macrospatial organization arising not just from administrative convenience but also from the imposition of political power, cultural domination, and social control over individuals, groups and the places they inhabit" (p. 32). Economic globalization and the post-Westphalian state system are some of the most obvious examples. Spatial justice, however, "is also configured from below through what can be broadly called endogenous processes of locational decision making and the aggregate distributional effects that arise from them" (Soja, 2010, p. 47).

Clearly, then, endogenous geographies are relationally inseparable from exogenous processes, but this does not mean that the exogenous simply determines the endogenous. For instance, case-by-case decisions about rural mortgages may ultimately be conditioned by processes in the global economy or regulatory mechanisms at the supranational level, but they do not simply derive from straightforward hierarchical impositions. "In this sense, spatial justice and injustice are seen as the outcome of countless decisions made about emplacement, where things are put in space" (Soja, 2010, p. 47). Over time, the continual tensions between exogenous and endogenous forces produce various mesogeographies, understood as a variety of regional scales between the global and the local: "metropolitan, subnational, national, supranational. At each of these scales... geographically uneven development inscribes significant spatial or territorial inequalities. When these... are maintained over time...they become another context or arena for seeking spatial justice" (Soja, 2010, p. 56). So, even though mesogeographies can be seen as products of the interplay between exogenous and endogenous forces, they are not simply effects of this interplay, but are themselves constitutive; indeed, they are necessary for this interplay to occur in the first place. Soja prompts us to ask, first, which mesogeographies are relevant for the (re)production of rural redlining, and second, which exogenous and endogenous processes were necessary for such mesogeographies to emerge and to be sustained.

Rural Redlining as Spatial Injustice

In analyzing rural redlining in the Danish countryside, we use the analytical framework as a heuristic device that allows us to navigate the complexity of the case at hand without getting lost in its labyrinthine intricacies. We begin where the issue confronts us most readily: as a distributional injustice whose symptoms come to the fore in lending decisions in the mortgage system. That places us in the distributional dimension and at the endogenous level shown in Figure 19.1. From here, we can trace the injustice as it traverses the matrix, even if we do not, over the course of this chapter, pay explicit visits to each and every box; moreover, the visits we do pay also vary in length.

As indicated in the introduction, we draw on tentative findings from an ongoing project. The purpose is to test the framework, not to present a complete and final version of the empirical study. At this point, our empirical material consists of a collection of reports and white papers on the Danish housing market and mortgage system; the lending policies of relevant banks and mortgage providers; and personal communications with key stakeholders, including the CEO of a regional bank, a representative of the association of real estate agents, CEOs of several mortgage providers, the president of the Joint Rural Council (an interest group working broadly for the interests of rural areas and trying to aggregate stories of spatial injustice on the housing market into political influence; see Thurston, 2018), and the mayor of a rural municipality.

Endogenous Geographies of a Distributional Injustice
Having made the decision to buy a house, one would expect that the decision to grant a mortgage would primarily be made on the basis of the household's

current and forecasted financial situation. As already mentioned, however, this is not the experience that would-be house buyers in the more peripheral areas of the Danish countryside are met with. Instead, they are essentially presented with the message that their desired home is in the wrong location. Their own financial situation has nothing to do with it, and they are told, implicitly or explicitly, that if they would just find a different location—i.e., an urban, or at least a less rural one—a mortgage would come their way. The logic of banks is thus to protect themselves against future risks associated with rural areas, notwithstanding the fact that this exacerbates a circular problem for the rural demography. There are, of course, no actual red lines drawn on a map that individual bankers and mortgage lender representatives frequent to make such decisions. But there are spreadsheets and standard procedures for the calculation of risk assessments to which these individuals are increasingly compelled to adhere. Obviously, the financial situation of individual applicants does comprise a large part of such spreadsheets, but they are also concerned with the geographical location of the property in question. It is especially in rural areas with declining housing markets and other structural issues that the latter part of the spreadsheet tends to overrule the former. Such areas can be found throughout the periphery of Denmark, although geographical distances between the centre and the periphery are comparatively small. Thus, the amount of leeway extended to bankers to make their own decisions based on personal judgment is so small that, effectively, the spreadsheets do draw metaphorical red lines on a non-existing map, demarcating no-go zones for mortgages.

This has a range of self-propelling consequences for areas with a declining housing market. Cost prices become much lower than market prices, which means that money cannot be borrowed for renovation and reconstruction. In turn, this leads to an increasing number of empty houses that cannot be sold (Kristensen et al., 2017), either because they are in miserable condition (Larsen et al., 2013) or because they are in a redlined location. The latter houses are thus only sellable to buyers who do not need a mortgage, i.e., they can pay up front. Since these houses can be acquired for small sums, a growing number of them are falling into the hands of real estate speculators who turn them into rentals. Seen only from a housing market perspective, this tends to exacerbate the downward spiral of house prices. From a broader perspective, however, what we also see is a development in rural areas from owner-occupied to rental housing, especially among younger age groups.[3] On top of all of this, the urban side of mortgage lending practices also needs to be considered. Potential homebuyers whose individual financial situations live up to the requirements in the risk assessment are effectively being funneled toward urban or peri-urban areas, thus accelerating urbanization processes. At the same time, real estate owners in rural areas are becoming poorer, while their counterparts in urban areas are becoming wealthier, for no other reason than their differential settlement choices. The issue, then, not only affects those who want to move to a rural area, but also the people who already live there.

Mesogeographical Roots of a Distributional Injustice

Moving on from these endogenous symptoms of rural redlining, we can start by tracing some mesogeographical explanations for the kind of spreadsheet-driven mortgage lending described above. For the moment, however, we will stay in the distributive dimension. Why have mortgage-lending decisions been stripped of personal judgment? The CEO of one of the larger mortgage providers explained:

> In reality, soft law functions as hard law. Even though we, in principle, can apply an individual assessment when providing [a] mortgage, we will have to argue very thoroughly, and we risk being sanctioned. Therefore, our lending policy levels with the guidance even though it may have unwanted effects locally.

Banks and mortgage providers are punished if they lend money for houses in a declining housing market in rural areas, because it increases the demand for capital requirements. Among other things, it means that it is not possible to obtain a mortgage or regular bank loan for houses below the estimated value of 500,000 DKK. This also results in geographically undifferentiated standards for market value assessments. While it is easier to calculate a real market value for a house in a more segregated urban neighbourhood, it is much more difficult in more diverse rural areas where the rich and poor often live in the same community (Lund, 2019). It is therefore difficult to find a reference property on which to estimate a specific home's price. The same goes for the evaluation of lenders where a standard threshold for household disposable funds has been introduced, notwithstanding the fact that life in the countryside is generally less expensive. For older adults of pensionable age, there are even stricter regulations, since often they are not allowed to borrow more than two times their net household income. Again, these thresholds are only guidelines, but according to the banks, they really must struggle to be able to grant an exemption to these regulations (CEO Jutlander, interview). The Danish Financial Supervisory Authority (*Finanstilsynet*) does random checks to control the estimation of property market values.

The tightening grip of regulation that pervades all of these practices at the mesogeographical level of the Danish mortgage system relates closely to meso-geographies at a European level, and ultimately this has to be seen in the context of exogenous pressures associated with economic globalization and the global financial crisis. We return to the latter in the next section. Here, it suffices to say that the threat of a collapse in the financial system at the European level prompted the introduction of a whole range of new regulations for banking and the financial sectors in general, most notably the requirements outlined in the voluntary Third Basel Accord (Basel Committee on Banking Supervision [BCBS], 2011) and implemented by the European Union (EU) in the Capital Requirements Regulation and Credit Institutions Directive in 2013 (EU, 2013a, 2013b). These regu-lations set direct thresholds for capital requirements, but also, indirectly, set requirements for control and assessment. One of the Danish implementations of this regulation is the "surveillance diamond" (Finansministeriet, 2014), which includes a range of measurement criteria and applies to both banks and mort-gage providers. If one or more of these thresholds is exceeded, *Finanstilsynet* will pay the lender a visit and give an injunction to improve practices.

So, to reiterate the point made by the mortgage provider CEO provided at the start of this subsection, soft law really does function as hard law in this area. This point has been corroborated by the conclusions of an expert committee under the Ministry of Business and Growth, which concluded in 2015, first, that "the legisla-tion is unsuitable and leads the financial sector to provide significantly fewer loans in rural areas," and second, that "the [financial] sector has overreacted on experiences of loss and has become too cautious in rural areas," while also failing to "exploit its opportunities to price differentiate and demand higher prices in rural areas" (Ministry of Business and Growth, 2015, p. 5). Whereas the committee report does place partial responsibility for the current situation on the financial sector, it also points out the key roles played by non-financial factors, including increased urbanization, a lack of industrial diversification in rural areas, and citizen preferences. It also hints at a discrepancy in the way disparate actors interpret regulations: "The committee has...found examples of regulatives that several market actors perceive to be more restrictive than *Finanstilsynet* interprets them to be" (Ministry of Business and Growth, 2015, p. 7).

Distributive Pressure from Exogenous Geographies

As hinted above, economic globalization and the global financial crisis have exerted significant exogenous pressures that need to be considered to explain both the practices that emerge mesogeographically and the production of redlining that has become manifest in endogenous distributional geographies. Around the turn of the millennium, economic growth accelerated worldwide, and the interest rate was gradually lowered. To keep up with economic acceleration, a range of new financial instruments and measures were introduced. Internationally, the rapid rise of subprime loans in the US is perhaps the most infamous. In Denmark, two measures were introduced in 2002 that went hand in hand to accelerate the Danish real estate market. First, a range of new loan types was put in place, including "interest pay only" loans, "adjustable rate" mortgages, and "interest pay only" mortgages. Second, the Danish government committed to a policy of not raising property taxes any further. This meant a threefold incentive to raise real estate prices, especially for bigger cities in Denmark. Simultaneously, parts of the social housing stock were increasingly converted to owner-occupied housing.

All in all, this led to an increased financialization of real estate, which became a crucial object for investment, not only among big capital and speculators, but also for ordinary citizens. The latter tended to invest in self-occupied flats for their university-attending children in larger cities, which was possible through using the equity from their own house to refinance. Banks and private mortgage lenders took an active and encouraging part in these developments, with banks competing to offer loans using equity for reinvestment or even for buying consumables such as cars and furniture (Rangvid et al., 2013). From 2000 to 2008, the assets of both rural and urban inhabitants increased, but at a very uneven pace. However, it was still possible to get mortgages for buying, building, or renovating houses across the country. The distributive spatial injustice only really became visible after the bank crisis in 2008, not as a direct consequence of it, but rather as a product of the mesmerizing mix of responses it provoked. Such responses were not necessarily restricted to the mesogeographical level of financial institutions, but could also be found at the endogenous level, where the dawning reality of a vulnerable economic system that could no longer be trusted to deliver endless progress was likely to have had a disciplining effect on all decision-making situations that had even the faintest suggestion of finance about them. This, however, is beyond the scope of the current chapter.

The developments outlined so far have oscillated between the fluctuations of financial markets and a bewildering mix of regulative measures, seemingly introduced in response to, or as attempts to anticipate, the convulsions of global capital. But there is of course more to the story. We turn, therefore, to the recognitional and representational dimensions of justice. Globalization and increasing market deregulation (including of the labour market) have applied increasing pressure on the Danish welfare model, which was originally based on assumptions closely related to trickle-down economics: if the rich get richer, we all get richer. This class-based argument was accompanied by a geographic sibling of sorts, a second argument that said a strong and competitive capital city is in the best economic interest of the country as a whole, i.e., a logic closely aligned with growth pole theory.

Mesogeographical Constraints on Rural Representation

The 2000s saw a wave of public sector centralization in Denmark, which was set in motion to make service provision cheaper and enable the lowering of business taxes. Most prominently, the structural reform in 2007 reduced the number of municipalities from 275 to 98, while effectively reducing the regional level of the state to management of the health care system and a consultative function in regional development policymaking. The reform also decentralized municipal tasks and responsibilities while centralizing state control (Agger et al., 2010, p. 11). The reduction of municipalities had drastic effects in terms of the number of elected representatives at the local level of the parliamentary system. Where previously it was entirely possible for most rural localities to be politically represented in municipal councils, the structural reform effectively left large parts of the countryside without direct political representation. The distance between citizens and political representation increased with the decrease in elected officials—a change that was particularly felt in rural localities. This has resulted in a general decrease in levels of citizen confidence toward local democracy (KREVI, 2009).

The combination of a rural representational deficit and a multifaceted malrecognition of rural areas and those who live there—we account for the latter in the next section—has not come about without generating a certain backlash. The 2015 national election was marked by increased support for the Danish People's Party (DF), a right-wing populist party. Whereas most commentators have explained this largely as a symptom of a broader shift to the right among European voters, this may not be the sole explanation, as the geographical patterning of election results correlates with rural areas that have lost democratic representation and been at the receiving end of territorial stigmatization. The "yellow"[4] election may therefore be partially explained by the fact that the only party in the election to explicitly position themselves as representing rural Denmark was DF (see Strijker et al., 2015 for an in-depth analysis of the interconnections between populist parties and rural voters). Previously, calls for political representation of rural areas had resulted in the creation, in 2011, of the Ministry for Urban, Housing and Rural Affairs. Ironically, the yellow migration of rural voters that helped sway the election also paved the way for a government that immediately terminated the young ministry, thus adding once again to the representational deficit.

At the level of the European Union, rural representation is strong, but mostly in connection with agricultural interests. Tendencies in the 1990s toward a more post-productivist conception of European ruralities have largely been replaced during the 2000s by a renewed focus on the narrower issues concerning agricultural production. Hence, the rural population, which for the most part is not directly involved in agriculture, also cannot readily turn to the European political arena for representation in questions of housing.

Malrecognition of Rural Areas and Issues

The new representational deficit has been accompanied by discursive developments that can only be described as an increasing malrecognition of rural Denmark. In national media, the most underprivileged areas have been adorned with the less-than-flattering label "the rotten banana"[5] (Christensen & Nielsen, 2013; Svendsen, 2012). This has to be seen in conjunction with official state designations of "remote areas," introduced with the purpose of targeting policy measures. Together, these discursive developments have had contradicting implications: on one hand, they have resulted in a recognition that these areas are indeed challenged, but on the other hand, they have also given rise to a territorial stigmatization in which it is subtly implied that the challenges are endogenously rather than structurally rooted (Møller & Clemens, 2012). The recognition that certain rural areas deserve special policy attention does have redistributional effects through geographically targeted support measures, such as the EU funded Local Action Group (LAG) program. These policy measures, however, largely follow logics associated with a neo-endogenous development paradigm, where developmental deficits are seen as local problems to be solved through local action (Bosworth et al., 2015). For some purposes, they are doubtlessly both beneficial and effective, but they are in no way positioned or geared to address complex translocal and multiscaled problems such as rural redlining. Hence, the recognition that policy needs to address rural challenges is accompanied by a malrecognition of the nature of those challenges, leading to policy that is unfit for dealing with actual spatial injustices.

Obviously, the term "rural redlining" is not used in Danish policy and media discourse; it was imported specifically for this chapter due to its capacity for highlighting and aptly naming the wicked problem that confronts us. It is telling, however, that when pushed for comments by journalists, mortgage provider representatives have had to deny quite explicitly that they practice redlining:

> [The mortgage decision] is obviously based on a concrete assessment, but it is correct that there are cases where house buyers cannot borrow money to buy the house. But it's not as if we have a map of Denmark with certain areas where we do not want to lend money to buy real estate (Berlingske, 2012).

Although voiced as a denial of the fact, the mental image of that map is nevertheless planted in public discourse. Whether it exists physically or not is less important than the awareness that mortgage providers conduct their day-to-day business as if it does. Similarly, the "rotten banana" and related trends of discursive malrecognition may themselves have material repercussions, because the proliferation of negative images also affects decision-making in the financial sector: "The negative representation may, unfortunately, itself have contributed to a more sluggish loan access in these areas" (Ministry of Business and Growth, 2015, p. 5). This kind of bad publicity has been perceived by many in the rural population as an unjustified stamp, provoking various instances of rhetoric that runs counter to the stigma, often relying on satirical inversions and alternative metaphors such as replacing the "rotten banana" with the "green cucumber" (Winther & Svendsen, 2012).

Conclusion

The complexities at play in the wicked problem of rural redlining in the Danish housing market are immense to say the least. This is despite the fact that they take place in a country with very short distances between rural and urban areas, and without many of the weather and income hazards (Dercon, 2002) that other countries might experience. In this chapter, we have tested an analytical framework designed to produce accounts of such problems that render them comprehensible without artificially reducing their complexity. In our choice of framework, we have opted to treat the problem as an instance of spatial injustice, because the symptoms that relayed the presence of a problem were of this kind: namely, that people who wanted to live in rural areas were being denied the opportunity to do so. We have found this lightly paradoxical in a time when much (rhetorical) effort is being directed at finding ways of tackling precisely the demographic challenges of rural areas. Clearly, the problem did not originate in malicious intent targeting rurality, but it has emerged as an ill-fated brew of disparate elements with no particular brewmaster in sight, a wicked problem in every sense of the term.

By integrating Nancy Fraser's three-dimensional concept of justice with Edward Soja's multiscalar spatial dialectic, we have generated a matrix capable of remaining true to the breadth and depth of the problem complex, while also equipping us with the means to navigate it without getting lost. In the preceding sections we have traversed it asymmetrically, that is, without paying equally detailed visits to each and every cell—as clearly demonstrated by the summary of elements given in Table 19.1. The symptoms that started us off were located in the economic sphere of redistribution, where they cropped up as endogenous instances of people being denied mortgages on a locational basis. Thus, we had to begin the journey there and start by tracing the problem toward the mesogeographical constructs and exogenous pressures responsible for these symptoms. The three dimensions of justice, however, prompted us to trace the problem beyond the fuzzy boundaries of the economic sphere and into those of the cultural and the political. Here, we can begin to see how the vicious financial circle that we have observed in the rural housing market links up with discursive developments, restructurings of the political-administrative state system, and electoral dynamics.

The strength of the framework is that it allows us to locate highly disparate elements of the problem in relation to one another. This should also prove beneficial in locating solutions, which will necessarily have to be partial and distributed; a problem with multiple origins calls for multiple solutions. The unbounded spatial dialectic prompts us to look beyond the immediate scaling of the problem, whereas the three-dimensional concept of justice forces us to take seriously the cultural and political dimensions of an economic problem. The limitation of the framework is that it does not specify exactly how individual cells in the matrix relate to one another. To treat it as an analytical framework with explanatory power would therefore be misguided. In this sense, it is more akin to "weak" theory as promoted by J. K. Gibson-Graham (2014), involving heuristic devices that allow us to approach an empirical field without pretending to know too much about it in advance.

TABLE 19.1 Elements in the wicked problem complex organized by the analytical framework

Soja (2010)	Fraser (2009)		
Spatial	**Justice**		
	Redistribution	**Recognition**	**Representation**
Exogenous geographies	Aftermath of financial crisis (e.g., new capital requirements)	Urban triumphalism	Agricultural dominance in EU rural policy
		Neoliberalization	
	Globalization of financial markets		
	EUS LAG program		
Endogenous geographies	Mortgage decisions	The "green cucumber"	The "yellow" election
	Spreadsheet evaluation	House buyer self-disciplining	
	Forced immobility	House value equals exchange value, not	
	Local foundations buying local property	use value	
Mesogeographies	Surveillance diamond	The "rotten banana"	Structural reform
	Soft law → Hard law	Growth pole logic	Ministry for Urban, Housing and Rural Affairs 2011–2015
	Lending policies and guidelines		
			United Credit

Notes

1. Wicked problems are those where "problem understanding and problem resolution are concomitant to each other" (Rittel & Webber, 1973, p. 161); i.e., "one cannot first understand, then solve" (p. 162). Thus, in putting forward our analytical framework, we are already venturing the tentative proposition that solutions to the problem may be found by contemplating it as a case of spatial injustice.

2. The research project is itself part of such a response. It was funded by Forenet Kredit, which is the association behind two of the largest mortgage providers in Denmark, and works toward the stated aim of providing "fair housing loans for all of Denmark" (Forenet Kredit, 2019). The project period ran from December 1, 2018 to November 30, 2020.

3. For instance, renters aged 25-39 years old increased by almost 20% from 2012 to 2018 in rural municipalities (Statistics Denmark, 2019).

4. Danish election results are typically colour-coded in red (left wing) and blue (right wing). Due to the DFS refusal to identify as either right or left, they are usually represented with yellow.

5. The term was originally coined in the 1990s as a sarcastic wordplay on the "blue banana," denoting the main growth regions in the European Union (Nielsen, 2016).

References

Agger, A., Löfgren, K., & Torfing, J. (2010). *Nærdemokrati efter kommunalreformen: Erfaringer med netværksbaseret borgerinddragelse* [*Local democracy after the municipal reform: Experience with network based citizen involvement*]. Roskilde Universitetsforlag.

Basel Committee on Banking Supervision (BCBS). (2011). *Basel III: A global regulatory framework for more resilient banks and banking systems.* https://www.bis.org/publ/bcbs189.pdf

Berlingske. (2012, June 5). Husjægere i udkantsdanmark får afslag på boliglån [House seekers on the outskirts of Denmark are refused home loans]. *Berlingske.dk.* https://www.berlingske.dk/privatoekonomi/husjaegere-i-udkantsdanmark-faar-afslag-paa-boliglaan

Bhattamishra, R., & Barrett, C. B. (2010). Community-based risk management arrangements: A review. *World Development, 38*(7), 923–932.

Bosworth, G., Annibal, I., Carroll, T., Price, L., Sellick, J., & Shepherd, J. (2015). Empowering local action through neo-endogenous development: The case of LEADER in England. *Sociologia Ruralis, 56*(3), 427–449.

Christensen, S., & Nielsen, H. P. (2013). Udkantsdanmark: Avisernes (med)produktion af Nordjyllands territorielle stigma [Outskirts Denmark: The newspaper's (co)production of North Jutland's territorial stigma]. *Praktiske Grunde, 2013*(3), 5–20.

Dercon, S. (2002). Income risks, coping strategies, and safety nets. *The World Bank Research Observer, 17*(2), 141–166.

Esping-Andersen, G. (1990). *The three worlds of welfare capitalism.* Polity Press.

European Union. (2013a). Regulation (EU) No 575/2013 (L 176/1). *Official Journal of the European Union.* https://eur-lex.europa.eu/legal-content/EN/TXT/?uri=CELEX:32013R0575

European Union. (2013b). Directive 2013/36/EU (L 176/338). *Official Journal of the European Union.* https://eur-lex.europa.eu/legal-content/EN/TXT/HTML/?uri=CELEX:32013L0036&from=EN

Finansministeriet. (2014, December 2). Tilsynsdiamant for realkreditinstitutter [Supervisory diamond for mortgage lenders]. Finanstilsynet. https://www.finanstilsynet.dk/Tilsyn/ Tilsynsdiamanten-for-realkreditinstitutter/Pressemeddelelse-tilsynsdiamant- realkreditinsitutter-021214

Forenet Kredit. (2019). Mærkesager [Key issues]. Retrieved September 23, 2019, from https:// forenetkredit.dk/maerkesager/

Fraser, N. (1997). *Justice interruptus: Critical reflections on the "postsocialist" condition*: Routledge.

Fraser, N. (2009). *Scales of justice: Reimagining political space in a globalizing world*. Columbia University Press.

Fraser, N. (2013). *Fortunes of feminism: From state-managed capitalism to neoliberal crisis*. Verso.

Gibson-Graham, J. K. (2014). Rethinking the economy with thick description and weak theory. *Current Anthropology, 55*(S9), 147–153.

Gunn, S., Brooks, E., & Vigar, G. (2015). The community's capacity to plan: The disproportionate requirements of the new English neighbourhood planning initiative. In S. Davoudi & A. Madanipour (Eds.), *Reconsidering localism* (pp. 147–167). Routledge.

Hørve. (2018). Levende Landsbyer 4534 ApS [Living Villages 4534 LLC]. https://foreningen4534. wordpress.com/levende-landsbyer-4534-a-m-b-a/

KREVI. (2009). Strukturreformen udfordrer nærdemokratiet: Borgernes lokalpolitiske tillid og selvtillid faldt, da kommunerne voksede [Structural reform challenges local democracy: Citizens' local political confidence and self-confidence declined as municipalities grew].

Kristensen, N., Kolodziejczyk, C., & Wittrup, J. (2017). Nedrivninger af huse og fremtidige nedrivningsbehov i Danmark [Demolitions of houses and future demolition needs in Denmark]. KORA.

Larsen, J. N., Andersen, H. T., Haldrup, K., Hansen, A. R., Jacobsen, M. H., & Jensen, J. O. (2013). Boligmarkedet uden for de store byer [The housing market outside the big cities]. Statens Byggeforskningsinstitut.

Letkiewicz, J. C., & Heckmann, S. J. (2018). Homeownership among young Americans: A look at student loan debt and behavioral factors. *The Journal of Consumer Affairs, 52*(1), 88–114.

Lund, R. L. (2019). *Dissecting the local: Territorial scale and the social mechanisms of place*. [Doctoral dissertation, Aalborg Universitetsforlag].

Lunde, J. (2016). Milestones in Danish housing finance since 1990. In J. C. Lunde & C. Whitehead (Eds.), *Milestones in European housing finance* (pp. 109–126). Wiley-Blackwell.

McCann, E. (2009). Redlining. In D. Gregory, R. Johnston, G. Pratt, M. Watts, & S. Whatmore (Eds.), *The Dictionary of human geography* (5th ed., p. 626). Wiley-Blackwell.

Ministry of Business and Growth. (2015). Udvalg om finansiering af boliger og erhvervsejendomme i landdistrikter [Committee on the Financing of Housing and Commercial Property in Rural Areas].

Møller, J., & Clemens, E. (2012). Yderområdeudpegning—velsignelse eller forbandelse? Brugbarheden som grundlag for policy-formulering [Outer area designation—Blessing or curse? Usability as a basis for policy formulation]. *Økonomi & Politik, 85*(1), 37–51.

Nielsen, H. P. (2016). Udkantsdanmark. Kampen om stedet og ordene [Outskirts of Denmark. The battle about the place and the words]. In H. P. Nielsen & S. T. Faber (Eds.), *Den Globale Udkant [The global outskirts]* (pp. 57-84). Aalborg Universitetsforlag.

Rangvid, J., Grosen, A., Østrup, F., Møgelvang-Hansen, P., Schütze, P., & Thomsen, J. (2013). Finanskrisens årsager [Causes of the financial crisis]. https://em.dk/ministeriet/ arbejdsomraader/finansiel-sektor-og-vaekstkapital/finansiel-stabilitet/finanskrisens- aarsager-rangvid-rapporten/

Rittel, H. W. J., & Webber, M. M. (1973). Dilemmas in a general theory of planning. *Policy Sciences*, 4(2), 155-169.

Soja, E. (2010). *Seeking spatial justice.* University of Minnesota Press.

Statistics Denmark [DST]. (2019). *BOL204: Personer i boliger efter område, anvendelse, udlejningsforhold, husstandstype, antal hjemmeboende børn, alder og køn [Persons in dwellings by area, use, rental conditions, type of household, number of children living at home, age and sex].* www.statistikbanken. dk/BOL204

Strijker, D., Voerman, G., & Terluin, I. J. (Eds.). (2015). *Rural protest groups and populist political parties.* Wageningen Academic Publishers.

Svendsen, G. L. H. (2012). Landlig italesættelse og virkelighed 1996-2011 [Rural discursive construct and reality 1996-2011]. In G. L. H. Svendsen (Ed.), *Livsvilkår og udviklingsmuligheder på landet: Viden, cases, teorier [Living conditions and development opportunities: Knowledge, cases, theories]* (pp. 9-28). Syddansk Universitetsforlag.

Svendsen, G. L. H. (2013). Skolelukninger på landet: Hvor, hvor mange, og hvilke konsekvenser? [School closures in the countryside: Where, how many, and with what consequences?] In G. L. H. Svendsen (Ed.), *Livsvilkår og udviklingsmuligheder på landet: Viden, cases, teorier [Living conditions and development opportunities: Knowledge, cases, theories]* (pp. 149-161). Syddansk Universitetsforlag.

Thurston, C. N. (2018). *At the boundaries of homeownership: Credit, discrimination, and the American state.* Cambridge University Press.

Winther, M. B., & Svendsen, G. L. H. (2012). "The rotten banana" fires back: The story of a Danish discourse of inclusive rurality in the making. *Journal of Rural Studies, 28*(4), 466-477.

20

What's Next for the Right to Be Rural?

JENNIFER JARMAN & KAREN R. FOSTER

AS KAREN AND I FORMULATED this book project, we wanted to challenge rural researchers to reflect upon what their own research work on rural communities could reveal about the idea of a right to be rural at this point in the twenty-first century. When we started, we were not even sure whether anyone would even think this was a useful starting point—we aimed to bring together seven or eight authors to explore this idea together. The response was immediate and enthusiastic. We very quickly found that the idea of a right to be rural not only attracted researchers from our immediate research communities, but also drew in those working in a wide variety of content areas—health, education, food insecurity, housing, language rights, immigration and settlement, youth, aging, telecommunications, environment, rural policy, natural resource management, agriculture, entrepreneurialism, and rural politics more generally. Furthermore, the researchers who responded represented not just a wide range of discrete topics, but also a number of countries. We realized that exploring the idea of a right to be rural resonated not just in Canada, but also in Europe, Asia, and Africa, and that despite the wide range of topics, there were significant and complementary theoretical and empirical overlaps in the issues that could be addressed. After some thought, we decided to deepen the scope of the undertaking and more than double the size of the effort to capture the complexity. After a full selection and development process, we have a collection that includes submissions from both the developed and the developing world, and from a variety of types of states—liberal democracies, social democracies, formerly socialist countries, and currently socialist countries. This book with its eighteen substantive chapters is the result.

Collectively, the book's contributors provide a lot to think about in relation to both the challenges and opportunities facing rural citizens in the twenty-first century and their implications for the right to be rural. This last chapter brings together the main points of what we have learned about the project of developing a rights framework for understanding what is happening in rural communities and for directing further social change and action. Let's return to those questions outlined at the outset of this book and see what can be said now.

Is there a right to be rural? The question that drives this book—whether or not it makes sense to talk about a right to be rural—has grown out of reading literature in two areas: the right to the city, and citizenship. Ideas about the right to be rural start with Henri Lefebvre's (1968) idea of a right to the city. Lefebvre did not like the urban forms created by the twin forces of industrialization and capitalism. His primary focus was producing ideas about the city with the power to transform and enrich the lives of people living in cities. He hoped for cities built to support lives centred around meaningful activity as opposed to being driven by the imperatives of industrial production. While he wrote primarily about urbanism, he did recognize that there is a relationship between urban and rural, and he did think that rural life was in equal need of rethinking and renewal. In "The Right to the City," Lefebvre wrote:

> *Rural society was (still is), a society of scarcity and penury, of want accepted or rejected, of prohibitions managing and regulating privations. It was also the society of the fête, of festivities. But that aspect, the best, has been lost and instead of myths and limitations, this is what must be revitalized! A decisive remark: for the crisis of the traditional city accompanies the world crisis of agrarian civilization, which is also traditional. It is up to us to resolve this double crisis (1968/1996, p. 150).*

David Harvey (2008) takes Lefebvre's ideas about the relationship between social form and urban form and emphasizes that urbanization is a highly class-based process. New developments typically entrench bourgeois interests and capitalist priorities, whether for labour force development or other uses that contribute to profitable enterprise expansion (Harvey, 2008). What the two authors share is an emphasis on the importance of enhancing the ability of low-income people to struggle against the dispossession of their resources as urban spaces are created and recreated. More recently, Laura Barraclough (2013) has focused on the rural part of the rural-urban dichotomy and asked how rural rights are different from urban ones. Karen Foster (2018) picks up the theme further, interrogating it from the perspective of its usefulness for understanding rurality in Atlantic Canada. In her work, Foster identifies a perception of rural people remaining in their communities long after they have a right to—that is, long after they are obviously useful to cities—and needing, and sometimes demanding, the extension of services to which they have, in the eyes of others, been disentitled.

This collection also views rural issues through the lens of the literature on citizenship. In the introduction, we referred to ideas about rights. Rights can be seen as bundles or packages of what we call citizenship—legal claims "brought to bear on a state" in a manner that both confers rights and involves duties in return (Somers, 1994, pp. 78, 67). T. H. Marshall's (1950) influential taxonomy divides rights into three categories—civil, political, and social rights, including a right to a decent standard of living. Foster (2018) elaborates this as "what we expect of each other" and notes a shift toward an increasingly contractual nature of citizenship in the late twentieth century and a narrowing of the idea of productive citizenship to mean that a productive citizen is one who is formally employed. This is occurring despite the shifts in the employment world, meaning that opportunities, especially for those at the bottom of employment structures, are increasingly threatened by technological advances and global competition (Jarman, 2017).

In different ways and to different extents, the preceding chapters have fleshed out these theoretical themes with examples of community efforts to create meaningful lives in rural areas, to voice concerns over and influence (with differing degrees of success) developments in their vicinities, and to maintain control of resources and structures, be they natural (Zimmermann et al.), social (Rinne-Koski & Riukulehto), or financial/economic (Fisker et al.; Hadley; Kinfu & Cochrane; Das). Collectively, the authors show the utility of rights and citizenship concepts for thinking through rural life. More specifically, they support the idea that the right to be rural is an important concept, the full exercise of which depends on a number of factors. Few of these authors would disagree with the premise that a person has the right to live where they choose, and that this includes rural places. Indeed, freedom of movement and residence is one of the rights enshrined in the United Nations Declaration of Human Rights (1948).

If there is a right to be rural, how might it manifest? Does living in rural areas affect access to services that are supposed to be universal? The chapters in this book strongly support the conclusion that rights work in an intersectional way. We would draw the reader's attention to the overlap between rights put forward by many of these authors and those outlined in the UN Declaration of Human Rights (1948). Specifically, in this collection, authors have argued that the right to be rural means that a person living in a rural place must have the right to accessible health and medical care. The UN Declaration of Human Rights Article 25.1 does not specify how this is to be delivered and links this with adequate standards of living necessary to obtain these. The point here is that the Declaration certainly includes health and medical care in its list of human rights (see UN Declaration of Human Rights, Article 25.1). It includes the right to have access to primary and secondary education that is "directed to the full development of the human personality" (Article 26.2); to be able to work and have free choice of employment (Article 23.1); to be able to earn equal pay for equal work (Article 23.2); and to obtain "special care" when they are mothers or children (Article 25.2). But the authors' statements leave room for interpretation in terms of how these rights materialize and how we know when they are being denied. As has been shown in some chapters, the concept of "access" is particularly flimsy; access to public services or education is often considered reasonable even if it means a long commute. In theory, an elementary school one hour away by bus is accessible, like a maternity ward in the nearest city. A rural home is still technically accessible even if a mortgage lender refuses to finance its purchase—all one has to do is come up with the money (Fisker et al.). Sarah Rudrum et al.'s chapter shows the significant need for investment in rural midwifery, as well as the value of drawing attention to areas of life where costs have been downloaded to individuals or shifted to the future rather than reduced. Kathleen Kevany and Al Lauzon's chapter also emphasizes the problem of the provision of something as basic as food security in rural places, pointing out that not only is the quantity of food available to low-income people in rural areas an issue, but so is its nutritional quality. They write persuasively of the need for agricultural policy that supports smaller, local farms and emphasizes better food distribution, as well as appropriate income supports. Katja Rinne-Koski and Sulevi Riukulehto argue for greater investment in housing for older persons and community infrastructure to build social cohesion, strengthen community ties, and allow people to age in place. Their work helps us understand that citizenship is not just a discourse of rights and responsibilities and access to the basic services of health and education and livelihood maintenance. A strong citizenry needs to be emotionally healthy. Rinne-Koski and Riukulehto help us to see that there are two aspects to this—belonging to a place, and having a place belong to you. Home building is thus a vital part of rural citizenship, and growing old in a place that one calls home is significant and needs to be taken into account in public policy development. All of these are fundamental to realizing the right to live in communities of choice.

Authors have drawn attention to the sticky question of how to define reasonable access—how far is too far to travel to give birth, and how is access defined? How far is too far to buy groceries? What limits should there be when deciding to find a place to spend the rest of one's days? The work in this collection suggests that the right to be rural means more than just the freedom to inhabit a place outside the city. The chapters that centre on service provision emphasize the importance of equitable and sufficient levels of servicing in core areas of human life: healthy birthing support (Rudrum et al.); access to schooling that not only provides a basic education, but that supports rural livelihoods and the learning of the basic skills of democratic life from a young age (MacLeod; Domingo-Peñafiel et al.; Seto; Hadley); access to health care throughout the life course (Bollman; Rudrum et al.; Rinne-Koski & Riukulehto); access to healthy and sufficient food (Kevany & Lauzon); the ability to maintain a decent livelihood (Das; Matai & Chirisa; Chipenda & Tom); the ability to finance the purchase of a home in a rural area (Fisker et al.); and healthy aging within a rural setting without having to relocate to an urban centre (Rinne-Koski & Riukulehto). What we can see here is an emphasis on being able to live a good quality life in a rural setting with the supports in place. We also see work that takes us beyond the obvious (the need for health and education) to the less obvious (e.g., financial regulation designed with the needs of rural housing markets in mind).

What does the right to be rural mean in the everyday lives of rural people, those who govern rural places, and those who depend on rural societies for food, recreation, access to nature, and natural resources? In different ways, Lefebvre, Harvey, and T. H. Marshall emphasize that the ongoing creation of meaningful spaces, whether they be urban or rural, involves an engaged citizenry with responsibilities as well as rights. Positive social changes in rural life are to be actively created through the actions of critique of existing social structures and institutions, as well as the day-to-day work of making positive change happen. For those living and working in rural areas, we can see this is even more important than in urban areas, given that almost all of the chapters describe situations where the dominant trends for several centuries now have been for young people to leave for the opportunities, advantages, and fashionable existence available in cities. To highlight just a few examples from the book, Hadley's chapter explores the pushes and pulls facing rural youth and the need for active retention strategies. Matysiak's chapter examines the dilemmas facing young adults with a university education who remain in rural communities, and what constrains their political and social action. Collectively, however, the chapters in this book show that there is a healthy worldwide culture and politics of valuing the types of lives and communities in rural spaces. To be sure, one of the strengths of the works gathered together here is that they help create an understanding that those who are working to remain in rural areas are not acting in isolation—that these values and goals are shared by many around the world.

How is the right to be rural claimed, protected, and enforced? Many of the chapters show clear evidence that the right to be rural is under active contestation around the world. Pallavi V. Das's chapter, for example, focuses on a community of rural fishers in India who have been very active in claiming and attempting to protect their access to shrimp fisheries. Her work shows us how both a degrading environment and the uncertainties of international fish market prices combine to reduce the ability of lower social classes to democratically manage rural resources that have provided sustainable livelihoods over centuries. Zimmermann et al.'s research looks at the implications of Canada's recent adoption of the United Nations Declaration on the Rights of Indigenous Peoples (2007) and its implications for democratic governance of natural resources. The special contribution of this chapter is its exploration of how First Nations leaders who have been active in resource development discussions view the potential of this United Nations declaration, as opposed to the many legal analysts who have written on the subject. Their work lays out what they view the concept of "consent" to mean, given its importance in the Canadian legal context.

Most chapters lay out a case for a rural lens in public policy. The authors offer ways of operationalizing rurality. The concept of distance-to-density, elaborated in Ray D. Bollman's chapter, is crucial, as it may hold a key to defining and enabling enforcement of the notion of "reasonable access" to public services. Matai and Chirisa show that globalization and urbanization can often be chaotic processes and that unregulated, unplanned processes are not desirable. In their case study of rural Zimbabwe, they emphasize the importance of spatial planning as a tool for thinking effectively about the different possible impacts of future developments on rural communities and moving beyond the dominant urban frame. In their study of Ethiopia, Kinfu and Cochrane give further insight into complicated planning processes. In their chapter, they explain how administrative reclassifications can shift someone from being "rural" to being on "urban" land, without them ever having moved at all. Importantly, they illustrate the meanings that this can have for land tenure rights, as these can be wiped out with a pen stroke. However, they also show that an active and engaged citizenry can develop effective resistance strategies to respond to such shifts. They affirm the importance of a rural perspective to counter urban centrism in public policy, and the potential for resistance at the grassroots level.

Do citizenship rights have a spatial character? Collectively, the chapters in this book provide a resounding "yes" to the question of whether or not citizenship rights are spatial in their character, meaning that distance matters, area matters, and community and region matter in the shaping of civic, political, and social outcomes. The most direct theoretical elaboration in the book is Ray D. Bollman's chapter, which operationalizes rurality in terms of distance and distance-to-density. He discusses the burdensome expenses incurred by rural people who often travel long distances for health care services. Bollman suggests that it might be better to place the onus on the medical service providers to come to the rural residents and presents telehealth delivery as an example of one attempt to make this a reality. Maybe the most significant part of his contribution, however, is through the provision of solid concepts to measure inequities in service, and thus highlight the existence of such inequities, as a first step in providing better outcomes. S. Ashleigh Weeden's chapter on telecommunications and technology policy and regulation extends understanding of the transformative power of technology to shrink distance and affect culture. She points out that there is often an urban-centric bias in telecommunications policy. Weeden emphasizes that the extension of digital infrastructure to rural areas raises complicated issues and is particularly wary of the content and privacy implications for rural citizens. Her work strongly suggests that rural communities must carefully consider what types of technology projects they want to support if they are to strengthen and not weaken political citizenship.

What are the implications of the principles of equity and access that underpin most legal charters and declarations at state and international levels? The chapters present numerous examples of inequitable access in rural areas to even the resources within those areas. For example, Zimmermann et al. focus directly on rights discourses in relation to the need to fight for, and keep, a rural and, more importantly, an Indigenous seat at the table in the management of land and resources. The protection of traditional rights to fish, farm, and otherwise use a community's natural resources to community benefit emerges as crucially important for rural sustainability and especially Indigenous self-determination. Then, Stacey Haugen describes the complicated politics facing refugees trying to make their homes in rural Canada. She explores the motivations and expectations of those who raise money and volunteer their time to bring refugees from outside Canada to rural communities, and also sheds light on some of the conflicts between sponsors and refugees that ensue. In doing so, she explicitly draws out the inequities between urban and rural support for refugees in Canada; this inequity theme runs through many of the chapters in this volume. Clement Chipenda and Tom Tom also examine the experience of people for whom belonging to a place is compromised—in this case, migrant workers in Zimbabwe, some of whom are descended from ancestors who migrated many decades ago. The authors explore the patterns of political participation within this group, but without the right to ownership of land and a home, there are always limits to how meaningful and extensive their participation can be. Jens Kaae Fisker, Annette Aagaard Thuesen, and Egon Bjørnshave Noe explore a different way that access to rural land can be limited. They focus not on formal ownership requirements, but on the problems of obtaining financing in the form of mortgages to buy rural homes. While there is no formal rule to say that people cannot buy rural homes in Denmark, mortgage lenders give them higher risk ratings. A differently regulated mortgage market would be needed to turn this situation around. From all of these, lessons can be learned about marginalization and mobility. For those authors who discuss situations where areas are becoming rural, the right to freedom of movement emerges as critical, which includes the right to move to and live in a rural community and enjoy the same basic human rights as anyone else, as well as the more fundamental rights to equal treatment and human dignity.

The chapters on the right to rural representation point to the need for concrete, practical supports (for mundane things, like childcare) to enable youth civic participation, as Matysiak points out, and for intentional targeting of young parents and working-age people to ensure that volunteering and political organizing are not limited to older persons alone. The development of an active, representative, powerful rural civil society is critical to meeting the standards set out in the United Nations Declaration of Human Rights around duties and obligations related to citizenship, but also to ensuring the advancement and protection of distinctly rural rights. The chapters suggest that, with adequate support and facilitation, there exists in rural communities the potential for a progressive, rural-led movement crystallizing around rural rights and citizenship.

One of the strengths of this collection is that authors do not shy away from breaking stereotypes and myths associated with twenty-first-century rural realities. One such example is Rachel McLay and Howard Ramos's exploration of the political values of rural populations. Since the election of Donald Trump, the presentation of rural communities as "conservative, closed, traditional, and parochial" has been widely discussed. But the results of McLay and Ramos's 2019 telephone survey of Atlantic Canadians reveals a much more complex picture, with rural residents being only slightly less open to increased immigration than their urban counterparts. Further, they found that rural residents were not afraid to openly protest when the need arose, and they conclude by thinking that there is potential for the coordinated, rural-led movements essential to keeping a right to be rural on a solid footing.

What are the underappreciated facets of community creativity and resilience in the face of these challenges? One of the insights that can be gained from reading these case studies is that resilience is not accidental. At the beginning of the book, we referenced Marx's ideas about classes in themselves as latent possibilities, not yet actively engaged as "classes for themselves" (Marx, 1978, p. 218). (The latter are classes who recognize their commonalities and have active strategies in play to advance their interests.) Every case study in this book provides evidence that the members of rural communities are acutely aware of their problems, with common goals, needs, and strategies, and a history of working together to sustain and improve the life of their communities. The case studies sometimes explore strategies that did not work, as well as those that did, or those that are still in progress. But in all cases, there was a collective, shared set of goals that emphasized the importance of maintaining meaningful rural existences.

What is the foundation for strategic action to direct resources and tailor public policy to rural places? We propose that the right to be rural requires, for its realization, public policy that reflects the distinctiveness of rural concerns (i.e., a rural lens in policymaking); democratic governance and management of land and resources; and an engaged, informed, and mobilized rural citizenry to press for and maintain these things. The notion of a right to be rural pulls these three different propositions together under one umbrella. But it remains conceptual. We would now suggest that further articulation and development of a right to be rural could boost progress toward a rural policy lens and more democratic rural governance.

The contributors to this collection do make practical suggestions for advocacy and action in the short term. Regarding education, the chapters underscore the importance of investment in locally relevant rural education. Laura Domingo-Peñafiel, Laura Farré-Riera, and Núria Simó-Gil demonstrate how students in three rural Spanish schools actively learn civic democratic habits through the development of responsible, critical-thinking student bodies. MacLeod's chapter and Hadley's chapter tell us much about the hard fight to maintain rural schools and relevant rural curricula (Corbett, 2007), and they show why a school's prox-imity to its students—geographically and culturally—matters. And Seto's case study of rural Newfoundland explores the way that class dynamics shape the sometimes different perspectives of students and teachers toward what is "fake news" and what is legitimate knowledge. His work illustrates the new challenges that teachers face given the increasing penetration of social media into rural settings. Finally, rural communities cannot exist without a viable source of liveli-hood. Given the challenges of providing sufficient, formal, rural employment to maintain community, Hadley's chapter emphasizes the critical importance of entrepreneurial development, and of wresting the latter away from its neoliberal articulations (prizing the individual hero) to pursue and nurture an entrepre-neurialism that is more community minded. His work emphasizes that rural education, regulations, and business infrastructure should support the develop-ment of rural economies that serve rural populations and enable people to pursue livelihoods according to their own objectives and to creatively respond to local challenges.

Does a right to be rural parallel the right to the city? Yes, and no. To answer this, we have to understand who in these rural settings has agency. Harvey's (2008) work suggests that elites dominate the way that cities are shaped. Many of the chapters in this volume have shown ways that collective action based in rural commu-nities has allowed members of groups who have not been part of the dominant social class to positively affect outcomes. Katie K. MacLeod's analysis of a very long fight to preserve a rural Acadian language dialect reveals that elites do have the ability to shape language outcomes, in this case toward a dominant French language that is more useful for professional career development than preser-vation of community cultural capital. Meanwhile, Das's research illustrates the difficulties facing communities attempting to mobilize around environmental damage to fisheries resources in India. Zimmermann, Teitelbaum, Jarman, and Smith's research also looks at disputes over resource development, particularly forestry, in and around First Nations communities in Northwestern Ontario.

Taken together, these chapters show that rural communities are more than just what Marx would have called a class with the potential for united action (Marx, 1978, p. 218). Rather, through their individual struggles they are becoming relatively united around the broader purpose of continuing to exist. They work hard to maintain access to critical resources. Above all, land rights are critical to the larger goal of maintaining the rural community life that has been the basis of rich, meaningful lives for generations. At a time in the world's history when many are questioning the healthiness of democracies, the chapters not only reveal the liveliness of active rural social movements, but also give insight into complex goals and political strategies for creating meaningful change. The research collected here has convinced us that the right to be rural has the power to unite those working in and researching rural matters, and that a rights-based discourse on rural issues is useful in drawing together disparate issues into a more coherent framework. In considering next steps, what we would say at this point is that the theoretical framework has drawn our attention to the actors who create rural environments in ways consistent with their values and their goals and strategies. One aspect that is present in many of the case studies, however, but analyzed less systematically in this book, is the role that the state plays in shaping rural outcomes. In late modernity, turning the right to be rural into more than an analytical frame and a rallying cry will involve a central role for the state's support of such rights with all the power of its laws, institutions, and spending power. But that is for another day. For now, we can conclude that we have made a comprehensive start on fleshing out what the right to be rural looks like on the ground.

References

Barraclough, L. (2013). Is there also a right to the countryside? *Antipode, 45*(5), 1047–1049.

Foster, K. (2018). The right to be rural. *The Dalhousie Review, 98*(3), 369–375.

Harvey, D. (2008). The right to the city. *The City Reader, 6*(1), 23–40.

Jarman, J. (2017). What are the challenges of economic transition? Exploring the consequences of regional dynamics and global shifts. In M. Hird & G. Pavlich (Eds.), *Questioning sociology: Canadian perspectives* (3rd ed., pp. 96–105). Oxford University Press.

Lefebvre, H. (1996). *The right to the city: Writings on cities.* (E. Kofman & E. Lebas, Trans). Blackwell.

Marshall, T. H. (1950). Citizenship and social class. In *Citizenship and social class...and other essays* (pp. 1–85). Cambridge University Press.

Marx, K. (1978). The coming upheaval, excerpt from *The poverty of philosophy*. In R. Tucker (Ed.), *The Marx/Engels reader* (2nd ed., pp. 218–219). W. W. Norton.

Morgan, R., & Turner, B. S. (Eds.). (2009). *Interpreting human rights: Social science perspectives.* Routledge.

Somers, M. R. (2008). *Genealogies of citizenship: Markets, statelessness, and the right to have rights.* Cambridge University Press.

United Nations. (1948). United Nations Declaration of Human Rights (UDHR). https://www.un.org/en/about-us/universal-declaration-of-human-rights

United Nations Declaration on the Rights of Indigenous Peoples (UNDRIP). (September 13, 2007). https://www.un.org/development/desa/indigenouspeoples/declaration-on-the-rights-of-indigenous-peoples.html

Contributors

RAY D. BOLLMAN retired from Statistics Canada in 2011, where he was the founding editor of Statistics Canada's *Rural and Small Town Canada Analysis Bulletin*. There are 65 bulletins available on the Statistics Canada website. He is also a past chair of the OECD Working Party on Territorial Indicators. He is now a research affiliate with the Rural Development Institute at Brandon University, a professional associate with the Leslie Harris Centre of Regional Policy and Development, Memorial University, and a research associate with the Rural Futures Research Centre, Dalhousie University. His recent activity includes a series of "Focus on Rural Ontario" FactSheets for the Rural Ontario Institute (http://www.ruralontarioinstitute.ca/knowledge-centre/focus-on-rural-ontario); a series of FactSheets on Rural Manitoba for the Rural Development Institute, Brandon University; a report on Rural Canada and summary FactSheets for the Federation of Canadian Municipalities (http://crrf.ca/rural-canada-2013-an-update/); and quarterly reports on job vacancies for the Canadian Agriculture Human Resources Council.

CLEMENT CHIPENDA, PHD, is a research fellow with the SARCHI Chair in Social Policy, College of Graduate Studies, at the University of South Africa and a visiting research fellow with the Collaborative Research Centre (CRC) 1342 "Global Dynamics of Social Policy," at the University of Bremen, Germany. He is the founder and executive director of AfriFuture Research and Development Trust and is a member of the Network of Young African Researchers in Agriculture (YARA) and Anthropology Southern Africa. His research interests are in agrarian political economy, land reform, social policy, youth development, gender and rural development, citizenship, and migration studies. He has published several book chapters and journal articles in the *Canadian Journal of African Studies, Africa Review, African Identities, Journal of Comparative Family Studies* and *African Journal of Economic and Management Studies*.

INNOCENT CHIRISA is a professor in the Department of Demography Settlement and Development at the University of Zimbabwe. He is currently the dean of the Faculty of Social and Behavioural Sciences at the University of Zimbabwe and a research fellow in the Department of Urban and Regional Planning, at the University of the Free State, South Africa. His research interests are in urban and regional matters including rural institutions and development, resilience, and policy.

LOGAN COCHRANE is an associate professor at H B K U, an assistant professor at Carleton University, and an adjunct associate professor at Hawassa University. Over the last fifteen years, he has worked in Afghanistan, Benin, Burundi, Canada, the Democratic Republic of the Congo, Egypt, Ethiopia, Qatar, Saudi Arabia, South Africa, South Sudan, Tanzania, and Uganda. Logan has served as a director for two non-governmental organizations, and worked as a consultant with clients that have included Global Affairs Canada, International Development Research Centre, Save the Children, Management Sciences for Health, the Liaison Office, UNICEF, and UNAIDS, among others.

PALLAVI V. DAS is an associate professor in the Department of History at Lakehead University, Canada. Her main research interests are environmental history, including people's history of climate change, the relation between environment and development, and modern South Asian history. Her book *Colonialism, Development and the Environment* (Palgrave Macmillan, 2015) examines the ecological consequences of colonial development policies in India. She has articles published in refereed journals such as *Environment & History, History Compass, Modern Asian Studies, Journal of Asian and African Studies* and *GeoJournal*. Her most recent research project, which was funded by a S S H R C Insight Development Grant, examines the socioeconomic impact of climate change on small-scale horticultural farmers in the Western Himalayas, India.

LAURA DOMINGO-PEÑAFIEL is a primary teacher and pedagogue, with a PHD in pedagogy (2014). She is a teacher at the Department of Pedagogy of the

Faculty of Education, Translation and Human Sciences at the University of Vic – Central University of Catalonia (UVIC-UCC), and a researcher in the research group GREUV, UVIC-UCC. Her main research area is rural education, specifically multigrade teaching and inclusive educational practices. Her doctoral thesis was titled "Pedagogical Contributions of the Rural School: Inclusion in Multigrade Classrooms. A Case Study." She participates in and coordinates research projects, has published several articles, and has presented at international conferences. She has done two pre-doctoral stays, at the University of Manchester and Stanford University in the United States, and one post-doctoral stay at the University of Wallis, Switzerland. She has produced teaching materials for rural teachers at the request of the Catalan government, runs initial and ongoing training courses for teachers, and consults for rural schools. She is a lecturer on the Official Master's Degree in Education and Rural Territories (University of Barcelona), supervising final master's papers and doctoral theses on the subject.

LAURA FARRÉ-RIERA (PHD) is an early childhood education teacher, a researcher for the Educational Research Group (GREUV) at the University of Vic – Central University of Catalonia (UVIC-UCC), and a teacher at the Department of Pedagogy of the Faculty of Education, Translation and Human Sciences at UVIC-UCC. Her PHD from UVIC-UCC is in educational innovation and intervention. Her doctoral thesis, "Engagement with Students' Voices to Improve Teaching Practices in a Secondary School. A Case Study," is a contribution from the research project "Democracy, Participation and Inclusive Education in Schools" (EDU2012-39556-C02-01 and 02). Her main research areas of interest are inclusive education, students' voices, and student participation in the school context. She participates in diverse research projects related to democratic education, youth participation, and pedagogical renewal. She has published several articles about democracy and participation in schools, and participates in national and international conferences. She has two pre-doctoral research stays, at the Southampton Education School in the University of Southampton, and at Queen's University Belfast.

JENS KAAE FISKER is a post-doctoral researcher in the Danish Centre for Rural Research at the University of Southern Denmark and an associate professor in the Department of Media and Social Sciences at the University of Stavanger, Norway. His research practice is situated at the intersection of rural, urban, and regional studies and usually approached from the perspective of a post-foundational take on political geography. This involves a focus on everyday life, spatial justice, and challenged localities, whether the latter are villages in the countrysides of the Global North or slums in the megacities of the Global South. Notable published works include two edited volumes on alternative urbanism, both of which build bridges between the urban, the rural, and the regional: *Enabling Urban Alternatives. Crises, Contestation, and Cooperation* (Palgrave Macmillan, 2019) and *The Production of Alternative Urban Space. An International Dialogue* (Routledge, 2019).

KAREN R. FOSTER is an associate professor in the Department of Sociology and Social Anthropology at Dalhousie University in Halifax, Nova Scotia, where she holds the Canada Research Chair in Sustainable Rural Futures for Atlantic Canada. She established and directs the Rural Futures Research Centre, and teaches and researches in the area of rural work, economies, and societies. She uses qualitative and quantitative methodologies to study rural life, with current projects focused on rural occupational succession, local food movements and production, housing for people with disabilities, and perceptions of environmental change. Her 2016 book, *Productivity and Prosperity*, won an Honorary Mention for the Canadian Sociology Association's John Porter Award, and in 2019 she received the Dalhousie University President's Research Excellence Emerging Investigator award.

LESLEY FRANK is a Tier II Canada Research Chair in Food, Health, and Social Justice at Acadia University. She researches in the areas of family poverty, food insecurity, maternal and infant health, infant feeding, health inequity, and social policy. She has authored the Nova Scotia Child and Family Poverty Report Card for over 20 years, and is the author of *Out of Milk: Infant Food Insecurity in a Rich Nation* (UBC Press, 2020). As a sociologist, she employs an interdisciplinary perspective to her work, and collaborates with scholars from the fields of dietetics, nutrition, and health, and public policy, along with community members, to advocate for food and health justice. Prior to her academic life, she worked as a community-based researcher and spent several years providing pre-natal services and support to families living in low-income circumstances in rural Nova Scotia.

GREGORY R. L. HADLEY is a lecturer with the Faculty of Education at St. Francis Xavier University. His research interests include entrepreneurship education, rural education and educational leadership. Prior to his current appointment, he was a high school teacher at small schools in rural Nova Scotia, Canada. His work focuses on the exploration of avenues for sustainability in rural communities. Along with his wife, herself an elementary school teacher, he has two children.

STACEY HAUGEN is a PHD student at the University of Alberta in the Political Science Department. Born and raised in rural Alberta, Stacey has a passion for rural development, small communities, and newcomers. Stacey's studies and work history have given her a unique set of experiences in rural and global issues. She holds a BA from the University of Alberta and a MA in Global Governance from the Balsillie School of International Affairs. After graduating, she worked as a research awardee at the International Development Research Centre in Ottawa, a research officer with the Alberta Government in Peace River, AB, and a project manager for the Alberta Centre for Sustainable Rural Communities and Prentice Institute for Global Population and Economy. This diverse set of experiences influenced her decision to return to academia to study rural refugee resettlement and integration in Canada and Europe.

JENNIFER JARMAN is a full professor and chair of Lakehead University's Interdisciplinary Studies Department. She is a former member of the Canadian Sociology Association executive and founded its Rural Sociology research cluster. Her work explores the development of equal pay legislation, gender segregation trends in labour forces, and the use of labour by the global call centre industry in peripheral regions. She is the lead author of "The Dimensions of Occupational Gender Segregation in Industrial Countries" (*Sociology*, vol. 46, no. 6). Her most recent book is an edited collection, *Exploring Social Inequality in the 21st Century* (Routledge, 2019) with Paul Lambert. She is a co-author of *Gender Inequality in the Labour Market* (International Labour Organization).

KATHLEEN KEVANY is an associate professor and the director of the Rural Research Collaboration with Dalhousie University, Faculty of Agriculture. She is the president (2020-2021) of the Canadian Rural Revitalization Foundation (CRRF) (https://crrf.ca/), an active steering committee member, and co-applicant of the SSHRC-funded Rural Policy Learning Commons. Kathleen is the editor of *Plant-based Diets for Succulence and Sustainability* (Routledge, 2020). She is a certified counsellor and psychotherapist, and offers free webinars on living with greater health, happiness, and mindfulness through her virtual office eatingavibrantlife.com. Her research expertise is in increasing well-being for individuals and communities, as well as strategies to foster greater food security, sufficiency, and sustainability through sustainable diets. Routledge has commissioned her to head up *The Routledge Handbook of Sustainable Diets*, due for publication in 2022. Formerly,

Kathleen was the Chief Energy Orchestrator of The Decentralized Intelligence Agency.

ESHETAYEHU KINFU is an assistant professor of urban and regional planning at the Institute of Technology, Hawassa University, Ethiopia. He is also working as a researcher at the Institute of Policy and Development Research, Hawassa University. He was awarded his Doctor Engineer Degree (settlement design and construction) from University of Rostock, Germany. Eshetayehu is engaged in different local and international research projects including "Youth Future Project" in collaboration with the University of Sheffield (UK) and University of Wits (SA). His work is concerned with the representation of peri-urban developments. His recent article titled "The Genesis of Peri-urban Ethiopia" analyzed the dynamics of political instruments in forming and transforming peri-urban development in Ethiopia. His main research fields include urbanization of developing countries, peri-urban development, urban–rural linkages, politics of urban planning, urban land development, urban governance, and urban employment. Eshetayehu has also worked in public organizations, including in municipalities as a city manager and senior expert of urban land development where he gained ample practical experience in the urbanization and urban development of Ethiopia in particular and developing countries in general.

AL LAUZON is a professor in the School of Environmental Design and Rural Development, University of Guelph. His research focuses on rural change and development and rural health and well-being. He is currently examining the issue of food insecurity in the rural elderly who live independently and the impact of COVID-19 on rural healthcare workers. Recent projects have included examining precarious rural employment, the development of rural social enterprises and the role of municipalities, rural youth development, and the role of colleges in supporting innovation in small and medium rural enterprises. He is an active member in his community and currently is the chair of the board of directors for Alexandra Hospital Ingersoll, and a member of the board of directors for the Ingersoll Hospital Foundation and the Social Planning Council Oxford. In addition, he is the co-chair of the research ethics committee for Winchester District Memorial Hospital, a small rural research hospital in eastern Ontario.

KATIE K. MACLEOD is a doctoral candidate in the Department of Sociology and Social Anthropology at Dalhousie University. Her SSHRC-funded research explores gendered practices of social reproduction in localized Acadian identities, culture, and traditions in Nova Scotia. She challenges popular and accepted narratives of Acadian identity and history, by sharing stories and experiences from the rural and marginal Acadian community of Pomquet. Through an exploration of these localized narratives—which have been overlooked in history and popular memory—her research reveals the significant role women have played in the preservation of culture, traditions, language, and foodways in the reproduction of ethnicity. MacLeod holds a Master of Arts in Anthropology from Carleton University and a Bachelor of Arts (Hons) in Social Anthropology from Dalhousie University. She has written and published on Acadian cultural institutions and histories, Acadian-Mi'kmaq relations, and Indigenous business.

JEOFREY MATAI is a lecturer at the University of Zimbabwe in the Department of Rural and Urban Planning. He joined the University of Zimbabwe in 2017. He holds a master's degree in Urban Design from the National University of Science and Technology (NUST) and a BSC Honours in Rural and Urban Planning from the University of Zimbabwe. Currently, he is pursuing a PHD with the University of Zimbabwe, focusing on spatial planning. Before joining the University of Zimbabwe, he worked in the Government of Zimbabwe's Department of Physical Planning for seven years as a town planning officer. After starting as the junior town planning officer, he rose to the position of principal town planning officer. In 2016, he joined Great Zimbabwe as a part-time lecturer in the Department of Urban Planning and Development. His research areas of interest are rural transformation, spatial planning, urbanization, regional planning and development, urban design and urban resilience.

ILONA MATYSIAK holds a PHD in sociology and works as an associate professor at M. Grzegorzewska University in Warsaw, Poland. Her research interests include social and demographic changes in rural areas in different countries, gender and local government, and gender and higher education. She has taken part in several cross-national studies, including "GENDEQU. Gender Equality at the University" (2013-2016) and "WILCO. Welfare innovations at the local level in favor of cohesion" (2010-2014). From November 2017 to July 2018, she was a postdoc Fulbright Scholar at the Institute for Social Research (ISR) at the University of Michigan, Ann Arbor, US. Her most recent research and publications cover the topics of young university graduates living in rural areas in Poland, the retirement migrations in the American countryside, as well as rural aging and the quality of life in different countries.

KAYLA MCCARNEY is a PHD candidate in the Department of Sociology at McGill University. Prior to this, she was a research coordinator on a project that evaluated midwifery care in rural communities in Nova Scotia. Her connection to rural sustainability is deeply personal: she grew up in a rural community in Newfoundland and saw firsthand the pattern of increasing austerity measures and their effects on the health and well-being of the rural population. Her research interests include medical sociology, sociology of reproduction, health inequities in Canada, feminist theory, and rural sociology.

RACHEL MCLAY is a PHD student in the Department of Sociology and Social Anthropology at Dalhousie University in Halifax, Nova Scotia. She studies political and social change in Atlantic Canada. As a research associate with the Rural Futures Research Centre, she has conducted survey research on Atlantic Canadians' perceptions of change and views on political, environmental, economic, and socio-cultural issues. She is a proponent of public sociology, publishing op-eds, reports, and blog posts on political polarization, public opinion, and inequality in Canada.

EGON BJØRNSHAVE NOE is heading the Danish Center for Rural Research. His recent research has mainly dealt with sustainable finance for Danish farming in relation to a larger EU project, "Sustainable Finance for Sustainable Agriculture and Fisheries" (SUFISA), and sustainable finance of rural owner-occupied dwellings in Denmark. His field of interest is how rural development can be sustainable through local strategies to development and systemic analyses of the mechanisms that lead to and enhance imbalances between peripheries and centres and increases in social injustices. His academic interests are social systems theory (Luhmann), narrative theory, actor-network theory, and cross and multiperspectival research. Noe has been involved in nine EU projects and has much experience in heading externally funded Danish research projects. For an example of his work, see: H. F. Alrøe & E. Noe, (2014), Cross-disciplinary Science and the Structure of Scientific Perspectives, *Journal of Organizational Knowledge Communication*, 1(1), 7-30.

HOWARD RAMOS is a professor of sociology and chair of the Department of Sociology at Western University. He is a political sociologist who investigates issues of social justice and equity. He has published on social movements, human rights, Indigenous mobilization, environmental advocacy, ethnicity, race, and

Atlantic Canada. He has also led the Perceptions of Change Project, which examined how people understand changes to their social, economic, built and natural environments. He has written op-eds on these issues and regularly comments on social issues in popular media.

KATJA RINNE-KOSKI (MSc Admin) works as a project researcher at the University of Helsinki Ruralia Institute, Finland. She has worked with the Ruralia Institute for several years on different R&D projects on rural research, development, and education. Recently, she has been working on several research projects with the themes of homey landscapes and experiences of home, which are part of the larger academic research area of the experiential theory of home. In addition to research on home and homey landscapes, her research interests concern multilocational housing and local citizenship as well as community-based social entrepreneurship and service provision in rural villages. Alongside these projects, she is finalizing her doctoral dissertation on the changing relationship between local citizenship and public administration.

SULEVI RIUKULEHTO is the research director in regional history and cultural heritage at the University of Helsinki Ruralia Institute, Finland. He received his Doc. of Phil. in 1998 at the University of Jyväskylä. He was appointed as adjunct professor in economic history in 2005 at the University of Jyväskylä, and in 2018 as extraordinary professor in the School of Social Sciences at the Vaal Triangle Campus of North-West University, South Africa. In Finland, Riukulehto leads the research group on regions, history and culture, which focuses on the development processes of regions and structures, regional history, and cultural phenomena in the rural context. Riukulehto's latest publications deal with questions of rural housing and the experiential theory of home. He has authored more than 20 books, including *A House Made to Be a Home* (CSP, 2016), *Between Time and Space* (CSP, 2015) and *The Great Ostrobothnian Peasant Houses* (Univ. of Helsinki, 2016).

SARAH RUDRUM is an associate professor of sociology at Acadia University. Her research focuses on issues of health equity, particularly in relation to gender relations and transnational health activities. She is the author of *Global Health and the Village: Transnational Contexts Governing Birth in Northern Uganda* (University of Toronto Press, 2021). She received her PHD from the Institute for Gender, Sexuality, and Social Justice at the University of British Columbia.

ARIO SETO is a postdoctoral researcher at the Ocean Frontier Institute, Memorial University of Newfoundland. A media anthropologist, his current research focuses on the intersectionality of media practices and values, particularly in terms of emerging public morality, democratic resilience, grassroots economic solidarity, the marketization of digital living, and mediatized community building. He is currently conducting research on mediatized innovation and rural community organizers' resilience in managing the sustainability of their social enterprises in Newfoundland, Canada. He has conducted multi-sited ethnographic research projects on mediatized populism in rural communities in Canada and in religiously conservative communities in Indonesia. His recent book, *Netizenship: Activism and Online Community Transformation in Indonesia* (Palgrave Macmillan, 2017), details the disciplining practices and ethics in shaping militant netizens in online forums.

NÚRIA SIMÓ-GIL is a pedagogue and lecturer at the Department of Pedagogy of the Faculty of Education, Translation and Human Sciences at the University of Vic - Central University of Catalonia (UVIC-UCC). She is the director of the Research Centre in Education (CRED), UVIC-UCC, and a researcher for the GREUV - Educational Research Group, UVIC-UCC. She combines teaching with research, teaching social education and in different master's programs. Her research projects focus on education, territory, and citizenship. Her recent projects relate to democratic education in secondary schools, intersectionality and youth, and pedagogical renewal from the past to now. Her areas of study are the training of social educators and teachers, democratic schools, and processes of social and educational inclusion with young people. She is involved in participatory research methodologies, to do research with people and not about people. She has published in journals such as *Studies in Philosophy and Education, Improving Schools, Estudios Pedagógicos* (EPED), *Power and Education,* and other educational journals, and published several chapters and books about democracy and participation in schools, active citizenship, and innovation.

M. A. (PEGGY) SMITH, RPF (Ret) (**MISKWAANAKWADOOK—RED CLOUD WOMAN**) is of Cree ancestry from the James Bay Treaty #9 area. She is Professor Emerita in Lakehead University's Faculty of Natural Resources Management, specializing in social justice issues in the natural resources sector, particularly the recognition and protection of Indigenous Peoples' rights. She retired in 2017 from her position at Lakehead as interim vice-provost (Aboriginal

Initiatives). She continues to supervise graduate students, and is carrying out research projects on free, prior, and informed consent (FPIC), and completing an online open access book on Indigenous Peoples and natural resources. Peggy is active in the Forest Stewardship Council, a non-governmental organization that focuses on voluntary certification of forest companies. She is a member of the Board of the Rights and Resources Group that coordinates the Rights and Resources International Coalition, whose members advocate for Indigenous land tenure rights.

SARA TEITELBAUM is an associate professor in the Sociology Department at the Université de Montréal. Her research focuses on the social dimensions of forests, specifically community-based approaches to forest management, Indigenous governance of forests, and issues surrounding community sustainability and public participation. Sara has published an edited volume on community forestry in Canada, which covers policy and practice from coast to coast. She has also published a number of research articles looking at the impacts of forestry certification, especially with regard to the protection of Indigenous rights. Her most recent research project focuses on the implementation of free, prior, and informed consent (FPIC) in the context of forestry certification in three boreal nations.

ANNETTE AAGAARD THUESEN, PHD, MA in social studies, is an associate professor at the Danish Centre for Rural Research at the University of Southern Denmark. Her research lies in community-initiated initiatives, strategic village planning, and governance through LEADER/CLLD in the EU Rural Development and Fisheries Programmes. She is currently working on externally financed projects related to local engagement in nature and outdoor life, as well as the relationship between local community associations and the municipality. Theoretically, she engages in governance, democracy, planning, and innovation. Recent publications are: Coordination of Village Plans and Municipal Rural and Health Policies: Can Low-hanging Fruit Be Picked? (*Sociologia Ruralis*, January 2021), Moving to the "Wild West": Clarifying the First-hand Experiences and Second-hand Perceptions of a Danish University Town on the Periphery (*European Planning Studies*, January 2020), and Rural Community Development through Competitions, Prizes, and Campaigns: The Villagers' Perspective (*Journal of Rural Studies*, March 2020).

TOM TOM, PHD, is a research fellow with the SARChi Chair in Social Policy, College of Graduate Studies, at the University of South Africa, and a senior lecturer in the Department of Development Studies, Faculty of Applied Social

Sciences, at Zimbabwe Open University. He is the programmes director of AfriFuture Research and Development Trust, and a member of the Network of Young African Researchers in Agriculture (YARA), International Sociological Association Junior Sociologists Network (ISA-JSN), and Development Practitioners Network (DPN). His research, publication, and teaching interests are crystallized around agrarian studies, social policy, youth, and rural development in the Global South, and he endeavours to transform the well-being of society through these roles.

S. ASHLEIGH WEEDEN is an award-winning rural futurist, feminist, and researcher whose work focuses on the way people, place, and power dynamics are reflected in and affected by policymaking, particularly in rural contexts. A long-time advocate for community-engaged, place-based approaches to public policy, Ashleigh has spent her career championing community-led innovation. Ashleigh holds an Honours Bachelor of Arts in International Development (Political Economy and Administrative Change) (University of Guelph) and a Master of Public Administration (University of Victoria). She is currently completing her PHD in Rural Studies at the University of Guelph. Recognized as an emerging thought leader on rural renewal and "the right to be rural," policy foresight, and public sector innovation, Ashleigh has provided expert commentary to outlets like Buzzfeed News, CBC News, and CTV News. Her work can be read in publications like The Conversation Canada, the Centre for International Governance Innovation, Policy Options, and Municipal World.

SATENIA ZIMMERMANN is a PHD candidate in the Faculty of Natural Resources Management at Lakehead University. Satenia holds a MA in Sociology, an HBA in Sociology, and a HBA in Women's Studies from Lakehead University. Her current research focuses on the impact of sustainable forest management, in particular the role of free, prior, and informed consent (FPIC) as outlined in the United Nations Declaration on the Rights of Indigenous Peoples (UNDRIP), on the viability of First Nations communities in northern Ontario. Her research is grounded in the areas of Aboriginal rights; forest management policy; impact benefit agreements; Aboriginal employment; and long-term viability and community well-being. Examining the experiences of First Nations communities with both federal and provincial governments, industry representatives, and environmental non-government organizations, her areas of interest include Aboriginal rights, Aboriginal law, and natural resource development in northern Canada.

Index

Page numbers in *italics* refer to figures and tables.

297; remote communities, *230*. *See also*
Canada, demographics and distances
alternative facts. *See* media literacy
Antigonish, Nova Scotia, 20–21, 24–28. *See*
also Nova Scotia, French language
education
aquaculture. *See* India, Chilika Lagoon,
fisheries
Atlantic Canada: about, 19–22; Acadians,
5–6, 20; demographics, 20, 181; French
language, 5–6, 30, 348; historical
background, 19–25; Mi'kmaw people,
20; regionalism, 19–20; right to be
rural, 341. *See also* New Brunswick;
Newfoundland and Labrador;
Newfoundland and Labrador,
education and media literacy; Nova
Scotia; Nova Scotia, Acadians; Nova
Scotia, French language education;
Nova Scotia, maternity care; Prince
Edward Island
Atlantic Canada, political citizenship:
about, 10, 177–78, 187–88; activism, 10,
182, 183–87, *184, 186*, 347; changes in
views, 182–83, *186*, 187–88; citizenship
models, 178–79; economic views,
182–85, *185*, 187–88; openness to
diversity, 182–85, *185*, 187–88; political
spectrum, 10, 178, 181–88, *185, 186*;
research findings, 10, 183–88, 347;
research project, 10, 178, 182–83; rural-
urban divide, 177–78, 180–88, *184, 185,
186*, 347; stereotypes, 10, 177–78, 181–82,
185, 346–47; voting, 182, 183, *184, 186*,
186–87

Barcelona, Spain, 41, 42, 257, 262. *See*
also Spain, Catalonia, democratic
education
Barraclough, Laura: meaningful space and
engaged citizenry, 240–41; right to the

countryside, 4–5, 8, 103, 160, 195, 240–41,
255, 341; urban centrism, 244, 300
Bauman, Zygmunt, 159–62, 195, 291–92
belongingness: about, 9, 141–42,
153–54; as bi-directional, 142–43,
154; in citizenship, 9, 77–78,
141–42, 242; displaced people, 290;
home experiences, 141–42, 148,
153–54; refugees and market/social
citizenship dilemma, 292–95, 299–301;
rural areas, 142; social capital, 181. *See*
also Finland, home experiences
Beretta, Megan, 258
Biesta, Gert, 6, 44
Bollman, Ray D., 11, 211–35, 344, 345, 351
Bosniak, Linda, 37, 161
British Columbia: access to health
care facilities, 215–17, 224–26, *225–27*,
342–44; Indigenous Peoples, 111,
197–98; maternity care, 110, 111, 112;
political spectrum, 181, 187–88; remote
communities, 111, *229–30*. *See also*
Canada, demographics and distances
Brodie, Janine, 77–78, 239, 290

Canada: ethnonationalist groups, 23, 25–26,
29; identities, 19–20, 202; regionalism,
19–20; remote communities, 110–11,
229–30; rights culture, 212. *See also*
specific provinces and territories
Canada, citizenship: about, 193–94; access
to health care, 111–12, 215–17, 342–44;
contractual citizenship, 2–3, 195–96,
291–92, 341; rights culture, 212. *See also*
Atlantic Canada, political citizenship;
Canada, Constitution (1982); Canada,
Indigenous citizenship; citizenship;
Nova Scotia, entrepreneurship
education
Canada, Constitution (1982): about, 26;
Charter of Rights and Freedoms, 21–22,

26, 132; Indigenous rights, 196, 198, 200, 203–04; minority language education (s. 23), 21–22, 26; mobility rights (s. 6), 211; rural protection, 215. *See also* Canada, government and politics

Canada, demographics: Atlantic Canada, 20, 52–53, 181; diseases, 127; Indigenous Peoples, 193–94, 198, 204n2; older people, 126–27; out-migration, 71–72; poverty, 126; urban-rural ratio, 52, 181. *See also* Canada, demographics and distances

Canada, demographics and distances: about, 11, 211, 215–17, 226–29; accessibility index, 217–18, 221–26, *222–23, 225–27*; access to health and welfare facilities, 11, 215–17, 221–26, *222–23, 225–27*; classification using statistics, 217–18; cost of travel, 115, 217–18, 228, 231n3, 345; demographic weight, 218–21, *219–20, 222–23*; density, 11, 213–15, *214*, 218–21, *219–20, 222–23*; differentiated universalism, 211–13, 229; distance-to-density, 11, 213–15, *214*, 218–21, *219–20*; inequities in access, 11, 215–17, 342–43, 344, 345; population size and accessibility, 221–26; public policy rural lens, 11, 215, 226–29; reasonable access, 212–13, 215–17, 228, 343, 344; remote communities, 110–11, *229–30*; remoteness index, 217–21, *219–20, 229–30*, 231n3, 231n5; research findings, 226–29; research project, 11, 211–12; rights, 211–13; rurality defined by distance-to-density, 11, 213–15, *214*; technologies, 11, 228, 345; urban-rural continuum, *214*, 214–15, 228–29

Canada, education: citizenship rights, 21; impacts of rurality, 25, 30–31; Indigenous control, 202–03; literacy levels, 127; nationalism, 23, 25, 29;

provincial jurisdiction, 21, 24; as right, 5, 72, 342; school closures, 7, 71–73, 116; schools as community hubs, 21; urban centrism, 72. *See also* Newfoundland and Labrador, education and media literacy; Nova Scotia, entrepreneurship education; Nova Scotia, French language education

Canada, food insecurity: about, 8–9, 123–28, 133–35; agricultural consolidation, 8–9, 125–26; defined, 123; demographics, 126–27; food banks, 9, 124, 130, 134; food sovereignty, 133–35; health and well-being, 127, 134–35, 216; neoliberalism, 8–9, 125–26, 134; nutritional quality, 9, 124, 127, 130–31, 342; right to be rural, 123–24, 128, 135; right to food, 123–24, 132–35; social supports, 128–31; state role, 21, 126, 128, 132–35; statistics, 124. *See also* Ontario, food insecurity

Canada, government and politics: activism, 178–79; citizenship rights, 21; federal/provincial division of powers, 21, 24, 297; public policy rural lens, 215, 226–29; right to vote and hold office, 178; stereotypes, 181; voter turnout, 178. *See also* Atlantic Canada, political citizenship; Canada, Constitution (1982); Canada, demographics and distances

Canada, health and well-being: food insecurity, 127, 135; government supports, 132–34; Indigenous well-being, 203; older persons, 127; social determinants of health, 133, 216; social supports, 128, 130–31. *See also* Canada, food insecurity; Canada, health care

Canada, health care: access to facilities, 215–17, *225–27*; belonging vs. exclusion, 8, 111–12, 114, 116; citizenship, 111; community connections, 111,

116-17; cost of travel, 109, 115, 217-18, 228, 231n3; essential services, 108, 119-20; Indigenous Peoples, 111-12, 203; inequities, 111, 215-17; medical recruitment, 216-17; medical specialists, 216, 228; midwifery, 107-12, 119-20, 342; provincial/ federal jurisdiction, 108, 119-20; public policy rural lens, 215, 226-29; reasonable access, 212-13, 215-17, 228, 343; regionalization/centralization of services, 108-09; remote communities, 110-12, *229-30*; reproductive care, 107-12, 119-20, 215; as a right, 342; rural-urban differences, 215-17. *See also* Canada, demographics and distances; Canada, food insecurity; Nova Scotia, maternity care

Canada, Indigenous Peoples: about, 196-98; assimilation, 194; belonging vs. exclusion, 111-12; constitutional rights, 196, 198, 200, 203-04; demographics, 193-94, 198, 204n2; FPIC (consent), 194, 197, 201-04, 344; health care, 111-12, 203; identity, 198-99, 202; Indian Act, 193, 197-99; Inuit relocations, 213; maternity care, 110-12, 120; reconciliation, 112, 199-201, 203-04; remote communities, 110-11, 197, *229-30*; right to be rural, 196, 203-04, 344; self-determination, 193-94, 198-201; treaties, 198; UNDRIP, 10-11, 194, 200-01, 204; *Van der Peet* (distinctive culture), 200. *See also* Canada, Indigenous citizenship; Indigenous Peoples; Ontario, Indigenous resource management

Canada, Indigenous citizenship: about, 10-11, 193-94, 198-99, 203-04; citizenship, 195-96, 198-200, 203-04; colonialism, 197-200; contractual citizenship, 195-96; First Nations, 194, 197-98; FPIC (consent), 194, 197, 201-04, 344; identity, 194, 198-200, 202; land stewardship, 199-200; rights-based analysis, 11; right to be rural, 195-98, 202-04; self-determination, 193-94, 198-201, 203-04; status vs. non-status, 197-98; UNDRIP, 10-11, 194, 200, 204. *See also* Canada, Indigenous Peoples; Ontario, Indigenous resource management

Canada, languages: bilingualism vs. language preservation, 5-6, 30; Charter rights (s. 23), 21-22, 26; French immersion programs, 29-30; language loss, 5-6, 22, 30-31; minority language rights, 21-22, 26, 30; Official Languages Act, 24, 26. *See also* Nova Scotia, French language education

Canada, natural resources: FPIC (consent), 194, 197, 201-04, 344; Indigenous relations, 196-98, 202-03, 345; land stewardship, 199-200; resource industries, 10-11, 202-03. *See also* Ontario, Indigenous resource management

Canada, older people: demographics, 126-27; food insecurity, 126-27, 132-35; government supports, 132-34; social supports, 128, 130-31

Canada, politics. *See* Canada, government and politics

Canada, refugee resettlement: about, 12-13, 289-90, 299-301, 345-46; belongingness, 290, 294-96, 300-01; blended visa office-referred refugees (UNHCR), 292-93; choice of location, 290, 298-300; citizenship, 290-95, 299-301; conflicts with sponsors, 13, 294-96; economic value, 292, 294-95; government assistance, 292-96, 299-301; language

humanist values, 38; more-than-economic entrepreneurship, 7, 77-78, 88, 348; participation, 38; power relations, 37-38, 44; service learning, 36, 41-42, 44-46, 48. *See also* Nova Scotia, entrepreneurship education; Poland, political citizenship and young adults; Spain, Catalonia, democratic education

civil rights, 2-3, 195, 242, 306, 341. *See also* Marshall, T.H., on citizenship

Clancy, Matt, 263-64

class. *See* social class

Clément, Dominique, 212

climate change. *See* environment

Cochrane, Logan, 12, 271-86, 344-45, 352

conspiracy theories. *See* media literacy

constitutions. *See* Canada, Constitution (1982)

contractual citizenship, 2-3, 195-96, 291-92, 341. *See also* citizenship

conventions on rights. *See* international declarations of rights

COVID-19 pandemic, 14-15

Cresswell, Tim, 243

Crouch, Colin, 36-37

Cunningham, Gordon, 76-77

Dalton, Russell J., 178-79

Das, Pallavi V., 7-8, 91-104, 344, 348, 352

declarations of rights. *See* international declarations of rights

democracy: definitions, 37-38; digital democracy, 257-58; dimensions of, 37-39, 45, 46-47; as relational process, 37, 45. *See also* Atlantic Canada, political citizenship; citizenship; citizenship education; Poland, political citizenship and young adults; political citizenship; Spain, Catalonia, democratic education

demographics: density of population, 213-15, *214*; rurality defined by distance-to-density, 11, 213-15, *214*; third age, defined, 143-44; urban-rural distance continuum, 214-15, 228. *See also* Canada, demographics; Canada, demographics and distances

Denmark, housing market: about, 13-14, 321-22, 333-34, *335*, 346; analytical framework, 14, 322-25, *323*, 332, 334, *335*; distributional injustice, 326-29; globalization, 329-31, *335*; mortgage practices, 13-14, 322, 333-34, *335*; out-migration, 322; political representation, 331-33; public policy, 14, 328-32, 334, *335*; redlining for rural mortgages, 13-14, 321, 326-34, *335*, 346; remote areas, 332; research findings, 14, 333-34, *335*; research project, 13-14, 326, 336n2; right to be rural, 13-14, 321-22, 325, 333, 346; rural-urban distances, 327, 333; spatial justice/injustice, 14, 322-26, *323*, 330-33, 336n1; speculation, 327, 330-31; as a wicked problem, 14, 322, 332-34, *335*, 336n1

de Schutter, Olivier, 133

differentiated universalism, 211-13, 229

DiGiorgio, Carla, 29

digital technology. *See* media literacy; technologies

displaced people. *See* Canada, refugee resettlement; immigration and settlement

dispossession. *See* land/sea dispossession

Domingo-Peñafiel, Laura, 6, 34-50, 347, 352-53

economy: agricultural markets, 125, 131-32; contractual citizenship, 2-3, 195-96, 291-92, 341; dispossession by capital accumulation, 91-95,

findings, 274, 283-85; research project, 273-74; right to be rural, 12, 272-74, 278-80, 282-85, 344-45; social rights, 12, 274, 284-85; state ownership of land, 274-75; urbanization, 12, 271-73, 276; urban planning, 282-85

Europe: citizenship education, 38; financial regulations, 329; political stereotypes, 181; spatial planning, 239-40, 244. *See also* Denmark, housing market; Finland, home experiences; Poland, political citizenship and young adults; Spain, Catalonia, democratic education

everyday life. *See* belongingness; citizenship; home experiences; right to be rural; right to the city

fake news. *See* media literacy

farms. *See* agriculture; fisheries

Farré-Riera, Laura, 6, 34-50, 347, 353

feminism, 109, 323-25

Finland, home experiences: about, 9, 141-44, 152-54; belonging, 9, 141-42, 148, 152-54; home as a building, 9, 145, 147-48, 153; home as emotions, 9, 141-42, 146, 148-51, 153; home as interaction, 9, 146, 150-51, 153; home as places for events, 9, 146, 151-53; hominess, 145-48, 153-54; locations, 143-44, 150-52; nature and environment, 145, 149-50, 152; ownership, 149-53; research findings, 146-54; research project, 143-47, 154; rural vs. urban views, 143-44, 150-51, 153-54; services, 145, 150; third age, defined, 143-44

First Nations, 194, 196-98, 202-03. *See also* Canada, Indigenous Peoples

fisheries: food insecurity, 99; global markets, 95-97, 100, 103; intensive fishing, 53, 102; Newfoundland history,

53-54. *See also* India, Chilika Lagoon, fisheries

Fisker, Jens Kaae, 13-14, 321-38, 346, 353-54

food: food sovereignty, 133-35; smart technologies, 263-64, 265n6, 266n7. *See also* agriculture; fisheries

food insecurity: about, 8-9, 123-24, 133-35; activism, 133-35; defined, 123-24; fisheries, 99; food banks, 9, 124, 130, 134; food literacy, 131, 134-35; food sovereignty, 133-35; government supports, 133-35; neoliberalism, 8-9, 124, 134; nutritional quality, 9, 127, 130-31, 342; reasonable access, 343; right to be rural, 123-24; right to food, 123-24, 131-35; UN declarations, 132-33. *See also* Canada, food insecurity; Ontario, food insecurity

forest management. *See* Ontario, Indigenous resource management

Foster, Karen R., 1-16, 339-49, 354

FPIC (free, prior, and informed consent), 194, 197, 201-04, 344

Frank, Lesley, 8, 107-22, 354

Frank, Thomas, 187-88

Franklin, Ursula M., 258, 259

Fraser, Nancy: dimensions of justice, 14, 322-25, *323,* 332, 334, *335*

French language. *See* Nova Scotia, Acadians; Nova Scotia, French language education

Fukuyama, Francis, 273

gender, 170-72, 307, 312

geographies: differentiated universalism, 211-13, 229; rurality defined by distance-to-density, 11, 213-15, *214;* rural-urban distances (Denmark), 327, 333; Soja's spatial justice/injustice, 14, 322-23, *323,* 325-26, 332, 334, *335;* urban-rural continuum, 214-15, 228. *See also*

Canada, demographics and distances; remote areas; rural areas; spatial justice; urban areas

Gibson-Graham, J.K., 334

Giroux, Henry A., 55, 60, 63-64

globalization: agricultural markets, 125, 131-32; citizenship and the state, 242, 290; fish markets, 95-96, 103; transformation of rural areas, 237, 241-44. *See also* economy; geographies

Guelph-Wellington, Our Food Future, 263-64, 265n6, 266n7. *See also* Ontario, smart technologies

Gurnstein, Michael, 261

Hadley, Gregory R. L., 7, 71-90, 160, 344, 347-48, 354

Halamska, Maria, 161

Harper, Steven, 177

Harvey, David, "The Right to the City": about, 4, 91, 340-41, 348; active democratic participation, 255, 261, 340-41, 343; capitalist expansion and urbanization, 4, 19, 91, 274, 340-41; dispossession by capital accumulation, 4, 7-8, 91-95, 101-03, 274, 340-41; meaningful spaces, 343; right to be rural, 102; urbanization as class-based, 4, 340, 348

Haugen, Stacey, 12-13, 289-302, 345-46, 355

Hawassa, 272, 273, 275, 277, 280-85. *See also* Ethiopia, urbanization and land tenure

health and well-being: government supports, 132-34; oral health, 131; social determinants of health, 133, 216. *See also* Canada, health and well-being; food insecurity

health care: access equality/inequalities, 109, 215-17, 342-44; centralization of services, 108-09; community connections, 111, 116-17; cost downloading to patients, 109; differentiated universalism, 211-13, 229; homecare, 130; maternity care, 107-08, 119-20; neoliberalism, 109; reproductive justice, 116, 120; as a right, 342-43. *See also* Canada, demographics and distances; Canada, health care; Nova Scotia, maternity care

Hindle, Kevin, 76

home experiences: about, 9, 152-54, 343; belongingness, 9, 343; citizenship, 9, 141-42; vs. houses, 148; social construction, 146-47. *See also* Finland, home experiences

housing markets: spatial injustice, 321; as a wicked problem, 14, 322, 332-34, 335, 336n1. *See also* Denmark, housing market

human rights: about, 1-2, 212, 341-42; access to services, 342; categories, 2, 242, 341; definitions, 2, 341; differentiated universalism, 211-13, 229; with duties, 2, 341; enforcement of, 5, 15-16; Indigenous Peoples, 200-01; legal claims, 2, 341; right to education, 72, 342; right to employment, 315-16, 342; right to food, 123-24, 132-35; right to mobility, 211, 346. *See also* international declarations of rights; Marshall, T.H., on citizenship; right to be rural; right to the city; UN Declaration on the Rights of Indigenous Peoples (UNDRIP); UN Universal Declaration of Human Rights (UDHR)

immigration and settlement: belongingness, 290; international conventions on rights, 315-16; market/

Lauzon, Al, 8-9, 123-39, 216, 342, 356

La Via Campesina, 133

Lawy, Robert, 6

Lefebvre, Henri, *The Right to the City:* about, 3-5, 240-41, 340-41; engaged citizens, 261, 340-41, 343; meaningful spaces, 343; resistance to neoliberalism, 255, 262; right to the city, 3-5, 240-41; right to the countryside, 4-5, 160, 255, 340

Lenzi, Michela, 61

LGBTQ people, 142

Lipton, Michael, 238, 240-41

Lister, Ruth, 159, 161, 172, 213, 241-42

livelihoods. *See* employment

Lourenco, Marina, 305

MacLeod, Katie K., 5-6, 19-33, 347, 348, 356-57

Manitoba: access to health care facilities, 215-17, 224, 225-27, 342-44; Indigenous Peoples, 197-98; midwifery, 112; political spectrum, 181, 187-88; remote communities, 229-30. *See also* Canada, demographics and distances

Mansouri, Fethi, 37

Marshall, T.H., on citizenship: about, 2-3, 195, 242, 291, 306-08; capitalist inequalities, 3, 306-07; civil rights, 2-3, 195, 242, 306, 341; critiques of, 307-08; engaged citizens, 343; historical background, 307-08; political rights, 2-3, 178, 195, 242, 306-07, 309; social rights, 2-3, 12, 13, 24, 77, 195, 212-13, 242, 291, 306-07, 313-14; state role, 2-3, 195, 291, 306-08; technologies' impacts, 257

Marx, Karl: egalitarian redistribution, 324; primitive accumulation, 93-97, 99-102, 103n1, 103n5; rural as "class in itself," 15-16, 347, 348

Matai, Jeofrey, 11-12, 237-52, 344, 357

maternity care. *See* Canada, health care; Nova Scotia, maternity care

Mathie, Alison, 76-77

Matysiak, Ilona, 9-10, 159-75, 344, 346, 357

McCarney, Kayla, 8, 107-22, 358

McLay, Rachel, 10, 177-91, 346-47, 358

media literacy: about, 51, 58-61, 64-65; blogs on technologies, 258-65, *260*, 265n6, 265nn3-4; deep discussions, 60; fake news and conspiracies, 58. *See also* Newfoundland and Labrador, education and media literacy; technologies

Meehan, Elizabeth, 39

midwifery. *See* Nova Scotia, maternity care

migration: in COVID-19 pandemic, 14-15; labourers in Africa, 304-05. *See also* Canada, refugee resettlement; immigration and settlement; mobility; Zimbabwe, land reforms and migrant labourers

misinformation. *See* media literacy

Miskwaanakwadook—Red Cloud Woman (M.A. Smith), 10-11, 193-207, 348, 360-61

mobility: about, 12-13, 346; right to be rural, 72, 211, 341, 346. *See also* Canada, refugee resettlement; Denmark, housing market; immigration and settlement; Zimbabwe, land reforms and migrant labourers

mortgages. *See* Denmark, housing market; spatial justice

Murphy, Elizabeth, 54

Myrdal, Gunnar, 241

Nash, Kate, 242, 290, 299

natural resources: agricultural land depletion, 125-26; Indigenous management, 10-11; right to natural resources, 5, 132, 345. *See also* India,

post-secondary education, 24; social resources, 24. *See also* Nova Scotia, French language education

Nova Scotia, education: course options, 85-86; francophone schools (CSAP), 22, 24-25, 27-31; more-than-economic entrepreneurship, 7, 83, 85-88, 348; pedagogies, 85-88; post-secondary education, 24; rural revitalization, 116-17; school closures, 71, 72-73, 116. *See also* Nova Scotia, entrepreneurship education; Nova Scotia, French language education

Nova Scotia, entrepreneurship education: about, 7, 71-72, 87-88, 348; citizenship, 77-78, 88; community connections, 84-88; to counter out-migration, 7, 73; definitions, 73-74; KSAs (knowledge, skills, attitudes), 72-88, *81*; KSA self-assessment, 80-87, *82*; Marshall's social rights, 77; more-than-economic entrepreneurship, 73-74; personalities, 7, 83-84; research findings, 7, 72, *82*, 83-88; research participants, 78-83, *81*; research project, 7, 78-86; rural contexts, 76-77, 348; scholarship on, 75-78; school experiences, 7, 83, 85-88; small entrepreneurialism, 74-75

Nova Scotia, French language education: about, 5-6, 19-22, 30-31, 348; anglophone boards, 26-27; anglophones in French immersion, 6, 21, 27, 28-31; belongingness, 25, 26-28, 30-31; Charter rights, 21-22, 26; curriculum, 21, 23-26, 28; dialects, 6, 30, 348; historical overview, 19-26; jurisdictional changes, 21, 28; language loss, 5-6, 22, 26, 27, 28, 29, 30-31; Pomquet schools, 25-27; provincial francophone board (CSAP), 22, 24-25, 27-31; research findings, 6,

30-31; research project, 22; school as community hub, 25, 27-28, 30-31; social class, 6, 30-31, 348; teachers, 22, 23-25, 28, 29. *See also* Nova Scotia, Acadians

Nova Scotia, health care: access to care and facilities, 114, 215-17, 224, *225-27*, 342-44; Indigenous communities, 110-12; neoliberalism, 109, 115; palliative care, 116, 215; reasonable access, 215-17, 228, 343; regionalization/centralization of services, 108-09. *See also* Nova Scotia, maternity care

Nova Scotia, maternity care: about, 8, 107-08, 119-20; activism, 118-20; belonging vs. exclusion, 8, 111-12, 114, 116-17, 120; distance continuum, 114; equality of access, 109; Indigenous communities, 110-12, 120; midwifery, 8, 107-20, 342; midwifery pilot program, 8, 113-14, 117-20; neoliberalism, 8, 109, 115, 118; regionalization/centralization of services, 108-09, 114-15, 119; remote communities, 110-12, *229-30*; reproductive justice, 116, 120; research findings, 114-20; research project, 112-14; as a right, 342; rural revitalization, 115-17, 120; scholarship on, 112

Nunavut: access to health care facilities, 215-17, 224-26, *225-27*, 342-44; remote communities, *229-30*. *See also* Canada, demographics and distances

older people: aging in place, 342; belongingness, 9, 142; home experiences, 9; social supports, 128; "third age," 143. *See also* Canada, food insecurity; Canada, older people; Finland, home experiences; Ontario, food insecurity

online content. *See* media literacy; technologies

individualism, 9-10, 159-62, 179-80; Marshall's political rights, 2-3, 178, 195, 242, 306; political spectrum, 10, 179, 187-88; populist movements, 179; rural communities as "class in itself," 15-16, 347, 348; rural-urban divide, 10, 180-81; stereotypes, 10, 177; voting, 10, 178, 306, 309. *See also* activism and engaged citizens; Atlantic Canada, political citizenship; citizenship; justice and injustice; Marshall, T.H., on citizenship; Poland, political citizenship and young adults

Pomquet. *See* Nova Scotia, French language education

population. *See* demographics

postsecondary education. *See* Poland, political citizenship and young adults

power relations: economic inequalities, 179; intersectional approach, 110-11; refugee resettlement, 294-96, 299; smart cities, 257-58, 259, 263-65

prenatal services. *See* Canada, health care; Nova Scotia, maternity care

Prince Edward Island: abortion services, 215; Acadian history, 23; access to health care facilities, 215-17, 224, *225-27*; demographics, 181. *See also* Atlantic Canada; Canada, demographics and distances

psychological ownership, 142, 153. *See also* belongingness; home experiences

public policy: about, 16, 215, 344-45, 347-48; constitutional rights, 215; differentiated universalism, 211-13, 229; rural lens, 16, 215, 226-29, 342-44, 347. *See also* Canada, demographics and distances

Quebec: access to health care facilities, 215-17, 224, *225-27*; Indigenous Peoples,

112; maternity care, 112; political spectrum, 181; remote communities, *229-30*. *See also* Canada, demographics and distances

racialized people and racism: land reforms, 238; reproductive justice, 116, 120; social bridging vs. bonding, 181; in social media, 51

Ramos, Howard, 10, 177-91, 346-47, 358-59

real estate and spatial injustice. *See* Denmark, housing market

refugees. *See* Canada, refugee resettlement; immigration and settlement

remote areas: defined, 110-11, 197; demographics, *229-30*; intersectional approach, 110-11; remoteness index, 217-18, 221, *229-30*, 231n3, 231n5; travel costs, 115, 217-18, 231n3. *See also* Canada, demographics and distances

reproductive justice, 116, 120

rights. *See* human rights; international declarations of rights; right to be rural; right to the city

right to be rural: about, 1-5, 15-16, 91-92, 123-24, 240-41, 340-49; access to services, 341-43; citizenship rights, 124, 195-96, 240-41, 341; in COVID-19 pandemic, 14-15; defined, 123-24; differentiated universalism, 211-13, 229; dispossession by capital accumulation, 91-95, 96-98, 102-03; dispossession by the state, 274; enforcement of rights, 5, 15-16; Indigenous Peoples, 203-04; key questions, 1, 15, 340-49; and Lefebvre's right to the city, 240-41; mobility rights, 211, 346; parallels with right to the city, 4-5, 348-49; quality of life, 343; resilience of communities, 347;

social rights: about, 212–13, 306–07, 313–14; differentiated universalism, 211–13, 229; of displaced persons, 291–92; economic security, 24, 77, 306–07, 313–14; Marshall's social rights, 2–3, 12, 13, 24, 195, 212–13, 242, 291, 306–07, 313–14; reasonable access to services, 212–13, 215–17, 228, 343; refugees and market/social citizenship dilemma, 291–95, 299–301; rights and duties, 2, 291; right to recognition, 291; social inclusion, 24, 77, 291–92, 313–14. *See also* human rights; Marshall, T.H., on citizenship

Soja, Edward: spatial justice/injustice, 14, 322–23, *323*, 325–26, 332, 334, *335*

Somers, Margaret, 2–3, 258, 259–60, 291, 299–300, 341

South Asia: dispossession by capital accumulation, 91–95, 97–98, 102–03. *See also* India, Chilika Lagoon, fisheries

Spain: Barcelona's technologies, 257, 262

Spain, Catalonia, democratic education: about, 6, 35–36, 46–48; belongingness, 6, 46–47; citizenship as a practice, 6, 36–40, 45, 47–48; community collaborations, 6, 36, 40–48; curriculum, 6, 38–40, 44, 47–48; democratic dimensions, 37–39, 45, 46–47; demographics, 36, 42–43; diversity of students, 38, 43, 45, 47; experiential learning, 6, 46; legal frameworks, 36, 39–40, 47–48; pedagogies, 41–42, 46–48; political context, 39–40; research findings, 6, 43–48; research projects, 35–36, 40–43, 48nn1–2; school climate, 6, 41–44, 46–48; school governance, 6, 42, 46; service learning, 36, 41–42, 44–46, 48

spatial justice: about, 322–23; dimensions of, 322–25, *323*; Fraser's three dimensions, *323*, 323–25; rural redlining for mortgages, 326–33; scale, 322–23; Soja's spatial justice/injustice, 14, 322–23, *323*, 325–26, 332, 334, *335*; wicked problems, 14, 322, 332–34, *335*, 336n1. *See also* Canada, demographics and distances; justice and injustice; right to be rural; right to the city

spatial planning, 239–40, 244, 249–50. *See also* Zimbabwe, citizenship and spatial planning

Swartzentruber, Barbara, 263, 265n6

Syrian refugees, 289, 293, 298–99. *See also* Canada, refugee resettlement

Szafraniec, Krystyna, 163–64

teachers. *See* Newfoundland and Labrador, education and media literacy; Nova Scotia, French language education

technologies: access to health and welfare services, 11, 228; citizenship, 12, 254, 258, 263–65; digital divides, 255–56, 261, 263–64; digital literacy, 264–65; rural broadband, 254–55; rural-urban partnerships, 263–64; surveillance capitalism, 254, 255–56, 258, 261–62; urban centrism, 11, 253–54. *See also* media literacy; Newfoundland and Labrador, education and media literacy; Ontario, smart technologies; technologies, smart cities

technologies, smart cities: about, 12, 253–55, 263–65; citizenship, 12, 254, 258, 263–65; consent, 256, 262; digital democracy, 257–58; digital divides, 255–56, 261, 262, 263–64; power relations, 257–58, 259; resistance, 254–60, *260*, 263–65; rural impacts, 256–57; smart cities, 254–57, 263–65; surveillance capitalism, 12, 254, 255–56, 258, 261–62; urban centrism, 12, 253–55; urban planning, 257. *See also* Ontario, smart technologies